EVERYDAY SAINTS

AND OTHER STORIES

Father Nikita.

Everyday Saints

and Other Stories

Archimandrite Tikhon (Shevkunov)

Translated by
Julian Henry Lowenfeld

Pokrov Publications
2012

For ordering information please visit our websites:
PokrovPublications.com
or
Everyday-Saints.com

Front cover: Archimandrite Nathaniel (Pospelov)

Cover design by Mikhail Rodionov

Second printing in English, 2013

Translated from the original Russian: Nesvyatye Svyatie, Olma Media Group, Moscow, 2011

Proceeds from the sale of Everyday Saints *will be used to build a memorial cathedral in Moscow dedicated to the victims of communist repression in Russia.*

Library of Congress Control Number: 2012911971

Everyday Saints and Other Stories
        Translated from the Russian.

ISBN 978-0-9842848-3-2

CONTENTS

Openly appearing to those who look for Him with all their heart, while hiding from those who run from Him with all their heart, God governs human knowledge of His presence. He gives signs that are visible to those who search for Him, and yet invisible to those who are indifferent to Him. To those who wish to see, God gives sufficient light; to those who do not wish to see, He gives sufficient darkness.

—Blaise Pascal

Translator's Introduction

Our hermit fathers and our nuns blessed and blameless,
To let their hearts fly up into the heavens nameless,
To keep their spirits strong in storms of wind and war
Composed a multitude of sacred hymns and lore.
But there's not one of them which gives me so much comfort
As one prayer our priest repeats and utters
Upon the melancholy days of Lenten Fast.
Unbidden, more than other prayers does it pass
My lips, bracing my fallen soul with strength mysterious:
"Lord of my days! Keep me from sloth that hides in bleakness,
From pride, greed, arrogance, and serpents therein hid,
Let not my tongue in idle gossip slip,
But Lord, show me my own faults and transgressions,
And may my brother never hear my condemnations,
May I for grace, patience, and love forever strive,
And wisdom's innocence within my heart revive.

—Alexander Pushkin (my translation)

*I*T MAY SURPRISE some of us who grew up during the Cold War, but Russia, feared for so many years as the land of "godless Communists," is in fact one of the most intensely spiritual and devout nations in the world. The profound faith of its people, Orthodox Christianity, rooted in a mystical understanding of life as a covenant and of worship as a sacrament, has always been the secret underpinning of the mysterious "Russian soul," whose elusive immanence makes Russian literature, art, and music so special. In the twentieth century, under the brutal totalitarianism of the Soviet system, Russia endured some of the very darkest days in human history. Yet where there is darkness, as this book shows, light shines forth ever brighter to meet it. Ultimately, though it may take a while, love and light and compassion conquer hatred and darkness and indifference.

Whether you are religious or skeptical, whether you care about Russia or not, you can still let this book transport you to a world and a way of looking at things of which most of us have no inkling. A world of ritual and sacred ceremonies; of ringing church bells and angelic choirs; of poetry and husbandry; of devotion to the land and also to spiritual objects of unearthly yet practical beauty, such as icons; a world of onion domes and candles; of incense, of prayers, of souls and spirits.

Welcome to a world where everything means something, and everything has a reason. A world of tradition and honor, yet of humor; of rigor, yet of profound compassion; of hard work performed with devout reverence, yet of ease and profound inner contentment. A world of modesty, yet majesty. A world of monasteries and cathedrals and convents, of bishops, of monks and nuns, of prayer, and of contemplation. This is a world where the Divine is present in everyday life; where every action, every thought, and every feeling has consequences; where uncanny "coincidences" are commonplace. Where we are not alone, bereft of plan or purpose, in an empty and meaningless universe. This is a world where everything matters, where, as Rainer Maria Rilke, who traveled to Russia and was fascinated by Russian Orthodoxy, wrote:

> You should not wait until God comes to you
> And says: "I am."
> A God, whose strength is vouched for, proved,
> Is senseless, mad.
> Yet you must know, though, that God blows through you
> Since time began,
> And when your heart glows warm and remains true,
> He works His plan.
>
> (my translation)

Skeptical readers—I at first was one of you—need not agree with the author or believe in everything he says to enjoy his remarkable way of saying it. Whether or not you are touched by the author's faith, I am certain that you will be transported by his stories of a spiritual treasure chest that has suddenly been reopened, a world that has been long hidden, a world that we can enter without belonging to it—just as one need not be a mariner to treasure a good yarn about perilous voyages at sea. Now and then, this book will have curious words and terms peculiar to the world it portrays. But we need not know the difference between a binnacle and a barnacle, a spinnaker or a spanker, in order to thrill to a tale of the sea. And so, when you are confronted with words for things you have never heard of before, let these stories, about and by some truly remarkable individuals, simply sweep you away. For as this book eloquently proves, the trifles that divide us politically or culturally pale in comparison to what unites us in common humanity.

I believe it is impossible to relate properly to Russia without understanding this world, sustained not just by the ancient faith of its followers, but by hallowed tradition. And this book is a marvelous point of entry, which explains why it has already sold over one million copies in Russia. For Father Tikhon is a natural raconteur, with a great sense of humor and a touching compassion that humanizes his faith and makes it accessible to believers and skeptics alike.

What's more, his world view has a way of growing on you: you may pass through stages of incredulity and bemusement, and then, almost imperceptibly, you may notice oddities in your life that begin to resemble his stories: friends suddenly turning up out of the blue, the hoped-for thing happening at the hoped-for time, books that conveniently open to just the right page, long-lost objects suddenly found . . . Uncanny and implausible "coincidences" seemingly in line with a mystical plan may have a tendency to seem ever more commonplace, until the extraordinary becomes almost routine, and the miraculous, natural.

Miracles are natural in Father Tikhon's felicitous world. All too often, we associate Russia with doom and gloom or with cynicism or corruption or cruelty. Perhaps—at least, so I hope—this book will help to correct our vision. Personally, in any case, I will always be grateful to Father Tikhon and to the "everyday saints" portrayed in this book for their own example, and for their infectious joy and integrity and sense of meaning, imbuing everyone and everything in their lives. I am profoundly honored to have helped to acquaint Western readers with them and their world and their way of life, in which

When, in life's minutes difficult,
   In my heart griefs do start:
   One wondrous prayer full of good
   I do recite by heart.

Some blessing in it lives; it heals
  Through words' harmonious sounds.
  Mysterious grace it breathes and peals,
  With holy charm abounds.

All burdens from my soul do sweep,
  All doubts fly out of sight—
  And I believe, and I do weep,
  And feel so light, so light!

—Mikhail Yuryevich Lermontov (my translation)

J.H.L.
June 23, 2012

Preface

*I*T WAS A warm September evening, as we, the still-young novices of the Pskov Caves Monastery near Pskov, were strolling about the corridors and galleries of the ancient monastery walls, making ourselves comfortable, looking out high above its gardens and fields. As we talked, we began reminiscing about how each of us had come to be at the monastery. And the more we listened to each other, the more amazed we became.

It was 1984 at the time, and there were five of us. Four had grown up in nonreligious families, and even for the fifth in our group, the son of a clergyman, our preconceptions of the sort of people who go off to join a monastery were utterly Soviet. Just a year earlier, each of us had firmly believed that the only people who ever entered a monastery nowadays were fanatics or complete failures in life. Losers, in short—or else victims of unrequited love.

But looking at each other, we could see that this simply wasn't true at all. The youngest in our group was just eighteen, and the oldest was twenty-six. All of us were healthy, strong, and attractive young men. One had graduated with highest honors from university with a degree in mathematics; another, despite his youth, was already an acclaimed artist in Leningrad. Yet another of our group had lived most of his life in New York, where his father was working, and had joined our monastery after completing his third year of university. The youngest (the priest's son) was a talented engraver and wood carver, and had just completed his education at an art school. And I had recently graduated from the screenwriter's division of the prestigious National State Cinematic Institute. In short, each of us youngsters had enviable worldly careers to look forward to.

So why had we come to the monastery? And why were we planning to stay here for the rest of our lives? We knew very well. It was because,

for each of us, a new world had suddenly opened up, incomparable in its beauty. And that world had turned out to be boundlessly more attractive than the one in which we had previously lived our young and so-far very happy lives. In this book I want to tell you about this beautiful new world of mine, where we live by laws completely different from those in "normal" worldly life—a world of light and love, full of wondrous discoveries, hope, happiness, trials and triumphs, where even our defeats acquire profound significance: a world in which, above all, we can always sense powerful manifestations of divine strength and comfort.

I have not needed to imagine anything. Everything you are about to read really happened. Most of the people you will read about are alive and well today.

The Pskov Caves Monastery, Pechory.

In the Beginning

I WAS BAPTIZED IN 1982, right after my graduation from film school.
I was twenty-four at the time. Nobody knew whether or not I had been
baptized as a child. Such things were common in those days: grandmothers
and aunts would sometimes secretly baptize infants without letting the
parents know. In such cases the priest performing the rite would utter the
phrase, "If he is not baptized, now hereby being baptized is God's servant
so-and-so."

I came to my faith like many of my friends in college. At the National
State Cinematic Institute there were several brilliant teachers who gave us
a solid humanities education and made us think hard about the important
questions in life.

As we discussed the eternal questions of humanity and studied the
history of the past centuries, grappling with the problems of our own
1970s and 1980s—in our classrooms, our dorms, and the cheap cafés
thronged by students, as well as during our frequent long nocturnal mean-
derings through the ancient side streets of Moscow—we came to the
firm conclusion that our Soviet state was deceiving us, forcing its crude
and ridiculous interpretations of history and politics upon us. We also
understood very well that everything had been powerfully arranged so as
to remove even the slightest chance of figuring out for ourselves the most
important question of all: the question of the Church and God.

There had been no doubts about this subject for our teacher of "scientific atheism," or for Marina, the leader of my Young Pioneer group (a
Communist scouting organization). She had always unwaveringly answered
this and indeed all other questions having to do with life. But gradually we came to a surprising revelation. All the great figures of world and
Russian history with whose philosophies we became acquainted during
our studies—all those whom we trusted and loved and respected—all of
them had thought about God in a completely different way than we did.
Simply put, they were people of faith. Dostoyevsky, Kant, Pushkin, Tolstoy,
Goethe, Pascal, Hegel, Losev—there were too many to list. What's more,
people of science, too—Newton, Planck, Linnaeus, Mendeleyev—all of

them were believers. We knew less about them, because of our humanities education, yet even here the picture was pretty much the same. Of course, these people's perceptions of God might turn out to be quite different from ours. Even so, for most of them, the question of faith was the most important, even if perhaps the most complicated, question in their lives.

By contrast, all the people in our histories with whom we had the most repulsive associations, those with a plainly horrible influence on Russia, those who evoked no sympathy in us whatsoever—Marx, Lenin, Trotsky—all those destructive revolutionaries who had led to our atheist state developing into what it had become—all were atheists.

And soon the rather harshly put question that life was posing to us became: was it Pushkin, Dostoyevsky, and Newton who had been so primitive and shallow that they had no idea of the realities of life? Were these geniuses really idiots? Or were we the idiots? We Soviets—along with our elementary-school atheism teacher Marina? This was a question that gave our young minds serious food for thought.

In those years there wasn't even a Bible in our extensive college library, not to mention that no ecclesiastical or religious literature was available. We had to glean what little we could about religion in meager grains and cryptic excerpts, in edited quotes from textbooks on atheism or certain classical philosophers. A huge influence on us at that time was therefore Russian literature.

But I loved to go to evening services in certain Moscow churches, although I hardly understood a thing of what I was hearing or witnessing. My first reading of the Bible made a huge impression on me. I borrowed it from an acquaintance who was a Baptist, and read and re-read it constantly, always delaying returning the book to him, because I realized all too well that I would never find the book anywhere else again. But that Baptist hardly insisted on my returning the book to me. He kept trying to convert me, over a period of several months, and even brought me to the Baptists' forbidden prayer house in Maly Vuzvosky Lane. For some reason I was not personally drawn to the Baptist faith and immediately realized his faith was not for me. However, to this very day, I am intensely grateful to that kind man for letting me read his Bible.

Like so many young people, my friends and I used to spend a lot of time arguing, sometimes passionately, about religion and God, and discussing readings of the Holy Scripture, a copy of which I'd managed to get my hands on, or other spiritual books that somehow or other we'd managed to obtain. But most of us put off the step of baptism and going to church. Most of us thought that it was quite possible to keep living without the Church, as long as we had God in our hearts, so to speak. Things might well have continued in this way, but then suddenly it became utterly clear to us both what the Church really was and why we in fact do need it.

Our teacher for foreign art history was Paola Dmitrivena Volkova. Her lectures were always interesting. And for some reason, perhaps because she was herself a person striving for answers to the big questions in life, she used to share her spiritual and mystical experiments with us. For example, she devoted a whole lecture or two to the ancient Chinese book of divination, the *I Ching*. Paola even brought sandalwood incense and yarrow stalks into the classroom and taught us how to use them to peer into the future.

One of her lectures concerned investigations conducted over many years (though unknown to all but the smallest group of specialists) by the famous Russian scientists Dmitri Mendeleyev and Vladimir Vernadsky. And although Paola gave us fair warning that dabbling in such things risked all kinds of unpredictable and unpleasant consequences, we, her students, with all our youthful enthusiasm, plunged ourselves into these tempting new mysterious worlds.

I will not get into the technical description of spiritualist techniques described in Mendeleyev's scientific papers, which we further discovered from researchers at the Vernadsky Museum in Moscow. But having experimented ourselves with several of the techniques, we found that we could indeed establish some sort of connection with . . . certain completely incomprehensible (for us) but nonetheless absolutely real entities. And these new mysterious acquaintances of ours, with whom we began to conduct long nocturnal conversations during séances, introduced themselves by various names: sometimes Napoleon, sometimes Socrates, and sometimes the recently dead grandmother of one of our acquaintances.

These entities would sometimes relate incredibly interesting things to us. Furthermore, to our utter astonishment, they somehow knew intimate details about each of our personal lives. For example, we might be curious about our classmate Alexander Rogozhkin (who would become a renowned film director). With whom was he secretly going out until late at night? And we would immediately receive the answer: "With Katya, a second-year student." Rogozhkin was indignant, huffing and puffing—and by his fury it was quite obvious that this answer had been spot on.

But there were other "revelations" that were even more amazing. Once during a break between lectures, one of my friends, who was particularly engrossed by these séances, started almost throwing himself at us, his classmates, urgently asking around in a conspiratorial whisper, with eyes red from sleeplessness: "Who is Mikhail Gorbachev?" Neither I nor any of my classmates had ever heard of anyone by this name (it was 1982). But my friend explained: "Last night we asked 'Stalin' who was going to be running this country and he answered: 'Some guy named Mikhail Gorbachev. But I've never heard of him myself. Find out who he is!'"

Three months later we were all shocked to hear the news that the young former First Secretary of the Regional Committee of the Stravropol Provincial Communist Party had been elected a Candidate Member of the Politburo.

Yet, the more we indulged in these extremely engrossing experiments, the clearer it became to us that something frightful and deeply worrying was happening to us. More and more, an inexplicable melancholy and profound depression would come over us, accompanied by a feeling of inescapable gloom and pointlessness. Everything seemed to slip from our lives. We were drained of energy, and an uncanny unrelenting despair took merciless hold of us. Month by month this feeling grew, until at last we began to guess that in some way it was connected to our nocturnal conversations with our "new acquaintances." Furthermore, I learned from the Bible, which I still had not returned to my friend the Baptist, that such experiments were not only forbidden, but were indeed accursed by God.

And yet we still did not admit to ourselves that we had come into contact with merciless and incredibly evil spirits, which had invaded our carefree and happy student life. We didn't realize how defenseless we were against their onslaught.

Then one night I slept over in the room of one of my friends in the dormitory. My classmate Ivan Loshchilin and Sasha Olkov, a student in the film directors' class, started again doing their mystical séances. By this time we all had already sworn that we would stop dabbling with this stuff, but we were completely unable to stop ourselves; the connection with these mysterious forces was more powerful than any narcotic.

This time my friends had picked up an interrupted conversation they had started with "the spirit of Gogol" (the great Russian nineteenth-century author). This spirit that spoke to us was certainly extremely eloquent, and indeed his vocabulary was in the style of the beginning of the nineteenth century. But today he no longer answered any of our questions. Instead, he complained, groaned, whimpered, and expressed to us that his heart was broken and that his pain was unbearable.

"What's wrong with you?" my friends asked

"Help me! Help me! Oh! I'm in agony! Help!" said this mysterious entity. "It's unendurable! I beg you! Help me!"

Of course we all adored the works of Nikolai Vasilyevich Gogol, and we all were certain that we were really speaking directly to him.

"But what can we do for you?" we asked, truly wishing to help our beloved writer with all our hearts.

"Help me, help me, I beg you! Please don't abandon me! The flame is frightful—the flame, and the sulfur, the agony! Oh! It's unbearable! Help me! Help!"

"We're ready to help," we said passionately, "in any way we can! But what can we do for you if you're in another world?"

The spirit slowed down and then said cautiously: "Oh, my dear youngsters, if you are truly ready to take pity on a sufferer . . ."

"Of course we are! Just tell us what to do!"

"Well, if you're really ready to help, then . . . then I'd give you some poison."

When the full meaning of these words hit us, we were petrified. And looking at each other, even by the dim candlelight of our séance, we could see that our faces had all gone as pale as chalk. Knocking over our chairs, we all raced from the room.

When I collected myself, I said: "He's quite right. In order to help him, we do in fact first have to become just like him. That means . . . we have to die."

"And I too have understood everything," Sasha Olkov said, through shivering teeth. "What he wants is for us to commit suicide."

"I'm even sure that when I'll go back into that room, I will see some sort of pill lying on the table," said Ivan Loshchilin, who had turned green with fear. "And when I see that pill, I'll understand that I absolutely must take it. Either that or I'll have an uncontrollable urge to leap out the window. Those spirits will force us to do this."

All night long we couldn't sleep, and in the morning, we went to the Church of the Tikhvin Icon of the Virgin Mary. We didn't know where else we could turn for help.

Savior . . . From using that name so often, even Christians lose connection to the word's real and original meaning. But now it was the most desired and most important word: Savior. We knew, however fantastic it might sound, that we were being hunted by powerful and unknown malevolent spirits, from whom only God our Savior could deliver us.

We were afraid that in church we would be laughed at with our "Gogol" story, but the young priest, Father Vladimir Chuvikin, quite calmly confirmed all our worst fears. He explained that we had of course been in conversations, only not with Gogol and Socrates, but with real demons and evil spirits. I must admit, this sounded a bit strange to us. Yet in that moment we had not the least doubt that we were hearing the truth.

The priest firmly told us that this sort of mystical activity was a terrible sin. Then he forcefully recommended that those of us who had never been baptized should get ready for the sacrament of baptism and should be baptized without delay. As for the rest of us, we must come to confession and to Communion.

But once again, we put it all off, although from that day forth we never once returned to our earlier experiments. By now it was time to prepare for our final exams, to work on our thesis projects, to make plans for our futures; and once more we were submerged in our freewheeling student life. But I read the Scriptures every day, and more and more, reading it became a daily need. Especially because the Scriptures seemed to be the only medicine to save me from the gloom and despair that from time to time came back to me, ravaging my spirit.

It was only after a year had passed that I realized that life without God would be completely meaningless for me.

I was baptized by a wonderful priest, Father Alexey Zlobin, in the Church of St. Nicholas in Kuznetsy, together with a dozen or so babies, and about half a dozen adults. The babies cried so loudly, and the priest read his prayers so softly, that during the hour and a half that the sacrament was taking place I didn't really understand anything.

My godmother, who was the cleaning lady in the church, said to me: "You will now have several very blessed days."

"What do you mean, blessed days?" I asked her.

"God will be very close to you," my godmother answered. "If you can, by all means go visit the Pechory Monastery near Pskov. There you will find an elder, Father John—his last name is Krestiankin. He'll explain everything to you, and will answer all of your questions. But when you get to the monastery, stick with it, don't just leave at once. Stay for at least ten days."

"All right," I said. "We'll see."

I left the church and immediately felt something amazing. Even the least hints of the depression and gloom that had surrounded me were gone. But I didn't linger or go deeper into my new feelings. Instead I immediately decided to share my new joy with my very best friend in the world at that time—my tutor in film school and the wonderful screenplay writer Yevgeny Alexandrovich Grigoryev. We had all been part of his tutorial group, and he was the idol of our entire class. He lived at the Metro stop Belyayevo, on the far outskirts of Moscow. I had no idea whether or not he was home (not everybody had a phone at this time, and phone books did not exist), and I decided to just go there, hoping to get lucky.

For a long time I rang the doorbell of his apartment in vain. Yevgeny Alexandrovich was not home. Dejectedly, I walked back towards the Metro. Then suddenly I remembered the "grace" or "grace-filled prayer" that my godmother had just taught me. I stopped, looked up to the sky, and said: "Jesus Christ, Lord, in whose faith today I was baptized. More than anything on earth right now I wish to see Yevgeny Alexandrovich Grigoryev, my teacher. I know that I shouldn't be bothering You with such trifles. But if it's possible, please, help me, do this for me today."

I got into the Metro entirely certain that soon I would see Yevgeny Alexandrovich.

I began to wait for the next train coming from the center of the city. As the passengers were getting out of the train I started to tensely scan them all, trying to pick out my teacher from that enormous stream of people. And . . . nothing. Then suddenly, somebody clapped me on my shoulder. It was Yevgeny Alexandrovich.

"Who are you looking for with such an eagle eye?" he asked.

"For you," I answered, not surprised in the least.

"Well, you found me, so let's go." And we went to his house. And I told him about the event that had taken place in my life that very day. Yevgeny Alexandrovich listened to me very carefully. He himself was not baptized. But he respected my choice. He asked questions about the rite of baptism itself. Then he asked me what had driven me to my decision.

"Because God exists," I answered firmly. "And I have become convinced of this. And everything that the Church teaches is correct."

"You think so?" Grigoryev asked doubtfully. "You know, in the Church, there are all kinds of things that, well . . ."

"Maybe so," I answered, "but the Church has the main thing."

"Perhaps," said Yevgeny Alexandrovich.

We went to a store, bought a bottle of Stolichnaya vodka, several packs of cigarettes, and something to eat, and then we sat together till the evening, discussing my new screenplay. But when I came home, I remembered what had happened in the Metro, how I had said the prayer and immediately after that Yevgeny Alexandrovich had appeared. Was it a coincidence or not?

It wasn't so easy to answer this question. But I felt there was clearly a link between the two events. On the other hand, nothing like this had ever happened to me before. It was time to go deeper into the mystery.

Two days later, following the advice of my godmother, I bought a ticket and set out by train for the Pskov Caves Monastery in the town of Pechory, near Pskov.

Pechory

The Moscow-Talinn train arrived at the Pskov station at about five in the morning. Rattling along in a claptrap old bus on the way to the Pechory Monastery, I gazed at Pechory, a surprisingly well-kept little town on the western border of Russia with lovely small homes, with turrets and neat lawns and little palisades. Pechory is five kilometers from the border with Estonia. After the Russian Revolution and until 1940, it actually was part of the territory of Estonia, which explains why it was the only monastery in the Soviet Union that remained undamaged and with its way of life relatively unscathed.

Along with the other passengers from the train from Moscow, I walked up to the great stone walls of the monastery. The monastery was still closed, and we had to wait until the guard opened up the old wrought-iron gates at the appointed hour. Inside the monastery it was surprisingly comfortable and beautiful—so much so that it was impossible not to be amazed. Everything here gave an impression, if not of a fairy tale—because this was obviously real life—then at least of something wondrous.

By the pathway over the well-kept cobblestones I walked down to the main square of the monastery. Now and then as I passed, looking at the colorful buildings of the monastery, I saw that everywhere were beautiful flowerbeds with lovely roses blooming. The churches here were so comfortable and so attractive. I had never seen such beautiful churches.

Inside the Pskov Caves Monastery.

In the main cathedral of the monastery, the cave church of the Dormition of the Holy Mother of God, the Virgin Mary, it was practically pitch dark. When I walked in, two monks in ponytails and black robes that fell down to the floor were lighting lamps. The low whitewashed ceilings dimly reflected the light coming from these lanterns. The faces of the icons in their ancient frames looked at me attentively.

In the church, the monks in their black mantles and monastic hats were gradually beginning to gather around us. People from outside the community also began to appear. A service began that unfolded for me as if in one breath. Once I found out that there would soon be another Liturgy and that the archbishop would be coming to it, I walked up to the Cathedral of St. Michael, which is located on a high hill. There I took part in yet another service.

I was completely struck by everything: the deacon with his long flowing locks and his beautiful stoles rippling over his shoulders, and the very serious head of the monastery, and all the priests, some old and some young. Their faces were completely different from the faces of ordinary Soviet people outside the monastery. The archbishop impressed me; he was a huge, elderly man, resplendent in his ancient raiment, and with a wise and unusually benevolent face.

At the end of the very long service, the monks with graceful singing marched off majestically, two by two, toward the refectory. I meanwhile went into the courtyard of the monastery and asked several of the pilgrims gathered there how it would be possible to stay in the monastery overnight. I was told that I would need to ask the monk in charge of keeping order in the monastery, known as the *blagochinniy*, or monastery dean. It was the first time I had ever heard such a word, and I repeated it to myself several times so as not to forget it.

As the monks began to leave the refectory, I started asking each of them in turn which one was the *blagochinniy*.

"The *blagochinniy* is with the bishop right now, but you can go ask one of his helpers. Try Father Palladius or Father Ireneaus," I was advised.

I immediately told myself that there was no way on earth I would ever remember such impossible names. One of the monks took pity on me and personally walked me over to the assistant of the *blagochinniy*, who in turn brought me to a cell reserved for pilgrims.

Ten Days: My First Tasks

The cell into which I was settled was on the first floor of the building of the chief monk of the monastery himself. His lodgings were directly above us. Right next to me, as I was immediately warned, lived the very strict Treasurer of the monastery, named Father Nathaniel.

I thought to myself, it sure wouldn't be a bad idea to give each of these monks simpler names! Fortunately, I thought the name of the monk whom I had been advised to find wasn't quite so difficult: Father John.

My cell was spacious and neat. There were about a dozen beds, some ancient bookcases with beautiful wood carvings, chests of drawers—in short, everything was there to help me relax and feel at home as I spent the night. There were all kinds of visitors in the monastery. Some had come as pilgrims; others were simply curious visitors like me. They had come from everywhere throughout the country, and yet relations between them, as I could immediately see, were entirely friendly, generous, and benevolent.

I was told that everyone had to go to services in the mornings and evenings, and during the afternoons there were tasks to be done. What sort of tasks? They'd let us know. We might have to chop wood, or help out in the kitchen or cellars, or sweep the paths.

In the evening we all went to services. This time for some reason it

Wandering holy fools.

seemed especially difficult to stand up all the way through. Somehow, this particular evening service just never seemed to come to an end—and, to my great discomfort, it lasted more than four hours. And yet I had a good look at the people who had come to the church. Most of these were simple peasant women—many of them middle-aged or older. Men were rarer in the throng of worshipers. But there was also a decent crowd of young people, or, at the very least, there were more young people gathered here than in the churches in Moscow. And of course there were also pilgrims, wandering "holy fools," and all those unique characters who make up the incomparable spirit of a Russian monastery and, in this case, the town connected to it.

After services we all went to supper. There were about five monks present. The others, as was explained to me later, ate only twice a day, and therefore the refectory was generally only full of pilgrims and novices doing their tasks. The food we were served was not luxurious, but it was quite tasty. An appointed monk read aloud to us from the lives of the saints as we were eating. Presiding over the meal was the ultra-strict Treasurer of the monastery, Father Nathaniel. At the time he was sixty-five years old. Wizened, with gray hair, he didn't eat anything himself, but merely watched over the rest of us, making sure that order was kept, now and then correcting the reader if he chanced to slip up in pronouncing an ancient Byzantine name.

When the meal was over, we all stayed where we were, and yet another prayer began—the evening prayer. Then we all began singing an ancient and very melodic hymn, and one after another we went over to the cross that the hieromonk* held in his hand.

When I walked out of the refectory, I saw for the first time the monastery at night. It was incredibly beautiful. The lamps were shining, illuminating the paths in the crowns of the trees; lanterns were also flickering brightly, lighting up the buildings. All this made nighttime in the monastery not frightening at all, but both mysterious and peaceful. I didn't want to go back to my cell, but I was told that it was just not the done thing to wander aimlessly around the territory of the monastery at night. Besides, we would have to get up very early the next morning.

How early? When I found out exactly, I was very distressed indeed. What? Were they serious? Five-thirty in the morning? I never got up that early!

But at 5:30 in the morning, just as they had promised, I was awakened by the loud ringing of bells.

"By the prayers of our Holy Fathers, Lord Jesus Christ, have mercy on us!" This was the "wake-up" monk, opening wide the door of our monastic cell, reading with a sleepy voice this regularly appointed prayer, and then shuffling off to the rest of the monastery to awaken all the others.

---

* A *hieromonk* is the title of a monk in the Orthodox Church who is also a priest.

How difficult and unpleasant it was to wake up at this hour, the crack of dawn, to brush my teeth with ice-cold water in a large communal bathroom! By now I had already regretted coming here a hundred times. What's more, I was regretting that I had given my word to God that I would stay here a whole ten days! What did we need to be getting up so early for? For whom? For God? Of course not! For ourselves? Also not! We were just torturing ourselves!

It was still dark outside. The monks in their rippling black robes silently climbed up the winding staircase, up the tall hill to the Cathedral of St. Michael. Pilgrims hurried on after them.

In the light of the oil lamps and candles, our brothers' *moleben* services— short, private prayer services—began. At this service we all asked God, the Mother of God, and the patron of the monastery, St. Cornelius, for blessing on this day to come. Using an oil lamp hanging before a miraculous icon, the monks lit a candle in an even more ancient lantern. From this lantern, in turn, they lit the wood-burning stoves of the monastery kitchens. After our brothers' supplicatory prayer services we listened to the morning prayers, at which we read long lists that had been handed us by pilgrims. These lists contained the names of persons for whose health or peaceful repose we were to pray for. Then, finally, those who would not participate in the second service—and this group included me—went to get breakfast.

When I saw what they feed the pilgrims for breakfast, my mood began to improve. They were serving fresh fish of a type that even in Moscow you would hardly ever see. They had pickled mushrooms and eggplants and various types of oatmeal and other grains—buckwheat—and they had fried onions. And plenty of everything—more than enough for everyone. I later found out that it was a tradition in Pechory to feed the pilgrims and workers in the monastery well. This tradition had been established from the time of the previous abbot of the monastery, Father Alipius, and had been continued under his successor, Archimandrite* Gabriel.

During breakfast the monks and novices talked to each other in a very friendly manner, sometimes even joking among themselves. I was very pleased by the atmosphere, because it was so calm and benevolent. I had never encountered such kindness in the secular world.

---

* *Archimandrite* is a title given to a monk in the Orthodox Church in priestly rank for his achievements in his work for the Church. It is usually given to heads of monasteries.

At eight in the morning, we pilgrims gathered in the stockyard. Father Maxim, the Brigadier, as he was called (still using the Soviet name for his job), read us a short prayer and started to assign our tasks to us. To me he said briefly, "You'll be cleaning."

What he meant by "cleaning" I had no idea at the time. When I found out, I got so angry that I very nearly turned around and went straight home. They had asked me to clean up the wells of the sewer systems! I was extremely upset, but I found the strength inside me to refrain from any wild reactions, and I forced myself to put on the dirty clothes and boots that they gave me so as to climb into the sewage canals.

I will not describe that day. I spent its endless entirety in freezing, stinking ditches, scraping filth and mud and muck from the floors with sand, and loading it all wearily into buckets.

Now and then, climbing out of my sewage canal to breathe, I stared at the monks who were all idly strolling around the monastery (as it seemed to me), and suddenly vividly remembered my lectures on atheism, all those stories we had been told about those fat black-robed exploiters of the peasants and workers, those hypocrites, all holier than thou, preying on the superstitions of the simple ignorant people—in this case, me.

At this point I still didn't know that each monk has not just one but several tasks to do, and indeed, the entire life of a monk consists of nothing but toil and prayer. But this is kept hidden from prying eyes. Monks work always: they work in the forges, in the carpenters' workshops, and in the kitchens, cleaning, washing, cooking the meals and baking the Communion bread. There are monks who work in the libraries, monks who work in the vestry, who keep the altar clean as well as the churches, making sure that everything needed for the service is ready; and there are monks who work in the laundries cleaning the vestments and church utensils. Others buy the food; others prepare this food for hundreds of people—both monks and civilians. Others work in the gardens, prune the trees, or work the fields, or maintain the vegetable storehouses. And so on, and so on . . . This isn't even to mention the fact that all these monks, besides working a full day, daily take part in many services that last many hours; what's more, these priests also care for their flock, listen to the confessions of congregants, sometimes till late in the night, and then on top of that, they have many other obligations to perform as well. Still, when you're young and mucking about in a sewage ditch, the world can seem extremely gloomy and unfair.

In the evening once again I stood for hours during a long service and read endless names in dusty notebooks, endless lists of people to be remembered: prayers for health and for repose . . . prayers for health and for repose . . . For Ivan, and Agrippina, and Peter, and Nadyezhda, for Catherine, who was sick, for Anna, who is pregnant, and for Nicholas, far away from home . . . And somehow all these names passed like living beings before my eyes.

Feeling myself responsible, I tried to not only say these names out loud, but to really try to picture these souls, to really pray as best I could for them. I can remember only one time when I was really cheerful: I received a list clearly written in the handwriting of an old person requesting a prayer for the health of "the prodigal infant Gregory." Somehow, I could easily imagine for myself this contrary youngster who had brought his unhappy grandmother to the edge of despair.

Oh! How I wanted to go home! Eight more days of this nonsense! And I still hadn't managed to meet Father John and to talk about my issues with him.

On the next day they made me chop wood and pile up the wood in enormous rows rising very high in the stockyard, like unusual cottages many stories tall. I had never in my life cleaned sewage canals, I had never chopped wood, I had never cleaned up cow manure, I had never swept cobblestone paths . . . But that's what they made me do while I was there. And so, by the time my ten-day stay in the monastery was over, I had many new impressions. I was also thoroughly irritated and tired. I had absolutely just had it up to here with all these "exotic experiences."

And yet . . . I had seen glimpses of an unfamiliar and striking new world. Now and then I would run into Father John for a few minutes. At that time he seemed to me to be a typical old grandfather, quite nice, to be sure, but otherwise very simple, and not particularly interesting. My questions for him were, as I remember now, really pretty foolish. But Father John nonetheless listened to me, and then, excusing himself on the grounds that he had no time, advised me to speak to a monk named Tavrion. For the umpteenth time, I wearily declared that there was no way I would be able to remember that name. However, in answer to a question that was particularly important to me at that time—namely, could I have a film career, and how would the Church feel about that— Father John gave a completely unexpected answer. What he said then was:

"After all, the movie business is simply about using your tongue. You can use it in various ways: either to crucify God, or else to glorify Him."

His words stuck to me at once, and I began to think: this grandpa is not so simple after all . . . How was I to know that this man was going to decide my entire future fate? How could I know that he would become one of the main revelations of my life? How could I know that he would forever become my model of a Christian, a monk, and a priest?

At the time the old man warmly embraced me as I was leaving, blessed me, and commanded me without fail to return once more to the monastery, a possibility of which I was immediately extremely doubtful. One trip to Pechory, it seemed to me, was far more than enough.

The day before leaving Pechory, I finally remembered the name of the priest to whom Father John had suggested I talk—the monk Tavrion. And I sought him out. He seemed to be a monk of about forty, not very tall, with a university education. (I have since understood what Father John was planning, since in the state that I was in at that time, I needed "intelligent conversation.")

Father Tavrion was very patient with me. He tried to answer all my very muddled questions as seriously as he could, and in the end he suggested that I read the Holy Scripture as well as the lives of the saints and the Church Fathers, and bade me to pray every morning and night according to the prayer book, to regularly make confession and take Communion, and—most important of all—to find a father confessor or spiritual father. Father Tavrion gave me a prayer book with a Psalter, which was something extremely valuable at that time, and also invited me to come back.

I endured all ten days—all that rising at the crack of dawn, all those tasks, all those endless services with the wailing of possessed voices* in my ear. I could not say that I ever regretted having wasted time there. But by the last day I was really longing to get back to Moscow.

Everyone said goodbye to me very warmly. With the blessing of the abbot of the monastery, the Treasurer gave me thirty rubles for my trip home—quite a vast sum in those days. They also gave me a pouch full of all kinds of delicious food. As I went to pray in the church, I felt a fleeting yet grateful melancholy for my leaving the monastery, as well as a

---

* In those days, many people who were demonically possessed would come to the Pskov Caves Monastery for healing. They would wail because the demons possessing them cannot bear the power of God that is manifest during the Church services.

Archimandrite
John Krestiankin.

joyful anticipation of returning to Moscow.

And then something happened that gave me a real shock. When for the first time in ten days I actually found myself outside the monastery's gates, the first feeling that came to me was an almost uncontrollable desire to drop everything and run back inside! Never had I expected that I would feel anything like this. Only by immense strength of will was I able to pull myself together and drag myself to the bus station, each minute with a growing understanding that I lived now in a completely different world, not at all the world that I had left ten days before.

It was early evening. Ordinary people were walking the streets. A young man came towards me, eating a roll in one hand and an apple in the other. I remember how revolted I was to see this absolutely ordinary event, and I couldn't understand why. Finally it hit me: all those days I had gotten used to the idea of only partaking of food after having first prayed to God. And so this vision of some guy just stuffing his face thoughtlessly and ungratefully in the middle of the street suddenly now struck me as quite unthinkable.

Young people were walking out of the movie theater. Someone chuckled loudly. Young couples in love walked past me embracing each other or holding hands. Everything was totally normal, except for one thing: I suddenly felt myself completely alien in this scene.

On the way back on the train there were two girls and a young man of about my age in my compartment. I clambered up to the top bunk, while they spread out their food and wine. They were clearly looking forward to a happy trip, and they started very insistently inviting me to join their company. Just ten days before, without even thinking about it, I would almost certainly have joined them, and we would have spent a lovely time together. But now, mumbling some kind of awkward answer, I stayed in my corner and, during the entire trip, despite my traveling companions' mirthful reproaches and appeals to climb back down to our sinful planet Earth, I instead kept to myself, reading incomprehensible ancient Slavonic words from my prayer book that had been given to me by Father Tavrion. Now, not for a minute did I condemn or look down on those young people. And (God forbid) I certainly did not consider myself some kind of righteous person as compared to them, benighted young sinners. I didn't think about things that way at all. It's just—now everything had changed, everything had become different.

In Moscow

Indeed, everything was different now. I didn't know what had happened to me, but suddenly the world had lost all its attractions, and ceased to be interesting. All that yesterday had seemed desirable and valuable to me was now revealed to be not worthless (I certainly wouldn't dare to say that) but irredeemably alien. I didn't recognize myself. And my friends didn't recognize me either.

When I came home to Moscow, suddenly I realized with surprise that throughout all those past ten days, not only had I not smoked, but I had not even thought about my incurable habit of many years. And this was despite the fact that until that time I had normally smoked not less than two packs of cigarettes a day.

Now the only place where I felt normal was in church. Neither my friends, nor my pastimes, nor the work I had once so strived for—none of it touched my heart any longer. Even my books, even my beloved Dostoyevsky and Tolstoy, somehow no longer held my attention. I understood that I had completely changed, and that in fact I was now hopelessly lost to this world that had once been so dear to me. Another life beckoned me, next to which all my prior experience of twenty-four years paled in comparison.

Of course, I did love that past world, and I was sad for it and felt compassion for it from the bottom of my heart! But that was just the point—my heart! It already belonged not to my old world and to my old goals, but to a new world that had mysteriously and unexpectedly revealed itself to me, a world devoted not to fleeting things, but to an unbreakable covenant between man and God.

At the good advice of Father Tavrion, I opened up the book of the lives of the Orthodox saints and discovered the works of the Holy Fathers. They completely astonished me. What bothered me most of all was that, having always had access to this incredible treasure trove of our own culture, we knew absolutely nothing about it. I was suddenly introduced to a whole flock of great authors who had over centuries acquired a vast store of knowledge and wisdom, more even than the great philosophical minds and geniuses of our classical literature. St. Isaac the Syrian, John Climacus, Abba Dorotheus, St. John Chrysostom, more modern saints—Ignatius Brianchaninov and Theophan the Recluse, and St. Tikhon of Zadonsk— all this tremendous spiritual assembly had been deliberately kept hidden from us for so long!

Within a month, church services became entirely understandable to me, and Old Church Slavonic words were now filled with depth and great meaning. My morning and evening prayers were now my most beloved times, and Communion and confession to me had become akin to truly physical needs.

Soon I returned to Pechory. Since then, I have always made it a point to live there as often as circumstances permit. The cinematic world completely ceased to interest me, and I believe that this was no great loss to either party. To be honest, I was merely going through the motions as I did the work required of us after graduating from the film institute. My teachers complained as they saw this, but soon understood that there was nothing they could do to change the situation. Having finished my jobs in the movie studio, I grabbed my first two weeks of free time, jumped onto a train, and went back to the monastery. What was it that so moved me to go back there? Its inhabitants, most of all. And I want to tell you about them.

Father John

I FIRST SAW Archimandrite John (Krestiankin) in 1982 when I visited Pechory Monastery. At the time he did not make a great impression on me: the benevolent old man in rather good physical condition (he was already seventy-two years old) was always running here and there, a bit fussed, even . . . yet ever surrounded by a crowd of pilgrims. In comparison with him, the other inhabitants of the monastery seemed much stricter, more ascetic, and somehow more dignified.

Usually before the start of the evening service a strange procession would fly out of the brothers' quarters of the Pskov Caves Monastery. Father Philaret, the young *econom* or steward of the monastery, would take Father John by the arm and almost at a run drag him off somewhere so quickly that he could barely keep up with his cell attendant. Following this pair, immediately there flowed a crowd of pilgrims waiting for their chance to speak to Father John, right there on the street. And so they all ran, racing headlong through the entire courtyard of the monastery, their robes and Orthodox *klobuk** veils flowing, with Father John stumbling over himself now and then as he panted, out of breath, trying on the run to bless some pilgrims and simultaneously even managing to answer theological questions! Father Philaret would get quite angry about this, and would yell—sometimes at Father John, and sometimes at the pilgrims, whom he might even drive away with his umbrella. Finally he would drag Father John into the church and would lead him to the altar as quickly as possible.

I should say that our young monastery steward acted this way not out of spite, but because he was concerned that in the cold winter months Father John might catch a cold. When the weather got warmer, there was a serious risk that Father John wouldn't make it to the church at all, as sometimes he would be surrounded by people seeking his blessings for hours and hours.

Together, my friends and fellow novices would watch the scene taking place day after day and would laugh heartily, until at last it began to occur

---

* A *klobuk* is a cylindrical hat worn by monks in church.

Father Philaret.   *Father John.*

to us that this seemingly humorous figure of Father John, racing after the irritated monastery steward, was actually one of those rare human beings on earth for whom the boundaries of space and time are shifted, someone to whom the Lord has given the gift to see the past and the future as clearly as the present. With complete surprise and not without awe we experienced this for ourselves. This man, whom some people mocked as "Doctor Aibolit" (something equivalent to a Russian Doctor Doolittle), was able to read the secrets of human souls, and all their hidden treasures, desires, deeds, and thoughts were open to him. In ancient times people like him were called prophets. We in the Russian Orthodox Church call such people elders.

But Father John never called himself an elder. And when people would say something like that to him, he would wave his arms disparagingly: "What elders? We just happen to be old men who have experienced a few things!" To the very end of his life he was convinced of this, in keeping with his profound inner humility. And yet many of those who knew Father John were convinced that in his person the Lord had sent us a true elder, someone who understood the Providence and the mysterious will of God.

Yes, this was the main thing about him: Father John was able to see the will of God as it concerned other people. But we novices did not immediately understand this. At first it seemed to us that this priest was just a very wise elderly man. Indeed, it was because of his famous "wisdom" that people would come from every corner of Russia to see him. It was only later that these thousands of people from all over the country would discover to their own astonishment that they had really come not so much for wise advice, but for something even more profound.

In worldly life we are always surrounded by people willing to advise us from their own experience. Yet the people who would appear before Father John, usually at the most tragic and fateful moments of their lives, wanted to hear from him not just how to act wisely, but how to act with certainty, in the only correct way. To be precise, it was in his unique understanding of the will of God that this elder was different from all other people—even from renowned wise men, even from intellectual theologians, and even from the most experienced and wonderful priests.

I remember when I was still just a young novice, one of the pilgrims from Moscow walked up to me and told me a story that he had just witnessed himself. Father John had been racing to church, thronged as usual by a crowd of people desperate to speak to him. Suddenly a woman in tears, holding a three-year-old baby, threw herself across his path.

"Father, bless my baby before his operation—the doctors demand that it be done immediately in Moscow."

Father John stopped and told the woman something that utterly shocked the pilgrims from Moscow: "Under no circumstances! He'll die on the operating table. Pray, and take loving care of him, but do not do the operation under any circumstances. He will get well."

Then Father John made the sign of the cross over the boy.

The pilgrim and I went off horrified as we reflected on this event. What if the priest made a mistake? What if the boy were to die? What would the mother do with Father John if something like that were to happen?

We of course could not suspect Father John to be someone with principled opposition to any form of medicine, a phenomenon that, though rare, does occur in certain spiritual circles. On the contrary, he often blessed and sometimes even insisted on surgical operations. There were several famous doctors who considered him their father confessor and themselves his spiritual children.

It was with dread that we waited for further developments. Would the mother of the boy come back to the monastery grief-stricken, stirring up a frightful scandal? Or would everything be exactly as Father John had predicted? Judging by the way the old priest continued to peacefully go back and forth on his daily path between the church and his monastic cell, we could only conclude that the elder who had given such decisive advice knew what he was talking about. And so it proved.

Confidence and obedience are the main rules for a relationship between a Russian Orthodox Christian and his father confessor or spiritual father. Of course, not every spiritual father is capable of inspiring such complete obedience, and indeed, spiritual fathers of such caliber are extremely rare. So in fact this is a very complicated question. There have been tragedies in which unreasonable priests have begun to imagine themselves elders, and have therefore given cruel commands and arrogant instructions and, worst of all, have begun to commit that which is absolutely forbidden in spiritual life: to suppress the freedom and free will of your spiritual children.

Father John never dictated and never insisted on his will, but had limitless respect for human freedom and treated it with the utmost reverence. Father John was prepared to persuade, cajole, exhort, and even beg his parishioners to follow advice that he somehow knew was utterly necessary for the happiness of the person who returned to him. But if such a person would stubbornly insist on going his own way, then, goodly priest that he was, he usually sighed and said: "All right, try it . . . act as you see fit."

And always, as far as I know, those who did not take the advice of Father John would bitterly regret their stubbornness in the end. And, as a rule, the next time they would come to see the priest with the fullest intention of following exactly whatever advice he would give. And Father John, with indefatigable sympathy and brimming love, would always take these people back into his great heart, sparing neither his time nor his strength, as he constantly tried to correct their mistakes.

* * *

The story about the young boy and the operation reminds me of a similar incident that took place about ten years later. However, that incident ended in a completely different manner.

In those years in Moscow there lived an unbelievably interesting and unique woman, Valentina Pavlovna Konovalova. She seemed to have walked straight out of the famous painting by Kustodiev—she was the spitting image of his portrait of the Moscow merchant woman that hangs in Moscow's Tretyakov Gallery. She was a widow of about sixty years of age, and was the director of a large grocery warehouse on Prospekt Mira in Moscow. Stout and intensely earthy, Valentina Pavlovna could generally be found presiding at a large managers' table in her office.

Even during the severest epoch of Soviet anti-religious persecution, she kept framed paper reproductions of icons hanging on her office walls, and on the floor beneath her desk she kept a big cellophane bag stuffed full of cash. Valentina Pavlovna controlled this cash as she wished: sometimes, she would send her staff out to buy vegetables, and sometimes she would support beggars and wanderers and holy fools, many of whom gathered around her grocery warehouse for material support. Her staff was terrified of Valentina Pavlovna, but also loved her. During Great Lent, she would have general Unction services right in her office. These Unction services were always reverently attended by the Muslim Tatars who worked at the warehouse. In those years when groceries were scarce, she would sometimes be visited by abbots of Moscow's monasteries, and even by archbishops. To some she was reservedly polite; to others whose "ecumenism" displeased her (that is, those not Orthodox enough), she could be curt and even a little rude.

I personally was sent several times from Pechory to her grocery warehouse in Moscow with a big truck to buy food for our monastery for Easter and for Christmas. Valentina Pavlovna always welcomed us in a warm, maternal way. Having long ago buried her only son, she was particularly nice to young novices. We became friends, especially because we had one common theme for our discussions: our common spiritual father, Father John.

Father John was perhaps the only person on earth who could make Valentina Pavlovna feel shy, even though she utterly loved and respected him. Twice a year she herself, together with her closest co-workers, would travel to Pechory, where she would fast and go to confession. On such days, she seemed unrecognizable—quiet, meek, timid, and in no way at all like a rich Moscow merchant woman, a mistress of this world.

In the fall of 1993 major changes occurred in my life: I was appointed abbot of the *podvorye* (local representation or residence) in Moscow of the Pskov Caves Monastery. This representation was supposed to be located in the ancient Sretensky Monastery. But in order to execute a large number of documents, I often needed to be in Pechory.

Often Valentina Pavlovna's eyes hurt . . . They thought it was nothing, just cataracts, which come with age. And so she happened to ask me whether I could ask for the blessing of Father John for a small operation she would be undergoing at the famous Fyodorov Ophthalmology Institute. Father John's answer, I must admit, surprised me:

"No, no, not now—under no circumstances. Not now, let some time pass," he insisted.

When I got back to Moscow I passed along his words to Valentina Pavlovna. She was very upset. The procedure had already been completely arranged at the Fyodorov Institute, an elite and prestigious institution whose services were not easy to come by. And so Valentina Pavlovna wrote a letter to Father John, explaining in detail and once again asking for his blessing for the operation, insisting that it was a very simple procedure, hardly even worth paying attention to.

Father John naturally knew just as well as she did how famous the Institute was and how safe operations on cataracts usually are. Yet having read the letter that she brought to me, he became extremely worried. I sat with the old priest for a long time and in great distress he pleaded with me that no matter what, I must absolutely convince Valentina Pavlovna to refuse to undergo the operation at this time. He once again wrote her a long letter in which he simply implored her to listen to him. With all his authority as her spiritual father he blessed her decision to postpone the operation for a certain length of time. Later it would be all right, but not now . . .

It so happened that back then I had just received two weeks' leave. For over ten years I had never had any free time, and therefore Father John blessed me to go to a sanatorium to rest in the Crimea for two weeks. He insisted that I must take Valentina Pavlovna with me. He wrote a special letter to her about this, insisting again that she undergo the operation later, a month after her vacation.

"If she goes through with the operation now, she will die," Father John said sadly to me as I took my leave of him.

But when I got back to Moscow, I realized that I had met my match. Talking to Valentina Pavlovna was like talking to a brick wall. Perhaps for the first time in her life, she rebelled against the wishes of her spiritual father. She raged that she had last been on vacation way back in her teens, and she seethed with rage:

"What other crazy idea has the Father gotten into his head? Vacation! And to whom am I supposed to leave the management of the warehouse?" She was truly indignant that Father John was "kicking up such a fuss" over a "routine procedure." But as decisively as I could when it was my turn, I refused to listen to her, and told her that I was buying two vacation

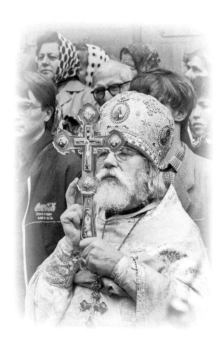

packages, and that we would be off to this nice sanatorium in the Crimea very soon. After a while it seemed that Valentina Pavlovna had agreed and calmed down.

Several days passed. I received a blessing from His Holiness the Patriarch for my vacation, ordered two sanatorium packages (which were not hard to find at the end of autumn), and called the warehouse to inform Valentina Pavlovna of the date of our trip.

"Valentina Pavlovna is in the hospital," her assistant told me. "They will be operating on her today."

"What?" I screamed. "But Father John forbids it!"

It turned out that a couple of days before a nun had stopped by the warehouse. In her secular job she was a doctor, and, having heard about the cataracts, she could not agree with the decision of Father John. Totally supporting Valentina Pavlovna's desires, she had ignored Father John's advice, and had instead sought out the conflicting blessing of the monks of the St. Sergius-Holy Trinity Lavra* of Sergiev Posad (Zagorsk) for the operation, and on that very day she received it. And so Valentina Pavlovna, quite content, went to the Fyodorov Ophthalmology Institute, counting on a simple operation, after which, in two or three days' time, she would go join me in the Crimea. However, during the operation she suddenly had a terrible stroke, and became completely paralyzed.

As soon as I heard of this, I rushed to telephone to Father John's cell attendant, the monastery steward Father Philaret. In certain emergencies, Father John came to Father Philaret's cell and used his telephone.

"How could you have done such a thing? Why didn't you listen to

---

* *Lavra* is the name given to a monastery of exceptional importance. The Holy Trinity-St. Sergius Lavra is historically one of the most significant monasteries in Russia, founded in the fourteenth century by the great St. Sergius of Radonezh.

me?" Father John was practically in tears as he heard my distressing news. "If I really insist on something, it's because I know what I'm saying!"

What could I say to him in reply? Nothing . . . I asked only how we could help now . . . Valentina Pavlovna was still unconscious. Father John begged me to go to the church and bring to his cell the reserved Holy Gifts (the Body and Blood of Christ reserved for ministration to the ailing), and without delay I was to take her confession and give her Holy Communion once she regained consciousness—whether it be day or night.

Through the nonstop prayers of Father John, Valentina Pavlovna regained consciousness the very next day. I was advised of this by her relatives, and within half an hour I was by her side in the hospital. She was brought into the intensive care unit of the hospital in a sort of metal stretcher. She was lying beneath a white sheet and was totally weak and helpless. When she saw me, she closed her eyes and cried. She could not speak. But no words were necessary to understand her confession. I read the prayer of absolution and gave her Holy Communion. We parted.

On the next day, she once again received Communion from Father Vladimir Chuvikin, who had baptized me. That very evening she died. We buried Valentina Pavlovna in a transcendent and hopeful mood, and with peaceful feelings. According to ancient Church tradition, the soul of a person who takes Communion on the day of death immediately ascends to the throne of the Lord.

* * *

Father John is also intimately connected with everything that involves the revival of monastic life in our own Sretensky Monastery. In the fall of 1993 during the commemoration of the Icon of the Iveron Mother of God, I came to visit Father John at an extremely difficult time in my own life. I had by then become a priest in Moscow's Donskoy Monastery. But my relationship with the head of the monastery, Archimandrite Agathadorus, had been completely ruined, entirely as a result of my own mistakes, and I had no idea what to do or how to fix the situation. Father Agathadorus himself sent me to Pechory to see my spiritual father, in the hopes that he might solve my problems.

Father John gently consoled me and urged me to have monk-like patience. Somehow he always found the right words. The main thing about him was his love for humanity, his faith, and his hope in God's Providence. These were so great that even people coming to see him with what seemed like the most insoluble problems would leave his priestly cell full not only of consolation but of new energy with which to face life. And there was yet another extremely rare quality particular to Father John: his authority. He spoke as one having the authority from God to give others life force, and to lead them joyously to follow Christ.

That time when I came back, we sat together for a long while. Evening Vigil service had already begun. Father John looked at his watch hurriedly and sent me to the church, saying that he would soon come himself. I and the other young hieromonks had already vested and were waiting for Akathist prayers to begin in the ancient altar in the cave of the Dormition Cathedral. Suddenly Father John walked up to us. I had just seen him half an hour ago, but now he looked totally different. His appearance was most unusual: highly focused and somewhat severe.

Without saying a word he took me by the hand and led me to the center of the altar right up to the Holy Table. Here he bowed deeply three times and reverently kissed the Holy Table and bade me to do the same. Then he turned to me and said:

"Now listen to the will of God . . ."

I had never heard Father John say anything remotely like this.

"You will go back to Moscow and immediately see His Holiness the Patriarch," said Father John. "You will ask him to bless you to transfer from the Donskoy Monastery to the brotherhood of our Pskov Caves Monastery. Ask His Holiness to bless the founding of a residence in Moscow of our Pskov Caves Monastery. And you will be the one in charge of this residence."

I didn't even know what to say. On the one hand, it was quite clear that at this very moment my entire life was changing. On the other hand, I knew from all my prior experience that on this occasion what Father John was saying was totally unrealistic.

"But Father," I pleaded with him, "this is totally impossible! The Patriarch recently officially announced that none of the diocesan monasteries will be entitled to have any resident monasteries here in Moscow. In fact, he strictly forbids anyone from even approaching him with such requests."

A brief explanation is in order. At this time the Russian Orthodox Church had managed to revive 360 monasteries, and each month the number of monasteries was increasing. Naturally quite a few of these communities, especially the provincial ones, wished to have their own representation in the capital, and their requests had by now so pestered the Patriarch that His Holiness at a recent gathering of his clerical administration had firmly warned that no such further requests were ever to be made of him. His reason for this was that if churches in Moscow were to be distributed to the various monasteries, soon there would be no local churches left for the benefit of local parishioners. I explained all of this to Father John. But he didn't even lift an eyebrow.

"Don't be afraid of anything!" he said. "Go and see His Holiness. Pass along to him exactly what I have told you. His Holiness will give his blessing. And then"—here Father John changed his tone of voice and suddenly became both businesslike and passionate in a single breath, "you will be given a choice of several cathedrals. Do not accept the first one they offer you! Out of the others you are offered, take the one you like the most, but be careful not to strive to get the biggest or the most famous church."

It was time to leave for the Akathist. The good Father added, "After the service I will be waiting for you in my cell."

All through the Akathist, and throughout the evening service that followed, all I could do was worry about the words that Father John had just uttered. As soon as Evening Vigil service ended, I immediately raced to see him. Father John again several times repeated to me exactly what he had said there in the altar, calmed me down, cheered me up, and bade me firmly, without any further doubts whatsoever, to act exactly as he had commanded.

Father John never before nor after ever uttered such grand and terrifying words as "I will tell you the will of God." He was not a man who spoke such—or indeed, any—words lightly. Therefore I took what he had said to me extremely seriously, and, overcoming my own fear, vowed to faithfully execute in every respect what I had been asked to do by my elder.

When I got back to Moscow there soon appeared a convenient moment to meet with His Holiness the Patriarch. With my heart in my mouth, I passed along to His Holiness word for word what Father John had told me to say: that I be transferred from the Donskoy Monastery to the brotherhood of our Pskov Caves Monastery, that His Holiness bless the founding of a residence or representative church in Moscow of our Pskov Caves Monastery . . . and that I be put in charge of it.

To my enormous surprise, His Holiness unexpectedly found the thought of establishing a Moscow residence for the Pskov Caves Monastery both timely and proper. As it turned out, just recently a question had

arisen as to the creation of a special border area with heightened security for the town of Pechory, now located just three kilometers from the new border with Estonia. It appeared that there might be a problem with the free access of pilgrims in their usual throngs to the Monastery of the Pskov Caves. Therefore the idea of establishing a local Moscow residence could be a great help to the Church, in the Patriarch's opinion, especially considering the possibility that the border police would make it difficult for pilgrims to get through to the original monastery. His Holiness therefore immediately commanded Archbishop Arseny (Epifanov) and Archpriest Vladimir Divakov to work with me to select a proper location for the residence.

The first place they suggested for a residence was the Monastery of the Protection, which had recently been transferred back to the Church. I went there to admire it, but remembering the advice of Father John that I was to refuse the first church that I was offered, I excused myself from their offer based on the fact that the Protection Monastery was far too big for our needs.

At that point Archbishop Arseny offered me two other addresses: the Cathedral of the Protection of the Holy Virgin Mary in Izmailovo, and the Sretensky Monastery on Lubyanka Street, in the heart of Moscow. The cathedral in Izmailovo also seemed to me far too big and grand in its decorations, while the Sretensky Monastery was just the right size, and exactly like what Father John had mentioned in his advice. Besides, it was not just a church, but a whole monastery, which had been closed down in 1925. Therefore it was a place where in any case it would be necessary to resurrect monastic life. I called Father Philaret in Pechory, and he connected me by telephone to my spiritual father.

"Sretensky Monastery? The one near Trubnaya Square?" Father John was perfectly acquainted with ecclesiastical Moscow. "Excellent! Take it!"

Eighteen years have passed since the time we founded this residence, yet always, in days of joy and grief alike, we have been supported by the prayers, blessings, and sometimes stern admonishments of Father John. He also gave us many of his own icons, including his very favorite, the icon of the Vladimir Mother of God. Father John blessed the creation of our own monastery publishing house, our own seminary, and our many supporting enterprises. And it must be said that, especially in our first and most difficult years, Father John watched over every step of our community as we were resurrecting it. And after concerns had subsided that border tensions might interfere with the possibility of pilgrims visiting Pechory, it was none other than Father John who blessed our asking His Holiness the Patriarch to transform our residence into the new and independent Sretensky Monastery.

The brotherhood of the Sretensky Monastery reveres Father John as an elder, as the one who blessed the creation of our monastery, as our father in prayer, as our spiritual advisor and guide, and as our patron. Every day we utter prayers for the repose of his soul. His sermons, letters, and words of wisdom are like textbook reading for the brotherhood here in our monastery, as well as for the students of our seminary and for many of our parishioners.

I particularly wish to remember how the souls of those people fortunate enough to have contact with Father John were transformed, literally as if reborn. But I find it difficult to recount all that took place during those twenty-five years in which I was blessed to know Father John. Indeed, even to assert that I knew him would perhaps be incorrect. In the end Father John remained entirely a striking and beautiful mystery.

Sometimes he would reveal himself to us in such a way that we would be left utterly at a loss for words, only able to gape in astonishment. For

The Cathedral of Vladimir Mother of God, Sretensky Monastery, during the 1990s.

example, I remember my enormous surprise when I once heard him quote a saying that came from imprisoned *zeks* (or persons who had been in the Gulag). What was more, the phrase was said so easily and casually, as if there were nothing unusual about it, that at first I couldn't believe my ears.

Once, in a sleepy country parish about a hundred kilometers from Pskov, my friend Father Raphael was visited by his nephew Valera. It was pretty obvious at once that the youngster had no religious inclinations, and he had certainly not stopped by to visit his uncle the priest in order to fast and pray. In fact, Valera was really just hiding out from the police. He did not keep his secret long but told us everything on the very first night. In his hometown he'd been accused of a very serious crime, but he assured us that he had not committed it. And although it was pretty obvious from first glance that he was far from an innocent lad, we believed his story this time. And in the end it turned out that his innocence was confirmed; Valera was proved to have no involvement in the foul deed for which he had been accused.

We brought the youth to the monastery to speak to Father John, and get his advice about what to do with the boy next. Father John was the soul of heartfelt courtesy and welcomed him warmly. Then suddenly he said:

"But nonetheless, Valera, you will still have to suffer."

"For what?" the boy cried out.

Father John beckoned him with his finger to come closer and then whispered something in his ear. Young Valera staggered and stared at the good priest in shock. Then he asked Father Raphael and me to leave the cell, and the two stayed together alone.

Half an hour later, when Father John asked us to come back, Valera was sitting on the little sofa. We could see that he had been crying, and yet, for the first time in all the days that we had gotten to know him, he seemed radiant and absolutely happy. Father John, having taken the boy's confession, was removing his *epitrachelion* (an Orthodox stole) and cuffs. Father John asked us to help Valera to fast and pray for three days in the monastery, to receive Unction, and take Holy Communion. After this Father John blessed him for his return to his hometown of Chistopol.

"Why?" we asked. But it seemed Father John had already explained everything to the boy—or all but one thing.

As he was taking his leave of Father John, Valera asked: "What should I do when I'm imprisoned?"

In reply, in a very cool and practiced manner, Father John pronounced the famous *zek* creed: "Don't believe, don't fear, don't beg." Then he added, with his face looking normal again:

"It's simple. The main thing is—pray. God is very nearby in that place. You'll see!"

Father John knew what he was talking about.

Three people had written a denunciation to the secret police of a priest, one John Krestiankin, in 1950, in Stalin's time: the head priest of the church in Moscow where Father John had been serving, the choir leader of that same church, and its deacon. They accused Father John of gathering young people around him, of not blessing persons who wished to join the Communist Youth League (Komsomol), and of "anti-Soviet agitation."

Father John was arrested. He languished for about one year in "pre-trial detention, in dark interior cells of the KGB's Lubyanka Prison in solitary confinement." Throughout that time, during endless "interrogations," he was routinely tortured.

During these "interrogations," Father John admitted that lots of young people did indeed gather around him. However, he maintained that, as a pastor in a church, he could not possibly turn them away just because they were young, nor could he agree to cease paying attention to them. As for the Komsomol, the arrestee Krestiankin also conceded that he did not accord his blessing to those who wished to enter into that organization, because it was an atheist organization. No true Christian could ever possibly be part of such groups. But as to having allegedly carried out anti-Soviet agitation, he denied his guilt, saying that as a priest such secular activities did not interest him.

Never, throughout the entire time that Father John was in prison and was being tortured, did he utter one name or betray a single friend. He knew that any name that he was likely to mention would immediately get that person arrested.

At some point later Father John told us about his interrogator. They were both the same age. In 1950 they had both turned forty. And the investigator had basically the same name that he did, Ivan. They even had the same patronymic—Mikhailovich. Father John told us that he mentioned his interrogator every single day in his prayers and would never forget him.

"He broke every single one of my fingers!" Father John exclaimed, showing us his hands, which had been maimed during the tortures.

"Hmm!" we thought. "After all that cruelty, every single day Father John prays for the man who did this to him? Now that is really being a Christian! Wouldn't it be interesting to find out the further fate of this interrogator, this Ivan Mikhailovich, for whom Ivan Mikhailovich Krestiankin prays every day?"

In order to finally break the will of this "criminal priest," the secret police interrogator Ivan Mikhailovich set up a confrontation between Father John and the head priest of the church that Father John had served in. Father John already knew that this man had betrayed him and was the reason for his arrest and all his immense sufferings. But when the head priest came into the room, Father John was so glad to see his brother and fellow priest, with whom he had so often performed the Divine Liturgy, that he simply threw his arms around him!

The head priest quivered in the embrace of Father John, and promptly fainted. The confrontation did not work out as planned at all. Nonetheless, even without the evidence of his accuser—indeed, without any evidence or confession of guilt at all—Father John was sentenced for anti-Soviet agitation to eight years in the camps of the Gulag.

It was written somewhere about one of the ancient Holy Fathers of our Church that, from the abundance of love that he had in his heart, he had totally forgotten what evil was. And we, young novices, in those years often reflected on why it was, or for what achievements and spiritual qualities, that God gave to his true servants certain gifts of prophecy or miraculous healing or ability to know His will. After all, it was difficult to even imagine that this man to whom people would open their hearts and reveal their most intimate thoughts and deeds could ever have been different than the way he was, limitlessly compassionate to everyone without exception. It simply could not be imagined that his heart would not have been full of this powerful, mysterious, and all-forgiving love, which was brought to us in this world by the crucified Son of God.

As for the history of Father John's years of imprisonment, what always struck me most about his story was the way in which he described the time he spent in those truly awful camps, so full of cruelty and suffering and callousness. Believe it or not, Father John would say that these were the happiest days of his entire life.

"Because God was always close by!" With joy Father John would exclaim this, although without doubt he realized that there was no way we could possibly understand him.

"For some reason I can't remember anymore a single bad thing," he would say about his time in the camps. "I can only remember now how I used to pray in there: the heavens opened and the Angels were singing in the heavens! I don't know how to pray like that anymore . . ."

* * *

In the monastic cell where Father John used to receive his numerous visitors it was always very noisy. Father John would fly in—yes, fly in—even when he was seventy and eighty years old, even when he was ninety, even when he was growing feeble with age, still, he would literally run to his icon and for a moment, not paying attention to anyone else, would freeze before it, totally immersed in prayer for the people who had come to see him.

Only having finished this main task would he turn to his guests. Every one of them would receive his joyous glance, and he would hasten to bless each and every one. To some he would whisper something, for others, he would worry . . . he would explain . . . he would console... he would complain, and he would encourage . . . He would groan and sigh, he would wave his hands . . . More than anything else, in these moments he would resemble a brood hen fussing about its chicks. Only after finished with all of this would he practically collapse on his ancient little couch and sit down beside his very first visitor. Each of these visitors of course had his or her own problems. I won't speak for the others, but I well remember those problems with which I myself came to the good father.

For nine years Father John did not give me his blessing on becoming a full-fledged monk and taking my monastic vows. He kept me as a novice, and said that he would only give his blessing on condition that my mother would give her blessing. But my mother, God rest her soul, although she approved of my serving the church in an ecclesiastical capacity, flatly did not want me to become a monk. Father John insisted on his precondition: I must get my mother's permission. He added: "If you truly wish to be a monk, then pray and ask God to help you get your mother's permission. The Lord will arrange it all in due time."

By then I had utter faith in Father John. And so I calmly waited, at first as a novice in the Pskov Caves Monastery, and then in the publishing department of the Russian Orthodox Church under Metropolitan Pitirim. And then one day, as I was returning to Father John in Pechory, I told him by the way that soon the Donskoy Monastery would be opened again, and that it was a place beloved by Muscovites. And suddenly Father John said:

"Now your time has come to see your mother and ask her blessing for your taking full monastic vows. I think now she will not refuse. And for the fact that you were patient for nine years and never took matters into your own hands, you will see how the Lord will not deprive you of His particular grace. You will receive a gift."

Later Father John began to tell me stories of the Donskoy Monastery of his youth, of the former Patriarch Tikhon whom Father John had loved dearly and who had lived there under secret police arrest. Father John told me that in 1990, in the same monastic cell in which we were sitting at that moment, Patriarch Tikhon had appeared in a dream and had warned him about the schism that would soon be in store for the Russian Orthodox Church. (And that's exactly what happened in the Ukraine; part of its Church later split off from ours.)

As he finished, Father John prayed to his beloved icon of the Mother of God, called "Search of the Lost," that hung in his cell, and then commanded me to hurry home. As soon as I received my mother's blessing, I was to request His Holiness the Patriarch to allow me to receive the monastic tonsure.

Because of the prayers of Father John, this time my mother unexpectedly agreed to give her blessing to my desire to take monastic vows, and blessed me herself with the icon of the Mother of God. And then His Holiness the Patriarch Alexiy II sent me to take my vows in the then still-sparse brotherhood of Moscow's Donskoy Monastery.

Father John's promise about my receiving a gift also came true. It so happened that the Abbot of the Donskoy Monastery, Archimandrite Agathadorus, who had twice put off the occasion of my taking my vows because of urgent monastery business that required him to travel, finally administered my monastic vows exactly on my birthday, just when I had turned thirty-three. Now, instead of my given name Georgiy Alexandrovich Shevkunov, I was to take the new name Tikhon—after my favorite saint and the beloved patron of the Donskoy Monastery.

There's quite a lot that I can still remember. Soon after the death of Valentina Pavlovna Konovalova, I was hospitalized. It was quite a serious illness, and Father John, in the letter that was passed along to me by his spiritual daughter Nastya Goryunova, authorized me to break the long Christmas fast and eat both fish and dairy products. My friends at that time had put me in an excellent clinic. There was even a television my hospital room. As I began to recover a bit I decided to watch the news on television, which I had not watched for several years. And then I watched an interesting film.

Later that day, in the evening, Nastya Goryunova arrived from Pechory, and, through the nurse, passed me a new letter from Father John. I can still remember how I received his letter, lying lazily in bed, watching some film or other on TV. I was even watching it and reading Father John's letter at the same time. Then, at the end of the letter there was a postscript: "Father Tikhon, I gave my blessing for you to relax about keeping the fast, but I do not give my blessing for you to watch television." I rolled like a peg-top out of bed and ripped the cord connecting the television out of the power socket. By this time I knew only too well what would happen if one did not obey Father John.

Father John also had his detractors. Some for whatever reasons simply did not recognize his service as an elder. But there were others who were outright bitter enemies. Father John always bore their hatred, slander, and even out-and-out betrayal with nothing but the most heartfelt compassion,

The feast of the Dormition of the Mother of God (held in the rain).

and never lost his sincerest Christian love for these people. For the rest of my life I will remember the words of the sermon he preached in 1987 in the Cathedral of St. Michael in the Pskov Caves Monastery:

"We have been commanded by our Lord to love our neighbor as ourselves, but it is none of our business whether they love us or not! The only thing for us to worry about is to make sure we truly love them!"

One priest from Moscow, who was a former spiritual son of Father John, once came to me with a rather strange request. I was to return an *epitrachelion* or stole, the symbol of priestly service, that Father John had given to him with blessings and parting words of wisdom before his ordination. This priest told me frankly that he had become disenchanted with Father John, because the latter did not support his dissenting views on clerical matters.* How many bitter words this priest then spoke! And yet it seemed he took absolutely nothing into account: neither the many

---

* There were so-called "Church dissidents" at that time, who spoke out against conformism among the Russian clergy with the Soviet regime.

years that Father John had suffered for his faith in the Gulag camps, nor the fact that he had undergone torture and had never been broken, nor the fact that Father John had never toed the line of Soviet conformity—and indeed, no one could possibly accuse him of such a thing.

With a heavy heart I returned the *epitrachelion* to Father John. His reaction astonished me. He crossed himself, accepted the *epitrachelion* with unfeigned reverence, and kissed the holy vestment. And then he said: "I gave it with love, and I take it back with love . . ."

Later on this priest who complained about him left for a different Orthodox jurisdiction, which he also disliked. And then he joined a third—and so on.

And here is yet another testimony, the memories of an elderly Muscovite, Adrian Alexandrovich Yegorov. He writes: "I was acquainted for the better part of my life with the late Patriarch Pimen. Once I asked him what a spiritual father is and what it means to be one. He answered me that in all of Russia there is perhaps only one true spiritual father— Father John." Indeed, Patriarch Pimen always invited Father John to stay with him in his country house in Peredelkino during Father John's rare visits to Moscow. And then they would converse for a long time together.

Father John had great reverence, love, and respect for the hierarchy of the Russian Orthodox Church. He felt deep within his soul that higher truth on this Earth can be found only in the Church. Father John would brook no schisms or rebellions, and would always fearlessly speak out against such things, even though he knew quite well how much slander and sometimes even hatred this would force him to undergo. He was truly a man of the Church. Many times he would command an act be done exactly as His Holiness the Patriarch would decide, or as the bishop would decide, or as the abbot of the monastery would decide, even though he disagreed.

At the same time, this absolutely did not mean that he was an unthinking, unquestioning automaton of soulless obedience, not at all! I remember a time when one of the monastery abbots and the presiding bishop tried to convince Father John to give his blessing to a decision they had already made even though Father John was utterly opposed to this decision on principle. These worthies demanded that he give his authority as an elder to their command. And yet his vast experience of ecclesiastical life (he had begun as a young child, serving as an altar boy at the age of four) gave Father John the confidence to be able to declare that nothing good whatsoever would come from their demands and therefore he simply could not give his blessing.

They began to insist, putting quite heavy pressure on him—you might say they put the knife to his throat. Priests and monks know all too well what folly it is to defy the will of the ruling bishop and head the of the monastery, the abbot. Father John bore with grace and patience their siege of many days. All the while he patiently explained that he simply could not give his blessing to something to which he could not agree in his soul. If those in charge and of superior rank truly believed that it was necessary to act as they requested, he would meekly abide by their decisions, for it was they who would bear responsibility before God and our brotherhood. But in this case, it was clear that the commands they were giving were coming entirely out of pique, from their passions, and therefore he could not give his blessing to something like this—in all humility, he simply could not.

Generally all those who remember Father John recall that he was kind, affectionate, good, and loving. There can be no doubt that in all my life I have truly never met any other man who better knew how to express his fatherly Christian love. And it must also be said that Father John, when it was necessary, could also be quite strict.

When need be, he knew how to express reproaches or rebukes whose recipient was certainly not to be envied. Once, as I remember, when I was still just a novice in Pechory, I heard Father John say: "You call yourselves monks? Nonsense! You're just nice guys—and nothing more!"

Father John was never afraid to speak the truth to someone's face, and would always do so expressly for the benefit of the person to whom he was speaking—whether a bishop or a simple novice or someone from the outer world. His firmness and spiritual principled integrity had been foundations of the soul of Father John since his early childhood, when he had had the fortune of being in contact with great spiritual authorities and future new martyrs of the Holy Russian Orthodox Church.

Here is his answer, in a letter he wrote in 1997, to one of the many questions I asked him:

Here's another example of a similar situation which I have dragged out from the warehouse of my memory. At the time I was only 12, but the impression that I received was so powerful that to this day I can see it all happening before my eyes, and remember all the main actors by name. In the town of Oryol, we happened to have a remarkable archbishop, Seraphim Ostroumov. He was the most intelligent, kind, loving and modest man; I cannot begin to count the complimentary epithets that he deserves. It is as if his entire life prepared him for the laurel of a holy martyr, and that is what in the end happened to him after the Revolution. Well, once, on Forgiveness Sunday (the Sunday before Lent, when everyone is supposed to ask for and give forgiveness to everyone else) this goodly archbishop drove out of his monastery two of its inhabitants: Abbot Callistos and Deacon Tikhon. He kicked them right out for some misdeed or other. He did this publicly and with great authority, firmly keeping all others from any temptations of even associating with them. Immediately afterwards he pronounced the words of forgiveness for the Sunday of Forgiveness and asked for forgiveness from all for all . . .

My still youthful consciousness was totally shocked by what I had just seen, because of the utter contrast: on the one hand, an act of driving out from the monastery, in other words, the absence of any forgiveness, and yet on the other hand, his meek plea for forgiveness for himself and others from all and to all. At the time I only understood one thing: that sometimes punishment can be the beginning of forgiveness, and that without punishment forgiveness may be impossible. Now more than ever I revere the courage and the wisdom of the remarkable Archbishop Seraphim, because the lesson that he taught me and the others stayed with all of us, as you can see, for the rest of our lives.

Father John was always unshakable and joyful in his faith in the most valuable and obvious of higher truths: that the life of a Christian on earth and the life of the heavenly Church were bound by unbreakable spiritual threads. And this faith of his was most touchingly confirmed in the hour of his death—as significant for Father John as it is for any other mortal.

Father John left us to meet his Lord in his ninety-sixth year of life. It happened on a feast day that was particularly important specifically for Father John—the commemoration day of the new martyrs and confessors of Russia. Many of these saints who gave their lives for Christ during the cruel persecutions of the twentieth century had been his teachers and closest friends; in a way, he too was among their number. And so it was

fitting that on the Feast of the New Martyrs of Russia, on the morning of February 5, 2006, just after Father John had received the Holy Mysteries (Communion) of Christ, the Lord summoned Father John to His presence.

* * *

But even after the death of Father John, those who had the good fortune of having known him can still feel his love, his support, his prayers, and care. And they will never leave us—even when Father John is in another world.

In 2007 the name day of His Holiness Patriarch Alexiy II happened to fall on the very first Sunday of the Lenten Fast, which is the day we celebrate the Triumph of Holy Orthodoxy. We in the brotherhood of the Sretensky Monastery had spent all the preceding week in unforgettable services marking the first somber week of the Lenten Fast. On Saturday after the Liturgy, guests began to appear for the celebration of the name day of the Patriarch. The time before Vespers and even after, till late into the night, was full of concerns such as welcoming and finding rooms for the monks, priests, and archbishops who usually stay with us in the Sretensky Monastery. When we were finally exhausted and desperately wanted to sleep, I decided that I would read the required canons and prayer rule for

Communion in the morning. But to my great shame, I overslept, and now suddenly I was driving to the Cathedral of Christ the Savior for Liturgy not having completed the required prayers.

Two or three times in the twenty years in which I have served as a priest I have had to administer a service not having been prepared for it. Each time there simply have been no excuses, no mitigating circumstances of weariness in particular, nothing that could possibly drown out the cruel reproaches of my conscience. But now I nonetheless tried to convince myself that well . . . after all . . . even though I hadn't read the required prayer rule . . . still, I had, in fairness, spent the entire week, morning, noon, and night, praying in the cathedral. And on Wednesday, Friday, and Saturday—in other words, literally as late as yesterday—I had taken Communion and had followed all the rules and said all the required prayers.

As I was putting on my vestments and entering the altar of the Cathedral of Christ the Savior, which was already full of clergy, I was even telling myself that nowadays there are certain quite well-known modern clerics who assert that reading the prayer rule before Communion really doesn't matter so much . . . In short, it seems that I had almost managed to work out a compromise with that little voice inside of me called "conscience," which was reproaching me for my failure, when all of a sudden Metropolitan Varnava of Chuvashia came up to me. I had seen this elderly and extremely respected elder of the Church many times at services given by His Holiness the Patriarch, but had never once spoken to him. Suddenly the Metropolitan said to me:

"May the Lord save you, Father Tikhon, for the wonderful movie you made about the Pskov Caves Monastery. I really liked it very much. I was acquainted with Father John for fifty years and often used to go visit him in Pechory."

The Metropolitan was referring to a documentary film that I had made about the Pskov Caves Monastery, where there were many scenes featuring Father John.

"You know what I was just remembering?" the Metropolitan continued. "Maybe you've heard about the time during the 1950s when Father John served in a country parish. And once in the evening right after the Vigil service, robbers burst into his house, tied him up, and beat him. Then they left him there, tied up, to die. Have you ever heard that story?"

"Yes, Metropolitan Varnava, I do know that story. In the morning just before the Liturgy was about to begin, parishioners came and found Father John and freed him."

"Exactly! Yes! It was just that way! Father John came to, thanked the Lord for the near-death experience and for saving him, and went off to serve the Liturgy. And do you know what he told me later? This had been the only time in his entire life when he was about to celebrate the Liturgy without being properly prepared, without having first said all the proper prayers . . . Anyway, go with God!"

It so happened that Archimandrite Dionysius Shchigin was standing next to me. I approached him and told him the entire story: both about my lack of preparation and about the conversation that I had just had with Metropolitan Varnava. I confessed all to Father Dionysius, and together we marveled at how great and mysterious was the Providence of God.

Who knows what it was that we had just witnessed? Perhaps Father John through the Metropolitan had yet again taught a lesson to "one of his foolish children," as he once called me in one of his letters. Or maybe it was that yet again we had met yet another of those priceless, hidden ascetics and servants of the Lord, whose faithful ranks will never thin in Christ's Orthodox Church.

Archimandrite Seraphim.

Archimandrite Seraphim

Father Seraphim for me was one of the most mysterious people in the Pskov Caves Monastery. He was descended from a long lineage of East Prussian barons. In the 1930s he had come to the monastery and given himself in obedience to the great elder and monk Father Simeon.

Father Seraphim had little contact with people. He lived in a dwelling carved out of a cave that was both damp and dark. He would stand through the services totally engrossed in prayer, with his head bent down every once in a while, with light grace and reverence making the sign of the cross. Father Seraphim would also walk across the monastery completely focused on his own thoughts. To us novices, it seemed a crime to distract him. Of course, now and then he himself would briefly deign to speak to us. For example, returning to his cell from services, he would always give leftover Communion bread called *prosphora* to the monk on duty in the main square of the monastery. Once there was one novice whose name was Sasha Shvetsov who was seriously thinking about leaving the monastery but hadn't said anything. Father Seraphim suddenly walked up to him and, stamping his feet, shouted to everyone's amazement: "The road out of this monastery is closed to you!"

He himself had lived in the monastery for sixty years and had never once left its precincts. And he used to say: "I never once left this community, not even in my thoughts!" Well, actually there was one time—it was 1945, and Red Army soldiers were leading him as an ethnic German out to be shot by a firing squad. But then they changed their minds for some reason and didn't shoot him.

Yet in general, despite his reserve and severe demeanor, Father Seraphim was a remarkably kind, loving man. Everyone in the monastery respected and loved him, although we novices were also afraid of him—or rather, we were in awe of him, seeing as he was a man who lived on this earth entirely with God, just like a living saint.

I remember my impression of those years. At the time I was a subdeacon* serving under the monastery's abbot, Archimandrite Father Gabriel. I noticed that whenever Father Seraphim would walk into the altar area, the monastery's abbot would quickly climb up towards him from his place as Father Superior and would greet him with particular respect. There was no one else to whom the abbot was so particularly deferent.

Winter, summer, spring, and fall, at exactly four o'clock in the morning, Father Seraphim would leave his cave in which he kept his cell and would quickly inspect the monastery to make sure that everything was in order. Only after this task was completed did he return to his cave and heat the stove, which as a result of the dank and damp conditions of the cave needed to be heated virtually all year round. It seems to me that Father Seraphim considered himself a particular guardian of the Pskov Caves community. And perhaps that was indeed his assignment. In any case, the singular voice of that former German baron, now a great ascetic monk and one of our sagacious leaders, was always definitive in deciding the most complicated questions faced by the brotherhood of our monastery.

Father Seraphim rarely had any particular words to say to those who approached him. In the entrance to his severe monastic cave dwelling he hung up pages with quotations from the works of St. Tikhon of Zadonsk. And anyone who would come to visit him would often have to be satisfied with these quotations, or else with a blunt phrase from Father Seraphim: "Read St. Tikhon of Zadonsk as often as possible."

Through all his years of monastery life, Father Seraphim made do with the very least—and not only with food or clothing, but even in his interactions with people. For example, he would never wash himself in the shower but instead would make do with two or three small buckets of water. Asked by the novices why he didn't bother to use the water, since there was more than enough water in the shower to wash oneself thoroughly, he would scoff that to take a shower was just as bad as to eat chocolate.

Once in 1983, I had the good fortune to be in Diveyevo Monastery in Nizhny Novgorod Province. That was much harder to do back then—a classified military factory was located nearby. The old nuns gave me a piece of a rock on which St. Seraphim of Sarov himself had prayed. When I got back to Pechory, I decided to go see Father Seraphim and give him the

---

* A *subdeacon* is an assistant to the clergy serving in the altar.

gift of this holy relic connected to his spiritual protector. Having received this unexpected gift, Father Seraphim stood silently for a long time and then asked: "What can I do for you in return?" I was rather shocked by this. "Nothing, thanks . . ."

But then I let slip my dearest desire: "Please pray that I will become a monk!" I remember how intently Father Seraphim stared at me then.

"For that the main thing you need," he said softly, "is just your own free will."

Later, under different circumstances, he talked to me again about the will for monasticism. At that time I was already serving in Moscow as a novice under Archbishop Pitirim. But Father Seraphim was living out his very last year of life on this earth and was already almost unable to get up. When I got back to Pechory Monastery, I went to see the ailing elder in his cave. And suddenly he himself began the conversation about the monastery and about the state of monasticism in our days. This was very unusual for him and made the moment all the more valuable. I remember a few key ideas from that conversation.

First of all, Father Seraphim spoke about the monastery with immense inexpressible love, as of the greatest treasure there was: "You cannot even conceive of how precious a treasure the monastery is! It is a pearl, it is uniquely valuable in our world! Only later will you really understand and value it."

Then he addressed himself to the main problem of those who wish to become monks nowadays. "The misfortune of monasteries nowadays is that people come here with weak wills."

More and more nowadays I understand how profound this remark by Father Seraphim was. The self-sacrificing renunciation and decisiveness needed for true monastic asceticism is ever more lacking among us. It was about this more than anything that the heart of Father Seraphim grieved as he observed the young inhabitants of our monastery.

Finally he pronounced an extremely important concept for me. "The time of the big monasteries has passed. More fruit now must be harvested from modest communities in which a Father Superior will more easily be able to take care of the spiritual life of each monk. Remember this. If ever you will be the abbot of a monastery, do not accept many brothers."

That was our last conversation, in 1989. At the time I was just a simple novice. I wasn't even a monk.

The clairvoyance of Father Seraphim was never doubted either by me or by my friends in the monastery. Father Seraphim himself was rather calm and even slightly skeptical when it came to conversations about miracles and clairvoyance. I remember once he said: "Everyone likes to say that Father Simeon was a miracle worker and could predict the future. But for all the years that I lived in his company I never noticed anything of the kind. He was just a good monk."

But I myself several times experienced the full force of the gifts of Father Seraphim.

Once during the summer of 1986 I was passing by the elder's cave cell, and I noticed that he was about to change the bulb in the light on his front porch. I brought him a small footstool and helped him. Father Seraphim thanked me and said: "A bishop took a novice to Moscow for further tasks. Everyone thought it would not be for long, but he ended up staying there."

"And?" I asked.

"And that was it!" Father Seraphim said. Then he turned around and went back to his cave. Not understanding, I went back on my own way. What novice? What bishop?

Three days later I was summoned by Archimandrite Gabriel, Father Superior of the monastery. He told me that Archbishop Pitirim of Volokolamsk, chairman of the publishing department of the Moscow Patriarchate, had just called him from the capital. Archbishop Pitirim had learned that in the Monastery of the Pskov Caves there was a novice with an advanced degree in cinematic studies, and therefore asked the abbot of our monastery to please send this novice to him in Moscow. It seems they were in urgent need of specialists to prepare a film and television program devoted to the anniversary of the millennium of Russia's adoption of Christianity. The commemorations would be within two years, and much needed to be done.

Father Seraphim fixing the roof of his monastic cell.

The novice of whom they were speaking was me. I don't remember a more frightful day in my entire life. I begged Father Gabriel not to send me to Moscow, but he had already made his decision.

"I'm not going to get into an argument with Archbishop Pitirim because of you," was all he said in answer to my pleas.

Only later I found out that my return to Moscow had also been a longtime request of my mother, who was very much hoping to talk me out of becoming a monk. Father Gabriel sympathized with her and had been waiting to find some excuse to send me back to my inconsolable parent. Besides, such curt and even gruff commands were very much in his style.

Of course I immediately remembered my last conversation with Father Seraphim about the novice, and the bishop, and about Moscow, and I ran to see him and his cave.

"It is God's will! Do not grieve! All this is for the best. You will see this for yourself, and one day you will understand," the elder said to me tenderly.

How difficult it was, especially in the beginning, for me to be living once more in Moscow! It was particularly difficult because, as I would wake in the middle of the night, I would realize that this amazing world of the monastery, so incomparable with anything else, blessed with its Fathers Seraphim, John, Nathaniel, Theophan, Alexander . . . all these dear men were now many hundreds of kilometers away. And here I was, far off in Moscow, where there was nobody and nothing who could compare with them.

Archimandrite Nathaniel.

Difficult Father Nathaniel

*I*F, DURING THE TIME that I was living there, someone had asked for the name of the most difficult person in the Monastery of the Pskov Caves, the answer without doubt would have been only one name: the Treasurer of the Pskov Caves Monastery, Archimandrite Father Nathaniel. What's more, this choice would have been made unanimously by all the priests, by all the novices, all the monks, by all the ordinary civilians, by all the Communists from the local administration of the KGB, and even by all the local dissidents. As a matter of fact, Father Nathaniel was not merely difficult. No, indeed! He was extremely difficult!

When I met him, he was a thin, elderly man with the keen, owlish, penetrating gaze of an elder. All year round he was dressed in an old and bedraggled monastic cassock with a torn hem. He usually carried an old canvas bag over his shoulders, in which just about anything might be found, ranging from moldy crumbs of dried bread given to him ages ago by some old grandmother, to perhaps one million rubles in cash. Either of these items in the eyes of this Father Treasurer of our monastery represented an extraordinary valuable that had been entrusted to our community by the Lord God Himself. All of these treasures Father Nathaniel would drag back and hide away somewhere in his innumerable secret cells and storerooms.

The finances of the monastery were completely under the control and management of Father Nathaniel. And there were plenty of funds that needed to be spent: every single day up to 400 pilgrims and 100 monks sat down at our tables to be fed—and fed well. An incalculable quantity of repairs and construction and restoration to the monastery always needed to be conducted. On top of this, our brotherhood had constant daily needs. Moreover, we needed to help the poor, to receive our guests, and to give gifts to officials and bureaucrats . . . There were innumerable further expenses.

How Father Nathaniel all by himself, without assistants, without computers or accountants or calculators, was able to deal impeccably with these numerous financial problems was something that no one could understand.

Furthermore, he alone was responsible for all the many businesses conducted by the monastery, and all their paperwork. On top of that, he was responsible for the creation of the schedules and programs for the long daily services, for setting forth the duties of the monastery secretary, for answering the many letters of persons who were in correspondence with the monastery, often for all kinds of different reasons. As if this were not enough, he shared, together with the abbot of the monastery, all the generally unpleasant work involved in dealing with the official organs of the Soviet government. All of these tasks and duties, the mere listing of which would make a normal person quail and grow faint, Father Nathaniel faithfully executed with such inspiration and such scrupulous attention to detail that some of us sometimes doubted whether there was anything left of this man other than the consummate ecclesiastical bureaucrat.

Yet in addition to all of these duties, our Father Treasurer was also responsible for the general supervision of us, the novices. And you may rest assured that he executed these duties as well with his invariable meticulousness: he snooped, he spied, he listened in on conversations, and in every way possible he diligently tried to discern whether we were worthy, whether we had committed some violation of the rules or otherwise harmed the monastery in any way.

To be fair, it must be admitted that it was truly necessary to keep an eagle eye on us novices: most of us had come to the monastery from the outer world as typical good-for-nothings.

Father Nathaniel also had one more fantastic quality about him: he always used to turn up exactly at the moment when we least expected him. If, for example, some of the young monastic novices were evading their duties and were hanging around somewhere by the ancient walls of the monastery to relax, chatter, and warm themselves in the sun— suddenly, as if out of thin air, Father Nathaniel would appear. Shaking his beard, he would begin in an unbearable grinding voice to scold. And by scold, I mean scold—so severely that the novices would wish that they could just disappear into the bowels of the earth, if only just to stop the torture.

In his zeal, Father Nathaniel scarcely ate or slept. He was far more than a mere ascetic: for example, no one ever saw him have even so much as a cup of tea. He would simply drink cold water. And indeed at meals he would barely eat a fifth portion of whatever it was that was served to him. Nonetheless, every evening he would always appear at supper in the brothers' refectory—not so much to eat, though, as entirely to ensure, as he sat before his near-empty plate, that order was being maintained everywhere exactly as it should be.

All the while his energy was simply incredible. We had no idea when, if ever, he slept. Even at night we could see the light coming out through the shutters of his cell. The old monks said that when he was in his cell he either prayed or counted the heaps of rubles (mostly one-ruble notes and three-ruble notes collected during the day's prayer services). All of these limitless riches he needed to accurately tie up in labeled packets of cash, while all of the coins also had to be sorted accurately into their own separate labeled pouches. As soon as he was finished with this, he would begin to type up directions on an antediluvian typewriter for the next day's service. There was no one in the monastery as fantastically acquainted with all the peculiarities and intricacies of the exact procedures required for the divine services in our monastery.

Yet even if it so happened that the light in his cell was out, in no way whatsoever did this mean that we had the right to consider ourselves free of his strict supervision for even a moment. Not a chance! All night long, at any moment, Father Nathaniel might swoop down on us, here and there and everywhere, checking to make sure nobody was simply strolling around the monastery, which was absolutely strictly forbidden!

I remember how one winter night we were sitting together in a group on the name day of one of our brotherhood. Our gathering went on till quite late. As we were all going back to our cells, suddenly out of the darkness emerged the dreaded figure of Father Nathaniel. We all froze in terror. But then we quickly all realized that on this particular occasion our Treasurer had not even seen us. In fact, his behavior was quite out of the ordinary. He could barely drag one foot after the other, and was staggering, barely able to keep up his canvas sack. Then we saw him climbing through a low fence of the forecourt—and... suddenly he lay down in the snow right on top of the flowerbed!

"He's dead!" some of us thought. We waited a little bit, and then cautiously, almost holding our breath, we approached him. Father Nathaniel was lying there in the snow—sleeping.

Just sleeping, Evenly and smoothly breathing and even snoring a little bit . . . sleeping. Under his head was his sack, which he embraced with both hands.

We decided not to go anywhere and not to leave him alone in that bitter cold until we saw what would happen next. We hid ourselves by the chapel over the holy well and started to wait. About an hour later, having nearly frozen ourselves, we saw how Father Nathaniel suddenly cheerfully lifted himself up, brushed the snow off of his sack and cassock, lifted his sack back up onto his back, then dashed off as if nothing had happened.

At the time, we absolutely didn't understand. It was only later that monks who had known the Treasurer a long time explained to us that Father Nathaniel had simply gotten tired and wanted to sleep more comfortably. More comfortably—in other words, for him. Meaning . . . with the wild luxury of lying down. Because in his own cell he would only sleep sitting. And in order not to indulge in this sinful luxury of lying in bed, if he had to lie down to sleep, he would only allow himself to sleep in the snow.

Anyway, just about everything that had to do with the Treasurer of our Pskov Caves Monastery remained for us a total mystery. Difficult Father Nathaniel would never let anyone into his beloved interior world. Never mind his interior world—he wouldn't even let anyone into his cell! This rule included even the all-powerful Father Superior of the monastery himself. You would have thought it completely unheard of for such an authority as our monastery head, Father Gabriel, to be unable to go wherever he pleased within his own monastery—especially considering the fact that the Treasurer's cell wasn't just located in any old place, but right on the first floor of the building in which the abbot himself resided—in fact, right below his lodging. You would have thought that of course the head of the monastery would never accept such an absurd situation.

Well, one day the abbot of the monastery, after some feast day, while in a wonderful frame of mind, announced to Father Nathaniel that he would be dropping by immediately to have a cup of tea with Father Nathaniel in his cell.

Several of our brotherhood who happened to be nearby at that moment immediately understood that something remarkable was about to take place, something that would dazzle the mind, soul, and entire human imagination. To pass up a chance to witness such an event would have been unforgivable. And so, thanks to the curiosity of these witnesses, the curious story has been preserved.

The abbot solemnly and determinedly crossed the courtyard of the monastery, proceeding implacably towards the cell of Father Nathaniel. But the Treasurer dragged his heels with a mincing gait behind, begging the abbot of the monastery to please change his mind about this plan.

He begged him instead to do something for the salvation of his soul, to do something useful, rather than wasting his time traipsing about dusty, old, miserable, and totally uninteresting dingy clerics' rooms. He eloquently described the disorder in his cell, exclaimed that he had not cleaned it in twenty-six years, and warned that there was an unbearably moldy stink in the air.

At last, in absolute despair Father Nathaniel began to utter what amounted to threats, ostentatiously thinking out loud how it would be absolutely wrong under any conceivable circumstances to subject the priceless life of the abbot to the dangers that might lurk for him in the frightful mess of the dwelling place of the Treasurer.

"Now that's enough, Father Treasurer!" growled the abbot, interrupting yet another litany of horrors as he stood before the very door of Father Nathaniel's cell. "Enough! Open up and let's see what you've got in there!"

In spite of the irritation in his voice, it was clear that the abbot was truly just wracked by curiosity. Father Nathaniel understood at last that he had no way out, and therefore, he resigned himself. Indeed, unaccountably he suddenly cheered up, and with a merry tone in his voice said, "You are most welcome, Father Abbot." Then he rattled his key chain and opened up before his boss that mysterious door which by now for over four decades had only been just sufficiently barely opened so as to briefly allow the slim figure of Father Nathaniel to slip through . . .

Pitch-black darkness like a complete abyss lurked beyond the threshold of the door. Both night and day the windows of Father Nathaniel's cell remained completely shuttered. Father Nathaniel disappeared into the gloom. Indeed, it seemed as if he had been swallowed up by it. At least, not a sound could be heard coming out of the cell.

The abbot cautiously stepped over the threshold and cautiously intoned in his deep bass voice: "Why is it so dark in here? Don't you have electricity? Where is the light switch?"

"It's on your right, Father Abbot," out of nowhere emerged the courteous voice of the Treasurer. "Just turn the handle."

In the next moment a horrible cry rent the air, as if some unknown force had cast the abbot straight out of the pitch-black darkness of the Treasurer's cell into the corridor. Speeding out after him into the light came Father Nathaniel. Within one second, he closed and triple-locked the door of his cell once again. Then he raced over to the severely shocked abbot. Huffing and puffing, the Treasurer fussed about brushing off the dust and adjusting the frock of the abbot, murmuring as he did so:

"Lord have mercy! How unfortunate! One has to get used to that light switch. It broke way back in 1964 on the occasion of the Feast of the Protection of the Mother of God, and, as I remember, that was just on the day when Khrushchev was removed. That was a sign! In the morning the light switch fell off, and in the evening they got rid of Nikita! And since that day I have never gotten around to putting that light switch back . . . No, no, no! No electricians! I took care of it myself. Two wires are sticking out of the wall: just put them together, and there's light in the cell; pull them apart and the light goes out. But I do admit, it does take some getting used to at first . . . That's all right. Never you mind, dear Father Abbot, you are most welcome! Come. Right now I'll just open up the door again, and we'll slip back in! There's nothing to worry about now that you know how to use my light switch . . . Come on. You'll see I really have lots of interesting things in there . . ."

But our abbot had long since vanished, well before this rambling speech had come to its end.

Father Nathaniel, in spite of this incident, was an absolute model of obedience and wrote extremely long verse odes in honor of the Abbot and dear Father Superior of the glorious Pskov Caves Monastery. Indeed, he even wrote five-page sermons and moral teachings—also in verse.

* * *

Father Nathaniel proved difficult to handle even for the mighty Soviet government, especially when it rudely attempted to interfere with our monastic life. It is said that none other than Father Nathaniel gave support and subtle advice to the great Father Superior and savior of the monastery Archimandrite Alipius, when the latter was under particularly heavy pressure from the crude persecutions of the Soviet authorities.

This took place at the end of the 1960s. As you may know, all citizens of the Soviet Union were required to take part in "elections." They brought a ballot box into the refectory of the monastery, where after dinner the brotherhood, under the discontented grumbling supervision of the abbot, rendered unto Caesar what was Caesar's.

But it turned out that the First Secretary of the Regional Communist Party Secretary for Pskov Province had found out that unheard of privileges were being given to these "savage" monks: they were being allowed to vote (unanimously, of course) for the one and only slot on the ballot, the Communist Party, over there, not at the local polling place like everyone else, but there in their obsolete historical ruin of a monastery! The First Secretary of the Communist Party was quite indignant about this and threw a fit, raging at his underlings and mercilessly rebuking them for allowing such unacceptable lenience to atavistic deviant non-working-class elements of society. He immediately demanded that from now on and forever those "black beetles" must come and "vote" for the members of the Supreme Soviet of the USSR like all good Soviet citizens, at their polls in their electoral districts strictly according to their place of residence!

It was then, so people say, that Father Nathaniel whispered into the ear of the monastery's abbot, Archimandrite Alipius, a piece of advice that was both innocent and extremely subtle in its defiance.

On election day (and, as always, it was a Sunday), after the festal Liturgy was served in the monastery, from the monastery gates came streaming forth a magnificent procession of the cross, with priests bearing crosses and icons. Paired into two columns, in a long line singing hymns and in full ceremonial dress, the troops of monks paraded through the entire town towards the polling place. Their ancient banners fluttered in the wind as they marched, carrying their traditional crosses and ancient icons. But this was not all. As is the required custom before any important action, right in the middle of the polling place the entire clergy began to pray out loud. The bureaucrats were frightened to death and tried to protest against this, but Father Alipius firmly interrupted them, lecturing that they were interfering with citizens' rights to express themselves and carry out their constitutional duties as they were required to do! Having "voted," the monks marched back with similar ostentatious ceremony into their holy monastery.

Needless to say, when the next elections came around, the ballot box was once again waiting for the monks on the table for the monastery refectory.

Yet, by the same token, in his ceaselessly vigilant looking after us, Father Nathaniel always stopped us from uttering any outright expression of opposition to the Soviet regime, or from getting involved in any attempts at being a dissident. At first this seemed to us to be disgraceful. Why was our Treasurer simply kowtowing to hated authority? But gradually we began to find out that Father Nathaniel had been tested on numerous occasions by spies and agent provocateurs or plainclothes KGB operatives, ever seeking any excuse to do real damage to the monastery. And yet, even when he quite well understood that the expressions of dissenting thought were genuine, Father Nathaniel would always interrupt our beloved free opinions. And this was not only because he was thinking of how to protect the monastery. More likely he was protecting us from ourselves, from our temptation to be too passionate or fanatical in our youthful excess, which was chiefly mixed up with nothing more than pride. He had no use for mere words—even for the most heroic of words. Yet he knew all about Soviet authority, and about everything that was happening in the country—and not in the way we did, just from books and rumors.

Father Nathaniel had a very sober and yet personal relationship to Soviet authority—perhaps because of the fact that his own father, the priest Nikolai Pospelov, had been shot to death for his faith in 1937. Father Nathaniel had served as a simple soldier throughout all of World War II, and then had served as a novice of the Great Abbot of our monastery, Archimandrite Alipius. He had also been the spiritual son of the holy elder and miracle worker of the Pskov Caves Monastery, Hieroschema-monk* Simeon. Both of them, seeing in him a man of impeccable honesty and remarkably lively intelligence, had appointed him, even during those most difficult years of the persecution of the Russian Orthodox Church under Khrushchev, the Treasurer and presiding secretary of the monastery, effectively entrusting him with its most valuable secrets.

Here's another memory about his attitude towards Soviet authority. One summer night it was my duty to be the monk on the vigil in the square before the monastery's Cathedral of the Dormition. The stars were twinkling dimly in the northern sky. Peace and quiet. The clock sounded three in the morning.

And suddenly I felt that somebody was standing right behind me.

---

* A *hieroschema-monk* is a monk who has reached the highest stage of monasticism—the great schema—but who is also a priest.

Startled, I turned around. It was Father Nathaniel, staring intently up into the starry heavens. Then he asked thoughtfully: "What do you think about the main principle of communism?"

What? Come again? Here we were in the Pskov Caves Monastery near Pskov. We were on Dormition Square. It was three o'clock in the morning. The stars were shining . . .

Not waiting to hear any answer, Father Nathaniel continued as thoughtfully as he had begun: "The main principle of communism is 'from each according to his capabilities, to each according to his needs.' But who is going to decide what each person's capabilities or needs are? Probably it'll be some commission as usual. But what kind of commission? Probably a 'troika' (that is, a group of three judges carrying out the Party's will). So they will summon me and say, 'All right, Nathaniel, what are your capabilities? You can chop twenty cubic meters of wood per day. And what are your needs? A bowl of gruel. There.' That is their main principle."

Although Father Nathaniel always tried as hard as he could to stress that he was no more than a pedantic administrator, a dry and stern ecclesiastical bureaucrat, even we novices after a while began to grasp that his modesty carefully concealed his considerable spiritual gifts. This modesty was something, by the way, that all the real monks in the monastery were endowed with. Our Father Treasurer had never become an official spiritual father in our monastery. Only a very few elderly people from the town of Pechory (or from even remoter regions, in the case of a few old-timers) ever came to say their confessions to him. Except for these few, he would not accept anyone else as his spiritual children, and would claim that he was not up to such a thing.

But once, for a brief moment he slightly opened up a priceless part of his own soul—although he once again immediately hid it, with his usual curmudgeonly strictness.

It happened when I made a mistake in performing one of my tasks. It seems I had been unforgivably casual in doing my duties. As a punishment for this, the Father Superior of the monastery himself had assigned me for three days to sweep away the snow from the entire area of Dormition Square. At this, I became considerably annoyed—especially because snow just kept coming down, more snow, snow and snow and snow! By the third day I wasn't just tired, but bone tired. I could barely drag one foot in front of another. I felt so sorry for myself that I took out my anger on the entire world, and was even beginning to nurse a plan for revenge. Of course, what sort of revenge can a novice take on the abbot of the monastery? The disparity in levels is so great it makes no sense.

Nonetheless, as with my last bit of strength I lifted up my shovel, I tenderly nursed within myself the following imaginary scene: the abbot would be walking past me on his way to dinner in the refectory and would sarcastically ask me, as he saw me shoveling snow:

"Well, how are you doing?"

And here I would answer cheerfully and casually as if I hadn't been doing hard convict's labor these past three days:

"Never better, Father Superior!" Then he would know that I was not broken so easily!

This little scene of terrible revenge began to so truly warm my heart that even amidst my weariness during the ceaseless snowfall I began to feel significantly more cheerful. And when Father Nathaniel passed by I even smiled at him, hoping for a blessing in return. His reply was a wry grin and a surprisingly gentle sign of the cross, as if warding off evil. I bowed to kiss his hand and suddenly heard his reproachful voice.

"So, you say, 'Never better, Father Superior—thanks to your prayers'?"

I bent over in shock as if paralyzed with arthritis. When I finally dared to lift up my eyes to the elder, I noticed him looking at me with undisguised irony. However, noticing my fear, he then added with genuine kindness:

"Have a care, young Georgiy (again, this was before I had taken my vows and acquired my new name), remember: sarcasm and defiance never brought up anyone to virtue."

Lifting up his old sack full of one million rubles in cash, or perhaps just moldy old bread crumbs, he scraped along through the bitter frost and snow towards the main campus of the monastery. I was left standing with my mouth open. And you could only see how at each step the torn shoe sole of our Treasurer was flapping open.

Oh! He was a real Scrooge! Except that he was a saint.

As one very respected elder of the Church in St. Petersburg said once: "Spending one year in the Pskov Caves Monastery is the same thing as spending fifty years in some seminary or theological academy." Of course, whether we really learned our lessons—that is another, and to be honest, sometimes far more bitter question.

By the way, Father Nathaniel truly was, no kidding, a man of legendary

A procession of the Cross in Pechory.

miserliness. Not only did he literally quiver over every least kopeck (penny) belonging to the monastery, but with a fury he would turn out any electric lights which he felt had no purpose to be lit, and would perpetually save water, gas, tea, biscuits, and indeed just about anything that could be scrimped and saved.

He was also an absolute stickler for the upkeep of the age-old rituals, as vital to the survival of the monastery as the upkeep of the buttresses and foundations of the medieval buildings of the monk's hermitages. He absolutely could not abide, for example, if any of our brotherhood ever went on vacation; he could not and would not accept it. He himself, of course, throughout all his fifty-five years of residence in the monastery, never once in his life took a single day off. Our abbot, Archimandrite Gabriel, also never once took a single day's vacation, and looked sharply askance at anyone who dared to come to him with such requests.

I do remember one time when our abbot gave his blessing to one monk who wished to take some time off for summer vacation. Well . . . that is, he gave his blessing. However, he instructed the poor hapless monk who had received it to go get money for his journey from our Treasurer. I was on night-vigil at Dormition Square and therefore happened to witness the scene.

It began with this monk who was planning to take off for vacation knocking for a long, long, long time at the door of the cell of Father Nathaniel, and receiving no answer. Our Treasurer, having understood right away what the matter was, simply hid, but didn't open the door. At this point the young priest decided to wait the Treasurer out. He sat down on a bench outside and began to wait. Four hours later, Father Nathaniel, with a wary glance around him, sneaked out onto the square. He was immediately overtaken by the young priest, who showed him the written blessing of the abbot to give him money for his journey.

When he saw the paper, Father Nathaniel froze as if he was being murdered, and then with a shriek collapsed onto the floor, nervously jerking his arms and legs towards the sky. At this the soles of his tattered shoes flapped open, and the holes in his weather-beaten long johns underneath his cassock were visible. He then began to scream:

"Help, help, help! Robbery! Thieves! They want money! For vacation! Oh! They're tired of the monastery! Tired of the Mother of God! Help, help, help! Robbery! Thieves!"

The poor priest was so shocked he couldn't stand up, and so squatted back down. Various foreign tourists who were in the square froze in amazement. Utterly horrified, the poor young priest dashed off to his cell. Meanwhile, the wise Father Superior, as he observed this scene from his window, watched with a very contented smile indeed.

But we always received particular pleasure whenever we were given the task of helping Father Nathaniel in guiding excursions around the monastery. Generally, he was entrusted with taking extremely important people around the grounds. Our tasks as novices only involved opening and closing doors, and sometimes opening and unlocking the heavy church doors on the watchtowers and cathedrals. All the rest of the time we would just listen to Father Nathaniel.

And there was plenty to listen to. Father Nathaniel eloquently carried on the tradition inherited from his teacher, the great Archimandrite Alipius, retired abbot of the monastery, who had defended it throughout years of persecution with unquenchable faith in God. Father Alipius's gift of wise, if sometimes mercilessly accurate, words had been inherited by Father Nathaniel.

In those atheistic years, the Soviet bureaucrats who visited the monastery

were itching for any excuse to close it down: any sign of insanity, illness, psychological inadequacy, just about anything or anyone would have served except what they actually found: unique but extremely interesting, erudite scholars, remarkably daring and internally free men who actually knew far more about life than anything of which their guests had the least inkling. Within a few minutes the tourists generally realized that they had never met such men in their entire lives.

Once in 1986 the Party bosses of the province of Pskov brought some big shot from the Ministry of Transportation to the monastery.

He was actually a surprisingly calm and decent fellow. For example, he didn't ask idiotic questions about where the monks' wives live. And he wasn't interested in asking us how it was that Yuri Gagarin had flown into space and hadn't seen God there. But in the end, after spending two hours with Father Nathaniel, this bureaucrat, being impressed by his new acquaintance, could not help himself:

"Listen! I'm amazed talking to you! I don't think I've ever met such an interesting and unusual man in my entire life! But forgive me—how can you with your intelligence possibly believe in . . . ! I mean, after all, science keeps opening newer and newer horizons for humanity! And all without God! The fact is there is no need for him. This year Halley's Comet will be approaching us. And the scientists have totally been able to calculate its orbit and its speed and its trajectory. And for this, forgive me, absolutely no concept of God is needed!"

"Halley's Comet, you say?" Father Nathaniel rubbed his beard. "You mean to say that if it's possible to calculate the orbit of a comet, that makes God unnecessary? Hmm! Just imagine this then: put me by a railroad and give me a piece of paper and a pencil. Within a week of observation I will be able to tell you exactly when and in what direction the trains will be running. But does that mean that there are no conductors, no dispatchers, no station workers, and no minister of transportation even? Of course not! Everything needs direction."

It must be said that not all such conversations ended so pleasantly. Once a group of children of the top ranks of the Communist Party Central Committee came to our monastery. At least, it was so whispered to us—I have no idea whether this was true, but those young kids certainly weren't well brought up. They were typical spoiled "golden Moscow youths" of the mid-1980s, the type of persons I knew all too well from my former life. These youngsters could barely contain themselves from mirth, pointing fingers at the monks, while asking the most idiotic questions—those same typical rude questions we were all so sick of. There was nothing that could be done, and Father Nathaniel patiently endured it as he showed them around the monastery.

The excursion went on to the caves. By the entrance to them there is a tiny cell with a little window. In the beginning of the nineteenth century a hermit monk named Lazarus locked himself into that cell. He is buried there too. But above his gravestone, still preserved, hang his ascetic chains as well as his heavy iron cross.

"Father Lazarus locked himself into this cell for a period of twenty-five years," Father Nathaniel began to tell the tourists. "Now I will tell you more about this remarkable individual . . ."

"But where did your Lazarus go to the toilet in a space this tiny?" interrupted one of the youngsters. His pals were all convulsed with laughter. Father Nathaniel patiently waited for them to calm down.

"You're interested in toilets? All right! I'll show you immediately!"

He led the mystified tourists out from the cave and through all the grounds of the monastery into a section of the workshop and warehouse that was closed to visitors. Here, somewhat at a distance from the other buildings, was a foul old outhouse that had clearly seen better days. Then, leading the tourists around this structure in a half circle as one might when showing visitors a particularly valuable object in a museum, Father Nathaniel triumphantly pointed out the foul-smelling outdoor facility and said: "Father Lazarus once went to the toilet here! Now stand here and have a good look!" With this he turned his back to the astounded tourists and left them alone.

When they had all recovered from their shock, the leader of the tour group went to express indignation to the abbot of the monastery. But the Father Superior replied: "Archimandrite Nathaniel has reported to me that it was the toilet which interested you the most, so it was the toilet that he showed you. I'm afraid I can't help you any further."

You must realize this happened in 1984 (well before perestroika). Things weren't so simple back then. The consequences could have been quite unpleasant. But then, the abbots of our Pskov Caves Monastery were extremely strong men.

Difficult Father Nathaniel died with remarkable peace and tranquility. When the cardiologist suggested giving him a pacemaker, he begged the Father Superior not to allow it.

"Father, just imagine," he said, "my soul wishes to go to God, but some tiny electric gadget is violently forcing my soul involuntarily back into my body! Let my soul go, now that its time has come!"

I had the happiness of visiting Father Nathaniel not long before his demise, and was amazed by the ceaseless goodness and love now pouring out of that elder. Rather than hoarding the very last ounces of his strength, this incredibly miserly (in all other aspects of his life) and dry ecclesiastical pedant gave the very last ounce of himself to whatever person who, even for a few minutes, had been sent to him by the Lord God. Actually, come to think of it, this is how he had lived his entire life. Only we hadn't understood it at the time.

Schema-Igumen Melchisedek with his spiritual children.

Father Melchisedek

FOR TWO YEARS after I completed my obediences or tasks as a novice I read the Holy Psalter unceasingly in the special prescribed rite. This is a particular tradition: prayers in the monastery cease neither by day nor by night, and are intermingled with the reading of the Psalter, after which there are further readings of particular prayers for health or for the repose of departed souls.

My turn for vigil-prayer came late at night from eleven o'clock until midnight. I was relieved by Father Melchisedek. He in turn carried on reading the Psalter until two o'clock in the morning.

Father Melchisedek was a remarkable and most mysterious man of faith. Except at Divine Services you could hardly ever get a glance at him in the monastery. He appeared for meals with the rest of the brotherhood only on feast days. Even then he would sit at the table with his head drooping beneath his cowl and would hardly touch any food.

The taking of monastic schema-vows in the Russian Orthodox Church involves the very highest degree of ascetic withdrawal from the world. The monk who does this forgoes all other services and tasks except for prayer. As in the taking of monastic vows, someone who receives the great monastic schema has his name changed. Bishops who undertake the schema are freed from their duties of governing their bishoprics, while monks and priests who undertake these vows are freed of all other duties whatsoever except for prayer and spiritual reflection.

Father Melchisedek would always appear beneath the vaults of the small and dimly lit Church of St. Lazarus, the place where the Psalms were always read aloud unceasingly, exactly one minute before the time when the bells of the monastery were about to ring twelve midnight. He would stand by the Royal Doors (as we call the Holy Gates of the altar in the center of the iconostasis) and slowly bow three times, waiting for me to approach. Having blessed me, he would gesture that I could go now so as to leave him in the perfect contemplation and peace needed for prayer.

For one entire year he never said a single word to me. It is written in an ancient monastic patericon (or Byzantine collection of the sayings of saints and ascetics) that "there was a custom that three monks would annually pay a visit to Abba (Father) Anthony the Great. Two of them would speak on themes related to the salvation of the soul, while the third would remain silent the entire time, never asking Abba Anthony anything at all. After many years of this, Abba Anthony finally asked this third monk, 'You've been coming to visit me for so many years—why is it that you never ask me anything, unlike the others?' The third monk replied: 'For me, Father, it is sufficient simply to look at you.'"

By this time I already understood how extraordinarily lucky I was to be able to simply see this remarkable ascetic every night—even if all I could do was simply look at him, but not speak to him.

However, once I actually was bold enough to dare disturb the ritual that we had long since established. Moreover, when Father Melchisedek as usual blessed me by the Royal Doors at the entrance to the altar, I found the courage within myself to finally ask the question that not only I, but virtually all the novices and young monks of the monastery, dreamed of asking him.

Before Father Melchisedek had taken the great monastic schema, he had served in the monastery like all the other priests, and was known as Father Michael. He was a very skilled and hard-working carpenter in the churches as well as in the cells of our monastic brotherhood. Indeed, to this very day we have kept icon frames, lecterns, chairs, tables, chests of drawers, and all kinds of other furniture made personally by his handiwork. He used to work and work with incredible devotion, to the unalloyed joy of the abbots of the monastery, from the first crack of dawn till very late at night.

At one point he was blessed with a commission for a particularly large and important work of carpentry for our holy monastery. He worked for several months straight, virtually never emerging from his workshop. And when he wasn't working, he felt himself to be slacking off. He worked so hard that when he finally finished the job, he was feeling ill, so ill that, according to eyewitness accounts, he fell down right there and then, and—died.

Several monks rushed in upon hearing the alarmed shouts of these eyewitnesses. One of the monks who rushed in was Father John (Krestiankin) (my father confessor). Father Michael appeared to be showing no signs of life at all. All those who'd gathered around him bent their heads in sorrow over his corpse. But suddenly Father John pronounced:

Father Melchisedek and the icon painter Georgiy.

"No, he is not dead. He will keep on living!"

And he began to pray. And suddenly the immobile carpenter of our monastery opened his eyes again and revived. However, everyone noticed that he appeared to be shaken to the very depths of his soul. Once he had come to a little bit, Father Michael began to beg us to summon the abbot to him. Once the abbot arrived, the ailing monk with tears in his eyes begged him for permission to be allowed to take the vows to enter into the great monastic schema.

It is said by some that, having heard this independent and unauthorized wish to suddenly take such a great responsibility upon himself, the Father Superior rebuked his monk with his usual gruff severity, and ordered the patient not to be an idiot, to get well as quickly as possible, and to get back to work—since it seemed that he couldn't die properly. Yet, according to the very same story that was told in our monastery, the very next morning the abbot himself, without any further discussion or invitation, and indeed, in noticeable discomfort, simply appeared at the cell of Father Michael, and announced to him that quite soon he would administer the vows to admit him into the great monastic schema.

This was so unusual and so in contrast with the typical behavior of our dreaded Father Gabriel that it caused more astonishment among our brotherhood than the fact of Father Michael's having been brought back from the dead.

The rumor spread through the monastery that in the night our abbot had been visited by the holy patron of our Pskov Caves Monastery, St. Cornelius himself (whose head had been personally cut off by Tsar Ivan the Terrible in the sixteenth century); supposedly St. Cornelius himself had sternly ordered our abbot to immediately grant the wish of his monk who had returned from the next world.

I do wish to stress that this is merely a rumor that was then current in the monastery. At any rate, soon afterwards, Father Michael was permitted to take the monastic vows to join the great schema, and was given the new name of Father Melchisedek.

Our abbot gave him this name in honor of one of the most mysterious of the ancient prophets of the Bible. His reason for choosing this particular name also has remained a great mystery. It's especially puzzling since Father Gabriel himself could never once properly even pronounce this Old Testament name—neither during the monastic ceremony, nor in all the years that elapsed since that time. No matter how hard he tried he would always mangle it and stumble on its pronunciation and make a complete hash of it. Immediately afterwards his mood would grow quite sour, and we were afraid to be anywhere near him at that moment.

What we did know in the monastery, however, was that, in those few minutes when Father Melchisedek was dead, he had a certain revelation after which he came back to life a completely different person. Father Melchisedek later did relate to some of his close associates and spiritual children a portion of what he had experienced. But even the echoes of what he related seemed utterly unusual. Therefore I and all my friends naturally wanted to learn something about this mystery from Father Melchisedek himself.

And so on that night in the Church of St. Lazarus, when I finally gathered up the courage to first ask a question of the schema-monk, that was exactly what I asked him: what did he see over there in that land from which no traveler returns?

Upon hearing this question, Father Melchisedek stood silently for a long time by the Royal Gates of the altar, with his head cast down. More than ever I froze and trembled with justified fear that I had had no right whatsoever to ask anything so impertinent. But finally, in a voice that was very weak from hardly ever speaking, Father Melchisedek began to reply.

He said that he had suddenly seen himself standing in the midst of a giant green field. Then he had walked on through this field, continuing straight but not knowing where he was going, until his path was blocked by a gigantic moat. There, amidst thick mud and clumps of earth, he saw a multitude of icon frames, church lecterns, and metal overlays for icons. There he also saw crooked tables, broken chairs, and strange wardrobes. As he looked at them, he recognized his own carpentry work. He stood looking at his own work both recognizing it and yet utterly surprised by it—and suddenly he had the feeling that somebody was standing over his shoulder . . . He lifted up his eyes and saw that it was the Mother of God. She gazed with melancholy at all his work of many years. And then she spoke: "You're a monk . . . And all we wanted from you was just one thing, the main thing: repentance and prayer. Instead of that, you gave us this woodwork . . ."

The vision disappeared. The dead man opened up his eyes and was once again back at the monastery.

After this event, Father Melchisedek was a completely changed man. The main focus of his life became exactly what the Holy Mother of God had mentioned to him—repentance and prayer. The fruits of his now exclusively spiritual labors were not delayed, revealing themselves in his deepest humility, his weeping over his past sins, his sincere love for all, and his complete and utter withdrawal from all affairs of this world, his absence from all human interference in his ascetic labors. Thereafter those fruits were also revealed in the effectiveness of his powerful prayers on behalf of others, and by his ability to foretell the future, something that was noticed by many of us.

Having noticed how he had utterly withdrawn from this world, and with what single-minded devotion he focused solely on his spiritual battles, invisible and incomprehensible to us, we the novices could only summon the courage to approach him in the most extraordinary of circumstances. Furthermore, almost everybody was afraid of him: it was well known throughout the monastery that Father Melchisedek was an exceedingly strict father confessor. Indeed, he had a right to be so. His unflinching insistence on the purity of spirit of every Christian was nourished by his great love for all people, his deep knowledge of the laws of the spiritual world, and his understanding of how vitally important it is for every human to constantly struggle against sin.

This true monk lived in his own higher world, a place where compromise is just not tolerated. But if Father Melchisedek would sometimes give us answers, they were always incredibly accurate, not just powerful but imbued by some kind of particular and quite uncanny force.

There was a period during my life in the monastery when I was inundated with an avalanche of undeserved and cruel (or so they seemed to me) trials. Sorely beset, I vowed to seek advice from the very strictest monk in the entire community, Father Melchisedek.

In answer to my knock on his door and to the prayer traditionally said before entering a monk's cell, Father Melchisedek emerged fully dressed in his monk's mantle and stole. I had found him in a moment when he was performing his strict prayer rule.

I told him about my misfortunes and seemingly insoluble problems. Father Melchisedek listened to me silently, standing as ever with his head drooping down in melancholy. When I was finished, he lifted up his eyes to me and suddenly burst into tears, and wept most bitterly:

"My brother!" he cried out in inexpressible pain. "Why are you asking me for advice? I myself am perishing!"

This elder, this great, holy ascetic spiritual warrior who was standing in front of me and weeping with unstained grief, now was feeling himself to be in truth the worst and most sinful man on earth! With each moment he did so, I saw with ever-increasing clarity and joy that all the ridiculous little problems of mine put together, indeed all of those matters that I had thought so insurmountable, were in fact not worth the least little thing!

Furthermore, at that very moment I suddenly felt that all of these insignificant problems had suddenly completely vanished and had been lifted from my soul. I already had no need to ask any advice from this elder. He had already done everything he could for me. I bowed to him full of gratitude and left.

Everything on our earth—both the simple and the complicated questions, both the little human problems and the challenges of finding the great path to God, all the secrets of the past, the present, and the future ages—all can be resolved only by such mysterious, ineffably beautiful and omnipotent humility. And even if we cannot understand its truth and meaning, and even if it seems for now that we are not ready for this mysterious and all-powerful humility, nonetheless, that humility by itself will reveal itself to us through those incredible persons who are capable of possessing it.

Father Antippus wearing his World War II medals.

Father Antippus

IN ADDITION TO the unceasing reading of the Psalter, there is a special church service that is often performed in monasteries: the reading aloud of Akathists and supplicatory prayers. This is when the service to a particular saint is added to ordinary prayers. As far as I know, this ceremony is not to be found either in the ancient rules of Orthodox monasteries or in the traditions of other Orthodox churches in other countries. Instead, it is peculiar to Russia. But our people are particularly fond of these services, and Akathist hymns have been requested from us in the Pskov Caves Monastery many, many times—sometimes fifteen or twenty at once, lengthening our services by up to three hours.

Young monks like us used to get quite tired by these long, drawn-out and sometimes monotonous services. It is easy to understand why: after all, Akathists are primarily designed to be read at home, and over time they have been composed by all sorts of people—sometimes by great ecclesiastical poets, but other times merely by pious and God-fearing provincial young ladies. Therefore the texts of these Akathist prayers are not always perfect, to put it mildly. And there were certain young monks who used to try to get out of their obligations to read these prayers out loud.

Happily for them, in the Pskov Caves Monastery there lived someone who was always willing to relieve his more educated brothers of the execution of this somewhat tedious ecclesiastical duty. His name was Archimandrite Antippus. He had come to the monastery long ago, just after the war, with a chest full of medals for military heroism. Then he had become the spiritual son of the elder Schema-monk Savva, to whom he was devoted until death.

In spite of his imposing appearance (Father Antippus resembled an extremely powerful elderly lion with a fiery-red thick mane), this priest was remarkably kind, cheerful, and easy-going with everyone. No one ever once noticed him to be angry or irritated—even though literally every day almost all kinds of people used to come up to Father Antippus to make confession, ask for advice, or just to chat and relieve their hearts. Because of his extreme kindness and good nature, many people tried to make sure that they would say their confessions particularly to him. And he was quite glad about this: he would forgive everyone's sins, and by virtue of the power of his priesthood would absolve them of their guilt forever. What joy!

Furthermore, Father Antippus was in charge of the reading of the Psalter. If it would happen that for some reason—either illness, or the execution of some other particular task, or even due to a mere lack of enthusiasm—one of our brotherhood was about to miss his required hour of unceasing reading of the Psalter, Father Antippus would relieve him, do it all himself, and would never scold or reproach anyone for this—even though it was already his duty to read the unceasing Psalter no less than three hours every night.

Truly, Father Antippus's greatest joy was reciting the Akathist. He would practically sparkle with joy during all these endless services—indeed, he would invariably add to the readings, inserting into the lists up to three or five books of names to commemorate, each of which weighed a good two or three pounds extra. He was ecstatic doing this, as he felt deeply that the saying of these prayers read in church for the living and dead Orthodox Christians was of vital importance. Indeed, the people truly loved these services.

But then came the day when Father Antippus could no longer walk on his failing legs and could no longer stand for hours and hours on end at prayer services. The monastery dean, or monk in charge of keeping order, declared that Archimandrite Antippus was to be freed from these obligations.

At this, Father Antippus performed his last service with tears in his eyes. The parishioners were also weeping. All of them were sad that there would no longer be any Akathists read by such a devoted man of prayer. Meanwhile the young hieromonks were seriously perturbed at the thought of how many more interminable prayers they would now need to add to their services without the aid of good Father Antippus. Only the novice sextons and sacristans rejoiced, because they knew that there were no other monks who shared Father Antippus's passion for reading Akathists and commemoration books of such seemingly interminable lengths. Indeed, some of the novices began to hope that they might finally make it to the midday meal on time.

The very saddest of all was Father Antippus himself. He had not only served his last supplicatory prayer service, but had been deprived of his chance to read his beloved Akathists in the future. At that time the

Father Antippus with his beloved book of Akathist prayers.

Akathist books, which we used to call "Akathistniki," were not published but were instead laboriously copied out by our parishioners into thick notebooks into which each of the texts was written out by hand. His beloved notebooks were kept in a special suitcase, and the suitcase, which had formerly been exclusively in the possession of Father Antippus, was now going to be given to several other priests.

At the conclusion of this service in the Cathedral of St. Michael, that most melancholy service in Father Antippus's entire life, a group of foreign tourists walked into the church. It appeared that they were descendants of Russian émigrés, because, although they looked like well-kept foreigners, they crossed themselves in the proper Orthodox manner, and approached the icons properly, just as Russians would. Having prayed, these pilgrims were about to leave when one of the women removed a little book from her bag, showed it to Father Antippus from a distance, and then placed it on the steps of the platform in front of the altar.

When Father Antippus left the church, accompanied by the wails and sighs of despairing old ladies, he suddenly remembered the little book that had been left behind for him. Hobbling back with difficulty he bent over to pick it up, and opened it. It was a book of Akathists written in Old Church Slavonic and published in Brussels.

From that moment until the very day of his death Father Antippus was never once parted from that little book. For him it replaced his entire beloved suitcase. Although it was not a big book, it was published in very fine print and on very fine paper, such that, to the great joy of that good old priest, it actually contained a great multitude of Akathist hymns.

At times we would see that big red-haired monk, perched with his little book on a little bench by the Holy Hill, put on his large glasses, open the book, read, and start to pray.

In the days before his death Father Antippus grew too sick to do anything but lie down. He was lodged in the monastery's infirmary, where he often gave his confession and received Communion, right there, while lying on his sickbed. However, he found the strength to get up and walk on the day of his death. He took a cross and Bible and went over to the caves, to visit the grave of his old father confessor. It was here that Father Antippus confessed for the last time all the sins of his entire life, to his long-since-dead elder, the great schema-monk, priest Savva, and begged for his prayers of support for the long journey ahead of him. Then he went back to the infirmary to die.

When I arrived from Moscow for his funeral, I was surprised that his coffin had not been placed in the Water-Blessing Chapel, the usual place of the three-day mourning and pre-burial period before the actual burial, as was standard in the Pskov Caves Monastery. It turned out that the chapel was closed for repairs, and therefore Father Antippus's coffin was taken straight to the caves, where he ended up right by the grave of Elder Savva. And it was there that he was finally buried. Even death could not separate them in the end.

Now Father Antippus and his spiritual father Father Superior Savva are together: by their relics together on earth, and by their spirits together in the Kingdom of Heaven.

I say "relics" not because I suggest that without proper ecclesiastical canonization it is possible to declare someone who has just died a saint, but just because the remains of any Orthodox Christian who dies within the bosom of the Church are properly called "relics" in our Church, though few people know this.

In the caves.

The Caves

ONE OF THE most surprising curiosities about the Pskov Caves Monastery is its holy caves, in which, over six hundred years ago, our monastery first began. A virtual underground labyrinth of caves extends for many kilometers beneath the monastery's churches, cells, gardens, buildings, and fields. It is here in the caves where the monks first settled. Here they built their first churches. Here too, they buried their departed brethren in the ancient biblical manner: right in these clefts of caves. It was only later when the number of monks and hermits began to grow and grow that the monastery started to expand to the surface.

Since that time, the caves were known as the "God-built" portion of our monastery—in other words, that portion of the monastery that is truly "made by God." This name came not so much from the natural properties of these caves—the monks later expanded and enlarged various caves and cavities, also constructing an intricate system of tunnels and corridors interconnecting them. It came from the fact that that human bodies and remains brought down to the caves immediately cease to smell the way dead bodies normally do.

By the time I got to the monastery, over 14,000 former inhabitants of Pechory at some point in its storied history were buried in its caves—and not just monks, but also civilian lay-workers and parishioners from the surrounding area, as well as warriors who heroically defended the monastery from attacks by foreign invaders in the Middle Ages. In the caves the coffins are not buried, but instead are simply stacked one on top of another in niches and grottoes, caves within the caves. In spite of this, however, visitors walking along the long labyrinthine corridors with candles are always astonished by how fresh and clean the air in the caves is.

There is an old Slavonic hymn that translates roughly: "If God wills it, Nature's laws are overcome." Yet skeptical tourists always leave the caves still surprised, refusing to believe their own eyes—or, to be exact, their own noses. Sometimes those skeptics who come and experience this marvel for themselves, if they are better educated, are left with no real recourse other than to quote:

There are more things in heaven and earth, Horatio,
Than are dreamt of in your philosophy.

Quite a few stories are told about these caves. One of the recent stories
took place in 1995 when Russia's then-President Boris Nikolayevich Yeltsin
visited Pechory. Our monastery Treasurer Archimandrite Nathaniel showed
him around the monastery, and naturally enough showed him the caves as
well. Thin, white-haired, and shambling along in tattered shoes and robes
that were long since dilapidated and full of holes, Father Nathaniel held a
candle aloft as he led our head of state and all his accompanying suite of
bodyguards and others through the caves.

Finally President Yeltsin realized that there was something inexplicable
going on, and expressed his surprise: why was there no smell of rotting
or decomposition, even though coffins with their corpses there had been
simply placed in niches in the cave grottoes instead of being buried? Why
was there no smell, even though the coffins were at times close enough to
touch?

Father Nathaniel explained to the president: "It is a miracle performed
by God."

The excursion continued. However, after a little while the president
once again skeptically repeated his question.

"As I said, it was all done by God." Father Nathaniel was quite curt in
his reply.

For several minutes there was nothing but silence. Finally as the president was leaving the caves he asked the elder: "Tell me, Father—what's the
real secret? What substance do you put on the coffins?"

Archimandrite Nathaniel replied: "Boris Nikolayevich, are there any
persons in your entourage who smell bad?"

"Of course not!"

"So what makes you think that anyone would dare to smell bad having
joined the entourage of the King of Heaven?"

It is said that President Yeltsin was perfectly satisfied with this answer.

In the days when we were officially an atheist state, and even nowadays
when it is not clear what we are, many people have tried and continue
to keep trying to somehow scientifically explain this mysterious quality
of the caves of Pechory. What crazy theories have not been put forward?
Starting with the fantastic idea that came into President Yeltsin's head,
that somehow 14,000 corpses in our caves are wiped daily with certain

The icon of the Resurrection in the caves, where the elders are buried.

secret pleasant-smelling substances . . . There have also been hypotheses that there are unique properties or a microclimate particular to these caves, capable of getting rid of bad smells. The latter version has always been the most popular. During Soviet times this was the usual explanation officially given to tourists.

Certain old monks relate how the great archimandrite and Father Superior of the Pskov Caves Monastery, Father Alipius, who was head of our monastery during the years of severe persecution in Khrushchev's time, always used to grab a handkerchief daubed thoroughly in some strong Soviet eau de cologne whenever he was taking a delegation of high-ranking Soviet officials through the caves. Whenever the visitors pompously began to discuss microclimates and their ability to remove smells, Father Alipius would simply give them a whiff of his handkerchief, thoroughly dunked in the most acrid achievements of Soviet perfumery. Other times, he would ask them to pay attention to the flowers and how pleasant they smelled in their vases by the graves of the revered elders. Then he would ask:

"Well, are you not willing to accept the fact that there are things in this life which you do not understand? And if you had occasion to be present in the caves when a new corpse was brought in and to experience how each time the smell of decomposition completely disappears, what would you say then? Would you also try to think of some kind of other reason?"

The labyrinths of the cave extend for many kilometers in all directions. Nobody ever knew how big they were, not even the abbot of the monastery himself. We all suspected that the only people who might know could be Father Nathaniel and Archimandrite Seraphim, who had lived longer than anybody else in the monastery.

At one point, my still very young friends the hieromonks Father Raphael and Father Nikita got ahold of the key of a very old communal grave. No one in this portion of the labyrinth had been buried after the year 1700, and the way inside was blocked by a heavy iron door. But proceeding by candlelight these doughty monks made their way inside through the low vaults, looking around with curiosity to their right and left: on either side all around troughs were stacked, crumbling with age (in the old days of Muscovite Russia that is how monks used be buried). In these troughs, the bones of the forebears of Fathers Raphael and Nikita in the monastic brotherhood were whitening and yellowing. After a while the intrepid pathfinders found a completely closed trough that was perfectly preserved. Curiosity got the better of them, and kneeling down, the young monks with great care and reverence opened up the heavy lid.

An abbot lay inside; his body was perfectly preserved and entirely whole; his fingers, still covered by waxy yellowish flesh, still clutched to his chest a large woodcut cross. Only his face was somewhat green for some reason. When they recovered from their initial surprise, the monks figured out that the reason for this rather strange sight was the decay of the green cloth with which it is customary to cover the face of a deceased priest, according to ancient tradition. Over the course of three centuries, the cloth had decayed into dust.

One of the monks blew softly on the face of the corpse: a green cloud curled up into the air, leaving the two friends to look at the face of this elder that had been completely unwithered by time. It appeared that he was merely asleep and that in just a minute he would open his eyes and look sharply on these curious young monks who had dared disturb his sacred rest. As these young monks realized that they were looking at the untarnished relics of a saint yet unknown to the world, the crew was startled by their own boldness, and rushed to put the lid back on the trough, and then hastened back to their twentieth century.

We novices often used to go to the caves. If ever there were any kind of serious problems, we would ask for the help of these great spiritual heroes. We'd get down on our knees and, touching their coffins with our hands, would beg these elders for support and inspiration, which was never slow to come. We particularly troubled with these requests the elder Simeon who had died in 1960 and had only recently been canonized. We also used to request help from the Great Abbot Archimandrite Alipius, as well as other elders who one by one after a life full of earthly labors went in their souls to God, and in their bodies to the caves.

Another particularly outstanding feature of the Pskov Caves Monastery would only be revealed in the twentieth century. The Holy Trinity Monastery in Sergiev Posad, Optina Monastery in Kaluga Province, and the Kiev Caves Monastery in Kiev, as well as the monasteries of Solovki, Valaam, and Sarov, were all famous not just in Russia, but throughout Christendom. By contrast, the Monastery of the Pskov Caves for many centuries was nothing more than a simple provincial monastic community.

However, in the years after the war, when the Russian Orthodox Church began to recover from the devastation wrought upon it after the Revolution, it unexpectedly came to pass that this backwater of a monastery had been chosen by God to carry out its own particular and magnificent mission.

Suddenly, it turned out that the Pskov Caves Monastery was the only monastery in the entire territory of Russia that had never closed even during Soviet times, and had therefore managed to keep its invaluable unbroken tradition of ongoing monastic life. Until 1940 the monastery had been part of the territory of Estonia. After the annexation of this territory into the USSR, the Bolsheviks simply had not had enough time to destroy the place, because the war began. Afterwards, even during Khrushchev's persecutions of the Church, the Great Abbot, Archimandrite Alipius, had managed to find ways of resisting the giant governmental machine, and had not permitted the closure of our monastery.

The fact that our monastery had never ceased to be a preeminently spiritual dwelling had an incomparable value. It is no accident that it was precisely here in Pechory, during the Soviet 1950s, that the tradition of the eldership was reborn—a tradition that is one of the most precious treasures of the Russian Orthodox Church.

Lower gates of the Pskov Caves Monastery.

Being a Novice

THE MOST IRREPLACEABLE and perhaps single happiest time in the life of a monk is his novitiate. Perhaps later the monk will experience spiritual flights and events that surpass his imagination, far beyond the ken of any secular person. There will be victories and defeats upon the ascetic field of battle; there will be astounding revelations about the world and about oneself. And yet there is nothing that compares to the years of a monk's novitiate.

Once former Patriarch Pimen himself was asked in his old age: "Your Holiness, you have attained the highest possible rank in the ecclesiastical hierarchy. But if you had the ability to choose, what rank would you prefer to hold?"

The Patriarch as a rule was usually laconic and kept his thoughts to himself. However, to this question he replied immediately. "I'd want to be a simple novice, a doorkeeper at the lower gates of the Pskov Caves Monastery."

If this most revered elder—a Patriarch no less—would have chosen this in his most ardent if unattainable dreams, then you can only imagine what genuine and passionate desire others might feel to return to that unique state of so long ago, that state when you have just begun and feel in every moment the fatherly love of an omnipotent God watching over you and advancing you according to His plan. It is reminiscent of those magic carefree moments in childhood, when everything that you do consists entirely of beautiful revelations in a new and endlessly undiscovered world.

By the way, 2,000 years ago, the apostles themselves basically served for three years as the first novices, in service to Jesus Christ. Their main task was to follow their Teacher, and to discover for themselves with joyous astonishment His omnipotence and love.

The very same thing takes place for novices in our days. The apostle Paul made a great discovery: "Jesus Christ is the same yesterday, and today, and forever" (Hebrews 13:8). These words have been proved throughout the history of Christianity. Times and people have changed, but whether for the generation of the first Christians, or for our own contemporaries, Christ remains the same.

True novices, whom Russians call *poslushniki,* or "those who hear and obey," receive a priceless gift from God—the holy carefree state that is better and sweeter than any other freedom. I have had occasion to see quite a few of such true novices, and they could remain this carefree way that they truly were in any rank, from the humblest laborer in the monastery all the way up to a bishop.

The apostle Matthew relates a story of how one summer in Galilee the apostles were walking along a path through the wheat fields with their young Divine Teacher. They had gotten quite hungry along the way. But that was no problem. The apostles began to pluck sheaves of wheat, to rub them with their hands and eat the ripened kernels of grain.

But then it was just their luck to run into a group of very strict Pharisees. These Pharisees began to sharply rebuke the young apostles, because from the Pharisees' point of view the apostles had committed a terrible sin: after all, it was the Sabbath, and the Pharisees and those who lived by the letter of the law believed that on the Sabbath even the most indispensable work was forbidden—with the praiseworthy idea being that on that day of rest and contemplation a human's thoughts should not be distracted away from God. But the simple-hearted apostles paid no heed to the insults of the enraged Pharisees. Peace and freedom reigned in their souls. They knew that they were not violating God's law, but only mankind's feeble interpretation of it. Furthermore, in following their Teacher, they were in fact carrying out God's will, for they were listening to God and following Him personally.

This rapturous feeling of happiness and freedom that nobody can take away from you, this sense that you are utterly protected and defended in this world because God Himself has taken you up under His protection and is leading you according to His will along a path known to Him alone—all of these feelings are part of the incomparable feeling a novice has during his novitiate. With time this feeling may pass. But they say that after many years of devoted service it comes back in a form that is only stronger and wiser.

I was incredibly lucky: for four months I actually happened to serve as doorkeeper of the lower gates of the Pechory Monastery—exactly the position old Patriarch Pimen had dreamed about. And His Holiness knew what he was talking about: it truly is the most beautiful place on earth!

The doorkeeper's tasks are few: to open and close the gates, so that cars and visitors and carts carrying hay may pass, and to clean up after

The cattle yard.

the cows who mornings and evenings wander through the centuries-old cobblestone paths from the monastery's cattle yard to pasture and back.

While I was on watch, I had a chance to read many interesting books, and began to really love solitude with all my heart. However, when fall came and the pasture-grazing season was over, they gave me a new task—working with the cows in the cattle yard. This was a more difficult task. They are always very particular in the monastery about cleanliness and order. It was required of us to be very attentive, and to immediately clean up manure, and to cast wood chips everywhere. Otherwise the cow might lie down in its own manure, damaging its udders and leading to sickness. There were thirty-five brown cows in the monastery's herd. They had large reserves of hay to feed on . . . and so, their production of manure continued merrily, efficiently, and around the clock—meaning someone always had to be standing by to shovel away it quickly.

I remember one winter night, at about four in the morning, I was so tired I could barely stand up on my own two legs; my eyes were falling shut . . . And those cows just kept it up: poop and poop, plop and plop! Finally, when it looked as if they'd just taken a break, I collapsed on the battered old sofa that had seen better days and fell asleep immediately. But no sooner had I fallen asleep when once again I heard the demanding sound: poop and poop, plop and plop! And once again, poop, poop, poop!

I forced my eyes open and saw in the dim light of an electric lamp a cow in its stall right across from me, standing in a great neglected pile of its own fresh steaming manure and waving her tail at me as if summoning me: she had eaten her fill of fresh hay, had done her duty, and was now waiting for me to do my job and clean it up. But I had no strength left to clean it up. The cow waited and waited, and finally, with a great sigh, lay down. But it was smart and lay down right on the wood chips; only its tail was sticking out into the manure and brushing it here and there. The brush of the cow's tail was swelling up from the contact with the dung, but at least it wasn't the cow's udders, so the cow wouldn't get sick. By now, although I was a city lad, I knew all of this, and so it was with a clear conscience that I fell asleep once again.

But finally it was time to rub my eyes and get back to my shovel. With my boot I slightly nudged that cow again so that it would get up and I would be able to clear away the manure underneath her. But upset by my neglect the cow had become completely mischievous: rolling around from leg to leg, waving her tail, and finally when I bent over—smack! I received a tail full of cow dung right in my face! Yes, in a second, my mouth, my eyes, my nose, my ears—all of me was suddenly covered in manure! At first I was so shocked that I somehow froze with sudden anger and humiliation. Then completely forgetting myself, I wanted to grab that shovel and hit that cow with it as hard as I possibly could!

Then suddenly I remembered that Christ had commanded us to turn the other cheek. That indeed is commanded us even when a human being offends us. And here this was just a dumb animal—moreover, one whom I had upset first. I dropped my shovel. I wiped away both the manure and my tears with the sleeve of my quilted coat, turned to the faded paper images of icons on the walls, crossed myself, and, still weeping for my humiliation, got back to work.

A very interesting though complicated portion of my novitiate took place in the bakery. Usually at about five o'clock in the morning, old people from the town of Pechory would arrive to help the monks and novices bake the Communion bread. Before they arrived, the bakers would prepare the dough. The entire time we worked in silence, listening to the Psalter, which would be read by a specially assigned novice or monk. Communion bread must always be prepared and baked to the accompaniment of prayers.

The most heated time in the bakery comes before Easter. Thousands

The bakery.

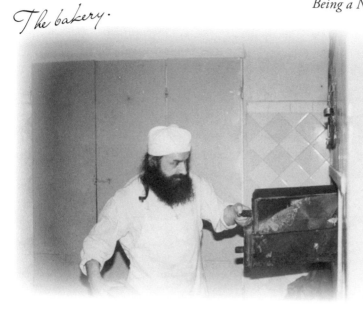

and thousands of Communion loaves must be baked for the two weeks to come—Holy Week and Bright Week,* when all work in the monastery is put off for prayer and then for celebration. It is also important to bake artos breads—special large loafs of bread baked specially before Easter to be blessed in the church and requiring lots of work to get right. We would bake these artos loaves not just for the monastery, but for the bishop's house and all the churches in the diocese. For Bright Week, furthermore, again not just for the monastery, but also for the bishop's table, we needed to bake huge quantities of the *kulich* loaves.**

We would start our work in the first wee hours of Holy Monday, when it was still dark. We would not come out of the bakery to even so much as glance at the light of day until it was time for the Liturgy on Holy Thursday. We would sleep in fits and snatches, where we could—sometimes right on the table, in shifts . . . It was quite a consolation when Father Anastasius would bring us novices a tin of canned peaches, which we would devour with still hot, aromatic bread.

---

* This week is also called Renewal Week. It is the week following Easter.

** These loaves are traditional Easter bread decorated with icing, on which is written X B, standing for *Khristos Voskrese*, or "Christ Is Risen."

Once the bakery literally saved my life. During my first Lenten Fast I happened to fall very seriously ill. I had double pneumonia. The worst of it was that I knew that I would never get better in Pechory. I had developed what they call "resistance"—none of the normal antibiotics kept in the monastery infirmary or in the town pharmacy were working for me. But I had decided that I would rather die in the monastery than live in the outside world. So I refused to leave to be treated elsewhere.

On the day that I made this decision, the inflammation in my lungs was aggravated by an inflammation in my muscles. The pain was so acute that I could barely get out of bed. Nonetheless I stubbornly proceeded to my work as a novice. My temperature never went below 38°C (100.4°F). On top of everything else, as we were moving heavy logs one of them fell right on my head. I clutched my poor head in pain and lay down by a stack of firewood. This sort of thing was what a nun in the Monastery of Diveyevo, old Mother Frosya, used to call "getting it from everywhere: from the people on one side, and God on the other."

Anyway, I grieved and grieved, and finally I got up and went back to my task of carrying logs. And then I was saved by an old monk named Father Dionysius. When he saw the state that I was in, he decided to save me in true peasant fashion. By this time, the baking of all the Easter bread was done. Father Dionysius fed some hay into the enormous stove as it was cooling and then stuck me into the stove. It was so deliciously warm inside that I fell asleep from exhaustion. The next morning I woke up wet from head to toe with sweat, yet felt utterly cured. I flew out of that stove like a spring songbird, and by the evening I stood throughout the entire Easter midnight service as if nothing had ever been wrong with me.

* * *

Although there were many tasks that we novices had to fulfill, our main task after all was and remains prayer. In the evening, once our tasks were done, we would relax for about forty minutes and then go to services. On ordinary days they would last about four hours, but on Church feast days, easily more than five.

We would read the ancient patericon books on the lives of the saints, and observe the inspired pastoral devotion of Father John, the ascetic nobility and clairvoyance of Father Seraphim, the supreme spiritual sacrifice of Father Melchisedek, the wisdom of our Treasurer Father Nathaniel, the exorcisms of Father Adrian, the remarkable humility of

Father Theophanes. And being full of admiration for these and other priests of Pskov Caves Monastery not mentioned in this list, we dreamed of imitating them in every way. While walking through the monastery corridors, even as we passed the cells of these elders, we would hush in reverence and awe, sensing that behind their doors invisible battles with ancient forces of evil were being fought, and universes were being destroyed and created!

As it was, our awkward attempts at ascetical struggle may have been laughable, yet they came from pure hearts. I will not tell stories about our many "ascetical feats" when we were still just novices in Pechory Monastery. I do not want to run the risk of making fun of this even in a good way, because I believe that the Lord accepted and blessed even these unfinished and naive spiritual labors of ours. After all, God looks into the heart of a man and perceives his inner intentions. And the intentions that we young novices had were pure and sincere.

Our drives to achieve new spiritual heights were strictly regulated by our spiritual fathers and by the abbots of the monastery. This was necessary in order to avoid spiritual delusion—pride and a sense of false self-confidence leading to overweening arrogance. I remember how our abbot Archimandrite Gabriel once very strictly rebuked a novice who was ostentatiously promenading about the monastery with his prayer rope. And the Father Superior was right. How many sad cases there are when people begin to pose, or to foolishly and dangerously swell with pride, acting without proper humility and respect, but instead rushing off all puffed up to "investigate" the spiritual world!

Yet the danger of anyone's falling into spiritual delusion hardly had much chance to ever develop or curb spiritual life in our monastery. We were always ever so attentively and carefully watched over, constantly guided towards prayer and modesty in all our desire to get closer to God. I remember how surprised I was once when the abbot approached me upon the altar and suddenly asked me an unexpected question:

"Georgiy, do you pray at night?"

"No, Father Abbot, at night I sleep, and that's all!"

Father Gabriel looked at me disappointedly. "Too bad. You should pray at night as well."

About ten years later I was told the same thing by Metropolitan Pitirim: "Remember the commandment of St. Joseph of Volokolamsk: the day is for work, and the night is for prayer."

Novice Alexander, now Father Joasaph.

They say that nighttime prayer is the particular strength of a monk. One time Father John wanted to strengthen me in my calling to help me to see a little bit of just what the spiritual world really is, and so he blessed me to follow a particular rule of prayer—particularly at night. This time had been chosen by Father John so as to minimize any chance of distractions from the outside world. From two o'clock in the afternoon until ten o'clock at night I labored at my tasks, serving in the cattle yard in the cowshed; then all night long I was on night watch in the Dormition Square.

Father John blessed me to perform a particular rule of saying the Jesus Prayer in such a way as to let it fill my entire mind and heart and let go of all external thoughts and feelings—even the most correct and praiseworthy ones.

It is remarkable but true that if one secludes oneself in prayer and limits oneself in food, sleep, and interaction with people, while not allowing any idle thoughts to enter the mind, nor any passionate feelings to enter the heart, then very quickly one discovers a truth: besides oneself and other people in this world there is also Someone Else. And this Someone is patiently waiting to see whether we will pay attention to Him during our endless race through life. He is simply patiently waiting, because God never forces Himself on anyone. But if one continues to pray properly (here I must stress "properly," in other words, without arrogance, and under the supervision of an experienced guide), then before one's spiritual gaze remarkable phenomena and images begin to appear.

The revered prelate St. Ignatius Brianchaninov writes:

> Use your time and energy to truly grasp your prayer as it acts in a holy way upon your inner body. There, deep inside you, prayer will open up new visions that will capture all your attention and bring you knowledge that the outer world cannot grasp, concepts of whose existence the outer world lacks even the slightest inkling.
>
> There in the very depths of your heart you will see the fall of man, you will see your soul murdered by sin, and you will see many other mysteries that are hidden from the world and from the children of this world. But once this vision opens up to you, then look inwards even more intensely with all your might; look inwards, and follow where that look inside leads, and you will grow cold to all that is transitory and subject to decay, and to all that you used to feel before.

The nights used to pass very quickly in saying the prayers Father John had assigned me and in the reading of the Psalter, and when my mind already began to get bored and distracted, I practiced bowing at the entrance of the caves. While doing this I also tried as much as possible to fast. But I was very hungry. Finally I decided to imagine a feast for myself that would absolutely not arouse my appetite. As I thought about it I decided it would be blessed bread, dipped in holy water. This was my own ascetic convention. The dish turned out to be certainly quite pious, but terribly untasty: it was wet, slippery, and bland. But even that was what I wanted. Having allowed myself a tiny plate of this repast, I had no further desire to eat. Father John smiled at my idea, but he did not object to it. Instead he strictly commanded me to come more often to confession and to tell him everything that happened during the day.

And indeed things began to happen. By the second or third day I began to feel that I hardly wanted to sleep. To be more exact, four hours of sleep seemed enough for me. Furthermore, my usually very sociable habits had somehow disappeared. More and more all I wanted was just to be left alone. Then one by one I began to remember sins that I had buried deep within my memory, long-forgotten incidents from my prior life. As soon as I would finish my night watch, I would race to confession. And yet although from these bitter memories I felt a sadness in my heart, I would also to my great surprise feel an inexpressible peace and lightness.

About a week into this routine something even stranger began to happen. In the nighttime, as I wearied from very long prayers, I was performing ritual prostrations by the entrance to the caves when suddenly behind me I heard a crashing din, as if a thousand sheets of tin had suddenly collapsed. I froze on the spot in fear. When I dared to turn around, I saw the main square of the monastery sleeping peacefully in the moonlight. All night long I did not leave the caves, but prayed to the holy Saints, expecting any minute for the horrible noise to be repeated.

When it dawned at about four that morning, Father Seraphim left the cell and his cave for Dormition Square as usual. I ran up to him and, still quivering with fear, asked him what had happened to me. Father Seraphim only waved his hand and scoffed: "Pay no attention, it was only demons." Then looking over the monastery with a proprietary glance, he retired to his cell.

Pay no attention? For the entire rest of my watch I stood quivering like an aspen leaf.

An even stranger incident took place the next day. In the evening I took up my task as night watchman on Dormition Square and was already beginning to say the Jesus Prayer as I had now become accustomed to doing. Soon I saw a novice walking up to me. It was Pasha the Chuvash, a well-known hooligan who had been sent by his parents after his service in the Army to the monastery to be reformed. I was disappointed to see Pasha, as I could see that he was headed straight for me, and that was not at all what I wanted right then. And suddenly somehow inside of me I heard the answer to his question and understood that it was precisely this that I needed to explain to him. His voice did not agree and argued. But another voice patiently convinced him and brought him back to correct thoughts. And this long dialogue lasting several minutes flashed within my head in an instant.

Father John.

Pasha came up to me, and I was by now not surprised at all when he asked me precisely the question that I had somehow already heard. I answered him in the exact words that had echoed in my consciousness just a minute before. Our dialogue went on exactly word for word as it had just played out in my heart.

This was incredible! Next morning I threw myself at Father John and

Two novices serving in the altar.

asked him what had happened to me. Father John replied that the Lord in His wisdom had given me a slight glimpse from the corner of my eye into the spiritual world that is hidden from us normal people. It became clear to me that this had happened through the prayers of Father John. The good Father strictly reminded me not to get carried away, and warned me that this new uncanny feeling would soon wear off. In order to remain in this state, he explained, extraordinary spiritual labors were needed— extraordinary in the literal meaning of that word. What labors? Each person in his own way must keep his or her own mysterious link with God.

The world considers real spiritual strivers as mad, eccentric, not quite together, regards their achievements as little more than the butts of jokes, and has no regard for these heroes of the spirit who for some reason leave the world of men and seek out barren deserts or climb onto pillars, or become holy fools, or kneel on the cold stones for years, forgoing sleep, forgoing food, forgoing water, and it considers mad those who truly turn the other cheek to their foes. In the words of the apostle Paul (Hebrews 11:38): "Of whom the world was not worthy, they wandered in deserts, and in mountains, and in dens, and caves of the earth."

In conclusion, Father John told me not to be sad when this unique feeling passed very soon, but always to remember what had happened.

That Father John had been right I realized myself the very next day. In spite of the incredible impression that had been made on me after the remarkable conversation with Pasha, nonetheless, somehow I got distracted in my mind with worldly thoughts, ate a bit too much in the refectory, began to chat with someone about this and about that, thoughtlessly let something impure come into my heart, and suddenly this incomparable feeling of being so close to God's presence quietly just melted away.

And so I was left with what my pleasure-loving and sinful sweet tooth of the heart had clung to: my favorite pea soup, a pleasant little chat with my dear friends, and all kinds of varied and interesting thoughts and dreams. Yes, I was left with all of these things . . . but without Him. The feeling was so bitter that I felt some lines of poetry within my soul:

> I feel sad and at ease: my melancholy's bright;
> My melancholy's full entirely
> Of Thee, and only Thee . . .

Later on I realized with a start that of course it seemed that someone else (Alexander Pushkin) had written these beautiful lines.

Bald Pasha the Chuvash ran away from the monastery a few years later and was murdered somewhere in Cheboxary. May God rest his soul! Not many of my friends from that time—my fellow novices in Pechory Monastery—were able to keep to the monastic path.

The Pskov Caves Monastery.
View from outside the wall.

How We Joined the Monastery

IN THE 1980s, we basically didn't join monasteries but instead fled to them. I think people considered this a little crazy on our part—sometimes more than a little. Our unhappy parents or inconsolable fiancées or furious professors in the colleges or institutes in which we studied would sometimes come by to "reason" with us.

There was one monk who had fled to us having already retired and raised the last of his children. His distraught sons and daughters arrived, yelling loud enough to fill the entire monastery with their shouting, insisting that they had come to take their daddy home right this minute and that they wouldn't leave without him. We hid him in an old laundry basket in an old garage for carriages. The children assured us that their father, a decorated coal miner, had lost his mind. In fact, as he had told us, for the last thirty years he had been dreaming of the day when he could retire to the monastery.

We understood him perfectly. We also had run away from a world that had become meaningless to us in order to find God, who had opened Himself to us—and we had run away in much the same way that some kids would run away to sea, to go voyaging to distant lands. But the call of God was incomparably more powerful. We had no way of overcoming it. To be more precise, we could feel unmistakably that if we did not follow His call, if we did not leave everything behind to follow Him, then we would irretrievably lose our own selves. And even if we were to gain the entire rest of the world, with all its joys and pleasures, we wouldn't need it and we would have no joy in it.

Of course, we felt great pity first of all for our uncomprehending parents, who were utterly lost in making sense of our firm convictions, and then also for our similarly lost friends and girlfriends. And also for our favorite professors, who, heedless of their time and resources, often used to visit Pechory in order to "save" us. We loved them and were willing to give up our lives for them. Our lives—but not our monastery.

To those from our former lives who cared about us, all of this seemed utterly ridiculous and incomprehensible. However, I remember I had

107

already been living for several months in the monastery when Sasha Shvetsov came to visit us. It was a Sunday—the only free day in the week. After a truly lovely Sunday service and a hearty monastery meal, we young novices were lying down blissfully relaxing in our beds in our big and very sunny cell. Suddenly the door burst open and a tall young man of our own age, about twenty-two years old, wearing designer Western jeans and an extremely expensive jacket, appeared at our threshold.

Without even saying hello to us, he exclaimed: "You know what? I like it here! I'm staying."

"Tomorrow they'll put you in the cattle sheds or make you clean the muck out of the sewers, and then let's see whether you'll stay or not," I thought to myself, yawning. The same thought must have come into the minds of everyone else looking at this fellow, who seemed like a typical Moscow spoiled brat who for some reason had blown into our ancient monastery.

It turned out that Sasha was the son of a highly placed worker in the Soviet trade representative's office. He had lived a privileged life with his parents in foreign postings—Beijing, London, New York—and had only recently returned to Russia for undergraduate study. He'd found out about God only half a year ago—and had not found out much, but he had found out the main thing. And it was clear that he truly had found it out. Because, from that moment on, he began to be tormented with the utter pointlessness of his life, and felt unable to do anything about it until he came to the monastery. Once he realized that he had found exactly what he had been looking for, he didn't even inform his parents as to his new place of residence. When we reproached Sasha that he was being cruel, he calmed us down, saying: "Oh, don't you worry. Dad will find me himself soon enough."

And so it proved. Sasha's father drove up to Pechory in a big black official Volga sedan and caused a gigantic scandal with the assistance of the police and the KGB, also dragging Sasha's friends from college into the mess and using all the usual strong-arm tactics employed back then to try to get us to leave the monastery. It took quite a long time to convince Sasha's horrified father that all was completely in vain and that his son would never leave this place.

Our Treasurer, Archimandrite Nathaniel, tried to calm our guest from Moscow and tenderly said to him: "It's all right. You've given up your son as a sacrifice to God. He will become a monk in the Pskov Caves

Two monks of the Pskov Caves Monastery.

Monastery, and the day will come when you will be proud of him."

I remember how savagely Sasha's father then screamed, so loudly that the entire monastery could hear: "Never!"

Sasha's dad did not know yet that Father Nathaniel was capable of seeing into the future; otherwise he wouldn't have gotten so nervous. Sasha truly is now a hieromonk. Indeed, he is the only one out of that group from the day he first walked into our novices' cell who has remained a monk, serving in the Pskov Caves Monastery. And ten years later Sasha's father, Alexander Mikhailovich Shvetsov, began to work with me in Moscow in the Donskoy Monastery, and then later in the Sretensky Monastery, as the director of our book warehouse.

Out for a walk.

It was in this capacity that Alexander Mikhailovich left us for the Lord, having first become an utterly sincere man of prayer and a true searcher for God.

A Story about People Like Us—
Only 1,500 Years Ago

From *The Prologue*

In the monastery library I once found a huge old book written in Old Church Slavonic, entitled The Prologue. *In it were collected a multitude of teachings in histories from the life of Christians starting from the time of the Evangelists and through the centuries up until the eighteenth century. The book was created gradually over a period of more than 1,000 years and was meant for daily reading in both church and home.*

I N THE SIXTH century in Constantinople, a huge city located by the waters of the Bosporus, with the most beautiful churches, palaces, and grand, snow-white marble homes in the world, during the reign of the Emperor Justinian there lived two young men and one young woman. Being children of wealthy patricians, well educated, and cheerful, they had been friends since early childhood. The parents of the young girl and one of the young men had already agreed among themselves even before the birth of their children that the young boy and the young girl would marry each other once they grew up. The day came and the happy pair did marry. Their friend was the best man at the wedding and was delighted for his friends.

It seemed that there would never be any cause for unhappiness. And yet, a year after the wedding, the young husband suddenly died. After the forty days of required ritual mourning, her friend came to see the young widow. Kneeling down before her, he said:

"Madame! Now that your days of heavy grief and mourning have passed, I find it impossible not to reveal to you that which earlier I would never have even dared to hint. I have loved you for as long as I can remember. The day in which I found out that your parents and the parents of my dear departed friend had decided to link you two in matrimony was the most horrible day of my life. From that time, even in my most private thoughts I had never dared to so much as think of happiness. You

know how dearly I loved your husband and my friend. But now what has happened has happened. And now I cannot conceal from you any longer that my feelings have only gotten stronger with time, and therefore I beg of you to become my wife."

The young woman grew thoughtful and replied:

"Well . . . such decisions should be made only after long prayers and fasting. Come back to me in ten days. But all throughout that time do not eat anything. And drink only water. Ten days from now I will give you my answer."

Exactly after the ten days of fasting had passed, the young man was once again in the home of his beloved. However, now his servants brought him in on a stretcher, so weakened was he by his fast. In the spacious hall of her dwelling he saw a table set and groaning with tasty delicacies. Meanwhile, on the other side of the hall a fabulous bed beckoned.

"Well, sir," the young mistress of the house asked him, "what shall we begin with?" And she demonstratively pointed out both the table and the bed.

"Madame!" the young man murmured. "Forgive me, but I must first partake of some nourishment."

"Well!" the wise young woman exclaimed. "Look how quickly you are ready to exchange me for another passion. All of mankind is like that. I too should confess to you that I have loved you for a long time. But knowing the will of my parents I did not disobey them and so became the wife of our friend. His death has revealed a lot to me. How fleeting and fickle everything in our life is! What do we prefer now? To serve the temporal world, or to serve God?"

They sat down to a meal in celebration. And then and there they decided to give away all their possessions to the poor and to follow Christ—each in a separate monastery.

Archimandrite Gabriel.

Father Gabriel

$\mathcal{T}$HE UNDISPUTED OVERLORD and master of the Pskov Caves Monastery in those years was our Father Superior, Archimandrite Gabriel. In ecclesiastical circles to this day legends are still told about his severity, even though it has been more than twenty years since he left Pechory to become a bishop in the Far East.

Father Anastasius, the cellarer* of the monastery, told me that once, at the market in Pskov where he was buying food, he was approached by two soldiers. They informed him that they had been sent to take him, Citizen Alexey Ivanovich Popov (as Father Anastasius was known to the outside world), to the Military Draft Board Office.

There the priest was informed that by a command of the military commissar he was being drafted into the Army for basic training over six months. Effective immediately. Father Anastasius, all depressed and dejected, was put into some office, and then ordered to fill out some forms.

Soon a man in plain clothes walked into the room. He sat next to Father Anastasius and showed him the identification of an officer in the KGB. Without further ado, he began to try to convince the priest to "collaborate" in exchange for not being sent off on a long trip to harsh military camps. The calculation was simple: a person already shocked with bad news, under stress from being torn from the life that he was used to, is indeed likely to be easier to convince.

For more than three hours Father Anastasius resisted as best he could the alternate threats and pleading that rained down upon him. The conversation would very likely have gone on longer. But all of a sudden the corridor rang out with shouts, someone's decisive footsteps, and . . . Suddenly, without knocking, Archimandrite Gabriel, the Abbot of Pechory Monastery, in a majestic Greek Orthodox *ryassa*** with a flowing black beard, and with a ponderous and most impressive staff in his hands, raced in, beside himself with rage. The officer wanted to start up, but

---

* The *cellarer* is the monk in charge of food supplies and the refectory.

** A *ryassa* is a loose, full-length outer garment worn by monastics and clergy.

our abbot stared at him with such fury that all the officer could do was freeze in terror. Grabbing Father Anastasius by the collar as if he were the puppetmaster Karabas-Barabas grabbing Pierrot the marionette, our abbot literally dragged him out of the Military Draft Board Office, all the while ushering dire threats to anyone in his way.

No one has the least idea how our abbot had found out that our cellarer was in the Military Draft Board Office. Of course, after this an enormous scandal erupted, such that our abbot even had to go to Moscow to smooth things over, but in the end Father Anastasius was never drafted—and was never bothered by any other KGB agents ever again.

The authorities of the town of Pskov and of Pskov Province also had a healthy respect for Father Gabriel as well as for his great predecessor as abbot, Archimandrite Alipius.

The fact of such respect was already something unique in Soviet times. Archimandrite Gabriel was reserved in his dealings with Soviet authority, and did not seek out trouble, but when the need came he was never subservient and bluntly spoke his mind. Somehow he was able to arrange things so that he alone vouched for the monastery's loyalty to political authority.

Therefore he did not countenance even the slightest attempts by agents of the "State Security Committee" (KGB) to poison our atmosphere by trying to establish any contacts or relationships with anyone in our brotherhood. How he was able to succeed in protecting the rest of us in the brotherhood remained his personal secret. But however he did it, we remain grateful to this day to him for what he did.

We young novices feared our abbot worse than death. Indeed, we used to roundly criticize him, sinners that we were! We were more than a little surprised to see how good-humoredly the elders of our monastery related to him.

Year after year, more and more people from all over the country used to come and visit Father John (Krestiankin). Sometimes they would live for several days in Pechory, waiting for an audience with that revered elder. The line to see Father John often stretched the entire length of the brothers' quarters, beginning at the crack of dawn all the way through to the wee hours of the night. Naturally, this could not fail to irritate the local authorities whose task it was to keep an eye on our monastery. The pressures that they must have put on our abbot were doubtless extreme.

Once Father Gabriel suddenly raced up to the long line of pilgrims

peacefully standing by the brothers' quarters. He yelled at these frightened and unhappy people and scattered them all like a kite scattering a flock of birds. Then he summoned a carpenter and demanded that he board up the door leading to the room where Father John used to receive visitors.

For several days the conversation in the monastery buzzed only about one subject: together with the Soviet authorities, our abbot is no longer allowing pilgrims to visit the elders. The only person who didn't complain about this was Father John himself (although our abbot used to scold him more than anyone).

Father John tried to calm us down: "Never mind, never mind! I'm doing my job, and our abbot is doing his."

And indeed three days later the very same monk carpenter who had nailed the door shut came back by command of the abbot and carefully removed the nails and got rid of the board blocking the door, after which Father John continued to receive visitors as he had before.

I can also remember another instance—perhaps my saddest memory of the monastery: a time when ten monks got together and collectively left the monastery. They wrote a letter to the Patriarch, declaring that they were leaving the monastery in protest against the harsh and despotic behavior of our abbot, and demanding that Archimandrite Gabriel be immediately relieved of his duties and removed from our community. All of these monks were basically wonderful young people. They moved into the nearby town of Pechory, staying in the houses of our parishioners and waiting around for an answer to their petition.

The departure of so many of our brothers was a terrible shock for our abbot. I believe that he understood that he had overdone it with his imperious and somewhat harsh manner of running the monastery. In any case, our usually implacable abbot went to town to go talk to those monks. It wasn't easy to find them. He begged their forgiveness. He tried to convince them to return to our community. But those monks wouldn't budge one bit. They demanded one thing and one thing only: that our abbot be removed from the monastery.

Soon a high commission arrived from the Patriarch with the decree relieving Archimandrite Gabriel from his post. The aged hierarch of Pskov, Metropolitan John, gathered together a council of the monastery's monks. The entire brotherhood assembled in the refectory, where the bishop who had arrived from Moscow asked our assembly how we felt about our abbot. A difficult silence fell upon us. And then the silence was broken by our Treasurer Archimandrite Nathaniel. He read aloud a letter he had written to the Patriarch with a request to keep our abbot in the monastery.

The bishop from Moscow was surprised at this but then asked if there was anyone else who also wished to sign Father Nathaniel's letter. Again a silence lingered in the room. Then suddenly the most revered elder in the entire monastery, Archimandrite Seraphim, stood up.

Curtly as ever, he asked: "Where do I sign?"

Then he walked up and signed. After him all the other spiritual fathers got up and signed. So did all the other monks. Only a very few were still holding back.

This story of the so-called "ten who left" would long be remembered in our monastery. It was particularly difficult for us during the first days after they had left, when the places they had just left behind in our brothers' refectory were so glaringly empty.

Many years later one of those "ten who left"—Father Anthony, who himself became the Abbot of the St. Gerasim of Boldino Monastery in Smolensk Province—spoke to his own somewhat unruly brotherhood in a speech that was printed in a Russian Orthodox newspaper:

Too bad for you all that you do not have Father Gabriel! If only you could have Father Gabriel for just one month! Then you would know what a monastery truly is. Bishop Gabriel (by this time Father Gabriel had been made a bishop) was a generous and incredibly kind man: he loved to give gifts, to receive visitors, and had a very broad spirit. However, he was tough. What's more, Father Gabriel was a person of profound faith. I still remember how he used to pray: his services were always intense, triumphant, long-lasting . . . True, his manner was hardly sweet as honey. But now I believe that if I had been in his shoes, I would have behaved exactly the way that he behaved. Because at that time there was no other way to behave.

Whether that is really true, and there really would have been no other way for him to behave is, perhaps, a somewhat difficult question. As a doctor of mine likes to say, "There is no cure for personality." And indeed, after a fairly short pause, once the "ten who left" had gone, our abbot did not change his ways in the least.

Father Gabriel had chosen the monastic life at the age of sixteen, and so our monastery and the Church in general was his only home. And in our monastery he knew that he was the unbounded master, the ruler of our group of monks tasked with obedience by him our abbot, and endowed with authority by the monastery's Patroness, the Queen of Heaven Herself. And in his own way with sharp intensity he felt a keen responsibility for our monastery and the brotherhood within it entrusted to him by our Lord.

He didn't care in the least what other people thought of him. During the thirteen years that he served as abbot, he never once took a single day off, and he kept all of us under strict supervision and under bit and bridle. Nowadays, however, in Pechory it is remembered that beneath his gruff façade of cruelty and even rudeness there was a warm and beating heart that was full of compassion. As it later turned out, Father Gabriel secretly helped many people—hundreds of people in the local area, without exaggeration. We now understand (although as novices we did not) that our abbot had neither the least interest in nor time for picking on us cruelly—although that's how it seemed to us then. However, Father Gabriel simply could not abide sloppiness or laziness—or, worse yet, any irresponsibility or casual attitude towards the service of God. But it must be admitted that his manners were, to put it mildly, not exactly sugar.

In those days when I was still trying to get the hang of how to take care of cows and calves and was learning the technique of cleaning up cow manure, I was summoned by our Dean, in charge of scheduling and tasks, and informed by him that I was going to become a subdeacon serving the abbot, Archimandrite Gabriel.

This news struck me like a bolt out of nowhere. To be a subdeacon serving Archimandrite Gabriel was considered perhaps the most severe and difficult of all the novitiate tasks possible in the entire monastery. It is not that the duties of the subdeacon by themselves are particularly complicated: timely assistance to the abbot in putting on his holy vestments, holding the service book for him to read, and handing him his staff. Yet, knowing his dreaded nature, everyone felt sorry for me that I had been assigned to serve Father Gabriel. Father John sent me off to my first service the way one might send someone out of the trenches into the front lines in wartime. And indeed it was difficult—not a single slight flaw would ever be forgiven or pass unnoticed.

Once after taking the night shift in the cattle shed I had to quickly bring myself back and freshen up so that I would be ready for the Liturgy in carrying out my task in the altar. But no matter how I scrubbed myself under the shower, the acrid stink of the cowshed could not be completely gotten rid of.

"Phew! Georgiy! Why do you always stink of cow manure?" Our abbot wrinkled his nose and sneered as if he didn't know why it was that I stank, as if it had not been because of him and with his blessing that I had been sent down to spend all night long cleaning up the ordure of thirty cows, a bull, and a dozen calves.

He even brought a bottle of French eau de cologne and generously sprinkled it all over me to let me get on with my work. And so it was that if I came to my service as subdeacon pungently reeking of the country, so to speak, I would come back to the cowshed after my services with a subtle hint of the most refined French perfumes—to the great displeasure of my cows.

In one ancient monastic book it is written:

"Once an elder grabbed a dried-out tree, planted it on the mountain, and commanded Abba John to water this dry tree with a bucket of water until such time as it bore fruit. Now, the water was very far from this peak. In order to reach the peak by evening, you had to approach the stream at dawn. As the third year was ending, the tree budded and bore fruit. The elder took the fruit, brought it to the church to his brothers, and said to them: come, taste of the fruit of obedience."

This story took place 1,500 years ago in an Egyptian monastery at the time of the first great Christian monastic movement. But during the centuries that have followed all the way up to our days, there are a great number of similar examples of the power of sincere obedience. The only thing is that today if our spiritual fathers will demand unquestioning obedience to the tasks that have been assigned, those demands will only be in exceptional circumstances. This is not so much because there are less sincere elders and heroes of our faith, and more because there are fewer and fewer real novices left who will obey.

In fact, the genuine and not a fake role of an elder and father confessor or spiritual father is and always will be to advise, to convince, to insist, and never to suppress the will of the Christian. But if a priest insistently demands absolute and complete obedience in everything and at all times, he should be fled from as if from a demon.

The Church makes a distinction between what is called blessed spiritual obedience to one's elders and spiritual fathers or mothers (if indeed these are true elders and spiritual fathers or mothers) and mere disciplinary administrative obedience to ecclesiastical hierarchy. I remember that there were several instances in which Father John and other elders would send questions to our abbot, saying that through his guidance as our Father Superior in our monastery, the Lord would reveal His will.

But are there any limits to monastic obedience? Father John used to say that we should obey our holy superiors in everything and at all times. Always—even in such cases when it seemed to us that the Father Superior was ordering us to do something completely incomprehensible, completely illogical, and even dangerous and risky to our own life. There is only one case on earth in which a novice may—actually not even may, but must—disobey, according to Father John. And that is if there is a command that is contrary to the Gospel commandments. But, thank the Lord, I have never seen or heard of any such command during my time in the Church.

Otherwise, the truth indeed is that we are novices sworn to holy obedience until we die—obedience unto death. And so it has sometimes been.

The small town of Pechory is a remarkably clean and pleasant place, with its unique character that has developed as a result of centuries in association with the ancient monastery. Here the most felicitous combination between the Orthodox culture of old Holy Mother Russia and the day-to-day orderliness of neighboring Estonia has arisen. And besides the fact that in Pechory, unlike the vast majority of Soviet towns, everything was remarkably neat and beautiful, there even in the 1980s young people sitting on the park benches in the evenings would stand up when an older person would walk past them. Most of the people in the town were pious believers. We would never hear a curse word while walking the streets.

People leaving their homes in Pechory wouldn't bother to lock their doors as a rule, but would simply lower the latch, or if they did lock their doors, they would leave their keys ostentatiously below their doormats.

It seems that some of the "comrades" in charge began to see this as abnormal. In order to "correct" the situation, on one fine day they decided to bring "chemical workers" into our national preserve. "Chemical workers" was the slang commonly used in those days for ordinary criminals who after spending years in jails and work camps had also been living for several years in exile working in special factories and were now supposed to live in designated towns.

These "new arrivals" at once brought their manners and ways of life to our little town. Fistfights, cursing, stabbings, robberies, burglaries, and other crimes that had been unheard of before began to appear. The situation so deteriorated that the robbers began to lurk around the monastery, where they would rob innocent pilgrims.

One day several of the bandits came up to the monastery, right up to its Holy Gates. They put a knife to the throat of the watchman Father Avvakum and demanded that the next day they be given 100 rubles. Avvakum ran as fast as his legs could carry him to our abbot.

"Do what you want with me, Abbot, but I will never again watch by the Gates ever again!" the old man wailed.

Father Gabriel could only look at him sadly and lift his arms to the heavens.

"Woe is me!" he cried out. "What a pass we have come to! A monk might die in carrying out his holy vow of obedience, and refuses to do so! Whosoever dies while carrying out his holy obedience immediately ascends to the Kingdom of Heaven! Woe is me! What a pass we have come to!"

These words struck old Father Avvakum like a bolt of lightning. "Forgive me, Father Abbot!" he cried out. "I have understood completely. Yes, I am here for the sake of holy obedience. Bless me."

And having received a blessing from the abbot, Avvakum strode off determinedly to the Holy Gates to die.

When we asked later what would have happened if those bandits had truly cut Father Avvakum's throat, our abbot calmly answered: "We would have said his funeral service."

But thank the Lord, it never came to that.

And although it later turned out that our abbot had in fact taken every possible precaution to ensure that Father Avvakum would remain safe and sound, that old schema-monk did not lose his promised reward in heaven. For as our Holy Fathers told us, the Lord accepts not only our deeds, but also our sincerest desires and intentions.

Disciplined obedience to the Father Superior in our monastery was unconditional for all of us, and indeed, it went without saying. I wish to stress that this obedience was unconditional—and I do not care how strange, foolish, and ridiculous this might seem to ordinary secular people. Sometimes even people of the Church can be shocked by such strict and straightforward obedience; sometimes it arouses indignation or even furious attacks. Whole volumes have been written on the theme of the absurdities and harm of "blind obedience." I do not condemn the enlightened authors of such tomes. But they simply do not understand that there is a different life in a monastery, which is regulated by its own particular laws. By far, not everyone is capable of understanding the goal and purpose of such laws.

It is related (this story predates my coming to the monastery by a long time) that one day our monastery was visited by a newly ordained deacon who had graduated from the seminary in Leningrad. He was learned, important, and looked down rather condescendingly on these ignoramus monks from some little provincial monastery.

The abbot had a beloved and remarkably beautiful old censer that he kept in the altar. It was so huge that we used to call it "the Babylonian furnace." It was big enough to fit half a bucket of blazing coals. Only the abbot had the right to use this ancient censer.

Indeed, it was so heavy, with fine gilded metal and encrusted with stones and chains, that only our mighty Father Gabriel was physically able to lift it. Although sometimes, it must be noted, when he was in an especially good mood, Father Gabriel might during the Evening Vigil service turn towards, for example, Father John, and say: "Father Archimandrite, do the honor of censing the church!"

And although it was not easy for Father John to even lift such a censer, he would humbly bow (speaking of unquestioned and disciplined obedience) and would grasp the nightmarishly heavy vessel with all his might and begin to swing it, although he would grow tired very quickly and sometimes would have to finish the ritual using both hands, while barely able to still hang on to the chains.

Our abbot was always terribly amused by this. But whenever anyone would try to express their sympathy to Father John, Father John would always protest in surprise: "What are you upset about? Who else is there to humble me other than Father Abbot?"

But let us get back to our guest from St. Petersburg. When he first beheld this wondrous censer in its place near the sacristan, he was seized

The beloved censer of Father Gabriel.

by a desire to immediately take hold of it himself. The sexton and sacristan both explained with fear that this censer could be used only by our abbot.

The seminary graduate decided to have a good laugh at these idiotic provincials and demanded that they bring him the censer at once. The novice sextons, for whom a real graduate of the seminary was practically a celestial being, meekly obeyed.

Well, this deacon from Petersburg presented himself in the altar, and came right up to the abbot, flaunting the ancient censer with its blazing coals emitting smoky and pleasant incense.

Triumphantly, he pronounced the customary request for a blessing: "Bless, Master, the censer . . ."

The abbot raised his hand as usual to give the blessing . . . and froze. He simply could not believe his eyes. When he finally realized that some upstart little deacon from Petersburg had dared to touch his beloved censer, then our abbot suddenly whispered in a voice that was both eerily quiet yet powerful, so powerful that it froze the blood of all who could hear him:

"Who gave this to you?"

The deacon stopped still with the blazing censer in his hand. However, his arm began to tremble so frightfully that the whole altar could hear the rattle of those precious chains.

"Drop that at once!" commanded the abbot.

The seminary graduate froze in terror.

"Drop it! I'm talking to you!" the abbot commanded even more sternly.

The floor of the altar was covered with very old wooly carpets. The censer was heaped full of fiery, blazing coals. The young seminarian looked as if he was about to faint. It was obvious that how to behave in such situations had not been in any syllabus in the Leningrad Theological Academy. Without removing his icy stare from him, the abbot beckoned with one finger our old hierodeacon Father Anthony, and barked out a short command:

"Take that censer away from him!"

Father Anthony grabbed the censer from the trembling hand of the young Petersburger.

"Now drop it!" our abbot commanded.

Without a second's hesitation Father Anthony loosened his fingers, and the heavy censer crashed with a melancholy thud right onto the rug, spilling out blazing coals. At once with sparks the rug began to burn. The monks standing around him dropped on the floor to stamp out the fire with their bare hands, kneeling at the foot of their abbot. He stood meanwhile surrounded by fire and smoke, gazing contentedly and majestically at the scene, and then roared:

"Now that is how to fulfill your vow of holy obedience!"

Then he turned to the young deacon from Leningrad and scoffed: "As for you, get out of the altar!"

What's the point of all this, you might ask? Is this not an example of devilish tyranny and power-mad despotism? Is this the kind of holy obedience that our Holy Fathers intended?

I really don't know what to answer. Perhaps we monks truly are completely abnormal, if we accept things like this as basically appropriate.

Once something similar happened—and it involved me. But in that instance it was the abbot who nearly paid dearly for the severe obedience that he himself had enforced upon us.

It so happened that I had been sick for a week in late autumn, and when I came to Evening Vigil service, I saw in the altar space on the little table (where usually books and personal items belonging to the abbot were placed) an object that was unfamiliar to me but very beautiful: an antique gold and malachite candleholder with a thick wax candle. Pechory is in the Russian North, and it gets dark fairly early in the fall. That's why the abbot had brought the candleholder into the altar, so that he would be able to read the books required for the services. However, to my young eyes it was still light enough, and so I figured out what was going on much too late.

At the appointed time as usual I took the book of services and opened it for our abbot. But he said to me: "Take the candle.'

I obediently put the book down and picked up the candleholder, then waited for further instructions. "Well, and what next?" the abbot asked grumpily, irritated by my lack of comprehension.

"And what should I do with it?" I asked naively.

Our abbot got even more irritated. "What do you think? Toss it out into the street!"

I can still remember what admiration seized me then. In an instant I remembered the heroism of our ancient ascetics, who at the bidding of their abbots would water dry sticks or leap into the ocean, or walk on water, or throw gold ingots away into a chasm . . .

I was imagining how I would run headlong out of the cathedral and with all my might hurl the extremely valuable but of course fleeting (from the point of view of infinity) candleholder to be smashed against the stonework of the monastery walls. The malachite would fly off in green fragments through the air . . . I raced towards the door so determinedly that the abbot was scarcely able to grab me by the edge of my cassock.

"What are you, crazy?" he asked me with fear in his voice, as he grabbed the antique valuable away from me.

"But you yourself said . . ." I replied with surprise.

The abbot looked at me for a long time as if I were truly insane and then said: "Georgiy, do not frighten me. Light the candle. Can't you see it's gotten dark in here?"

Only then did I understand what it was that I was supposed to do. Although I was a little sad that I could not carry out an old-style task of obedience and thereby become a witness to such a rarity as a "malachite salute," I lit the candle and with a sigh opened the book of services before the abbot.

As I have already mentioned, our abbot absolutely could not abide it if his commands were ever disobeyed. But here is a mystery: the truth is that sometimes we did not carry out all of the commands of our abbot, but instead there were occasions when we flatly contradicted his will. And yet he would not get angry in the least and would even pretend not to notice anything. And we for our part began to have an absolutely casual attitude towards such minor disobedience without the least twinges of remorse.

If, for example, the abbot would get enraged by some pilgrim or foolishly rude tourist and would yell, angrily shaking his finger, "Grab him! Throw him out of the monastery!" of course we would race to carry out the command. But when we would reach the unhappy person to whom it was directed, we would whisper calming words and peacefully accompany him to the gates.

Our abbot was perfectly aware of this and approved silently: on the one hand he had been obeyed, but on the other hand, we had not gone too far overboard in blind obedience.

Overall our abbot perfectly understood what his monks needed. And what they really needed was just humility and reinforcement of their faith. In several of the ancient monastic patericons there are stories about how the Father Superiors of the old monasteries used to restrain even the most experienced monks with reins and harnesses, to tame them and settle down their ardor and anger.

One summer I held the watch on Dormition Square. It was during the hour that our abbot used to walk around and make his inspection of the monastery. Suddenly, an unfamiliar but thickset and burly young stranger approached. I heard him beg to be accepted into the monastery.

"Are you willing to take a vow of complete obedience and carry out commands?"

"Of course, Father, any commands at all!"

"Any commands at all?" Our abbot perked up his ears at this.

"Absolutely any commands! Any and all!" The youngster replied with passion.

Just at that moment an elderly monk, Father M., was hobbling through Dormition Square. And the abbot commanded:

"Well, if you are really ready to carry out any commands, walk up to that old man and hit him so hard that he'll fly right out of the monastery!"

In an instant the youth flew up to the old man and kicked him so hard that he was hurled several paces forward through the air like a fish trying to leap out of a boat back into the water, and then he landed flat out on the ground. But the old man immediately jumped up and then cast himself at the feet of the youngster, begging:

"Pity a poor sinner, my son! Forgive me!" The elderly monk was literally on the brink of tears, not understanding what had provoked this lad's rage.

"Just you wait!" the fellow waved the old man away. Then he turned to the abbot and eagerly awaited his further commands.

Our abbot looked the youngster over from head to toe with utter astonishment. "Well, well, brother," he said, "you really are an idiot!"

With this he took twenty-five rubles out of his pocket and handed it to the young man. "This is for your ticket. Make sure you go straight home."

Meanwhile Father M., a bit shaken, bowed low to the abbot and once more, hobbling with difficulty, kept walking on his way.

The story provoked some fairly indignant condemnation of Father Gabriel in our monastery. However, there was one extremely independent-minded and educated monk who said, "The truth is none of you understand anything. Here you are rushing to judge and condemn the abbot. But I will neither praise nor condemn his actions. It is not for us to judge our Father Superior. Of course, all of us love and respect Father M. All the time, we hear how he gets praised and sometimes even held up as an example. And indeed, Father M. has deserved these compliments. But these compliments are not at all useful to him as a monk."

We waited with great interest to see what he would say next. And he continued:

"On the one hand, the abbot committed a most uncivilized act against Father M., but on the other hand, whether or not the abbot wished to do this intentionally, he gave Father M. perhaps the most valuable and useful present which it is possible to give to a monk, namely, an opportunity to be humble. Did he do this rudely? Yes! Extremely rudely? Absolutely! But do you remember the story about the Great Abbot Arseny, who before he joined the monastery had been a highly placed noble in the Imperial courts in Constantinople and even responsible for the upbringing of the Emperor's children? Once the abbot of his monastery suddenly and unceremoniously rudely ejected Father Arseny from the refectory and wouldn't even allow him to sit down at the table, but forced him to stand outside beside the doors. Only when the meal was coming to an end did he deign to throw him a crumb of dried bread as if to a dog. The other monks in the monastery later asked Father Arseny how he'd felt at that moment. The elder answered: 'I was thinking that the abbot, like an angel sent by God, had recognized that I was like a dog, and even worse than a dog. That's the truth! And that's why he threw the bread at me the way one would throw bread at a dog.' Meanwhile the abbot, realizing the great humility of Father Arseny, said: "He will become an excellent monk one day.'

Our erudite advisor continued after a pause: "It is only in that way, through mysterious humility incomprehensible to the world, that a true Christian comes to one of the two greatest revelations in life. The first of these revelations is that one must discover the truth about oneself, and see oneself as one truly is. You must meet your own self. And believe me it's the most important acquaintance. A vast number of people live their lives never even bothering to discover themselves at all. Sometimes we only have the vaguest notions or fantasies of who we are, and so depending upon our own vanity, pride, resentments, and ambitions we see nothing. But the truth, however bitter it might seem to us, is that we are 'wretched, and miserable, and poor, and blind, and naked.' . . . Remember that verse from Revelations? And this truth only comes to us through scriptural and ruthlessly honest examination of oneself. Through true humility. True humility does not humiliate a man. On the contrary, anyone who survives this ordeal, this bitterest and harshest of truths becomes a saint. It is only those who are humble who can peer into the future, who can become prophets and miracle workers, wondered at by all of you."

"But what is the second revelation?" we asked. "He said that there are two main revelations in a person's life. The first is to become acquainted with one's own self. But what is the second?"

"The second?" The monk smiled. "You know the second revelation not one bit less than I. It is the truth that our Church patiently reminds us of in every single Divine Service without exception: 'May Christ, our true God, through the intercessions of His most pure Mother and of all the saints, have mercy on us and save us, for He is good and lovest mankind.'"

We thanked our teacher from the bottom of our hearts. As he took his leave of us, he said, "But if any of you ever becomes an abbot, do not so much as think about daring to imitate Father Gabriel and attempting to humble the brothers in such a fashion! Our abbot has his own particular charisma." This was said with a slight smirk.

"But you should be grateful not to me, but to Father M. for the lesson in humility that he has taught you and all of us. Do you remember how in the ancient patericon there was one heroic ascetic who was asked how to become a true monk? The great monk tore off his mantle, cast it into the dust, and then trampled it into the dirt saying, 'Until a man humbles himself in exactly this manner, he will never become a monk.'"

* * *

If a man does not humble himself, he will never become a monk. God will not reveal himself to him, as the Lord, as He Who Is what He Is, and not as in books and stories of other people, but through personal revelation and experience. Without humility, years and decades will be wasted, and all of the highest ecclesiastical ranks will bring him only condemnation: the priesthood, an abbacy, a bishropric . . .

Soon after Metropolitan Pitirim brought me back to Moscow, my relationship with Archimandrite Gabriel began to deteriorate. The reason for this was a film that I made over a period of several years about the Pskov Caves Monastery.

Metropolitan Pitirim purchased on behalf of the publishing house an amateur video camera, which was a great rarity in the Soviet Union in

the 1980s. I brought it with me to Pechory, in order to capture the life of the monastery and its great elders before their memory would be lost to history. Many years later a movie was made from some of the clips that I had shot in the Pskov Caves Monastery.

But at one point (I cannot say whether someone spread this rumor to the abbot or whether this thought arose by itself in his mind) Archimandrite Gabriel decided that I had been carrying out an independent assignment from the Patriarch to snoop around for various faults in his monastery and to pass along the filmed evidence that I had gathered to His Holiness. No matter how hurtful to me it was to hear such an accusation, and no matter how I tried to explain that I had never even dreamed of anything of the kind, now all of my visits to the monastery—even to visit Father John— suddenly became extremely problematic.

And then I remembered all the many tales that had been told about the cruelty and capriciousness of our abbot, including the complaints of his extremely suspicious nature.

Naturally, my resentments and gloomy thoughts in no way benefited any improvement in our relationship. But soon Archimandrite Gabriel was made a bishop in the Far East of Russia. Even this did not change anything. Things got so out of hand that we hardly even said hello to each other when we met during services in Moscow—I remember this to my shame. After all, who was I compared to him—a bishop, a hierarch of the Holy Church of Christ? But what happened is what happened, I'm sorry to say.

Three years passed. During that time I used to calmly visit the monastery now that there were other abbots. However, there were new changes in the fate of Bishop Gabriel.

In the Far East, the priests were completely different people from the monks of Pechory. It was impossible to count on the kind of unconditional obedience to which Bishop Gabriel had grown accustomed in his monastery. And so at one point some parish priest began a quite serious conflict with Bishop Gabriel, who had as usual grievously offended him. In Pechory the incident would have been nothing out of the ordinary. However, in the Far East, the local priest became enraged, and using words that should be remote from the lexicon of any good Russian Orthodox priest, grabbed one of the objects used in the Divine Liturgy—a sharp ceremonial lance— and charged his own ruling bishop with it. However, this was Bishop Gabriel we were talking about; he may perhaps, as I imagine, have been a bit surprised, but he was not in the least bit frightened. He grabbed the rebellious priest by the collar of his robes, tossed him out of the church, and threw him down the stairs.

This priest then wrote a complaint to the Patriarch and even appealed for assistance from the civil authorities. Soon a Patriarchal judicial commission was formed. And this time the result was a very strict ecclesiastical sentence: Bishop Gabriel was removed from his post and forbidden to serve as a clergyman for three years.

The ecclesiastical trial took place in Moscow. On the day when the decision was declared I went with some trepidation to the hotel where Bishop Gabriel was staying, not knowing how my visit might turn out. After all, he had been my first abbot; he had accepted me in the monastery, and I was beside myself at the thought that in such a difficult moment in his life, everyone possibly might have abandoned him—regardless of whether he was right or wrong. I began to remember all the good things that had been connected with the abbot, and I decided that I wanted to support him somehow (although I had no idea how).

I found the hotel room he was staying in and I was just about to knock, when suddenly I heard behind the door a loud conversation—to be more exact, a serious shouting match. I was about to run away before I got myself in trouble, when the door suddenly opened with a loud bang and two men walked out of the room seeming to be extremely displeased. Bishop Gabriel followed them with the words: "Get out of here, you scoundrels, or I'll throw you down the stairs!"

"He is up to his usual tricks," I thought to myself, "and maybe in the Far East he got into the habit of throwing people downstairs. I just hope he doesn't decide to do the same with me!"

"And what are you doing here?" Bishop Gabriel growled at me.

"I just came by to visit you," I replied with trepidation.

The bishop looked me over from head to toe with a piercing stare. "All right, come in." And he let me into his room.

We sat together till very late at night. By now the bishop was in no hurry. He ordered a bottle of cognac and some food through room service. So we remembered the old days in Pechory, and the bishop told me about how he had opened churches in his very remote diocese. He told me that the two men whom he had just now so rudely ejected from his room had been representatives of some kind of alternative church called "the catacomb church." When they had heard that Bishop Gabriel had been removed from his post, they had come to the condemned man and had offered the naturally offended hierarch a chance to become a bishop in their "church." To which Bishop Gabriel had replied:

"Never! I was baptized in our Church, and in it I became a monk, priest, and a bishop. All right, maybe I was a bad bishop, if the Church has suspended me. But I was born in our Church, and in our Church I will die. And therefore . . ."

Thereafter followed his tirade to which I had been an unwilling witness, basically calling them impostors and scoundrels and threatening to throw these scoundrels down the stairs in a manner not befitting a bishop.

* * *

The bishop left for Khabarovsk. We used to correspond rarely. And in his letters he revealed to me a new side of himself, of which I had never had had any inkling. One of his letters began with the words from the Psalter in which King David with gratitude reflects on one of the most difficult times

Bishop Gabriel.

in his life and says, "It is good for me that I have been afflicted, so that I might learn Thy statutes" (Psalm 119:71). That was a remarkable letter, although I regret that in all the fuss and commotion of my other tasks I never answered.

Three years later the ban on Bishop Gabriel was lifted, and he was sent to serve as a bishop of the city of Blagoveshchensk. By this time I already was serving in the Sretensky Monastery. When the bishop used to come to Moscow on business, he would stay in our monastery, which always made me and our brotherhood sincerely happy. At one point Bishop Gabriel even traveled back to Pechory. They say that when he administered the service on that occasion, there was a huge crowd. Naturally, old resentments had been forgotten. Several of the monks and parishioners wept when they approached him for his blessing. The bishop himself was also very touched. But he never returned to Pechory again.

After a while priests from the bishopric of Blagoveshchensk used to come and stay with us in the Sretensky Monastery. At one point I couldn't help myself and I asked them their opinion of their bishop. Was he good or was he terrible?

"Oh! He is a very good man indeed . . . but he's terrible!" After which they told stories from which I drew the irrevocable conclusion that there is no cure for personality.

Many years later I accompanied His Holiness the Patriarch Kirill on a journey to the Far East. Bishop Gabriel traveled to see His Holiness at a service in Yuzhnosakhalinsk on the island of Sakhalin. He had already turned seventy. While I had been in the Pskov Caves Monastery, he had been a bit over forty. After the Patriarch finished services and the official meetings were over, we sat down in a small group for dinner. There were several priests with us and one young bishop. Bishop Gabriel was also there.

The atmosphere at the dinner table was warm and brotherly. Remembering the past, I gathered the courage to ask Bishop Gabriel how he had lived when he had been under suspension. Everyone including the young bishop was very interested to hear what the elder bishop would say. All of us understood that life is not so simple, and that any of us might make a mistake from time to time. In the words of the Russian proverb: never vow to avoid poverty or jail. The bishop did not try to avoid the question but instead told his story simply and without embellishment of any kind.

After the Synod had suspended him, he had returned to Khabarovsk. For several months he had lived on his meager savings, and then he tried to find work in his former diocese as a sexton or as a guard. But the new bishop refused to allow his priests to take their former bishop into any employment in the churches at all, and even commanded that he not be allowed to enter the altar. For all those years Bishop Gabriel came to Holy Communion just like all his parishioners, and stood in line to take Communion. As he would approach the chalice, arms folded across his chest, he would tell the priest his name, "Bishop Gabriel"—and next to everyone else partake of the Holy Mysteries of Christ.* During these years, so the bishop told us, the love and support of his flock meant very much to him, as did the letters he received from those he had known earlier, most of all from Archimandrite John (Krestiankin).

The bishop also found work with his parishioners. From spring to late fall he would weed and guard their gardens on an island in the Amur River, not far from Khabarovsk. All winter long he would live modestly on the money he had earned during the summer.

Then I asked him, "Your grace, Bishop Gabriel! You have lived a remarkable and interesting life. You were a young novice in the Monastery of Odessa, at the time when the great elder, Father Kuksha, labored there. You also lived in the Holy Land working as a secretary of the Russian Mission in Jerusalem. For many years you were our abbot in the Pskov Caves Monastery, associating every day with our wisest elders, whose names are too many to count. Then you created a diocese in the Far East. Now you are the Bishop of Blagoveshchensk. What was the very happiest time of your life?"

---

* A clergyman, especially a bishop, receives Communion inside the altar. This shows how Bishop Gabriel peacefully accepted his demotion to the status of a layman.

The bishop grew thoughtful and at length answered, "The very happiest times of my life were the years when I was suspended and disgraced. Never before or since in my life was the Lord as close to me as back then. It might surprise you to hear this, but, believe me, it is the truth. Of course, when I was allowed to return to my priestly duties and was sent to Blagoveshchensk, I was very happy and pleased. But my prayers, and most important of all, my sense of the closeness of Christ, that closeness that I felt when I was in my gardens, was unique and cannot be compared to anything else . . . That was the happiest time of my life."

He fell silent again and then added: "My brothers, have no fear of the punishments of the Lord! For He does not punish us as criminals, but as His own children!"

He had nothing more to say. But I think it was not just I alone, but all of us, young and not-so-young priests, sitting then with the bishop around the dinner table, who have remembered these words of his for the rest of our lives.

Archimandrite Alipius.

The Great Abbot Archimandrite Alipius

*T*HE GREAT ABBOT of the Pskov Caves Monastery Father Alipius used to describe himself as follows: "I am a Soviet archimandrite." And he would eagerly confirm this statement in word and deed.

At the beginning of the 1960s various members of a provincial Party commission visited the monastery with one goal—to figure out some way to close down our monastery. As they inspected the monastery, they saw pilgrims fixing the hedges and the flower beds, and immediately complained to Father Alipius: "How is it that these people are working here illegally?"

The Soviet archimandrite answered calmly: "They're not working illegally. These are the people laboring to improve their own Fatherland!"

No further questions were asked. But then another commission was sent from Pskov, this time a financial commission called "the Commission of Popular Oversight"—also with just one goal: to find something wrong and close down the monastery. The abbot asked the delegation to present its letters of authority.

"We represent a financial organ which—"

But Father Alipius interrupted them. "I have only one overseer, the Bishop of Pskov, Bishop John. Go see him and get his authorization. Without his signature I have no right to show you any financial documents."

The inspectors left, but naturally several hours later the Bishop of Pskov was calling Father Alipius, all in a tizzy, and asking that he allow the inspectors to review his documents.

"Your Grace, as a bishop you know that I cannot enter a telephone call into a file. I need that authorization in writing. Please send me a telegram."

Soon enough the telegram arrived. When the Commission of Popular Oversight inspectors came back, the abbot was waiting for them with the telegram in his hand.

"Tell me, please, are you fellows real Communists?"

"Yes. We are almost all members of the Communist Party."

"And yet you sought out the blessing of the Bishop of Pskov? Just a moment. I think I'd better send a copy of this telegram to the Provincial Communist Party Committee."

That was the end of the financial inspection of the monastery.

Before Archimandrite Alipius had taken his monastic vows, his name was Ivan Mikhailovich Voronov. He fought for four years as a soldier on the front lines in World War II, and endured and marched together with the Red Army all the way from the Battle of Moscow to the Battle of Berlin. After that he defended the Pskov Caves Monastery for thirteen years—this time struggling against the very same state for which he had previously spilled his blood.

In both wars Father Alipius truly was involved in a life and death struggle. The then-head of the Central Committee of the Communist Party, Nikita Khrushchev, very much needed a great victory against the Church—no less a victory than the one his predecessor whose glory he greatly envied had presided over in World War II. In order to celebrate his planned-for triumph, Khrushchev aimed for the extinction of the Russian Orthodox Church, which had been in existence for 1,000 years, and therefore he declared war on it, solemnly declaring to the entire world that soon he would show the very last Russian Orthodox priest on television.

Soon thousands of cathedrals and churches were blown up, closed, and converted into warehouses, taxi garages, and tractor factories. The majority of the seminaries and higher ecclesiastical academies were closed. Virtually all the monasteries were dissolved. Quite a few priests were arrested and put in jail. In the entire territory of Russia only two monasteries were allowed to exist: the Holy Trinity Monastery (needed for window dressing in order to show foreign tourists that the Russian Church was still fine, as a sort of Russian Orthodox "reservation"), and one provincial monastery—the Pskov Caves Monastery. It was here that the Great Abbot struggled against the entire machinery of the mighty atheist state. And—most wonderfully of all—he triumphed!

In those days the entire sorely persecuted Russian Church watched with bated breath, waiting to see how the unequal struggle would turn out. News from Pechory was passed by word of mouth, and it was only many years later that the participants in and witnesses of those events wrote down their memories. Here are just a few recollections of those now long-gone struggles.

One winter evening several men in plain clothes marched into the office of Father Alipius and handed him an official command: the

Pechory Monastery near Pskov was officially closed. The abbot was hereby commanded to so inform the personnel of the monastery. Having read the document, Father Alipius tossed the paper into a blazing fire right before the very eyes of these officers.

To the astonishment of his visitors he calmly declared: "I am willing to undergo martyrdom and death by torture if it comes to that, but I will never close the monastery."

The paper that he had just cast into the fire was an official decree of the government of the USSR, and had been signed by Nikita Khrushchev himself. This incident has been recorded by a witness, that most loyal disciple of the Great Abbot, Archimandrite Nathaniel.

I personally never met Father Alipius, as he was no longer alive when I first came to the monastery. However, it is impossible to speak about the Pechory Monastery without saying a few words about him.

* * *

I was very lucky: there were still many monks who had lived under the Great Abbot when I first came to the monastery. I have also met many famous artists, writers, scholars, and art restorers from Moscow, Leningrad, and Riga who used to come and partake of his abundant hospitality during those years. For them he was always the very model of a fearless spiritual warrior, and the ideal of a demanding and yet loving father.

In spite of his considerable pragmatism and even quite obvious earthiness (for Father Alipius was always quick to size up any situation, and indeed, despite his brilliant and often biting wit, invariably found amazingly practical solutions to just about any predicament), many of his contemporaries, including those who had made the ultimate sacrifices on the path of ascetic monastic discipline, considered him to be a saint. Archimandrite Seraphim, an unquestioned moral authority in our monastery, always used to be surprised whenever any monks informed him of plans for distant pilgrimages to the various sites of ascetic spiritual struggles of our great saints:

"Why bother traveling far away?" He couldn't understand. "Just go to the caves—there are the relics of Father Alipius."

The Lord does not like cowardice. This spiritual law was once revealed to me by Father Raphael, but in turn that law had been passed to him by Father Alipius. In one of his sermons Father Alipius had preached:

Monks of Pechory — WWII veterans, Victory Day, 1984.

"During the war I was a witness to how certain soldiers were so worried they might die of hunger that they would carry little bags of crumbs on their back. So worried were some about their little bags of bread crumbs, so eager were they to prolong their life rather than fight the enemy, that these people were invariably the first to be cut down by enemy fire. They perished along with their bread crumbs. But those who were willing to strip their backs if need be, and to die to fight the enemy—those were the ones who survived."

When the order came to close the monastery caves, Father Alipius ordered the keeper of the keys: "Father Cornelius! Hand me an axe! Today I will be chopping off heads!"

The officers who had brought the command fled in terror—after all, who knew what crazy ideas might have come into the head of these ignorant fanatics?

In fact, the abbot knew all too well that he wasn't just uttering these commands into thin air. Once, during yet another visitation bearing yet another demand that the monastery be closed, he declared, "More than half of our brotherhood served as hardened front-line soldiers. We are heavily armed and very well trained. We will fight to our very last bullet. Take a look around you. See what discipline we keep here in this monastery, what distribution of troops there is here. Look at these walls. You won't get tanks through here. In fact, the only way you'll take us is by use of air power: dropping bombs. But if you start dropping bombs on us, I can promise you this: once the first airplane flies over our monastery, within minutes everything that's going on here will be related to the world directly by the Voice of America. Well, it's up to you."

I cannot judge what kind of arsenals they had at the time in the monastery. Very possibly, this speech was just another "military maneuver" in which our Great Abbot yet again out-bluffed his opponent. But if he was joking— as we say, there is always quite an

Ivan Voronov 1944.

element of truth in every good joke. For it certainly was true that in those days more than half of the monks were highly decorated veterans of World War II—indeed, many of them still had their medals for valor and bravery on the front lines. There were other monks, also a fairly large contingent, who had been hardened by their brutal ordeals in Stalin's camps. There was even a third group of monks who had gone through both the war and Stalin's camps. You can imagine how tough they were.

"The winner is the one who attacks," Father Alipius used to say. And he followed his own strategy precisely. Every day, he would battle to save the monastery. Every day the Great Abbot would restore the ruins of our still-mighty fortress walls, would restore the dilapidated churches and cathedrals, would scrupulously and professionally clean and restore the ancient frescoes, and restore the abbot's and brothers' quarters to their former stateliness. He himself had been an artist, and therefore by his work he diligently saved several masterpieces by Russian and foreign artists from being looted and sold overseas. In his own personal collection there were works by such celebrated artists as Levitan and Polenov. Upon his death, Father Alipius willed the collection of masterpieces freely and in its entirety to the Russian Museum in Leningrad.

Lastly, he was a master gardener, and covered the entire monastery with such beautiful orchards, flowers, flower beds, hedges, lawns, and groves that the monastery was converted into one of the most beautiful places in all of Russia. And so, anyone arriving in Pechory for the very first time, regardless of whether he was a pilgrim or just a tourist, beheld the monastery as the representative of a divine and utterly miraculous world, by comparison with which the mundane and meretricious Soviet reality around them paled.

But Father Alipius's main achievement was his restoration of the tradition of eldership in the Pskov Caves Monastery.

The tradition of eldership is something entirely unique, especially because it does not belong to one particular place or to one particular monastery. Sometimes the Church elders' wandering leads them to make pilgrimages or build monasteries all across the earth: sometimes, through them, you will find retreats unexpectedly flourishing on the far side of the Volga River sketes,* in the small monastic communities of the Northern Thebaid,** or in White Shores Hermitage in the Bryansk forest wilderness, in Sarov, in Nizhny Novgorod Province, or in Optina Monastery in Kaluga Province. But in the mid-twentieth century, the tradition of the elders found refuge in the Pskov Caves Monastery. It was Father Alipius who tenderly grasped this mysterious path. He cared for our elders, treated them as the most precious jewel in the monastery, and multiplied their numbers.

Somehow the abbot was able to get permission for the great elders of Valaam to come to the Pskov Caves Monastery from Finland. It was Father Alipius who gave refuge to Father John (Krestiankin) after his years in the Gulag and exile, when he was secretly brought here by Bishop Pitirim (Nechayev). He gave sanctuary to Father Adrian, who had been forced to flee the Holy Trinity Monastery. Indeed, under Father Alipius, an entire generation of elders and spiritual fathers grew, that same generation which to such a large degree figures in this book. To have been able to create and nurture such leaders during such a time and under such pressure was truly an amazing achievement.

* * *

---

* A *skete* is a small monastic community, usually rural, and traditionally with twelve or fewer monks or nuns.

** The northern monasteries of Old Russia are often compared to the many monasteries that once flourished in the Egyptian Thebaid during the early centuries of Christianity. —TRANS.

In those days of hysterical anti-religious propaganda, most people's conceptions of monasteries were little less than savage. Father Alipius was therefore never surprised even when he was asked the most ridiculous questions. He would always answer with good-natured humor and wit that always left a positive comparison of his simplicity, honor, and true faith with the malicious persecution, dirty lies, and ridiculous distortions he was faced with.

Once a group of tourists—faithful Soviet believers in Communism—stopped Father Alipius by the threshold of one of the churches. In indignant tones they demanded that he tell them the whole truth about the exploitation by high-level clerics of the simple monks and novices, about their physical humiliations, and in general tell them everything about all the horrors of monastic life about which they had already read plenty of newspaper articles. In response to their question, Father Alipius only answered mildly: "Can you hear?"

"Can we hear what?"

"Can you hear anything at all?"

"Yeah. A bunch of monks singing . . ."

"Exactly! Now do you really think that, if they were actually so miserable in their lives, they would sing with such obvious joy?"

One Communist, a visitor from Finland, in the company of his Soviet comrades asked Father Alipius the typical question that was always asked by atheists at that time: "How do you explain the fact that the astronauts flew up into cosmos and didn't see any sign of God there?"

"The same thing could happen to you. You've been in Helsinki, yet you never saw the president of Finland, perhaps."

People who had the luck to be in Pechory then recall with particular delight how the Great Abbot used to appear sometimes on the balcony of the abbot's quarters. He would emerge for all kinds of reasons. Sometimes, particularly in the spring, the daws and ravens would so trouble Father Alipius with their ceaseless cawing that he would come out onto the balcony with a pistol and shoot at the birds until they scattered. It wasn't actually a real military pistol; it was just a glorified noisemaker. But imagine the effect: a sunny morning in the monastery, the Great Abbot standing on the balcony and aiming a pistol with a very well-practiced hand at a flock of birds! It must have made an unforgettable impression!

But of course these were not the only memorable emergences onto the balcony of the Great Abbot. Far more powerful and deeply lasting impressions were made on visitors to the monastery when they became witnesses to the conversations that Father Alipius sometimes conducted from the railing of his balcony with the visitors who had gathered below it.

The abbot's balcony looks out on the monastery square. From it, our abbot could see the entire monastery (when the weather was good enough), in this way both keeping his eyes out for any violations of order and discipline and at the same time communicating with his flock.

Below him on the square there was always a crowd of pilgrims and tourists, as well as townsfolk from the small town of Pechory. Discussions of faith or simply questions and answers with Father Alipius could sometimes last for hours. Father Alipius would never let an opportunity slip by for helping anyone who had turned to him with their everyday life problems.

And although at that time there was an absolute ban on any form of what was then called ecclesiastical charity, Father Alipius was always governed by his conscience alone, and acted in all such cases as he felt was just. Here is one memory of Archimandrite Nathaniel's: "Father Alipius always helped the needy, always had them fed and clothed, always distributed charity, and many were the people who begged him for help in times of crisis in their lives and received it. For his goodness he was threatened with persecution many times. But Father Alipius was guided by the words of the Scripture, which dictate that compassion and mercy are our highest calling, and therefore compassion could not be forgotten, since it is an inalienable part of the life of the Holy Orthodox Church."

And here are the memories of Deacon Georgiy Malkov, who at the time was just a young student of languages who used to travel to Pechory frequently: "The words of the Scripture teach us: 'Thou shalt love thy neighbor as thyself. There is none other commandment greater than this.' This was something Father Alipius always tried to carry out each day in his daily life. And so the sick, the needy, the hungry, and those in need of consolation were ever in his mind, and often received material help from him—sometimes considerable help."

You would often see cripples and beggars and persons, whom for various reasons fate had been unkind to in this life, gathered beneath his balcony. And the abbot—in spite of constant commands from the authorities that he was forbidden to give them any charity—would always help as best he could: with food, medicine, clothing, with money . . .

When he had no money, he would sometimes joke, "The money is still

The famous balcony of Father Alipius.

drying, so come tomorrow, my dear servant of God, tomorrow!"

In some cases the help that he gave to others was really significant: he helped one person who lost his home in a fire completely build his house anew. Another person who had lost his cow was given enough money to buy a new cow. Once Father Alipius learned that not far away in the village of Izborsk a well-known local artist named Peter Melnikov had lost his home to fire, and reacted by wiring him what was then quite a considerable sum of money with a note: "May this tide you over just for a start."

Father Nathaniel used to recall: "Father Alipius was a wonderful preacher, and truly had the gift of gab, so much so that we would often hear from the pilgrims that they plan to stay an extra week until they could hear another sermon of Father Alipius. His teachings were always about lifting up the downcast and comforting the depressed."

Here are some examples:

"Brothers and sisters, you have heard the calls for an intensification of the anti-religious propaganda against us, but do not hang your heads. Do not lose hope, for all these calls really mean just one thing . . . It is they who are running out of steam.

"What a frightful thing it is to be part of the crowd. Today the crowd is screaming 'hooray, hooray, hosanna in the highest!' And tomorrow the same crowd will scream 'take him, take him, and crucify him!' You cannot be left out perhaps, and maybe you will be forced into the crowd along with everyone else, but at least when you hear those lies, do not shout 'hooray!' And do not clap. And if they ask you why, just answer 'because it isn't true.' And if they ask you how dare you say it isn't true, just reply 'because my conscience tells me so.'

"How do you recognize a Judas in real life? Our Savior said at the Last Supper, 'He that dippeth his hand with Me in the dish, the same shall betray Me' (Matthew 26:23). And so it is in our own lives. Watch out for the arrogant student who wants to be equal to his teacher, for the proud upstart who argues with his boss and wants to take away his place and become boss himself. Look out for the guy who reaches for the teapot first. The elders have not yet breakfasted, yet this upstart is already licking his lips, having stuffed his face . . . 'A young Judas is growing up. There were twelve disciples, and one of them was Judas.'

"So remember, if your elders have not yet sat down to eat, remain standing and wait. After your elders have sat down then you, after your prayer, may sit too. If your elders have not taken their spoons into their hands, do not touch the spoons yourself. Once the elders take the spoons, then you may touch them. Once the elders begin to eat, only then allow yourself to eat."

* * *

But not all his lectures from the balcony were so peaceful and delightful. One scary moment came when an extremely powerful and unpleasant woman came to visit Pskov Province. She was the minister of culture Yekaterina Furtseva, and she arrived with a big delegation of bureaucrats both from Moscow and from the provincial capital, Pskov.

In those days everyone was quite afraid of her—and I mean everyone, not just cultural figures. Naturally, she was given a tour of the Pskov Caves Monastery. But Father Alipius knew from his artist friends about her pathological hatred of the Church, and did not even bother to come and meet her. Her excursion was guided by Father Nathaniel.

This powerful delegation was already making its way towards the exit of the monastery, when all of a sudden Furtseva noticed the abbot, who was standing on the balcony and chatting with the people gathered below. She decided that she would teach a lesson to this upstart monk who had dared to not even come out to meet her. What's more, she thought, she'd kill two birds with one stone—teaching the local Party bosses how severely the policies of the Party and the government must be executed, regardless of whatever opposition some ridiculous cleric might put up. She approached the balcony and interrupted his conversation with the pilgrims, yelling, and calling our abbot by his civilian name:

"Ivan Mikhailovich. May I ask you a question?"

Father Alipius looked at this woman who had just interrupted him with disdain, then calmly replied: "Ask away."

"How can an educated man like you end up here in the company of this crowd of ignorant obscurantists?"

Father Alipius was generally a patient man. However, when the monks whom he served were publicly insulted, he did not let it slip.

"You want to know why I'm here?"

With this he stared at her in the same way in which former private Ivan Voronov, serving in the artillery forces of the Red Army, had once squinted through the sights of a cannon at the enemy. "All right. I'll tell you. Did you ever hear that I was a front-line soldier in the war?"

"Let's say I did."

"And did you hear that I made it all the way to Berlin?"

"Well, yes, I heard something about it, but I don't see what that has to do with my question. In fact, it makes it all the more surprising. How could you—such a model Soviet man, go through the whole war and—"

"Well, here's the thing . . ." the abbot drawled. "It so happens that in the Battle of Berlin I received a wound in the . . ." (And here Ivan Mikhailovich Voronov let out a soldier's word for a piece of the male anatomy.)

"Anyway, after that, there was nothing left for me to do, except go to the monastery."

For a moment there was a terrible silence, followed by a female shriek, followed by indignant yells and shouts and threats, as the members of the delegation commanded by this extremely important woman streamed off in a fit towards the monastery gates.

Within an hour the abbot had already been summoned to Moscow. This time it looked like they weren't joking. But Father Alipius calmly answered any and all of the questions he was asked by his KGB interrogators: "She asked me a direct question, and I gave her a direct answer. I put it to her in exactly the kind of language that she understands."

Somehow or other even this time everything worked out all right. It was the one and only time that Father Alipius ever indulged in the use of such a weapon, so to speak.

But this famous and somewhat defiant answer later turned into the cause of all kinds of gossip and rumors. Savva Yamshchikov, the celebrated art historian and restorer, who had been a friend of Father Alipius, set us straight on the real story of how Father Alipius joined the Church, straight from the abbot's lips:

"All the time I used to be asked just how it happened that such a handsome man had retired to the monastery. They always used to say: Aha! You must have been severely injured in a certain place, and now can't carry on your lineage, so to speak. In fact, Savva, all that is utter nonsense. The truth is simply this. The war was so horrible, so full of monstrosity and suffering, that I gave my word to God: if somehow I manage to survive these terrible battles and survive the war, then I will give my life to God and will retire to the monastery. Imagine the German tanks charging our front lines, their machine guns firing, cannon shells blazing, just cutting us down, sweeping away almost everyone in their path, and suddenly in the midst of this utter hell I saw how our battlefield commissar tore off his helmet, even as the bullets were flying around him, and fell to his knees, and began to pray . . . yes, indeed, somehow this 'Communist' was able to mutter the half-forgotten words of the prayers he used to know as a child, begging the Almighty to spare us. And He did. That's when I realized: God lives inside of all of us, and one day He will make his appearance to us, some way or other . . ."

* * *

The powers that be were always trying any way they could to destroy our monastery. At one point, the local Soviet of Pechory region confiscated the agricultural property and pasture of the monastery. They did this just at the beginning of summer. The cows had only just been let free to roam in the pasture, but now the poor animals were forcibly driven back into their stalls.

Also just at that time, on orders from Moscow, the Provincial Party Committee had brought a large delegation of fraternal Communist Party members from other countries to treat them to a bit of old-style ancient Russian tradition. At first, all was calm. But just when the "children of fraternal Socialist peoples," quite enchanted by the silence and beauty of our monastery, began wandering among the flower beds and blooming rose gardens, the doors of the cattle sheds opened with a loud creaking noise, and all thirty of the monastery's cows and its one enormous bull, lowing and mooing for joy at being suddenly let free, careered headlong right at the delegation. It was Father Alipius who had given the command for this well-prepared action in advance.

As these great beasts with flaring nostrils and tattered tails charged in their madness of sudden freedom straight for the flower beds, devouring grass or flowers or anything else in their path, the representatives and leading lights of the international Communist movement, cursing the monastery with yells and epithets in a great variety of languages, ran for their lives. The Provincial Party Committee workers complained to Father Alipius.

"Well, don't blame me," the abbot replied. "Actually I feel sorry for the cows. Now they have no other place to go, since their pasture has been taken away from them. That's why there's no other choice—we have to graze them inside the monastery."

That very day the monastery received all its pastureland back.

Father Nathaniel remembered as one of the most difficult days of his life a day in which the monastery received a decree forbidding that funeral services be held in the caves. This effectively meant closing off all access to the caves, and eventually the closing of the monastery. The decree had been signed by the Bishop of Pskov. In spite of this, Father Alipius gave the order that the funerals continue as before.

When the authorities in town found out about this, they hastened to the monastery and demanded to know whether Father Alipius had received the decree from the bishop, who was his direct superior. Father Alipius answered that he had.

At this the bureaucrats were indignant. "Then why don't you carry out these orders?"

To this Father Alipius replied that he would not carry out the order because it had been given out of weakness of spirit. "I pay no heed to those who are weak in spirit. I only obey those who are strong spirit." And so the tradition of holding funerals in the caves was never halted.

The war against the monastery did not cease for a single day. Valentin Kurbatov, a writer from Pskov, remembered another incident:

Yet another state commission that had been commanded to close down the monastery arrived to do its job. But Father Alipius did not let them in, and instead posted a notice on the Holy Gates, that the plague had broken out in the monastery, and therefore he would not permit the commission to enter. The head of the commission was the chairman of the Provincial Cultural Committee, Anna Ivanovna Medvedeva. Father Alipius addressed himself directly to her.

"I'm not worried about my own monks, idiots though you think they all may be. After all, they'll all end up in the Kingdom of Heaven. But I'm worried about you, Anna Ivanovna, and your bosses, and that's why I can't let them in. I have no idea what defense there would be for you when you all are called to the Day of Judgment. So for your sake, forgive me, I simply will not open the gates."

That very day he hopped into a plane and flew to Moscow. And again he lobbied and besieged the doorsteps of the powers that be and pleaded and argued and cajoled and eventually won the argument.

Just as a real warrior always has an unerring instinct for guessing the plans of the enemy, so Father Alipius was always an implacable foe of deliberate enemies of the Church. But he was quite a different man in his dealings with common folk, even if it seemed that they sometimes had no idea what they were doing.

Strange as it might sound to anyone who has just heard all the previous stories, the main thing in the life of Father Alipius—in his own words—was always love. It was love that made him so invincible and so incomprehensible to the rest of the world.

"Love," said the Great Abbot, "is the very highest form of prayer. If prayer is the queen of the virtues, then Christian love is God, for God is love. If you just look at the world only through the prism of love, all your problems will disappear, and within yourself you will see the Kingdom of Heaven, within the human being you will find the Icon, and within the earthly beauty you will see the shade of Paradise. You may object to me that it is impossible to love your enemies. But remember what Jesus Christ told us: 'Whatever you have done unto the least of these my brethren, you have done it unto me . . .' Inscribe these words in golden letters upon the tablets of your heart, and inscribe them and hang them together with an icon, and read them to yourself every day.

One evening, long after the monastery had closed its gates for the night, the frightened night watchman ran up to the abbot and told him that drunken soldiers were breaking into the monastery. (It later turned out that these were graduates of the Pskov Paratroop Cadet Training Institute, who were celebrating graduation in a particularly rowdy way.) Despite the lateness of the hour, the young lieutenant paratroopers were banging on the gates, loudly demanding to be let in at once, asking that all the churches be open to them, that they be given a tour, and that they be allowed to find out where the priests were keeping their nuns hidden.

The night watchman related in terror that these drunken officers had already gotten ahold of a huge log and were this very minute using it as a battering ram to bash down the gates.

Father Alipius dashed into his cell. When he returned he had put on his military parade dress jacket onto which were pinned all his many medals for bravery and heroism and distinguished conduct in the field of battle. Keeping his military regalia and medals hidden beneath his priestly black robes, he sped off with the night watchman to the Holy Gates.

Even from a distance it was clear to the abbot that these youngsters were serious about taking the monastery by storm. As he approached, he commanded the night watchman to open the gates. Instantly a crowd of about a dozen furious lieutenants flew into the monastery. With threats they surrounded the old monk in his black mantle, yelling at him that he had no right to insist on his Church laws on their Soviet land, and demanding that he immediately display the People's Museum, which was the people's legacy right now to its future heroes.

Father Alipius bowed his head and listened to them. Then he looked up and dramatically cast off his black mantle. The young lieutenants looked at Father Alipius and hushed, stunned. Father Alipius in turn stared at them all threateningly and demanded that the officer closest to him hand over his cap, which he did meekly. Turning over the cap and finding the officer's name written on the inside rim as required, he turned and marched off to his own lodgings.

The young lieutenants followed him, sobered up at once. Muttering their excuses, they begged for the cap to be returned. It had begun to dawn on them that they could be in for a lot of trouble. But Father Alipius did not reply. The young officers followed Father Alipius to the very threshold of his lodgings and hesitated. The abbot of the monastery opened the door and gestured for them to enter.

That night they sat up with him until the wee hours. He treated them as generously as only a Great Abbot could have done. Then he himself guided them on a personal tour of the monastery, showing them all the

ancient holy shrines and telling them in detail about the glorious history of the monastery. In parting he gave each of the youngsters a fatherly embrace and generous gifts. They in turn were embarrassed and refused. But Father Alipius insisted that these funds, which had been collected by donations from their grandmothers, grandfathers, and mothers, would prove truly useful to them.

Of course this was an exceptional case, but by far not the only such case. Father Alipius never lost faith in the power of God to transform humanity and to change people, no matter who they were. He knew from his own experience how many former persecutors of the Church had become secret and then later open believers, perhaps precisely due to the powerful words of truth and confrontation that they had first heard from the abbot. Months and sometimes even years later, former enemies would return to Father Alipius, not to persecute the monastery anymore, but instead to find in the Great Abbot a witness to another world, and a wise pastor and spiritual father. Perhaps the fearless truth that he had spoken to them, no matter how incomprehensible and bitter it had seemed at first hearing, had taken seed and remained in their memories. And that seed would remain until such time as the person either accepted it or rejected it forever. Either choice was completely up to each person.

* * *

In his letters to Bishop John of Pskov, Father Alipius reported that "newspaper articles brim with undeserved attacks and slander against grieving mothers and widows of fallen soldiers. Here is the true face of their ideological struggle—the humiliation of hundreds and thousands of priests and clerics—many of them the best people in society. Many of them come to us with tears in their eyes, complaining that they cannot find even civilian work. They have wives and children with nothing to live on."

Here are some headlines from the central and local newspapers of the time: "The Pskov Caves Monastery Is the Home of Religious Obscurantism," "Squat-Dance Alleluia," "Black-Robed Spongers," "Black-Robed Hypocrites." And here is yet another letter to Bishop John of Pskov. In it Father Alipius related yet another incident:

"This Tuesday, May 14, 1963, our steward, Father Ireneus, organized, in keeping with the traditions of all the former years of monastic life in this monastery, the watering of the gardens of the monastery with rainwater and snow melt water that we are able to capture thanks to the little reservoir that we have constructed by the fortress wall. When our people were working, six men approached them followed soon after by two others. They were carrying surveying instruments that they were using to mark off land that had formerly belonged to the monastery. They started screaming at our workers and telling them they were forbidden to draw water from our own reservoir, telling us that this water was not ours and demanding that we stop pumping. A worker strove to continue, but one of the men ran up to them, grabbed the hose, and started to rip it away. Another who carried a camera started photographing our people. Our steward told these unknown visitors that the abbot had come and that they should explain everything to him. One of them came up to me while the other stood by photographing us. Three of them were left.

"Who are you and what is it that you want?" I asked them.

The man in the hat refused to give me either his name or his rank, but instead told me we had no right to this water and this land on which we were standing. I added, "And we probably shouldn't dare to breathe or to warm ourselves in the sun here because the sun and the air and the water—they're all yours, right? So what's ours?" Then I asked him again: "Who are you and why are you here?" He refused to tell me his name. Then I told him:

"My name is Ivan Mikhailovich Voronov. I am a citizen of the Soviet Union, and decorated veteran of World War II. I and my comrades who live beyond these walls are war veterans, some of whom were wounded in the war. Some lost their legs and arms, or received severe wounds or concussions. Some of them literally watered this land with their blood, cleansing the fascist evil from this air you now so begrudge us. What's more, my comrades who live here are hard workers in the factories and workshops and fields. Many were crippled in battle; some are receiving their war pensions; others are fathers who lost all their children in the battles for the liberation of this land and of this water.

"Are you saying that all of us who have us spilled our blood and given our lives for this place do not even have the right to use this land and water and air, this sacred land that we literally tore from the grip of the fascists for the use of ourselves and of our people? Who on earth are you to dare say such a thing? And in whose name do you claim to be acting?'

They started to mumble, naming the Regional Party Committee, and the Provincial Party Committee, and so on. Creeping away from us sideways, the man in the hat said:

"Sorry, Father."

I answered that I am a Father for those people on that side of the wall. But for you, sir, I am a Russian named Ivan, and am still strong enough to fight with vermin and fascists and other evils.

* * *

In the beginning of 1975, Father Alipius had his third heart attack, Archimandrite Nathaniel told us during the sermon commemorating the memory of our Great Abbot. He had already prepared his grave. He

On a snowy day in Pechory.

ordered that his coffin be placed right next to him in the corridor. And when people would ask him where his monastic cell is, he would point to the coffin and say, "There is my cell." In his final days he was accompanied by Hieromonk Theodoretus, who daily gave him Communion while nursing him and giving him medical assistance. On March 12, 1975, at two in the morning, Father Alipius said. "The Virgin Mary has come! How beautiful she is! Give me paint and paintbrushes and let us draw her!" They brought him the paints and brushes, but those hands, which had carried so many heavy shells to cannons in the front lines during World War II, could no longer move. At four that morning Archimandrite Alipius died peacefully.

By this time our Soviet archimandrite Father Alipius had many faithful and dedicated helpers among the military, and even had some fairly high-ranking supporters in the government. Many were the artists, scientists, politicians, and writers who came to visit him. He had a marked influence on the lives of quite a few of them—and not only a material influence, but most of all a moral influence as a priest and spiritual pastor. But these people too in their way, whether playing large or small roles in our society, also strengthened him spiritually. In the archives of Archimandrite Alipius at Pechory Monastery there is a fragment of a manuscript by Alexander Solzhenitsyn. It is a short prayer in verse, which epitomizes the principle in life always followed by our Great Abbot:

How easy it is to live with You, O Lord!
How easy it is to believe in You.
When my spirit sinks
or scatters in confusion,
and the very smartest people
cannot see further than this evening,
and do not know what to do tomorrow,
You send down clear certainty to me that You exist and that You care,
and will ensure that not all the paths of goodness will be blocked.
On the peak of earthly glory
I look back in surprise on the path I have taken
which I would never have been able to invent for myself,
an incredible path
through hopelessness
from which I was yet able
to send humanity a reflection of Your rays of light.
And for as long as it is necessary that I keep reflecting them,
You will let me do so.
And what I do not finish—well then,
You have assigned others the task.

The mountains of Abhkazia.

Augustine

THIS STORY OCCURRED in 1986. A month earlier I had been sent back from the Pskov Caves Monastery to Moscow. Archbishop Pitirim, who headed the publishing branch of the Moscow Patriarchate, had been told that in the Pskov Caves Monastery there was a novice with a degree in cinematography. It just so happened that in that year the government had finally allowed the Church to prepare to celebrate 1,000 years of Christianity in Russia. Specialists were urgently needed to prepare a show for the ceremony commemorating the millennium: for the first time we would be showing the life of the Church on television, and making movies about Orthodoxy. So I was requisitioned.

For me it was a real tragedy to be moving back to the city that I had left for the Pskov Caves Monastery several years before, but my spiritual father, Father John, said to me, "A novice must above all obey: go where your holy superiors have commanded you." Nonetheless, I always used any excuse I could to come back to my beloved monastery, even if only for a day or two.

One day I received a call from Father Superior Zenon, a monk and icon painter who also lived in Pechory Monastery at the time. He sounded very nervous and wouldn't explain anything over the phone, but begged me to immediately come back to the monastery. I can't remember what excuse I used to convince Archbishop Pitirim to give me leave, but the next morning I was already in Pechory, in the cell of Father Zenon.

What did he have to tell me? Under conditions of greatest secrecy, he informed me that several weeks ago in the mountains of Abkhazia, amidst regions where monks had secretly been living illegally for several decades, there was one monk who had suddenly had no choice but to descend from the heights and come back into the secular world. Now he was in serious danger.

Monks had been living illegally in the mountains around Sukhumi for years, since the very beginning of the Soviet Union. They would relinquish the world forever and go into hermitage in remote mountainous regions, hidden from civil authority and even sometimes from ecclesiastical author- ity. Some of them were real heroes and spiritual warriors who sought

163

seclusion in order to be with God through ceaseless prayer and contemplation. Others left the world in protest against the lies and injustice of the Soviet government and the Church that it controlled—ripping up their Soviet passports. Others wanted to have nothing to do with what the Soviets called "ecumenism," collaboration, or any of the other empty slogans that our ecclesiastical authorities at the time were parroting.

Three years ago I had a chance to visit these mountains myself. With the permission of Archimandrite Cyril and Archimandrite Onuphrius of the Holy Trinity Monastery, I went with several friends to bring a monk from the monastery with us to the illegal monastic hideouts. The story of our trip is worth telling separately, but in any case I was well acquainted with the house of Deacon Gregory on Kazbegi Street in Sukhumi. From there almost all of the journeys from legal to illegal life departed, winding to the summits of the Caucasus past two or three shelters along the road into the mountains where pious Christians would hide the monks. The travelers would climb up steep mountain paths from one cell to another, ascending to ever more remote and beautiful places. Such were the hiding places of our spiritual heroes.

Of course the authorities persecuted these monks mercilessly. They would set up search crews trying to hunt them down, and when they caught them, they would put them in jail. And yet monks kept coming back and living here—an example to many of the unconquerable Church.

And now Father Zenon told me that one of these monks had been forced out of the mountains and was now in Pechory. He was still quite a young man—just twenty-two years old. His name was Augustine. I'd heard about him from the monks in Sukhumi, but had never laid eyes upon him.

When Augustine was only four years old, his mother had become a nun. She had gone up into the mountains and taken her son with her. The boy was brought up by monks and at the age of eighteen took his monastic vows. He lived in a cell with his mother and was educated by those mountain elders. He had never had the slightest thought of abandoning his desolate seclusion.

However, once as he was working on the mountainous terraces of his orchard, while his mother was busy taking care of the household, a band of Abkhazian hunters came upon their community. They were all drunk and angrily demanded that Augustine's mother prepare food for them. She completely understood that she had no options. (All those hunters had to do was return to their village and report her and her son to the authorities.) Therefore she obeyed and invited them to sit down and eat. However, after eating and drinking more and more wine, these interlopers became even more unruly and began to make unwarranted advances on Augustine's mother. She replied that she would prefer that they burn her alive than that they defile her honor. The hunters, maddened by wine and lust, then poured kerosene on her and burned her alive.

From a distance Augustine heard the horrible scream of his mother. He raced back to the cell and saw the horrific scene: his mother burning and on fire, running around their hovel and screaming horribly, while the hunters trying to sober up chased after her in a panic, trying to put out the fire. When they saw a young man running into the house the hunters began to panic even more and ran away. Augustine finally was able to quench the flames that were burning his mother. She was already just about to die. Augustine brought his mother to the nearest village—into the home of one of their friends—but there was already nothing that could be done to help her. The nun died, after first taking Holy Communion and asking her son not to take any revenge, but instead to pray for her miserable murderers.

But the hunters, once they sobered up and realized what they had done, were terribly worried. Whether or not she was a nun, she was a woman. Whether or not she was living legally in these mountains, they understood that if anyone ever found out about their crime, they would be answerable under the law for murder. As a result they began a manhunt against the only witness to their crime—Augustine. When the elders learned about this, they told the young man: "Those hunters will find you eventually, and they will have no mercy. So it's best you leave the mountains, and take refuge where you can, but not here. Here they will kill you."

Augustine listened to his elders' advice. At first he took refuge in the Holy Trinity Monastery, but it was dangerous living there without an internal passport. Therefore from there he was sent on to the Pskov Caves Monastery. This was because there already was one monk in the Pskov Caves Monastery who had come back down from the mountains. But now he was very old, and after more than forty years up in the mountains, he was allowed by the elders with their blessing to go back to the outside world for medical treatment. The abbot of the monastery at that time, Father Gabriel, had for all his gruffness and terrible temper taken pity on him, and had figured out a way to obtain permission from local authorities, police, and the KGB for the old and ailing monk who had no documents at all to live out his days in the monastery. Indeed, with the help of our abbot, the imperious Father Gabriel, he had been given an internal passport. And so he lived in the almshouse, located in the St. Lazarus wing of the monastery.

Father Zenon was hoping for similar assistance when he brought this young monk to the abbot. However, this time it appeared that the abbot was just not in a good mood. Scarcely had he taken one look at Augustine when he screamed furiously: "You call him a monk? He's a crook! Take him away to the police!"

"Oh! That Gabriel is a real KGB type!" Father Zenon complained. "Whatever made me bring this young angel to see him?"

And Father Zenon told everyone that young Augustine was an utterly angelic creature. "You cannot imagine what an amazing man he is! He eats less than a five-year-old boy. His eyes are pure and angelic. And he's always praying!"

Father Zenon even added: "He is the only real monk whom I have ever met in my entire life!"

Of course, when he said this, he was still upset by the rude reception that our abbot had given him. Still, as he was saying, anyone who ever met Augustine was truly amazed. Unfortunately, at this time Archimandrite John (Krestiankin) was not present in the monastery. Like no one else, he would have been able to give the correct advice as to what to do with this surprising young monk.

I inquired where Father Augustine was now. It turned out that after the incident with the abbot, Father Zenon had sent him away from Pechory for safety's sake to Moscow, to his spiritual children Vladimir Vigilyansky and his wife. For the moment Augustine was taking refuge there.

The next day when I got back to the capital I made the acquaintance of this lovely pair. Nowadays lots of people know Vladimir Vigilyansky as the director of the press service of the Patriarch. But at that time everyone just called him Volodya (the nickname for Vladimir, like "Bill" for William). He was still a researcher in the Institute for Art History, and he lived with his wife Olesya and their three young children in the so-called Writers House on Prospekt Mira. Their neighbors were such celebrities as the bard Bulat Okudzhava, the astronaut Leonov, and the sports announcer Nikolai Ozerov. Father Augustine was hidden like a secret jewel of the

Olesya and Vladimir Vigilyansky.

Vigilyansky family on the ninth floor of this building. Of course, I couldn't wait to meet him.

Into the room walked a man who seemed to have come from another world, a young monk with long flowing tresses of hair down to his shoulders, and with huge deep dark-blue eyes. We greeted each other in the special and pleasant manner of the mountain monks. Olesya and Volodya gazed at us with admiration. We sat down at the table and I started asking him about our common friends living high up by the Psou mountain brook—Fathers Madarius, Orest, Paisius, and little Father Raphael. Augustine answered calmly and with few words: he had known all these people since he was a boy. When the conversation was over he retired to his room.

But we were left with a remarkably radiant impression from this meeting. On the other hand, we were left stressed by the unresolved question of what we were going to do with him. At the time it was 1986. He had categorically refused to put on secular dress. But at this time a man wearing a monastic cassock and without documents was guaranteed to be stopped for a document check by the police, and would then be immediately arrested. Lawyers who were friends of Volodya Vigilyansky warned that Father Augustine would immediately be slotted into any old unsolved crimes on the police blotter from Kaliningrad to Vladivostok. And it would be very convenient for them to write off a crime as solved—especially while getting rid of an unwanted monk at the same time.

At the very thought of this young monk who knew nothing of worldly life, this little angel-Mowgli, raised in the mountains and on Scripture and the holy books of the Church elders, suddenly being kept captive and tormented in a preliminary holding cell, or being packed off to our Army, to which a healthy young man would in any case otherwise be sent without further discussion, we were all horrified. And what if the worst were to happen, and this chaste and unspoiled lad were to end up in jail just for having given up his life to God?

Over the next few days we tried as best we could to find a solution to this predicament. Vladimir traveled to the famous Holy Trinity Monastery to consult with his spiritual guides. We consulted our friends, some of whom knew other lawyers. Someone even promised to get the celebrated pop star Alla Pugacheva involved, just in case we needed "pull" to get Augustine out of jail.

Meanwhile Father Augustine lived his own life. He prayed in his room, which we immediately began to call his cell, and then waited for our decision. As I observed him, I noticed curious differences in traditions between regular monasteries and mountain hermitages.

For example, I happened to notice that Father Augustine was wearing an ornate priestly cross with decorations underneath his cassock. "Where did you get this cross? Are you secretly a priest?" I asked this because I knew that sometimes that's exactly the answer.

"No, I am not a priest," Augustine answered. "But when my elder died he gave me this cross with his blessing. And he commanded me to wear this cross openly on the day when I become a priest. Till that time this cross will protect me."

He also had a very beautiful incense burner, and every day he would burn incense in his room, for which he would ask us to obtain both coal and the incense itself. I had not noticed such a custom in any of our monasteries. Or another time I suggested to him that we read the *kathisma,* or a portion of the Psalter, together, and I was quite surprised to see that Father Augustine made quite a few simple mistakes. I was almost about to judge him for this—what sort of monk is it who knows his Psalter so badly? Then I thought better of judging him, realizing that in the high peaks of Abkhazia there was simply nobody available to teach him the fine points of correct Old Church Slavonic.

And so the days went by. Gradually we began to notice that Father Augustine was changing. To be more exact, or to call a spade a spade, our company was ruining him. After all, quite unlike him, we were far from angels. And as the Book of Psalms says: "with the merciful thou wilt show thyself merciful; with an upright man thou wilt show thyself upright, with the pure thou wilt show thyself pure; and with the froward thou wilt show thyself froward" (Psalm 18, 25–26). The last verse was about us, and everyday we saw signs of our bad influence on him. For example, after long discussions of all possible plans for the salvation of Father Augustine that came to nothing, we would decide to console ourselves with ice cream. Our young monk suddenly became so fond of walnut ice cream for twenty-eight kopecks that he ate five whole portions in a row. Soon every day he was sending Vladimir's son Nick to the nearest kiosk. We didn't feel good about refusing him, and so we began to observe with growing horror that we had truly perverted Father Augustine: he could eat that cursed ice cream twenty-four hours a day!

Young Nick has now grown up, graduated from college, and serves as a deacon in a church, but remembers all too well how he repented with tears having fattened up the mountain refugee with a seemingly limitless quantity of ice cream.

Or another example: Olesya's brother had a tape recorder. And suddenly we saw how young Augustine would sit next to him and together they would listen entranced to the Beatles! A monk who liked rock and roll? What would be next? At this we were truly horrified and fell into a deep shock. Feeling helpless and gloomy, we would gather in the Vigilyanskys' apartment. Also joining our discussions were another husband and wife pair, Elena and Zurab Chavchavadze, and Father Superior Dmitri from the Holy Trinity Monastery (who is now the Bishop of Vitebsk).

The last straw for me personally was when Father Augustine suddenly exclaimed joyously while standing on the balcony: "Look! It's Nikolai Ozerov!"

I was shocked. On the balcony of our neighbors' apartment one floor beneath us the legendary sports commentator was truly standing there, and in fact benevolently he nodded to the monk who recognized him. But that was not the point.

"What Nikolai Ozerov!" I yelled! "How on earth do you know about him? Where did you find out about Nikolai Ozerov?"

It turned out that Father Augustine had found a subscription to the popular magazine *Ogonyok* and had spent hours shortening his days reading these magazines cover to cover in his cell. I realized that before it was too late we must immediately remove this innocent monk from our society. Otherwise we would corrupt him beyond redemption and never be forgiven.

In the midst of all of these unhappy events suddenly a decision was arrived at by my friend Zurab Chavchavadze (he and his wife Elena to this day are parishioners of our Sretensky Monastery). Zurab suggested that he bring the boy to Tbilisi to the Georgian Patriarch Ilya. It was truly a brilliant idea. Those who lived in the Soviet Union before may remember that at that time Georgia was in many ways an exceptional territory within our enormous country. Many things were possible there that were totally unthinkable—for example, somewhere in Pskov Province or in Siberia or in the Russian Far East. For example, it would be possible to back date and "naturalize" a person or "correct" his documents. Besides, Father Augustine had lived his entire conscious life on the canonical territory of the Georgian Patriarchate. Zurab himself had served for several years as a subdeacon of His Holiness Patriarch Ilya. The Patriarch respected the ancient princely lineage of the Chavchavadze family, and Zurab was certain that Patriarch Ilya would want to help both us and a brother of the Church, and therefore would be able to do something that would be totally impossible in Moscow.

And so, having rejected the doubtful ideas of buying a fake passport, or appealing to the mercy and goodness and understanding of the Soviet state organs, or a third idea of ceaselessly shuffling poor Father Augustine from apartment to apartment to apartment, we decided to take him to Georgia. Father Augustine prayed and then agreed to the plan. There was only one hitch: how was I going to get a week off to go to Georgia? I needed a serious excuse. I did not think that it would be possible to tell my boss Archbishop Pitirim about the underground monk Augustine, if for no other reason than that I did not wish to place a high-ranking ecclesiastical leader who was constantly under surveillance by the secret police into a vulnerable position.

Then suddenly I had an idea to make a film in connection with the millennium of Christianity in Russia about the unity of the Russian and Georgian Orthodox Churches. I should add that the supervisors from the Council on Religious Affairs, whose job it was to oversee ecclesiastical life, had several times asked me to make an "ecumenical" film about how all religions were really the same. Having been educated in the Pskov Caves Monastery on strict monastic anti-"ecumenism," I had categorically refused all previous offers. But now a plan was budding within me to pass off a film about the unity of the Churches of Georgia and Russia as being ecumenical, thereby receiving support from the Council on Religious Affairs both for the trip and for the film.

I wrote the screenplay in one night. The images of the films were as follows: the symbols of Russia are wheat and bread, while the symbols of Georgia are grapes and wine. The Russian farmer plows the field, sews the grain, harvests the grain, gathers the wheat kernels, grinds them, and thus makes flour. The Georgian farmer drops the grapeseed into the warm earth, grows the vineyard, then harvests the grapes, tramples the grapes with his feet into enormous vats . . . And all of this is very beautiful and one can feel it leading up to an extremely valuable goal. . . . In the end, all was made clear: the highest goal of this ancient and mighty labor is one common Liturgy: the Bread and the Wine, the Holy Gifts of the Eucharist. This is our true unity.

Archbishop Pitirim was very pleased by this screenplay, and with skilled diplomacy he quickly talked the bureaucrats from the Council on Religious Affairs into at last making the "ecumenical" film that they had been bothering us to make for years. Of course if this bureaucrat had been better educated he would have understood that the story had absolutely no relationship whatsoever to his notion of "ecumenism," since both the Russian and Georgian churches are Orthodox, whereas his "ecumenism" presumed dissolution of our faith into others.

But the main thing was that the question of our trip to Georgia was immediately resolved. However, now there was another question: before traveling to Georgia, we needed to film the harvesting of the wheat in Russia. Otherwise we would need to wait an entire year for the next harvest. And this was the problem: it was already the beginning of September, and in the central portion of the country, not to mention the South, all the wheat had long since been harvested. I called the Agriculture Ministry and asked if there was any place where they were still harvesting the wheat. Unfortunately I was taken for an inspector and immediately given the runaround: always, on the entire territory of the Soviet Union, one sixth of the globe's land mass, all the wheat had been successfully harvested and stored properly in its granaries. Even as I tried to find out if there was just one collective farm anywhere in the country that was just somewhat later than the others so that we could just take a few pictures and shoot a few frames of the harvest, the bureaucrats of the Ministry steadfastly swore to us that there was no way it would be possible to find any farm anywhere that had been so frightfully backward in its duties. But finally I got lucky. The editors of the newspaper *Country Life* took pity on me and told me that according to their data there was still one part of the USSR harvesting the wheat—Siberia, or to be more exact, a region of Omsk Province. And if we were to fly out there no later than today, we just might make it.

That very evening I raced out with the cameraman, whose name was Valery Shaitannov, to Domodedovo Airport and barely made the last flight to Omsk. Meanwhile Zurab Chavchavadze was supposed to buy tickets on the express train to Tbilisi, leaving in two days. Back then internal passports were not required for the purchase of train tickets, although they were for airplane tickets. Therefore we were not worried about Augustine.

In Omsk, thanks to the assistance of the Council on Religious Affairs, we were awaited by the news that some 300 kilometers from the city there was one farm where they would still be harvesting wheat for one more day. We were driven to that distant collective farm in the Volga sedan of the Archbishop of Omsk by his deacon John. The archbishop himself was not in town, as he had recently been transferred by a decision of the Holy Synod to a bishopric in Belorussia. Instead Archbishop Theodosius of Berlin had been assigned to become the Archbishop of Omsk. As they used to say in those days, he had been "promoted to Siberia."

But it did not seem that Theodosius was in any particular hurry for his "promotion." At any rate, he had not yet arrived. Thus the full complement of ecclesiastical authority for us in the bishopric of Omsk was represented by Deacon John—who was also our driver.

Our cameraman and I were able to film everything wonderfully, with lovely shots of an endless wheat field in the sunset, and the rays of sunlight streaming on the waving sheaves of wheat, and the friendly teamwork of the workers on their tractors and combines, the golden grain and the joyful faces of the farmers . . .

By evening we were worn out but content as we raced back in the archbishop's car to Omsk in order to catch our late-night flight to Moscow. Tomorrow evening we had to get into a train to Tbilisi. The cameraman was asleep in the backseat while the deacon and I chattered about everything under the sun. When there was nothing more left to talk about the deacon begged me: "Please! Keep talking! Let's discuss something else, or else I'll fall asleep at the wheel!"

I understood that he really wanted to hear more stories about life in the capital, and I didn't begrudge the deacon this pleasure. I told him everything I could remember about the life of the Moscow church, until finally I told him about how there had been a scoundrel pestering

Archbishop Pitirim and claiming to be the son of the last Tsar. The deacon stirred.

"We have scoundrels like that too! A year ago a young orphaned lad appeared in one of our churches . . . The grandmas took him in. He began to help them out chopping wood and clearing out candleholders, and soon he learned how to be a sexton, and even read from the choir . . . He earned so much trust from the church warden and the rector that they even gave him money to pay their dues for the Peace Fund. It just so happens that this was the patronal feast day of this church. That night the archbishop and I served the Vigil, and in the morning when we came to serve the Liturgy the church had been robbed. That youth had stolen all the church offerings and all its money, had stolen the cross from the altar, and many other things."

"Even stole the cross from the altar?" I exclaimed.

"He even stole my cassock!" exclaimed the deacon. "I had left it in the church after Evening Vigil. It was so beautiful too. The archbishop had brought back the buttons from overseas. What beautiful buttons! I will never again have such beautiful buttons! How happy I would be to look at those buttons again—they were green on one side and red on the other . . ."

"Yes, it seems that certain representatives of our clergy are very fond of these accoutrements," I mused to myself, already not listening to the deacon. "Some like fancy belts half the size of their bellies, some go crazy about some buttons . . . buttons . . ."

And then I remembered that not long ago I had seen just such a cassock with just such curious buttons. But where and on whom? And suddenly I remembered distinctly: I had seen these exact buttons on the robes of Father Augustine. In fact, it had always made me somewhat curious: how was it that a mountain monk was somehow wearing such a "stylish" cassock?

But when I had asked him about it at the time Father Augustine had answered me simply: "I wear the cassock I was given by my well-wishers. I must take what I am given. There are no stores in the mountains."

But then I reproached myself—"Here I am focused on his clothes, thinking his buttons look odd! Shame on me! It's just a coincidence!"

Nonetheless, to keep passing the time, and drive off the foolish doubt that had begun to bother me, I asked the deacon what that young lad who had stolen his robes and the money and the cross from the altar looked like. As Father John eagerly described the youth in great detail, I began falling off my seat. He was exactly describing Augustine!

I couldn't believe my ears. I interrupted the deacon almost with a scream and asked: "By any chance does he like ice cream?"

The driver looked at me with great surprise and answered: "Like it? Are you kidding? Give the lad 100 ice cream cones in a row and he'll eat them all. Our grandmas used to joke that he would probably sell his own mother for an ice cream cone."

"Tell me," I said, "what else did he steal from your church?"

"What else did he steal?" The deacon repeated my question. "Let me think—oh yes, I remember, we spent two months hanging around the police station about this . . . he stole our censer for incense, it was golden, and belonged to the archbishop . . .

"Did it have little bells on it?" I whispered this question.

"Yes, it did have little bells. And he stole the medal of Prince Vladimir, 2nd Class, which our rector got last year. What else? Money. Lots of it. About 3,000 rubles in total, collected for the Peace Fund. Also a decorated cross."

"And what did that cross look like? Was it slightly damaged in any way?"

"I'm not sure about the cross. Why are you asking?"

"Because it appears that youth at this very moment is sitting in my apartment in Moscow wearing your cassock!"

Now it was the deacon's turn to be astonished. I related the story to him as best I could and asked him to take me as quickly as possible to the priest of the church that had been robbed. According to Augustine the cross that had been given to him as a blessing by the elder had one peculiarity: its frame and green malachite stones had been damaged.

At first the priest of the church didn't even want to speak to us, because the investigation had been extremely traumatic. Indeed, they had suspected him of the theft of the valuables from his own church. But finally he described the cross that had been stolen. The detail about the damaged stone on the frame of the cross left no doubt—none whatsoever.

That night I flew home but was completely unable to sleep, of course. The only place in the entire Soviet Union where the wheat had not been harvested until last evening was thousands of kilometers away, way, way out in Omsk Province. The only person who was eagerly willing to take us there had been the deacon, my driver. And the only reason why this curious story had slipped out was because the deacon couldn't forget about his beloved buttons. And the only reason why I had had the chance to hear the story from him was that the old Archbishop of Omsk had left for a new bishopric, while the new archbishop had yet to arrive. Otherwise the deacon would have been driving around his own archbishop, and not some young novice monk from Moscow. And how on earth had the idea about the screenplay with the wine and the bread come into my head? Maybe this was all just so that I could fly here and discover everything?

What did I know? What could I be sure of? Who then was Augustine? A villain! Was he responsible for murders or blood or violence? Or was it all just a devilish coincidence? How was it possible that our Augustine was not a real monk when he knew my dear friends, the mountain monks Father Paisius and Father Raphael?

The more I thought about things during that sleepless night as I looked up into the dark starry night, the clearer things became for me: I had been brought to the distant town in Siberia by the Almighty hand of the Lord! Nothing, absolutely nothing was a coincidence!

The peculiarities I had noticed in Augustine before now blazed in my memory like flashing alarms: his poor reading ability of Old Church Slavonic, his priestly cross, his fancy censer, his passion for ice cream, his joy upon meeting the famous sports commentator Nikolai Ozerov, his love for rock and roll. And much, much more.

We had tried as hard as we could not to judge him for all these things we didn't understand. In fact, we had been afraid of ourselves for being judgmental against him. Was it because we had been afraid to judge him that the Lord so miraculously revealed the truth to us? Or was it because it would have been just too terrible if Zurab Chavchavadze and I had brought this fellow to Patriarch Ilya and gotten him to vouch for this fellow and procure documents for him? If we had unwittingly deceived the Patriarch into becoming his next victim, that would have been too horrible to think of!

Over and over again I kept coming back in my mind to the question: Who was this man? Why was he hiding? Why was he always around the Church? What other crimes had the lad been involved in? And although my reason was telling me that everything that I learned in Omsk, where I had only been for one day, was the truth, still my heart refused to believe. Too monstrous and impossible would have been our disillusionment at Augustine's deceit!

No, we needed to calmly and carefully get to the bottom of everything. I remembered that Augustine had told us how before coming to Pechory he had lived for a while in the Holy Trinity Monastery. So as soon as our flight landed in Moscow, I said goodbye to our camera operator and took a cab from the airport directly to that monastery, in Zagorsk.

I was well acquainted with the dean of the monastery, Archimandrite Onuphrius. He was a remarkable monk and father confessor who now serves as the Metropolitan of Chernovtsy and Bukovina. When I told him the whole story, he immediately remembered that three months ago there had in fact been a rather strange young deacon from the diocese of Omsk living with them very like in description to Augustine. Father Onuphrius asked his assistant the Hieromonk Daniel (who is now the Archbishop of Arkhangelsk), who had been taking care of the guest from Omsk, to give us more details, and we interrogated him thoroughly.

Father Daniel told us that at the beginning of the summer a completely unknown and very young deacon had arrived from the diocese of Omsk. He called himself Father Vladimir. He said that he had been robbed on his journey and therefore he had nothing—no documents, no money, and just a cassock. The monks of the Lavra had taken pity on him and had brought him to the monastery wardrobe, where he had been given a complete set of monastic garments—a cassock, and a *klobuk* hat. Within half an hour the guest was presented to the Abbot of the Lavra in full monastic regalia. He was allowed to live in the monastery while he got his documents back in order.

Father Daniel told us that he was an ordinary young monk, albeit with certain peculiarities, but then again young provincial monks are often not without their quirks.

What quirks? Well, for example, he had a medal of St. Vladimir—a very high award indeed, rarely given out even to the most dedicated members of the clergy. Asked about the medal, he had answered that he was given this award for having restored a church in the diocese of Omsk.

"So young, and he already managed to do such a great thing!" The other monks were beside themselves with admiration. But what surprised Father Daniel more than anything was that this young deacon refused to take part in the services, but instead would stand off to the side or somewhere in the corner. When he was asked to serve together with the other monks, he would refuse, saying that he was indisposed or that he did not feel worthy of such an honor.

Finally the monks of the monastery got seriously worried about the spiritual health of their guest and decisively insisted that he serve the Liturgy on Sunday. "And did he?" Father Onuphrius and I asked in one voice.

"Oh yes, he did serve," answered Father Daniel, "but not in our monastery, no, instead he gave the service in the neighboring parish church. But what kind of service was it? It seems the bishops in the provincial dioceses give their blessings to completely ignorant candidates for the deaconate. He seemed to know absolutely nothing at all. He didn't know how to put on his vestments. He didn't know what prayers to say. We had to do everything together with him. In our seminary with such complete lack of preparation he not only wouldn't have gotten near ordination, but he wouldn't have even been given a chance to take the examinations."

I was beginning to feel ill. To act a sham role as a clergyman without ever having been ordained? It was unthinkable!

"So what happened to him?" Father Onuphrius was curious.

"Somehow he never got his documents. He complained about the bureaucracy in Omsk. He asked us if we could help him to get documents here in Zagorsk and even made some kind of contact somewhere here. But in the end nothing came of it. He lived in town for about a month, and rented a room from some grandmothers. I stayed friends with him and helped him as I could. Then he left for Abkhazia, for the mountains. He had always been interested in the mountain monks, the hermits, and had always been asking me about them. By the way, about a month ago I received a postcard from him. He says that he has made it to Sukhumi, and in the end there is a rather strange postscript: "I have a new name now—Augustine."

And so, with God's help, the situation had become clearer. Someone (whose real prehistory we did not know) had appeared in Omsk. There he had passed himself off as an orphan and had lived around the church for eight months. Then he had robbed the church, after which he came to the Holy Trinity Monastery, where he had passed himself off as the deacon Vladimir. There he had tried to obtain documents for himself, but when that didn't work out, he had gone to Sukhumi. The life of those mountain monks, outside the orbit of Soviet officialdom, and best of all without any documents whatsoever, had appealed to him very much. However, having spent some time with the hermits, he quickly realized that in their ascetic conditions (in the complete absence of any ice cream) he would not last long. Then having heard about the true tragic story of a real monk named Augustine, he decided to pass himself off as that real person. What's more, he had heard that the Abbot of the Pskov Caves Monastery near Pskov, Father Gabriel, had, in spite of his reputation for being a crude despot, once taken in a refugee, an ailing elder monk, and had even in spite of all obstacles obtained an internal passport for him.

And so he came to Pechory. At first everything went swimmingly. The monks believed his legend and were passionately willing to help him. But then something went wrong. Archimandrite Gabriel, that "unspiritual" and "beastly" harsh "despot," had said: "You call him a monk? He's a crook! Take him away to the police!"

As Father John (Krestiankin) later revealed to me, the truth had been revealed to Father Gabriel by the Mother of God, the Heavenly Protectress of the Pskov Caves Monastery, who had spiritually revealed to the abbot as her representative just who this young scoundrel was and thereby had protected our monastery. Meanwhile the other goodly monks, deceived by appearances, and shocked by the cruelty of their abbot, had saved "Augustine" from his clutches and hastened him off to Moscow. The rest we know.

Except we don't know! Who was Augustine in real life and what did he do before he got to Omsk? And what would he do once he realized that we knew the truth about him? What if he were armed? Or what if, once we revealed the truth about him, he would grab a child—for instance Nastya, the Vigiliyanskys' four-year-old daughter—and put a gun to her head or a knife to her throat, and tell us to do what he commanded, or else?

And even now, in spite of the undeniable facts, I was still not entirely convinced that our Father Augustine was truly a liar and a criminal. How could it be? Our Father Augustine, whom we had all gotten to love? With whom we had all prayed, drunk tea, argued, and discussed spiritual questions? Was this all just some kind of horrible hallucination? Was it all just a string of remarkable if unlikely coincidences? Was I, a sinner, unfairly judging an innocent lad who was pure as the driven snow? All these doubts did not leave me for a moment. Finally I came to the firm conclusion that I could not accuse him of anything until I was completely certain in my heart. How would this happen? I did not know, but if the Lord had already revealed everything that we had just learned in the past two days, then He would reveal the rest.

That evening we were supposed to get on the train for Tbilisi. In the publishing department I picked up a letter from Archbishop Pitirim to Patriarch Ilya, asking him for help in the making of our film *The Eucharist*.

Left to right: Sasha, Nastya, and Nika.

I called my friends who had taken part in the matter of Father Augustine, and asked them to all gather together with us in the apartment of Vladimir Vigilyansky that evening to have one last discussion before our trip.

I already knew what I was going to do. When we would be all sitting together with Augustine at the table, I would announce that I had just arrived from Omsk. Then I would carefully observe the reactions of Father Augustine. Then I would suggest that we all listen to the story about how nine months ago a young man had arrived in Omsk and had gone to the church calling himself an orphan. I would talk about how everyone had taken pity on him, had helped him with food and shelter and work, had introduced him to the priests and the elders, and how that "orphan" had repaid their kindness by pitilessly robbing the church, stealing the offerings of the parishioners, and even stealing a cross from the holy altar. Everyone would express their indignation about such a sacrilegious crime—but I would continue.

"And here's another story," I would say. "You are not going to believe this one! Imagine someone coming to the Holy Trinity Monastery in Zagorsk and passing himself off as a deacon! Why, he even had the nerve to go into the altar and pretend to serve the Divine Liturgy, without knowing anything, without ever having been ordained! Imagine the blasphemy!"

At this, of course, everyone would be amazed, but I would continue, still keeping my eyes fixed on "Augustine," and would say: "And I have learned yet another story. Once there was a man who came to the mountains. Those were the very same mountains where you lived, Father Augustine. He found out a little about the lives of those mountain monks, and began to pass himself off as one of those mountain monks himself, so that he could cover up the traces of his previous life, and tried to obtain documents under a new name. And guess what—it turns out that in all three stories the same protagonist was one and the same man!"

Someone, probably Olesya or Elena Chavchavadze, would be bound to exclaim out loud: "So who was he?"

Then I would turn to Augustine, and say: "Father Augustine, who do you think it was?"

Here without doubt he would certainly give himself away! It would be impossible not to! "Who?" He would repeat feebly with trembling lips.

And then I would reply like Detective Porfiry Petrovich in my beloved Dostoyevsky's *Crime and Punishment*: "What do you mean 'who'? Who else could it be but you, Father Augustine?"

Here by his reactions everything would be utterly clear, and he would not be able to conceal his feelings.

Two hours remained for the invited guests to appear. When I went into the Vigilyanskys' apartment I immediately asked Father Augustine to take a taxi with me to the publishing department to pick up the letter for Patriarch Ilya. He agreed happily. He seemed pleased about the idea of taking a spin in the car, and having a look at the publishing house.

Then I had an idea. What if after we revealed his identity, he managed to escape again and would once again commit crimes against the Church? So therefore I suggested: "Father Augustine, let's get our picture taken together! It'll be a nice memory for Olesya and Volodya!" He wasn't very happy about this, but gritting his teeth he agreed.

Then for some reason I had to go and joke: "And let's get our picture taken both looking straight ahead and in profile. That way if the police ever detain us they won't need to waste film."

Having said this, I immediately regretted it. Augustine gave me such a nasty look that it almost made me ill. But I did my best to turn these words of foolish vanity into nothing more than a silly joke. Fortunately, I succeeded, and the moment passed. Augustine let us take a picture of him, although from time to time he gave me extremely suspicious looks.

Zurab and Elena Chavchavadze, with their daughter, Anastasia.

It seemed plain that he was getting nervous.

During a moment when Augustine was busy getting ready to go visit the Patriarchal publishing department, I drew Volodya off into the kitchen, and closing the door behind me whispered to him: "Augustine is probably not the man he passes himself off as. It is quite possible that he is a terrible criminal. I am not joking. He and I will be leaving together now, and while we are gone immediately search his things—make sure he doesn't have any weapons or anything like that."

Volodya's eyes bulged and for an entire minute he could not speak. Finally he opened his mouth: "Do you have any idea what you're saying? Are you crazy? How dare you suggest that I search other people's belongings?"

"Listen!" I answered. "This is no time for intellectual niceties. The situation is far too dangerous. I'm talking about saving the lives of your children."

Finally Volodya began to comprehend. I said nothing more, but grabbed Father Augustine and went off with him in a cab to the publishing department. We chatted on the road about this and that. And then I even took him out for ice cream.

I wanted to give Volodya more time to conduct a thorough search.

When we got back, our host was as pale as chalk. At once I dragged him off to the kitchen, yelling at Augustine to stay in the foyer and meet our guests.

In the kitchen Vladimir could barely even whisper what he had learned: "His documents are in the name of a Sergei _____." (He stated the last name too.) He has a cross from the altar, a huge amount of money—2,500 rubles—and a medal of the Order of St. Vladimir! What on earth is going on?"

"Did you find any weapons?"

"No. He doesn't have any weapons."

The doorbell rang in the foyer. Father Dmitri had arrived from the Holy Trinity Monastery. We could hear how Augustine met him and how they went together into the living room.

But even now with the new evidence, I could still not believe in the reality of what was happening. It was so amazing! I swapped impressions with Volodya. Even he, who had just seen with his very eyes this fellow's real documents, as well as the large sum of money, had also not been able to believe that Augustine was not really the man he was passing himself off as.

Zurab and Elena Chavchavadze arrived as well. Once Volodya and I joined everyone in the living room, we had all gathered as planned. We sent the kids off to take a walk.

"Well? Why have you asked me to come here all the way from Zagorsk?" Father Dmitri was somewhat annoyed that he had had to make the trip.

As I glanced at Father Augustine, I immediately understood that he had guessed everything, and that it was all, all true! I also understood that if I would begin to tell my story in the manner of Detective Porfiry Petrovich, everything would turn out exactly as I had planned, even concluding with the dramatic question: "What do you mean 'who'? Who else could it be but you, Father Augustine?"

And everybody would react just as I had imagined. But suddenly I had a different feeling . . . I felt sorry for him. Although, to be honest, I was also feeling a different feeling—one of triumph, the feeling of a hunter who can see that within a moment his prey will at last be in his hands. But this feeling was hardly a Christian feeling.

I therefore cast off everything that I had so carefully rehearsed and planned and turned to him with just one word: "Seryozha!" (This is the diminutive or nickname of Sergei.)

He turned deathly pale.

What a fuss! Everyone jumped up and began to yell: "Seryozha? What are you talking about? Both of you explain what's going on!"

But we stayed seated and looked at each other silently. As the others calmed down slightly, I turned to the young lad and said: "This morning I came back from Omsk. There I received the last facts that had been unknown about your true story. The most correct course of action for me to take right now would be to dial 02, and the police will be here in five minutes. And yet we will give you one last chance. You saw how sincerely we tried to help you. If you right now tell your entire story from beginning to end, telling the truth and nothing but the truth, then maybe we will decide to help you again. But if you say even one word that is a lie, then I will immediately pick up this phone and call the police. I don't need to explain to you what will happen if I do that. So now everything depends on you."

Seryozha was silent for a long time. My friends were also silent, staring with amazement at their beloved "mountain monk" and "angel-Mowgli." Meanwhile, my heart was quivering in utter silence as I waited for him to decide. Finally he spoke:

"All right. I'll tell you everything. But on one condition, if you will guarantee to me that you will not hand me over to the police."

"Sergei, your one and only guarantee now is to tell the absolute truth. The instant that I perceive that you're lying, the police will come."

Once again he fell silent for a long time. I could see his mind spinning, calculating, trying to figure out what he could get away with. To watch this process was so unpleasant that my last bits of charity and pity for him disappeared.

"Where do you want me to start?" This question was clearly a trap. He was trying to feel out how much I actually knew.

"You can start where you like. From Omsk, where I just was. Or from Sukhumi. Or from your adventures in the Holy Trinity Monastery. But why not start right from the very beginning?"

From the disappointment with which he hung his head, I was relieved to see that my words had landed right on target. Even if, though he did not know it, I had shot my last bullets, and had no more ammunition in reserve.

And Sergei began to tell his story. He had been a criminal, a swindler, and a thief. He had been thieving since childhood. At eighteen he had escaped inevitable imprisonment by being drafted into the Army. But in the Army his criminal proclivities had been noticed by the eager-beaver boss of the regimental warehouse, who got him to help sell off property that belonged to the Army. Among his "clients" by the way had been a priest, who was trying to repair a half-destroyed church. In those years it was impossible to buy construction materials needed for the church without the permission of the Council on Religious Affairs, and therefore the priest, in typical Soviet style, had bought bricks and cement and lumber from Sergei.

Sometimes Sergei used in to come to the priest's home, where he had been touched by the true goodness and kindness of the fatherly priest's concern for the "little soldier." He was also touched by the fact that the priest was doing all this not for himself, as he lived very poorly, but for others, for the Church, for the faith . . .

But one day an inspector came to the regiment. Sergei quickly realized that his "friend" the boss would finger him with all the blame in order to get off scot-free. So he grabbed his profits and got on the first train for anywhere. The train brought him to Omsk. It was the last stop. From there he had no idea where to go, but suddenly he remembered the good priest. Sergei looked for a church, called himself an orphan, and found himself a nice, safe, warm place to stay for many long months. The grandmothers doted on him, and Sergei himself began to get used to the life of the church, learned some new words and phrases, and was pleasantly surprised by all the kind and trusting relationships he observed between the people there.

But finally spring came, and Sergei had gotten tired hanging out with the little old ladies of the church in Omsk. He began to dream of the open road. Just at that moment a grandma who was an elder of the church and called him her grandson trusted him so much that she gave him the entire fund of one year's dues and donations from the parishioners to carry over to the Peace Foundation. He stole the money, even though he knew with what enormous effort, kopeck by kopeck, these funds had been collected for the Soviet Peace Foundation. He stole everything that he fancied from the church and ran away to freedom.

After carousing to his heart's content for several days, he almost landed in jail. He was so scared when he escaped being caught that he again turned to those idiotic believers, those strange black-robed people who are such suckers, since it was so easy to pull the wool over their eyes.

He arrived in the ancient Holy Trinity Monastery in Zagorsk and called himself Hierodeacon Vladimir. He was surprised even himself at how quickly he was able to be clothed in formal monastic robes and then be surrounded by very pleasant if somewhat exhausting friendly concern and care. However, he found it impossible to obtain a new passport. Furthermore, it was getting more and more dangerous to live in the city of Zagorsk, which was under constant surveillance from both the police and the KGB.

"But how did you dare pretend to serve the Divine Liturgy?" I asked him this because I really wanted to understand. Furthermore I thought it would be useful to show him that I knew even these details.

"Well, what choice did I have?" Sergei replied gloomily. "The monks were insisting on it, asking how it was possible that I was a deacon and not serving the Liturgy. And so I did . . ."

"How awful!" Olesya cried. Sergei sighed and continued his tale.

Having learned that there was a place in our country where it was possible to live without any documents, where it was relatively warm and free, he set off for Sukhumi. During his month and a half in the Caucasus he visited quite a few mountain cells and hermitages, calling himself the Hierodeacon Vladimir and bearing kind words of regards from the monks of the Holy Trinity Monasery. The mountain hermits showed him places where few people had ever been and told him things that they hardly ever told anyone. Of course, Sergei had no plans at all to stay in the mountains. However, it was there that he learned that the Abbot of the Pskov Caves Monastery had helped an ailing monk who had to come down from the mountains to receive his documents. And he also learned about the tragedy of the real young monk Augustine.

We knew all the rest. When Sergei finished his story, I sent him off to his "cell." We remained in the living room, stuck once more with a question that had been torturing us for the last two weeks, namely: what were we going to do with him? Only now the question had acquired completely new dimensions.

In fact, when I had begun our discussion with Sergei by telling him that at any moment I would call the police, I hadn't been telling the truth. It would have been impossible to hand him over to the police. And not only because Sergei himself could turn on us and tell the police that we had seriously planned to help him buy a false internal passport! All that was a trifle. The worst danger was that this man who had been in the mountains had found out most of the major paths leading to the illegal shelters in the mountains. He knew Mother Olga and Deacon Gregory in Sukhumi. He knew the location of the mountain refuges, and knew how to find the elders, and knew a lot about their links with the various secret cells. He even knew the location of elders who had been safely hiding out in the mountains for decades. There could be little doubt that the police would pay him quite a pretty penny for such information. On the other hand, it was impossible to just let him go, or else he might go back to swindling gullible kind hearts in churches and monasteries.

The next day we traveled to the Holy Trinity Monastery to seek advice from the most authoritative spiritual counselors. The holy fathers were horrified by our tale and also struck with wonderment at the Providence of the Lord, but they had no concrete suggestions for us.

Our position seemed to be worse and worse: our hero, realizing that we still didn't know what to do, began to feel safer, and even began to order the kids to get him ice cream again. After all, to them he was still Father Augustine.

Finally we realized that there could be one—and only one—way out in this situation: Sergei himself would have to change. He would have to repent of his sins before God and come to the police and confess. And the chances that such an outcome was possible, strangely enough, were not small.

Sergei himself had been deeply amazed by the mysterious workings of the Lord in uncovering his hoax, in which a loving and compassionate Christ had revealed Himself. We could see that in spite of his problems, Sergei was truly undergoing a profound spiritual crisis. Furthermore, nearly a year of being in contact with loving Orthodox Christians, with their incomparable if somewhat naive kindness, was truly beginning to have an impact on him.

He thought about everything for a long time. Finally, after long conversations, and a confession in the Holy Trinity Monastery to Archimandrite Naum, for which we were truly overjoyed, he decided to accept his punishment for his sins.

However, having made this decision, he took his time about acting. Zurab and I left for Georgia to finish our film, and when we came back Sergei was still living in the Vigilyanskys' apartment. When he finally gathered himself up and steeled his spirit to doing the right thing, he took his leave of the children in a lingering and affectionate way, and finally left, taking (without permission of course) several old religious books and an old prayer book. As he had once said, it was difficult for him to pray from a freshly printed prayer book. A week later, Sergei called and said that he was going to turn himself in.

A month later a detective from the Army Prosecution Squad arrived in Moscow. Because I had taken custody of everything that "Augustine" had stolen, the detective lived in my apartment, so as not to spend money on a hotel. The detective was a senior lieutenant of about my age. At his request I took him all around the main stores in Moscow, where on his senior lieutenant's salary he bought presents for his wife, and stuffed his "perhaps" bags (which in Soviet times people would carry around at all times, in case "perhaps" something good appeared for sale in the shops) with smoked sausage, cartons of Marlboro cigarettes, and tins of instant coffee. Of course, he told us all about "Augustine"/ Sergei. Apparently he was behaving perfectly in his holding cell, never swearing or causing trouble, never playing cards, praying . . . The other criminals had given him the nickname "the Saint." He kept this nickname throughout his years of imprisonment. Sergei cooperated with the investigators and fully confessed to all his crimes.

Soon his trial took place, and for all of his thefts and crimes he was given the combined sentence of eight years' imprisonment in a medium-security facility. For all eight years of his imprisonment, Olesya and Vladimir helped Sergei. They sent him money, books, food, and even, at his request, back issues of the *Journal of the Moscow Patriarchate*.

Eight years later, Sergei was back in Moscow. We were very glad to see him and talked about some of our happier memories with him. He was a completely changed man, like the once-possessed Gadarene from whom Our Lord expelled the legion of demons from the swine. The swine then ran off a steep cliff into the sea, where the previous demonic deceits, crimes, and nastiness drowned in the deep, and were forgotten, as if they had never existed.

Once more Sergei was living with the Vigilyansky family. The children—Nikolai, Alexandra, and Nastya—had grown up by now and already knew the true story of their former miraculous friend, the "mountain monk" Father Augustine. At first the bitter truth had greatly disturbed the children and they had even cried, but then in the end it only strengthened their faith, and they said that they loved Seryozha every bit as much as they had once loved Father Augustine.

A year later Sergei unexpectedly announced that he had taken monastic vows, and his name had been changed to Father Vladimir. He was serving an archbishop in some provincial diocese. He was elevated soon to hierodeacon, and then to hieromonk, and he was even given a parish to look after.

And yet I admit that we were still worried about him. On the one hand, of course, we were glad for him, but on the other hand a certain fear seemed to cling to this joy. By this time I was a hieromonk of the Donskoy Monastery. It happened that Father Vladimir was visiting me in Moscow. He drove into the capital in a very expensive (for that time) foreign car, as he put it, "on business to see his sponsor."

I decided to speak to him very seriously. The conversation was long and difficult, but it seemed to me that he had heard me. I reminded him that Our Lord Jesus Christ Himself had worked wonders in order to give him a new way of perceiving the world, that it was no coincidence that He had compassionately led him back to salvation, teaching him proper living and not just book faith. I warned him that now that he was a real monk and priest he faced enormous dangers from a false sense of security, from a perilous sense of self-contentment, when outer prosperity might become a reason for great misfortune, and even possibly a bitter end. "For when then shall say 'peace and safety,' then sudden destruction cometh upon them," we are warned in Thessalonians 5:3.

After all, upon taking monastic vows and becoming a priest, many things change in our lives, but not everything. The ancient evil that always dwells within us will always haunt us, and will never quit trying to steal in upon us in order to accomplish the Devil's main goal—to steal our soul. Only ceaseless courageous battle with evil, solely for the remarkable goal that is incomprehensible to many—the purity of our soul—will justify us before God. But if Christ does not see this struggle within us, He turns away from us, from that priest, monk, or layperson who has turned from Him, leaving him alone with what he has chosen for himself. And that choice is the same as it always was—insatiable pride and desire for the pleasures of this world. As time passes, sooner or later these passions will subvert or even pervert someone who has forgotten about God. Then these passions reveal their true horrible dangers.

Then the Sea of Galilee will rise up, and from its abyss the enraged swine who were drowned long ago will race ashore and hurl themselves on the unfortunate who thought there could be any compromise between them and God. When the evil spirit leaves the man, it wanders through the arid places, seeking rest but not finding it. And then it says: "I will come home to the place from which I left." And if it comes back and finds the place empty, swept out and neat, ready for visitors, then it will go and get seven other demons, even more evil than it is, and when they come there, the evil will be worse than before.

So unfortunately it proved to be with Augustine-Sergei-Vladimir. In 2001 we read in the newspapers that the Hieromonk Father Vladimir, who was serving as a priest in one of our provincial cities, had been intimately linked with the company of utterly perverted local criminals, men whose mere society is completely forbidden to a monk. And he'd been found brutally murdered in his own home.

Lord, grant Thy peace upon the soul of Thy servant, the murdered hieromonk Vladimir!

A gorge in the Caucasus.

What Was Happening in the Spiritual Realm at Those Moments?

*W*HAT IS COINCIDENCE? Why does a brick chance to fall on the head of this one passerby in particular—this one out of the thousand and not that one? Similar profound speculations have concerned mankind for millennia.

Once the dean of the Holy Trinity Monastery, Archimandrite Onuphrius, and the spiritual father of the monastery, Archimandrite Cyril, asked me to help them convey one of the monks of the monastery, Hierodeacon Raphael (Berestov), to the Caucasus Mountains, to the refuges where for many years hermit monks have been living illegally. Father Raphael was a very short man, the size of a child, beardless, and with a clear high voice and simple spirit—truly like a child.

In a conspiratorial whisper Father Raphael told me that with Father Cyril's blessing he was forced to go to the mountains because he was struggling all by himself with "ecumenism." He had hung up a piece of paper on the door of his cell in the monastery which said: "SHAME ON THE ECUMENISTS!"

I also had no truck with Soviet "ecumenism," and therefore was eager to help, although I had my doubts as to how serious the dangers to the hierodeacon truly were. How could they be so grave that he had no choice but to flee the monastery?

"There will probably be a desperate chase after me! They will try to arrest me and lock me in a casemate!" Father Raphael whispered. He always used to express himself in a very passionate and high-flown manner. To be honest, I didn't much believe him about the casemate. Why should the authorities care about this little hierodeacon?

Father Raphael was also an artist. In addition to his personal effects he was planning to take with him up into the mountains his paint brushes and paints and the easel and boards for painting icons. I realized that all

191

by myself I would not be able to handle this task, and therefore asked my friend Sasha Shvetsov, who was temporarily visiting his parents in Moscow, to come along on the trip. With the permission of Father Cyril we also acquired yet another young traveling companion named Constantine, who was a graduate of the Moscow Theological Academy. He is now known as Father Nikita, and he serves in the diocese of Bryansk.

We were met in the railroad station of Sukhumi by Deacon Gregory, a somewhat disheveled and gloomy-looking man, and by his wife Olga, his complete opposite, a very outgoing and caring person. We stayed in their home on Kazbegi Street. It turns out that this is the place where those who are secretly setting out into the mountains to visit the mountain monks begin their journey.

Father Raphael could not wait to begin to climb up to the hermitages in the mountains, but it turned out not to be so simple. Olga got a call from Zagorsk. She was warned that rumors were already flying about there that Father Raphael had arrived in Sukhumi and was planning to flee up into the mountains to live free of Soviet law, without passport registrations or regulations of residency. But if they were talking about this in Zagorsk, how long could it be before it became known to local authorities? And so it proved. There were loyal Orthodox believers in various governmental posts in Sukhumi, and so we learned the command had been sent to the police in Sukhumi that the dangerous criminal hierodeacon known as Father Raphael Berestov be arrested at once before he could disappear into an illegal status and be involved in anti-Soviet activities, living like a vagabond.

I was very surprised to see that the forebodings of little Father Raphael had been justified. He himself, although he had been prepared for such a possibility, became so scared when he heard about the manhunt that had been launched against him that he hid under his bed like a little boy and didn't want to crawl out. Laughingly we tried to bring him out, to no avail. In any case there was no way we can imagine why the whole squadron of police had been assigned to catch little Father Raphael, since he in no way resembled the dangerous criminal he was described as officially.

Be that as it may, we realized that it was best for now to postpone the hike up into the mountains. At the advice of Father Adrian, who was here visiting from Pechory, we decided to wait until the vigilance of the police slackened. This was only to the liking of our young group of three: Sasha Shevtsov, the seminary graduate Constantine, and me. All week long we

Father Adrian.

went swimming in the warm waters of the Black Sea and got ourselves a tan, until this ostentatious idleness began to thoroughly irritate our house-host Father Gregory.

And so, upon catching us yet again sleeping late, he triumphantly announced that the good days for the lazy were over. Work had been finally found for us—just as the day was remarkably sunny and hot, and the lovely sea was deliciously lapping the beaches not far away. We had absolutely no desire to work, but we had no choice and after breakfast we followed Father Gregory through the entire city to a place that he had decided would be the site of our new triumphs of labor.

The place to which he led us was on the very outskirts of Sukhumi. He brought us to a half-ruined brick home, which he had purchased the day before for almost nothing. He commanded us to carefully disassemble these ruins so that we could use the bricks again in building a summer kitchen. The work promised to be long, hard, and literally dirty.

We broke up part of the wall, and then began to stack the bricks, brick by brick, scraping off the old cement, and carefully loading up the bricks into a car. Once he had given us this hard work, Father Gregory cheered up considerably. After he wound his head up in a big white handkerchief, he resembled a bearded bandit chieftain, especially when he got onto his motorcycle to follow the truck, promising to be back in five hours.

For five hours straight we wearily disassembled the high wall and stacked up the huge heap of cleaned-up bricks as commanded. It was unbearably hot. We were sweating and covered with cement dust from head to toe. By three o'clock in the afternoon, Father Gregory returned in his truck. Fortunately for us, he had decided to take care of us a little bit better, and had even brought us a huge ten-liter bottle of water, which helped us to keep slaving away over his bricks before we dropped dead of thirst.

Having slaked my own thirst, I sat down in the only place where there was just a bit of shade, beneath the half-disassembled wall. There was room enough in the shade for just one person and I barely fit. But this joy was not long lived. The deacon summoned me and I had no choice but to leave this cool place. I don't remember anymore what it was that Father Gregory asked me to do—it was probably some trifle—but when I went back to get another bit of shade, the seminary graduate Constantine was there soaking up his bit of bliss. I walked around and around, but there was nowhere else that shade could be found. And so I went away.

Just then Constantine noticed that Sasha Shvetsov was drinking his fourth or fifth mug of water. "Hey! Watch out or you'll drink it all! Leave us a little," the seminary graduate asked.

But Sasha paid him no heed and pointedly poured himself yet another large mug of water. Constantine raced to grab the mug out of his hands as Sasha, cleverly letting the mug go without any struggle, slipped into the precious shade.

We all looked at him enviously. But Sasha was not destined to have a long rest in the shade either. Deacon Gregory, catching us being idle once again, yelled: "Why are you bothering to cool off? Load up those bricks now! I've only paid the driver for an hour! I'm not going to pay him an extra three rubles for your laziness!"

As quickly as we could, we raced to carry out his commands. Meanwhile Father Gregory sat down in the lovely space in the shade with great contentment.

Everything happened next very quickly. We were carrying the bricks into the van when we suddenly heard a terrible noise. When we turned around we saw that in that place where Father Gregory had only just been sitting, there was nothing but a thick cloud of dust. The wall had

Father Raphael.

unexpectedly collapsed. As we ran up, we caught sight of the unhappy deacon completely covered in dust and a huge pile of broken brick. I was very struck by the bandanna on his head, which had suddenly changed from being white to scarlet, like in one of those movies about our heroic Red Commanders. The first thought that came into my head was "how did he get tied up so quickly?" But then I realized that what was making his bandanna so red was blood, and so I hurried to help Father Gregory out.

He had lost consciousness. We tried to free him from the bricks. As quickly as we could the truck driver sped off to find an ambulance. The doctors arrived in half an hour. After taking a look at Father Gregory, they gloomily pronounced that he was in bad shape and took him off to be operated on at once. After the accident Father Gregory spent eight months in various hospitals, and was operated on several times. It was a long time before he could serve again, or even able to move around as before the accident.

That evening Constantine, Sasha, and I were tortured with the question: why was it that Father Gregory had been the one to be beneath the wall at exactly the moment when it crashed? Every one of us had spent several minutes fighting to be in that spot. It could have happened to any one of us. Why should that wall have crashed on the deacon? And what had been going on in the spiritual realm at that time to make our Guardian Angels drag us out of that accursed spot under any excuse? Or was it all just chance?

We were so preoccupied by this question that we asked Father Adrian for his advice. The good priest became thoughtful and replied: "I cannot answer your question. But I can say, without breaking the secret of confession, that Father Gregory has been serving the Liturgy for several years without ever having been to confession himself. And both I and the priests of his church have warned him many times that this would lead to no good. But Father Gregory could never be bothered: 'not now—I'll go to confession later.' Then he was always postponing and postponing his confession. And so I was sure that something bad was going to happen to him, for one mustn't joke with such things."

Several days later Father Adrian at last gave us his blessing to go up into the mountains carrying the heavy backpacks with the belongings of Father Raphael. We were accompanied by a local nun who was about forty years old, and was remarkably strong. She carried the very heaviest backpack of all without complaint.

We climbed up only by night, clambering up the steep mountain paths by the moonlight, clutching rocks and rhododendron branches for balance. By day we rested in the hidden monastic cells from the unwanted eyes of the hunters. We saw bear prints and deer prints on the paths. We ate delicious mountain honey. We met the monks of the mountains, some of whom were truly spiritual heroes. We spoke to them, and helped them fix up their cells, which had been carved from great tree trunks.

At one point we had to spend a couple of days in the home of one elderly schema-nun while hunters were roaming around looking for us. During those two days we ate her entire food reserves, which that nun had been saving up for the whole winter. Of course we had no desire to eat her out of house and home, but the high altitude in the mountain air had given us young folk such animal appetites that we thoughtlessly wolfed down cans and jars and fried potatoes and all kinds of grains. That meek nun could barely keep up cooking and cooking for all of us. She never said a word to us, but after we were gone she had to climb back down from the mountains and once again all the way back up to stock up with provisions for the winter.

Finally on the sixth day of our hike, we met the Hieromonk Paisius by a mountain brook. He was a friend of Father Raphael, a very young, cheerful, and learned monk, and had already been living here for several years.

"Paisius!" It was striking how happy little Father Raphael was to see him, and he threw himself straight ahead, fording his way right through the surging mountain stream.

And so the story ended. We brought Father Raphael's things through that raging brook, said goodbye, and set off on our way back down the mountain, still discussing why all these unusual adventures in these mountains and with our new acquaintances were happening to us.

The General-theologian.

The Theologians

O NE DAY A YOUNG seminary graduate came up to Father John and without even bothering to introduce himself said: "I am a theologian."

Father John was quite surprised by this and asked: "Really? The fourth one?"

"What do you mean by 'the fourth one?'" asked the confused seminarian.

Father John explained: "In our Church we know of three theologians. The first was John the Theologian, the Apostle and beloved disciple of our Savior. The second was Gregory the Theologian of Nanzianzus. And the third was Simeon the New Theologian. In its entire 2,000–year history the Holy Church has only granted these three men the title of theologian. So are you the fourth?"

From where does God send us His wisdom? "The wind bloweth where it listeth, and thou hearest the sound thereof, but canst not tell whence it cometh, and whither it goeth: so it is with all born of the Spirit" (John 3:8).

Once we were on tour with our Sretensky Monastery Choir in the Russian Far East at a military base for the Strategic Air Force. After services and a concert, the officers invited us to dinner. This was the first Russian Orthodox service that had been heard in this distant military outpost in a very long time. Naturally, everybody looked at us as extremely unusual. Before the meal, like all good Christians, we said grace by uttering the Lord's Prayer.

Praying together with us and crossing himself was a highly respected and decorated general. Two hours later, as the meal was ending, the officers approached the general: "Comrade General! We noticed that you crossed yourself. We all respect you, but we do not understand. Maybe with your long experience you have realized something that we have not thought about yet. Perhaps you might want to share with us some of your knowledge gained from long years of learning—or impart some of your wisdom to us. Tell us, what is the main thing in life? What is the meaning of life?"

Naturally, such questions are only asked having spent a long time with one another in intimate company, Russian style, with utter trust and goodwill.

The general, a grizzled Army veteran, thought for a bit and then replied: "The main thing in life is to keep your heart pure before God."

I was amazed. This was the sort of thing that only a really outstanding theologian would say—someone who was both a thinker and a practitioner. But I don't believe that this Army general guessed my amazement in the least.

The point is that priests have a lot to learn, and indeed a lot to be ashamed of sometimes in comparison with people who might at first glance seem to be very remote from the study of theology.

At one point during negotiations for the reunion of the Russian Orthodox Church Abroad (begun by Russians in the diaspora after the Russian Civil War), with our Russian Orthodox Church, the Moscow Patriarchate, Archbishop Mark of Germany and Great Britain, told me about an incident that led him to believe that the spiritual changes in our country were not propaganda but a reality.

He was in a car in Moscow Province with a priest. Archbishop Mark is a German. He was not used to cars racing at 140 kilometers per hour when the road signs clearly marked the speed limit at ninety kilometers per hour. His nerves put up with this for a long time, but finally he delicately asked the priest who was driving him about the . . . discrepancy. The priest merely snorted at the remark of the naive foreigner and assured him that everything was just fine.

"But what if the police stop you?" The archbishop was very concerned. "There'll be no problem with the cops," the young priest reassured his amazed guest.

And sure enough sometime later they were stopped by a traffic cop. The priest rolled down the window and casually called out to the young policeman cheerfully, "Good afternoon, boss! So sorry, we're in a hurry."

But the policeman had no reaction to this greeting. "Your documents!" He barked his command.

"Oh, come on, boss!" The priest was getting nervous. "Can't you see we're in a hurry?" "Your documents, please!" The policeman repeated insistently.

The priest was upset and ashamed to be shown up in this manner before his guest, but there was nothing he could do. He handed over his driver's license and car registration to the policeman, but could not refrain

Archbishop Mark's reception in Russia.

from adding sarcastically: "Here! Take them! Your job is to punish, and ours is to forgive."

The policeman looked him over coldly and then said, "First of all, it is not we who punish, but it is the law. Second, it is not you who forgive, but the Lord God."

It was then that Archbishop Mark realized that if even a policeman on a provincial Russian road could reason in this manner, then in this mysterious land of ours that cannot be comprehended by the mind alone, everything had truly changed once again.

The Vladimir icon of the Mother of God.

A Sermon Given on the 23rd Sunday after Pentecost, November 19, 1995

*I*N THE NAME of the Father and the Son and the Holy Spirit!
Today during the Liturgy, our Church asks us to bear in mind the story that Luke the Evangelist witnessed for himself in a small fishing village—the healing by our Lord Jesus Christ of a woman who had suffered for twenty years from an incurable disease.

This healing took place in a rather remarkable manner: Jesus Christ had been surrounded by the multitudes, all of whom wanted something from Him. Some asked to be healed, others were asking for miracles, and still others did not even know what they wanted. And amidst this huge throng our Lord turned and suddenly asked his disciples a strange question.

"Who was it that just touched Me?"

His disciples were surprised: "Teacher, You are being crowded around from all sides, and everyone is seeking Your attention for at least a moment. And yet You ask, 'Who just touched Me?'"

Christ answered that a throng was indeed surrounding Him, and yet He had truly felt that in its midst His Divine Energy had suddenly gone out to one person in particular amidst the throng crowded around him.

And then a woman who had been standing nearby confessed abashedly that she had touched the robes of the Teacher. She was abashed because under Jewish law she was considered unclean because of her female illness, and therefore she was not supposed to have touched anyone. But she confessed that she had touched Him because from that very moment she had felt that she was no longer ill! Christ replied with words that were sufficient to explain not just to His disciples and to the woman herself, but to all of us, exactly what had happened.

"And He said unto her: 'Daughter, thy faith has made thee whole; go in peace, and be whole of thy plague.'"

Thus, throughout the ages humility and all-powerful faith in God are interwoven with worthless temporary human laws, false shame, and fear of human condemnation.

All of you, dear brothers and sisters, will of course remember how just two months ago we celebrated the six-hundredth year of the founding of our Sretensky Monastery, or the Monastery of the Meeting of the Vladimir Icon of the Mother of God, who delivered our city of Moscow from the onslaught of the dreaded Timurlane. What a great celebration that was! For one day we received on loan from the Tretyakov Gallery the actual Vladimir Icon of the Mother of God, that ancient, miracle-working icon which is the holiest relic in all of Russia.

In the Procession of the Cross that began in the Kremlin and ended up here in our monastery, more than 30,000 people took part, even though a September rain was falling. His Holiness the Patriarch and the senior hierarchy of the Russian Orthodox Church followed the icon even though their vestments were utterly soaked with rain, and people thronged the streets as they passed, and as the great holy relic went past them they fell on their knees—right into the puddles, right onto the wet asphalt, nobody bothering even to look where . . .

By the time the last person in that enormous line which was several kilometers long finally made it into our church and bowed before the holy relic, it was already three o'clock in the morning. In the now empty church the only people left around the wonder-working icon were those who were responsible for bringing in and guarding it: scholars and art historians and custodians from the Tretyakov Gallery, as well as city officials and high-ranking police officers. They all stood in silence. The picture that they had beheld during those hours of the true strength of the Russian people's Christian faith was overwhelming.

My brotherhood and I said our last farewells and made our last earthly bows before the icon. Then we kissed the holy relic and I said to the bureaucrats: "Now is the only chance you will have in this life for something amazing. On this day and in this place you can approach the miraculous icon and pray to the Queen of Heaven. In a few minutes they will take this icon back to the museum. Now I quite understand that you are all very serious people, but do not miss this chance."

Those bureaucrats looked at each other uncomfortably, shuffling about a bit, and smiled with embarrassment, but they did not move. I think that each of them, if they had been there all by themselves, would have happily

*Procession of the Cross with the Vladimir icon
from the Tower of the Savior
in the Kremlin, September 8, 1995.*

come up to the great ancient icon and would have asked the Holy Mother of God for their greatest desire. But now, as spoken in the Scriptures, for fear of the Pharisees, they stood like stumps of wood.

Then suddenly one very high-ranking officer in the police with a face blushing as red as an old Soviet flag stepped forward. Angrily he wheezed up and handed his cap to some major who was standing next to him and lifted himself up the steps to the icon, clumsily bowing to the ground. He loudly kissed its glass protection and began to fervently whisper something to the Mother of God. Then he bowed once more to the ground with great difficulty and carefully walked backwards. He grabbed his cap from

Before the Vladimir icon in Sretensky Monastery, Moscow.

the open-mouthed policeman he had handed it to, and gloomily looked around at the others, before stepping back into the crowd.

I said: "Good for you, Comrade General! The Mother of God will never abandon you after that." Then I turned to the museum workers and said: "All right, take away the icon."

A week passed. We gathered all of those who had been part of our celebration—our brotherhood, the many workers who help us in our monastery, the bureaucrats, and our choir—for a celebratory banquet. We just wanted to thank them all. That same general of the police also came to the banquet.

"You know, what a miracle happened to me then!" he said as he lifted his glass for a toast. And he shared with us what had happened.

When the general had heard my suggestion to approach the miraculous icon at night in the church, he had, like everyone else, at first been simply embarrassed. All around him were people of his station, including people whom he depended upon. But just in those days the general had been visited by misfortune: his older sister who lived in the town of Vladimir had gotten into an automobile accident and had broken both her legs.

The doctors in Vladimir had operated on her for many hours. They had gathered what was left of one of her legs and put it into a cast. An operation was scheduled on the second leg requiring complete anesthesia. But the general's sister was quite an elderly woman; the doctors were afraid that her ailing heart would not be able to withstand the ordeal.

That night the general, after deciding to go up to the icon of the Virgin Mary, whispered to Her: "O Mother of God, I don't need anything. I already have everything. But my sister . . . She's being operated on tomorrow. I'm afraid she won't make it. Help her!"

The next morning the general called the hospital in Vladimir to find out how the operation was going. But they told him that there hadn't been any operation. To his astonishment, the doctors told him that in the morning before they were going to take her into the operating room they had done one last x-ray, which revealed that the broken bones had set exactly as they should have in order to grow back again. It seemed that in the night the patient had somehow turned over in a particularly fortunate way, and the bones had lined up just as they were supposed to. Now all the doctors had to do was put that leg in a cast.

What we have heard today in the reading from the Scripture about the woman who was healed happened 2,000 years ago in the sleepy little Galilean village of Capernaum on the outskirts of the Roman Empire. The story of the general of the police and his sister happened two months ago here in Russia.

For many of us the stories of the Scriptures are lovely but are no more than fairy tales. Inspiring, beautiful, wonderful tales that make a person—indeed not just a person, but all of humanity—better! But still, for many of us they are just fairy tales.

But this is not so! The Apostle Paul once made a great discovery—one that all of us should keep firmly in our memories. It may seem to us that discoveries are only made in physics or medicine. But Apostle Paul discovered the most important and fundamental law of our world, which he formulated as follows: "Jesus Christ is the same yesterday, and today, and forever" (Hebrews 13:8). What can possibly be added to this? Only one ancient yet joyful word: "Amen!"

The Egyptian desert.

The Tale of the Prayer and the Little Fox

From *The Prologue*

*I*N EGYPT, in whose ancient Christian past there had once been many grand monasteries, there once lived a monk who befriended an uneducated and simple peasant farmer. One day this peasant said to the monk, "I too respect God who created this world! Every evening I pour out a bowl of goat's milk and leave it out under a palm tree. In the evening God comes and drinks up my milk! He is very fond of it! There's never once been a time when even a drop of milk is left in the bowl."

Hearing these words, the monk could not help smiling. He kindly and logically explained to his friend that God doesn't need a bowl of goat's milk. But the peasant so stubbornly insisted that he was right that the monk then suggested that the next night they secretly watch to see what happened after the bowl of milk was left under the palm tree.

No sooner said than done. When night fell, the monk and the peasant hid themselves some distance from the tree, and soon in the moonlight they saw how a little fox crept up to the bowl and lapped up all the milk till the bowl was empty.

"Indeed!" the peasant sighed disappointedly. "Now I can see that it wasn't God!"

The monk tried to comfort the peasant and explained that God is a spirit, that God is something completely beyond our poor ability to comprehend in our world, and that people comprehend His presence each in their own unique way. But the peasant merely stood hanging his head sadly. Then he wept and went back home to his hovel.

The monk also went back to his cell, but when he got there he was amazed to see an angel blocking his path. Utterly terrified, the monk fell to his knees, but the angel said to him:

"That simple fellow had neither education nor wisdom nor book-learning enough to be able to comprehend God otherwise. Then you with your wisdom and book learning took away what little he had! You will say that doubtless you reasoned correctly. But there's one thing that you don't know, oh learned man: God, seeing the sincerity and true heart of this good peasant, every night sent the little fox to that palm tree to comfort him and accept his sacrifice."

A six-winged seraphim.

Guardian Angels

G UARDIAN ANGELS do not only send us blessed thoughts for eternal salvation, but truly stand guard over us in our daily lives. The word "guardian" is not metaphorical and is not an allegory, but represents a valuable experience of many generations of Christians. It is for good reason that the Church calls upon us in our prayers to spare a thought for those of us who are traveling, bidding us to seek the special protection of our Guardian Angel from the Lord. And truly where, if not on our journeys, which are often fraught with the most unexpected circumstances, do we need more help and intercession from God?

About thirteen years ago I was in the Pskov Caves Monastery with my parishioner Nikolai Sergeievich Leonov, a professor and historian, and a lieutenant general in the intelligence services, who for many years had taken part in the television broadcast "The Russian Home." In Pechory Nikolai Sergeievich met with Father John for the first time. Father John didn't just make an enormous impression upon him, but, as Leonov later recalled, truly helped him with his prayers.

At that time Nikolai Sergeievich was only beginning to enter the life of the Church, and he had a lot of questions. In particular he asked me to clarify the teachings of the Church about the world of angels and about Guardian Angels. I tried as best I could, but despite all his tactfulness, I could see that Nikolai Sergeievich was disappointed with my clumsy answers. I was sad about that, but there was nothing left to do but to pray for God's assistance.

We left the Pskov Caves Monastery to return to Moscow on an early summer morning, having been sent off by Father John. We had a long road ahead of us, and before leaving I had asked the mechanics from the monastery garage to look our car over and put in some extra motor oil.

We raced along quickly over the open road. I was driving and listened without distraction as Nikolai Sergeievich told me a story of one of his long voyages that he had long promised he was going to tell me. I had never met a more interesting raconteur than Nikolai Sergeievich. The way he told stories always took my breath away. And so it proved this time.

Nikolai Sergeyevich Leonov in Pechory.

However, I also caught myself having a strange thought: this time was different, and right now, in this very minute, something very special was happening. The car was moving along fine. Nothing, not any of the instrument readings, nor any sounds, nor any smells, nor the way it was proceeding along the road, seemed to give any cause for alarm. And yet more and more I was feeling out of sorts.

"Nikolai Sergeievich, I'm afraid something's wrong with the car," I said, taking the liberty of interrupting my companion.

Leonov is a very experienced driver and has been for many years. He looked around and assured me that everything was okay. But my inexplicable alarm did not pass, and on the contrary only grew with every passing second. "I think we must stop," I finally said.

Leonov looked once again at the instruments and indicators, listened to the sound of the motor, and once again assured me that there was nothing to worry about. However, for the third time I felt so completely distressed that I began to insist that we had to stop, at which point Leonov agreed. Barely had we braked when a great black cloud of smoke emerged from the hood of the car.

We ran out into the road. I opened the hood, and flaming oil burst out of the motor. Nikolai Sergeievich grabbed his jacket and doused the flame with it. When the smoke cleared, we figured out what was wrong. The mechanics in the monastery had added motor oil, but had forgotten to close the cap. It was still lying there next to the battery. Throughout the journey the oil had poured out of the wide-open gap that had not been closed, onto the hot motor. But because of our great speed the smell had been carried under the wheels of the car, and with the windows rolled up we hadn't smelled anything. If we had driven on for even a kilometer more, our journey would have ended in tragedy.

As we brought our car more or less back into shape, I asked Nikolai Sergeievich if he needed any further explanations about Guardian Angels and their roles in our fates. Nikolai Sergeievich replied that for today he was completely satisfied and had now quite understood this question of religious dogma.

About One Holy Monastery

A Tale That Could Go into a Future *Prologue*

S OMEWHERE IN THE depths of Russia before the Revolution there was a monastery that had a bad reputation in the neighborhood. It was said that its monks were all idlers and drunkards. During the Civil War the Bolsheviks arrived in the town that was closest to the monastery. They gathered together its inhabitants in the market square, and then they dragged the monastery's monks out in a convoy.

The commissar loudly yelled at the people as he pointed to those men in black: "Citizens! Townsfolk! You know these drunkards, gluttons, and idlers better than I do! Now their power has come to an end. But so that you will understand more fully how these vagabonds have fooled the workers and peasants for centuries, we will throw their cross and their Scriptures into the dust before them. Now, before your very eyes, you will see how each of them will stamp upon these tools of deceit and enslavement of the people! And then we will let them go, and let the four winds scatter them!"

The crowd roared. And as the people cheered, up walked the monastery's abbot, a stout man with a meaty face and nose all red from drinking. And he said as he turned to his fellow monks: "Well, my brothers, we have lived like pigs, but let us at least die like Christians!"

And not a single one of those monks budged. That very day all their heads were chopped off by the sabers of the Bolsheviks.

The Monastery of Diveyevo during the 1980s.

The Most Beautiful Service
of My Life

*D*URING SOVIET TIMES there perhaps was no more horrific symbol of the devastation of the Russian Orthodox Church by Communist rule than Diveyevo Monastery.

The monastery had been founded by St. Seraphim of Sarov, yet it had been turned into a frightful ruin. The gutted remains of what was left towered over the pathetic Soviet "regional center" into which the once glorious and flourishing town of Diveyevo had been transformed. The authorities didn't bother destroying the monastery completely. Instead they deliberately left the ruin standing there as a memorial of their triumph, as a trophy of their perpetual enslavement of the Church. By the Holy Gates of the monastery, they put up a monument to the leader of the Revolution—Lenin—whose arm was raised to the sky in mocking greeting of anyone who came to the devastated monastery.

Everything about the scene said convincingly that there would never be any return to the past. The prophecies of St. Seraphim about the grand destiny of Diveyevo Monastery, which had been so beloved in all of Russian Orthodoxy, seemed to have been forever profaned and destroyed.

Nowhere in Diveyevo, neither within the town, nor in its surroundings, was there a single working church, not even the memory of a church—all had been utterly destroyed. And in the once renowned Monastery of Sarov, and in the towns around it, instead of a holy site, now one of the most top-secret and heavily guarded constructions of the Soviet Union was housed instead—a project known as Arzamas-16. Here nuclear weapons were made.

If any priests ever made a secret pilgrimage to Diveyevo, they hid their intentions, dressing in secular clothes. It was to no avail. The secret police would find them out anyway. In the year when I first visited the devastated monastery, two monks who came to pray and express their reverence for the holy relics of Diveyevo were arrested, cruelly beaten by the police, and then kept imprisoned for fifteen days in a jail cell, sleeping on a frozen floor.

That winter, Archimandrite Boniface, a wonderful and extremely kind monk from the famous Holy Trinity Monastery, asked me to accompany him on a trip to Diveyevo. According to our ecclesiastical rules, a priest who sets out on a journey with the Sacred Gifts of the Eucharist—the Body and Blood of Christ—must always be accompanied by someone, so as to help defend and protect the great Holy Gifts in the event of any emergency that might arise. And Father Boniface was on his way to Diveyevo in order to give Communion to a few old nuns still living in the area around the monastery—some of the last few still living in our time of the thousand who once inhabited the pre-Revolutionary convent.

To get there we had to take a train through Nizhny Novgorod, then called Gorky, and next drive by car to Diveyevo. In the train all night long Archimandrite Boniface could not sleep. Hung around his neck by a silken cord was a small sacred receptacle for the Holy Gifts. I was sleeping on a neighboring bunk, but from time to time would wake up at the sound of the wheels and see Father Boniface seated at table reading the New Testament in the dim night light of our train wagon.

We made it to Nizhny Novgorod, which was his home town, and stayed in his parents' house. Father Boniface gave me a seriously transformative book to read—the first volume of the works of Holy Hierarch Ignatius Brianchaninov—and all night long I couldn't sleep a wink, as I first discovered for myself that amazing Christian writer.

Next morning we set off for Diveyevo. We faced a drive of about eighty kilometers. Father Boniface tried to dress in a way so that no one would ever suspect him to be a priest: carefully tucking away the pleats and folds of his cassock beneath his coat, and hiding away his very long beard into his thick scarf and upturned collar.

It was already getting dark by the time we reached our destination. Looking out of our car window through the snowflakes whirling in a February storm, I was distressed to see the tall watchtower, wrecked dome, and ruined shells of the desecrated churches. Despite this mournful scene, I was still struck by the unusual power and secret energy of this great monastery. What's more, I had a sense that the Monastery of Diveyevo was not yet dead, but still alive with some ineffable spiritual life, well past the comprehension of this uncaring material world.

And so it turned out to be! In a ramshackle little hut on the outskirts of Diveyevo I saw something that I could have never imagined even in my most radiant dreams. I saw alive the Church Radiant, invincible and

St. Steraphim of Sarov.

indefatigable, youthful and joyful in the consciousness of its God, our Shepherd and Savior. It was then that I was struck by a great verse of the apostle Paul: "I can do all things through Christ which strengtheneth" (Philippians 4:13)!

And what's more, the most beautiful and unforgettable church service in my life took place then—not in some magnificent grand cathedral, not in some glorious ancient church hallowed with age, but in a nondescript building in the community center of Diveyevo, on Number 16, Lesnaya Street. It was not even a church at all, but an old bathhouse somehow vaguely converted into communal housing.

When I first arrived with Father Boniface, I saw a dingy little room crowded by about a dozen elderly women, the youngest of whom could not have been younger than eighty, while the oldest were definitely more than 100 years old. All of them were dressed in simple old country maids' clothes and wearing peasant kerchiefs. None of them was wearing a habit or any kind of monastic or ecclesiastical clothing. Of course, these weren't nuns—just simple old ladies; that's what anyone would have thought, including me, if I had not known that these old women were in fact some of the most courageous modern-day confessors of our faith, true heroines who had suffered tortures and decades in prisons and concentration camps for their beliefs. And yet despite all their ordeals, their spiritual loyalty and unshakable faith in God had only grown.

I was amazed to see how before my very eyes the venerable Father Boniface, an archimandrite and rector of the churches in the Patriarchal quarters of the Holy Trinity Monastery, a respected and well-known father confessor in Moscow, got down on his knees before blessing these old women, and bowed low to the floor! To be honest, I could not believe my eyes. But after lifting himself up from the floor, this priest fervently began to bless those old women who were hobbling up awkwardly to him, each in their turn. It was clear how truly delighted they were by his visit.

As Father Boniface and the old women were exchanging greetings, I looked around. Icons in ancient ceremonial frames, dimly lit by flickering lamps, were hung on the walls. One of them particularly attracted my attention. It was a large and beautiful icon of St. Seraphim of Sarov. The elder's face exuded such kindness and warmth that I could not tear my eyes away from him. As I found out later, that image had been painted right before the Revolution for the new Cathedral of Diveyevo, which they had never even had time to consecrate, and which only by miracle had been spared from complete desecration.

Meanwhile I started to prepare myself for the Vigil service. It took my breath away as the nuns started to take out of their secret hiding places and set down on the crudely put together wooden table genuine artifacts belonging to St. Seraphim himself. Here was the stole of his ecclesiastical vestment; there was his heavy iron cross on thick chains, worn for the mortification of the flesh, a leather glove, and the old-fashioned cast iron pot in which the saint had cooked his food. After the Revolution when the monastery was pillaged and destroyed, these holy relics had been passed down from sister to sister by the nuns of the Monastery of Diveyevo.

Having put on his vestments, Father Boniface gave the priest's pronouncement that begins the Vigil service. The nuns immediately perked up and began to sing. What a divine and utterly amazing choir they were!

"In the sixth tone! Lord, I have cried unto Thee, hearken unto me!" sang out one of the voices quavering with age; it was the canonarch nun, who was now 102 years old. She had been imprisoned and exiled for over twenty years. And all those wonderful sisters sang out together with her:

Mother Frosia (far left) with other Diveyevo nuns.

"Lord, I have cried unto Thee, hearken unto me! Hearken unto me, O Lord!"

There is no way to capture the sublimity of this service in words. Candles flickered, and the limitlessly kind and wise face of St. Seraphim looked down from his icon upon us . . . These incredible nuns sang the entire service virtually by heart. Only very rarely did one of them glance at the thick old books, for which they needed to use not just eyeglasses but gigantic magnifying glasses with wooden handles. They had risked death or punishment saying this service in concentration camps and prisons and places of exile. They said it even now after all their sufferings, here in Diveyevo, settling into their wretched hovels on the outskirts of the town. For them it was nothing unusual, and yet for me I could scarcely understand whether I was in Heaven or on Earth.

These aged nuns were possessed of such incredible spiritual strength, such prayer, such courage, such modesty, goodness, and love, and they were full of such faith, that it was then at that wonderful service that I understood that they with their faith would triumph over everything— over our godless government despite all its power, over the faithlessness of this world, and over death itself, of which they had absolutely no fear.

Mother Frosya in her house on Lesnaya Street.

Mother Frosya

*I*N THAT LITTLE house on Lesnaya Street in Diveyevo where the relics of St. Seraphim were kept, there lived a schema-nun named Margarita. Except that for many, many years nobody knew that she was secretly a nun. Everybody just called her Mother Frosya or just simply Frosya. She was as old as the century itself. When I met her in February 1983 on my first trip to Diveyevo, she had just turned eighty-three years old.

"Secret monasticism" is something that began to happen during the persecutions of the Church of the twentieth century. Having been secretly given monastic vows, monks and nuns would remain living in the world, would wear normal secular clothes, and would work in normal secular institutions, while strictly fulfilling all their monastic vows in secret. Only a father confessor or spiritual father would know about their vows and about their new names. Because of the climate of severe persecution, even when taking Communion in parish churches, these ascetics would always name themselves by their worldly names and not by the names given to them upon taking their monastic vows.

For example, the famous Russian philosopher and scholar Alexey Fyodorovich Losev secretly became a monk. In taking his monastic vows he became the monk Andronicus. Usually in all his photographs Professor Losev is shown in some kind of strange black cap and wearing glasses with enormous lenses. Alexey Fyodorovich wore these glasses because, after several years in the labor camps along the White Sea–Baltic Sea Canal, he nearly went blind. But he wore that strange black cap not because—as everyone else thought—he was afraid of catching a cold. No. It was a *skufia,* or clerical cap—the only object he received when taking his monastic vows that the secret monk Andronicus permitted himself to wear all the time.

After the war, another period in the history of the Russian Orthodox Church began: gradually churches and monasteries began to open again. It seemed as if the idea of the secret taking of vows and secret monasticism had begun to lose its meaning. But then the well-known law of history proved once more that history indeed repeats itself, first as a tragedy and then as a farce.

223

In our ecclesiastical circles we hear stories of how sometimes during the service some woman dressed all in black would stream purposefully through a humbled crowd of parishioners, rushing to be first to take Communion. And as it is customary for a communicant in the Orthodox church to state his or her name before the chalice, she would declare for all to hear: "Secret nun Lukeria!"

Metropolitan Pitirim once told me a joke that was still making the rounds during the 1950s. A woman in Moscow came to visit her friend, who was playing solitaire, laying the cards out on the table. The guest nervously whispered: "Maria Petrovna! Maria Petrovna! I'm not allowed to tell anyone! It's such a secret, such a secret! But I'll tell you . . . Yesterday I secretly became a nun with a new name of Concordia." But her hostess kept on dealing out the cards, quite unimpressed, and said, "What's the big deal? I received the great schema two years ago!" Of course, she won—a schema-nun is higher than a mere nun.

Everyone thought that Mother Frosya had simply once been just a novice in the former monastery. And if any curious persons would ask her questions about her past, Mother Frosya would answer completely honestly that there once had been a time when she was a novice in the Monastery of Diveyevo.

She was only forced to reveal her true monastic name in the beginning of the 1990s, with the blessing of Abbess Sergia, the first appointed abbess of the resurrected Diveyevo Monastery, to which Mother Frosya moved back for her last three years before her death. But until this time everyone just called her Frosya. And she herself was quite self-deprecating and unassuming. One might even say she was disparaging of herself at times.

Once when I was working in the Patriarchal publishing department, we published a beautiful illustrated magazine devoted entirely to St. Seraphim and the history of Diveyevo Monastery. This was the first edition of its kind ever in the Soviet Union. During the first chance I got, I brought this magazine to show it to Mother Frosya. It was shiny, elegant, modern, sparkling with color; it seemed like something totally alien in that ramshackle little hut on Lesnaya Street. Nonetheless she was delighted by the journal, and she began to look at all the pictures and leaf through the pages with great curiosity.

"Oh! Father Seraphim!" she exclaimed, waving her arms as she saw the beautiful icon of her beloved saint. "Mother Alexandra! Our dear nurse!" She cried out joyously as she recognized the portrait of the first abbess of

the Diveyevo Monastery, Agafya Semyonovna Melgunova. Mother Frosya was perfectly acquainted with the 200-year history of her monastery. "And here is Nikolai Alexandrovich Motovilov!"

Finally Mother Frosya got to the very last page where her very own picture had been placed. For a moment she lost the gift of speech, and then, waving her arms with most sincere indignation she cried out: "Frosya! Are you here too? Oh my shameless eyes!"

Even during my very first trip with Father Boniface, Mother Frosya had asked me as I left to please come back soon and help her repair her roof and barn. I promised her that I would, and later that summer I came back to Diveyevo along with two friends of mine. We slept in her barn on the hay and all day long worked making repairs for her. During the evenings we walked through the ruins of the monastery and prayed with those incredible nuns and listened to the incredible, incomparable stories of Mother Frosya. She told us the history of the old town of Diveyevo, and of how during all the long decades of Soviet persecution, throughout all the jails and concentration camps and exiles, the Monastery of Diveyevo remained under the protection of St. Seraphim, and remained so even now, with the convent all in ruins. It was clear that she wished to recount all that she remembered, so that her story would not die with her.

Schemanun Margarita (Mother Frosya).

The True Story of Mother Frosya

Audiotaped on my ancient cassette recorder and laboriously
typed up by me with just a few minor corrections.

*W*HEN I WAS still just a little girl, I suddenly had a desire—never
to get married!

My father used to get drunk a lot. Sometimes, when he didn't come
home until morning, we knew he'd be drunk, a-hollering and carrying
on something awful all night. And Mama and I would be stuck waiting,
trembling . . .

Suddenly we would hear "clap!" Dad opening the gates. Daddy
stumbling home. Drunk.

He'd walk in. "Gimme my dinner!" he'd yell—didn't matter what time
of day it was, dinnertime or breakfast time. He would yell. And Mom
would give him dinner.

It didn't matter whether or not Dad liked his dinner. Like it or not,
he'd throw his plate right at Mama's head!

I had a good long look at all of this, and I said to myself: "O Heavenly
Queen! Save me please from ever getting married!"

We used to have a neighbor named Ulita. Somewhere she'd lost two
fingers. And I used to think to myself—"Lord, tear something off of me,
too, just as long as I never get married! Otherwise, whether I like it or not,
they'll marry me off!"

I would always pray only to the Virgin Mary. I would beg of her:
"Dear Mother of God, please, deliver me!" But I never told anyone about
it. Only Mom.

Then came the time when my cousin Grisha and my Aunt Maria, my
father's sister, were leaving for the monastery—one to Sarov, the other to
Diveyevo. They were older than me; I was still young, but I begged them:
"Please take me with you!" But they didn't want to take me.

I prayed "O Heavenly Queen, Mother of God! If they don't take me
with them now, I'll run away anyway." That was my mood. I didn't want
to live a worldly life anymore.

They were already getting ready to leave. I was trembling with fear and prayed: "Dear Father Seraphim! Help me!"

There had been a moment when neither my mother nor my father was working. It was some kind of minor feast day. And then my Mom, though afraid to speak, spoke up anyway: "You know, Dad, Masha and Grisha are both heading off to the monastery . . ."

"So what?"

"Why don't we let Frosya tag along with them as well?"

"What? Are you crazy?"

They didn't say another word. Mom was afraid to say anything more. Dad was so stern and strict. Nobody said anything.

Dad said nothing, nothing at all . . . Then suddenly he said: "Frosya! Did you hear what your mom was talking about?"

"I did."

"Well?"

"I don't mind. I'll go . . ."

That's all I said. Then I shut up. I was trembling inside, praying, "Queen of Heaven! My fate is being decided! Father Seraphim, please help!"

But my father grew very thoughtful . . . After all, he did have the fear of God within him. And without saying anything to anyone, this is what he decided.

We had three calves. Dad was keeping them. There were three girls in our family that needed to be married off. One calf each was needed for each of their dowries. That's the way it was in the old days. They would marry a girl off and pay a cow for her dowry.

So my dad took the cow that he had been saving for my dowry and brought her to the market to sell her. And, as he later explained: "I made a little bet with myself. For your calf I will ask double the price. If they pay, I'll let you go to Diveyevo. But if not, if they all laugh at me, you're staying home."

Well, he got there. And he looked around. He could see the whole fairground was full of cattle. So full that he took his place on the far edge of the fairground.

"I looked all around," says he, "and what good was our little calf? There were lots of other calves much bigger and better! But scarcely had I looked around when suddenly in rushes some old man in a homespun coat, with his hat sort of tilted to one side. And he didn't look to his right or to his left, and he didn't ask anyone anything, but instead he came straight up to me. 'That's a mighty fine calf you got there!' says he. 'How much are you charging for it?' At first I didn't even know what to say, but just spit out double the real price—twenty-four whole rubles! Twenty-four! And the very most you could possibly have ever gotten for a calf like that was maybe twelve rubles. But the old man even seemed to be as delighted as I was. 'All right,' says he. And we shook hands."

The old man led away the calf. Meanwhile Dad was amazed. He just stood there holding the money in his hands.

He came home. And said nothing. Just started his dinner. Mom gives him his food, and Dad asks her: "Well? Is Masha going to Diveyevo?"

"She is," says Mom.

"And is Grisha going to Sarov?"

"He is."

"And Frosya?"

"That depends on what you—"

Dad just looked at Mom and said: "Pack her things!"

So off we went. It was the fifth of May. The year was 1915.

*   *   *

Well, we got to Diveyevo. There was so much that I loved about the place! Everything was so clean and neat and organized! Not one moment wasted. Beautiful little bridges had been built from the monastic cells leading straight into the church. Yes, it was lovely! And the singing! It was as if angels were singing. There were a lot of sisters for our choir, plenty from which to choose! At least one thousand of us sisters. The task they gave to me was to look after the calves by a cottage on the far grounds of the monastery over by the little river Satis. There we lived.

Now my Aunt Masha soon went home. She didn't stay in the monastery . . . because—you want to know what our conditions were like? They didn't even give us so much as a shirt, not even so much as a rag. Whatever you had taken out of your parents' house, that's what you were supposed to wear. Then my cousin Grisha left the Sarov Monastery after about a year and a half.

I do remember once, though, that cousin Grisha came to visit me over in Satis. Actually it wasn't to visit me; they had driven over for some hay. Grisha saw me mucking around with the calves, in old bast peasant shoes called *lapty*, and he laughed at me: "Ha! You're wearing *lapty?* I wouldn't put them on for nothin'!"

That's what he said! Monks had their own official clothes back then, and even their own boots were given to them. And he was full of pride about this. And you want to know how he proved himself a real "lord" to his little cousin? He gave me a whole ten-kopeck coin!

The nuns all laughed about that later, saying, the rich kid gave his cousin ten kopecks! Never mind, Lord save him. He was just swelling, bursting with pride! I guess it just wasn't his fate to become a monk. Because he suddenly was overcome by depression. Nope. He didn't stay in the monastery. Not him. He couldn't stick it. But the Lord gave me strength and I stayed. Yes!

But Grisha, he didn't get it at all. When he got home, he told my parents how I was wearing nothing but *lapty* bast shoes, and how tough things were for me! Mama burst out into tears. And they sat down to dinner, and Grisha took a piece of bread in his hands and said: "Here is the real kingdom of heaven! But over there—there's nothing!"

Imagine that, comparing a simple piece of bread with the Kingdom of Heaven! Well, that only made Mom blubber all the more.

But that Grisha, why, he hadn't even seen anything of the real life of a monk! And the tasks they'd given him were real easy—just baking bread rolls. Sometimes the bishop would come to serve, and Grisha's job was to hold his staff. He had real long flowing hair all the way down to his shoulders. And the Devil, he sowed confusion in him. But Grisha didn't get it. Nope!

You know what, my boys? I'll tell you something, forgive me, for Christ's sake! Do you all want to live in a monastery? You do? Well, listen up, here's the first thing you need to know: never judge anyone, not the monks, nor their superiors. Judge not, lest ye be judged.

As soon as you start judging others, there's no way you'll last. You'll fly right out of there in a jiffy!

Not so long ago some hierodeacon named Vasily came to see us, from the Holy Trinity Monastery. My, my! What things I heard him say! Those monks are no good, says he. They're living all wrong. And this isn't right, and that isn't right—and it's all wrong, it's all wrong!

"Just you wait!" I told him; "watch out—you yourself won't last in the monastery."

And that's just what happened. He left the monastery. Yes, indeed. Here is the commandment: if you see some monk or hieromonks or superior doing something wrong or committing some sin, your job is to pay no attention at all! Turn away, and don't look at anyone! Let them sin as much as they like. As our father, St. Seraphim, used to say, "Let them live and eat our bread for the time being. But when the time comes, the Lord Himself will cast them out!" So listen carefully, beware of condemning people. Do not judge others. That's not for us. The Lord Himself will fix everyone.

Otherwise, who cares what flaws each of us have? That's not any of your business. Don't snoop, don't pry. Don't look at him. Look away! No one should judge him. That's right! But my Grisha wasn't like that at all. Instead he judged everybody: this is wrong and that is wrong and this is no good and that's the way it's supposed to be . . . What kind of monk is that? So the Lord upped and tossed him out—threw him right out of the monastery. Listen, you—if you want to live in a godly way, live that way yourself.

Except for this. As our blessed elder Sister Agatha used to say, "Pray every step you take, pray, Holy Queen of Heaven, preserve my virginity, do not deprive me of the Kingdom of Heaven, do not drive me out of your holy monastery! Just keep saying that over and over and you'll live, though there are many enemies all over the place."

Once I saw a painting of St. Seraphim in which all around him are horrible beasts—vicious crocodiles surrounding him. But he's just standing there and praying. Did you ever see it? Well, you know what those crocodiles really are? Demons, and human passions. Now, prayer saves everyone. But if instead you judge others you won't last anywhere—that is repugnant to God. Watch instead what you're doing yourself!

But this is how I pray now: "O Queen of Heaven, my death is coming . . . Don't abandon me!" Yes, only she, the Queen of Heaven, saves and delivers us all, and helps you always no matter where you are. I was in jails and in concentration camps and in exile . . . And all the while I just prayed and sang to myself, "O victorious Leader of the Heavenly Hosts!"

I just prayed, prayed like that, and the Lord delivered me.

* * *

At the time we were living in the cottages by Satis. We had lots of land there. Someone had donated it to us. And we had lots of cattle. I looked after the calves.

Russian nuns cutting the hay.

One time they brought us a cow from Sarov. They wanted us to raise cows like theirs: gray-colored, big, healthy, strapping cows! But ours were sort of reddish in color and not very big. We took special care of this new calf from Sarov. For two years we didn't allow it to go out into the general herd. We only let it out in the third year.

Anyway, when this calf was still only two years old one day it heard the lowing of the big herd of the other cows on the other side of the river. Those cows were all mooing. How excited my little calf became! She pulled and strained, wanting to get over to them, to the other cows in the big herd. But it wasn't allowed.

I ran after her! I ran and ran, but that calf just plopped right into the river Satis, and swam. And the Satis is pretty deep, actually. But that calf swam right across it to the other side and ran up towards the big herd.

I was stuck on the other bank! I fell to my knees and cried out loud: "Dear Father Seraphim! Can't you see what's happening? That calf's run away!"

Yes, there I was—insulting the saint himself in that very same tone of voice! "Can't you see what's happening?"

And guess what? That calf suddenly stopped and stood still! As if frozen! Then it turned around gradually and slowly, step by step, climbed back down and came back to me. It was as if someone was dragging her! And then she went into the river and slowly swam all the way, back!

When she got back to our side of the river, I was waiting for her with a rope. "Oh you mischievous little beast! You sure made trouble for me!" But I understand that it was really Father Seraphim who stopped her!

That calf never got up to any of those tricks again. And what a wonderful and lovely calf it turned out to be! But soon, we were the ones driven like calves out of Satis.

Oh yes, terrible times came upon us. First the big war came, and then they overthrew the Tsar. It was the Revolution. You never lived through that. You have no idea what it was really like.

At first they spared the monastery, but they robbed the farmsteads. They came to rob us too. And now it was our turn to suffer. But who was robbing us? Our own villagers! From our own village: Lomasovo, which is about six kilometers from Satis. We called the men and women from this village "Lomas-folk." But what was it they wanted? To rob us and take everything!

But we were forewarned about what was going to happen. From the monastery they sent workers to us at Satis to drive the cattle into the monastery. Otherwise tomorrow they would be gone—taken away. And so, all night—all night, dear fathers, all night!—we drove the herd. Oh, what trouble we had with the cows—not to mention the calves! Some of them were only five days old, and we had to load them onto carts and drag them. There were many cows, and many calves.

Then we lost our way as we were walking through the woods. And the woods were thick—impenetrable. Oh, how we suffered! We thought it wouldn't be a long walk, but in the end, as it happened, we wandered some twenty kilometers, perhaps. We also passed an estate in which the nobleman and landowner Lazhkin had lived. On that estate he had owned a winery. The peasants had already begun to pillage it, marauding from all around, and drinking—swilling everything! Several people were drowned in the liquor vats; many others were burned by the alcohol.

It was complete and utter anarchy, and everyone was trying to cram in, and get in absolutely everywhere they could.

Yes, and the cows could scarcely walk, and the calves were tired, and falling by the wayside. What took place then—oh! I can never forget it!

But we all made it to Diveyevo somehow by seven o'clock. The late Liturgy was going on, and here we were all lumbering in here with the cows. We drove all the cattle into the horse yard. Somehow all were safe and sound. But then our Mother Superior ordered us all to go back. So we had a spot of tea and left.

My friend (a girl named Pasha) and I hadn't slept for a whole day and night, yet we walked, walked, walked. We were so tired—no more strength—that we said to each other, 'Let's sit for a bit.' So we sat down right on the road and immediately fell asleep. I don't know how long we slept. No idea, because we were very tired. And suddenly a peasant came riding up to us on a cart. He yelled and screamed at us, telling us to get off the road, but we couldn't hear him—not even if we were run over. We were sleeping. So what did he do? He started just lashing us with his whip! We were terrified. "Lord Jesus Christ! Where are we? In hell?" Woods and woods for miles around, and we couldn't understand . . . we were terrified.

"Mister, please tell us, for the love of Christ, where are we? Where have we ended up?" And he curses. And rides past. Well, and may God take you!

And we sat there. With great effort we pulled ourselves together, remembered where we had come from, where we were going. Then we saw that we were not far from the place where the "Lomas-folk" were busy robbing the winery. I guess the peasant on his cart had been riding off there.

We saw them dragging out the pots and braziers and rolling-pins and beaters, and also just stealing everything that had ever been in Lazhkin's home. And they were drunk. Well, we couldn't go down that road. They would kill us. Are you kidding? Nuns! We could hear them yelling: "Now we'll go get those church mice!"

And so, as fast as we could, we made it back somehow to our girls. Our sisters were waiting for us. "What took you so long?"

We told the whole story, how we got lost, how we fell asleep, how we made it back. And we told them that the peasants would be coming any minute to rob us next. Barely had we finished telling our story when we heard the sisters yelling: "The Lomas-folk are here. With their red flag!"

They burst in. How many of them there were! We had a granary over there. And they went straight for it. "Give us the keys!"

Our eldest came up to them. "All right. I'll give them to you now. What is it you need?"

A bonfire of icons.

"We need everything! All of it. We'll take all the grain. Give us all you have!" The poor old nun—she had thought they were going to spare us! No way!

They forced open the granary. Inside it were wheat and grains and flour. They were just pouring it all out, spilling it everywhere. Were these the kind of people to wait and pour out measures? No, they kicked and dragged us out, and then started pouring everything out in a mess, a frenzy. They took away everything! Stole it all!

One guy even dove right into the bins, into the flour! How crazy! Funny enough to cry. He was all white! And they were pouring and pouring out all the sacks.

Then suddenly we hear: "boom-boom!" Bullets, shooting. What's happening? We look over yonder, and we can see the peasants from Vertyansk have risen up to defend the monastery and drive off the "Lomas-folk."

We scream: "Save us! They're going to kill us!" And the Vertyansk-folk answered: "Silly geese! Why are you yelling? It's not you who'll get killed, but those folk over there!"

But they didn't kill anyone, thank God. They just fired over our heads.

But they did manage to drive off those "Lomas-folk." Still, how much had those Lomas-folk managed to steal? What a robbery! Lord save us!

It was fall already. October . . .* 1917. Yes, it was already getting cold. We had already gotten ready for the winter: mushrooms, cabbages. And I can remember as if it were right now: a peasant comes up and dives right into our cellar, dragged out the little vats and a couple of buckets. The peasant really liked the little vat. The very best mushrooms we had were stored there. And what did the peasant do? Shook them all out, and not even sparing his own bast shoes, began to stamp-stamp-stamp, stamping them all into the ground, those lovely mushrooms! So that nobody would get them! Because he didn't need the mushrooms, he just wanted the little vat.

There was also a Tatar there. He also seemed to like the little vats, except he preferred a different one, which had tomatoes in it. "What's this stuff?" he asks.

And there was one nun there, a quick-witted girl from Mordovia, who answered: "That's our medicine."

"For what?"

"When the cows get lice, we use these to wash them." She said it with a straight face. And he believed her. He didn't understand what tomatoes were.

We had had lots of nice dishes for milk and dairy products, excellent quality glassware. Oh Lord! One lad climbed up to the attic, and sees the bottles there. Shoves them into a sack.

Lumbering down the ladder, knock-knock-knock, one by one they were all smashed. Dumps everything out in our yard. "I know where I can get some more!" And back he went.

And all of them were drunk! They'd swilled themselves silly with the liquor from Lazhkin's winery. I can't even begin to tell you all the lunacy they got up to! Right in the yard one man completely passed out. So drunk he was blue! Lord have mercy on us, sinners!

And then some sort of . . . "authority" appeared. This "authority" was about fourteen men. They held their meeting right in our large kitchen. They were discussing what to do with the alcoholic spirits. And they said:

---

* The Julian calendar in use in pre–Revolutionary Russia was thirteen days behind the Gregorian calendar used in the West. Thus, the Bolshevik October Revolution of October 25, 1917, took place on November 7, 1917, according to the modern Gregorian calendar. —TRANS.

"If we leave them just here where they are, who knows what the folks here will get up to?"

So they decided to empty all the spirits out. Just spill them out. Just like that! Right into the ground. But the others were against this. "Alcohol! We need it. It comes in handy everywhere. It's medicine, after all."

And the others said: "No! Not now. At this time we can't keep spirits anywhere near the people. Otherwise the people here will get up to all kinds of drunken mischief."

And so in the end they decided to pour out all of the spirits. We'd made them from potatoes. People had brought their potatoes to us in our distillery and we had made white vodka. But now…before pouring out all our spirits into the ground, these "authorities" came up to us and said: "Have you got any bottles?"

We did have bottles. Big bottles, full of holy water. We showed them to these fellows.

"What've you got in there?" they asked. "Holy water."

They grabbed the bottles—and poured them out. Right on the floor. What did they care about holy water? And then they filled our bottles full of our spirits. For themselves. What was left of the spirits they poured into the ground. Right into the sand.

After this, the peasant men and women from all the neighboring villages came to wash out the sand. And drank it! And how many peasants were drowned at that time in the distillery! One somehow fell leg first into a large tank, and was burned up like a piece of coal in the alcohol! There were many horrors like this.

And so they robbed the whole of Satis, and kicked us out. Oh yes. When was this? That's right. 1917. Just when the Revolution was beginning.

But they closed the monastery only in 1927. By that time it wasn't quite so frightening then, because at least there was some sort of government in place.

All of the other monasteries in the neighborhood had been pillaged and destroyed, but until now they hadn't touched ours. Somebody in Moscow had helped us somehow. They whispered to us: "You all stick around and don't go anywhere yet. Hold on."

And we set up a workshop and we started calling ourselves not a monastery, but a workshop. But then in 1927, the authorities demanded that our Mother Superior hand over the list of all our sister nuns, and all of their personal documents.

Sisters of Diveyevo.

Then we answered: "But we don't have any personal documents!" And it was the truth. We were always accepted into the monastery without documents.

Of course they did count us. Yes, they knew how many of us there were. Before the Revolution there had been more than 1,000 of us nuns. I myself had already gotten there in 1915. And the only thing they had asked me then was: "Whose girl are you, and where might you be from?"

And in the monastery there was a girl from our village named Agatha who was just a bit older than me. So I said: "I'm from the same village as Agatha."

"Oh! From Agatha's village!" And that was it. That was the whole document about me. It just said, "From Agatha's village."

Some of the older women told me that when the nuns lived there in the time of St. Seraphim, around 150 years ago, St. Seraphim told the sisters: "The time will come when my orphans will be cast through the Nativity Gates like peas!" This always mystified us, and we wondered, "What Nativity Gates? There aren't any gates by that name in our monastery!"

And then in 1927—it was just on the occasion of one of our patronal feast days—the Nativity of the Mother of God. I remember it was two o'clock in the afternoon, time for Small Vespers. At the time I was one of the bellringers. Off we went to ring the bells in the bell tower. Just as I was opening the lock—ouch! Somebody grabbed my arm. Oh Lord! A "red hat!" The militia! I hadn't seen him coming. He grabbed that lock and hung on to it, and wouldn't let us open it, wouldn't let us go up to the bell tower.

"Halt!" he yelled.

And I said: "What do you mean 'halt'? It's time for us to ring the bells!"

"It may be time for *you* to ring the bells" says he, "but it isn't time for us!"

The choir girls ran up asking: "What's wrong? Why aren't you ringing the bells?"

"This 'red hat' fellow over there isn't letting us!"

They didn't let us ring the bells for the feast day. Instead they let us have just seven days to collect all our things.

This was in 1927 in September. It was 8th of September according to the old-style calendar. I don't know what day it was according to the new style. It was the Feast of the Nativity of the Mother of God, September 8th. And suddenly our sisters remembered:

"St. Seraphim used to say. 'The time will come when my orphans will be cast through the Nativity Gates like peas!' And here we are on the gates of the Nativity being cast out into the world! That's what he meant by the Nativity Gates." So we remembered the words of our saint.

Then the nuns asked: "So you're allowing us seven days before we have to finish up and leave? Does that mean we can have our services and ring the bells?"

"Heck! Whatever." They didn't refuse us.

One week later, before the final Evening Vespers we rang all the bells, sounding all their chimes, all of them—letting them ring for the last time. We rang and rang them, and then we said our Divine Service. Then we were scattered like little birds, scattered to the wind! Just like that—in the pouring rain. The cops came and kicked us out into the street! Lord! We were getting it from everywhere: from the people on one side, and God on the other. Oh, Queen of Heaven!

What could we do? It was impossible for us to wear our nuns' habits anymore. The authorities had forbidden it. So we had to wear secular clothes. And all icons were forbidden. They made us put up pictures of Lenin instead. None of us would agree to that!

Everything had been collected in the Tikhvin Church for the building of a new cathedral. But everything that had been there they started to loot right in front of us: vestments, crosses, . . . they stole everything, absolutely everything . . .

And the peasants whom they had forced to come with their carts to collect all our treasures were miserable, and said: "We brought everything here with joy for the building of a new cathedral; but now as we're taking it all away, we aren't joyful at all." At this point, some of those peasants bent their heads and even began to weep. What a mournful sight it was! But all they could do was weep. What could they do against the power of the Soviet government?

On the second day, they took our Mother Superior off to jail. And we got scattered all over. There was a bishop there secretly, and he said to us all, "They drove you out of the monastery. But we have not released you from your monastic vows."

I don't know about other people, but this is what we nuns thought: "All of this is a scourge, a punishment from God. The Lord has set up this government against us!"

* * *

It was the year 1937. I and several of the other nuns were still living near the monastery. I was right here on Kalganovka Street. And on the other side of the street there were also little houses in which nuns were living . . . Some of them were so afraid of going to jail that they got married . . . Lord save them!

But this time they came for us and put us in jail. They had this system of three judges, well, sort of, called a troika. I remember they were sitting in a smallish room, three really big men. Suddenly one militia man brings in twenty women, all of whom are nuns. The three judges look at him and say, "Whoa, brother! So many at once!"

"There's plenty more where they came from! I know where to find them!"

"All right, girls!" Girls!

"You know you're guilty! Now, what are you guilty of? Hmm? Well? Did you ever go to church?"

"We did."

"List them as 'vagabonds,'" says the judge. That was our crime—we were "vagabonds"!

They took us away to Tashkent. They locked us up in cattle cars, and shipped us, just like cattle . . . The cars were drafty and horrible. I got sick in the cattle car. The whole time I was crying: "Lord, what am I in jail for? Why did you make me a jailbird?"

I was very upset to have been imprisoned. So I was crying. Actually everyone was crying, probably. Once the train started moving, the wind blew through the cattle cars with freezing drafts and I caught a cold immediately, and from all my crying, my face got all swollen. How they brought us to Tashkent I already don't remember. I can't remember anything, except that I ended up in the hospital. That's probably what saved me, so I didn't die. I stayed alive . . .

Then they brought us to Tashkent, to a bare field, where there was nothing, and said "work" . . . We built a whole city. Working like slaves, without pay.

They used to do what was called the general inspection . . . They made us walk down a long dark file of soldiers. On both sides guards with guns and bayonets were standing. It was terrifying! So many guards! They had dogs barking at us. And for what? What were they afraid of? Us nuns? And so we had to walk, walk, walk in single file past those guards and dogs . . . Keep going or else. And at the end—search them! We were searched! They took everything from us! They took away our crosses! Lord forgive them! Oh, Mother of God . . . One policeman ripped off my neck cross, then threw it on the ground and trampled on it, barking at me: "Why are you wearing that?"

You know, when they were taking away our crosses, the feeling I had— it was as if our Lord and Savior himself were standing there crucified, suffering and enduring it all Himself! They took away our crosses! How could they? It was so awful!"

And then what? How could we live without our crosses? Well, in those days we all were set to work as seamstresses, using locally picked Uzbek cotton. They had these little forklike twigs, those cotton balls, and if you cut them a little bit they were like little crosses. So we all made ourselves little crosses. But then we went with our makeshift crosses into the prison bathhouse. Some of the women there ratted us out to the bosses: "Those nuns are wearing crosses again!"

But they didn't bother taking away our little homemade crosses. There was no point. Take them away and we'd make new ones.

And the Lord strengthened us! One of the nuns from Diveyevo had been put into this jail before us, and she told us how she saw St. Seraphim in a dream. Father Seraphim was leading a whole bunch of nuns here to the jail, and he was saying cheerfully: "Open the doors! I'm bringing your sisters to you!" And that was us!

But before we were arrested, there was a holy woman who had lived with us in Diveyevo named Maria Ivanovna. I was with her when she was dying—that was soon after they drove us out of the monastery. All of us were asking her then: "Dearest Mother, when can we go back to the monastery? We want to go back to the monastery!"

She said: "You'll get your monastery. You will. Our late Mother Treasurer and I will be summoning you soon to the monastery."

And you want to know what else she said? "But in this monastery they won't call you out by name, but instead by number. And so, Frosya, our Mother Treasurer and I will call for you, and we'll cry out three hundred and thirty-eight."

Three hundred thirty-eight. I was surprised by that, but I remembered. But then . . . When I got put in jail, that was the number they gave me. Yes, she predicted it, blessed Maria Ivanovna! "That'll be your monastery!"

Anyway, those were the times we lived in. We had to put up with lots of things. We couldn't openly keep the fasts. Lord forgive us. They boiled us some kind of soup made out of bones. But we manage to keep the Lenten Fast. We drank just the water or ate what is allowed . . . But we didn't eat forbidden stuff, like milk or meat . . .

Nonetheless it was good that so many of us nuns were there. Forty of us together. What a feast day—crammed in together on our prison camp plank boards for sleeping! It was on the Feast of the Annunciation! Lord have mercy! What a crowd, how crammed in we all were! On the bottom sleeping boards all the criminals were spread out. Bully girls. They were totally in charge. But though we were on the top planks we were much happier than they were. May God be with them! Some of our group had been in the choir. And so sometimes we would gather together on the top prison planks and we would just quietly sing the Annunciation hymn—"The Voice of the Archangel."

Several of them in there knew everything by heart, the church services, the Akathists, so it didn't matter that they didn't let us have any books. Yes, they took all our holy books away.

Then there was a time that we were shipped off to some transfer camp. The trip took forever, and in the train wagon next to us were all criminals and bullies. And how they fought! The nuns were in a separate car, but the criminals smashed up all their prison planks. Then they kicked one of their own bullies out and put her in with us after they roughed her up. And she was . . . almost totally naked. She was hardly wearing anything. She didn't even have a little pouch. She had nothing. All us nuns had our little pouches, with a spare shirt or a piece of bread and bits and pieces of what we needed. And the criminal girls, they didn't have anything . . .

So we started to feel sorry for her. Somebody gave her some spare bits of bread, and they fed her. Somebody gave her a spare skirt, somebody gave her a headscarf, and by the end she was fully dressed . . .

Anyway, we kept on riding and riding that train. And suddenly a soldier opens the door. By now it wasn't the Bolsheviks who were guarding us, no, it was just simple soldiers.

"Well, sisters, how are you?" he asked. "All's well, thank God!"

"Any of you need anything? Any of you sick?" "No, nothing. We'll get through it!"

And this hooligan girl whom we had just dressed suddenly tried to rat on us and said: "Citizen overseer! These nuns are all still praying to God and singing!"

And he answers: "Well, that's good then! Why don't you sing with them? That's why they were arrested, so let them pray."

There was a soldier in each train car, sitting in guarding us. We were in the wagon, and the soldier was above us and guarding us. And it was cold up there. We could hear him pacing and pacing, jumping up and down and stamping his feet. And we all felt sorry for him: "Lord, here we are warm inside, and he's up there freezing cold, guarding us!"

And soon as the train moved off again, that soldier would knock and yell: "Hey! Sisters! Sing the song 'Our Lady!' "

We didn't know what he meant exactly, but we would sing the hymn from the beginning of Liturgy, "Bless the Lord, O my soul." Or some other hymn. And always, just as our train began the move, although he didn't know what to call it, he would yell: "Sing the song 'Our Lady!' Don't be scared!"

Yes, my Lord, some of them were good lads. There were all different kinds there.

Later they brought us nuns to their children's shelter. They had the shelter attached to the prison. Their mothers were in the camps. There was no way those poor children could be trusted to the criminal girls. Give them half a chance and they would kill a child and not think twice about it. So they had us nuns brought over there to take care of the kids.

And we were happy over there! When it was Easter time, as soon as we had put the little ones to sleep, we would gather at midnight in that room . . . I don't remember what they called it—oh yes! The Pavilion! The kids used to play in the Pavilion in the afternoon. And we gathered there quietly, and we would sing: "Thy Resurrection, O Christ our Savior . . ." And "Christ Is Risen . . ." Quietly, so no one would hear.

But one time the nurse and the director heard us. "Where's that singing coming from? They're singing like angels!"

So they went and found us. "So it's you singing!"

We got so scared! And the director was Jewish. But she didn't say a word to anyone. "It's all right. Just sing quietly."

We also had occasion to baptize the children. Oh! Lord forgive me! I should have told the priests about it! We used to baptize the kids while we were bathing them. We would say the prayers: "I believe . . ." And besides that some other prayers too. I've already forgotten which. We used to baptize four kids at the same time. Unless the children were sick, because we didn't want infection to spread. There was so much disease there, so much sickness and so much neglect!

That's how it was. And how many kids died there? So many!

Finally we were let out of that place.

Oh my dear Lord God! What didn't we get up to then? How much there was to do in this life! We would spin, and we would sew, we would look after kids, and we would educate them. We, we nuns!

Oh, prison life! It pities no one. You know what they say: "Whoever's not been, will be there yet; whoever has been—will not forget!"

Now I just have one more ordeal to endure . . . Lord, save me! Queen of Heaven!

I've been babbling on to you a whole lot!"

* * *

As she walked with us to the station and said her goodbyes to us, Mother Frosya stopped, undid her handkerchief, and took out from a folded pleat of her cassock a tiny little wooden cross.

"I've kept it here. All these years. I never lost it. My little cross—a gift

from my jail. Here. It's just a little simple piece of wood. You know what? I'll tell you simply, in plain words. If I don't talk fancy, don't you fuss about that! All of you were prisoners for seventy years. You do understand that, don't you? Yes all of us, all of us were prisoners of the Soviet authorities. It was one big prison. I don't know what'll come next. Which way will we go? But I heard someone say—I won't tell you his name, but this is what he said—

"The reign of the Children of Ham has ended!"

Mother Frosya.

While Visiting Mother Frosya

$\mathcal{S}$EVERAL YEARS PASSED. I was already an ordained priest. One winter, in my priestly capacity, I had to go visit the restored Diveyevo Monastery. When I was done with my business in the monastery I immediately rushed to see Mother Frosya in her house on Lesnaya Street. But the gate to her house that I knew so well was locked up with a great big lock. I thought this was strange: after all, she was already ninety-two years old at this point and never went out.

Pulling up the folds of my cassock, I scrambled over the fence. When I knocked at her door, Mother Frosya told me that these days they locked her up in her home and wouldn't even give her the keys, because she had so many visitors that she was literally besieged from dawn to midnight.

But we did want to see each other. So Mother opened the window and I crawled up through like Romeo.

"Tikhon! I know that you're already a priest!" That was the first thing she said to me. "Quickly, take my confession, because I can't give my confession to any of these married priests!"

After her confession, she had me sit down at her table and began to fuss over me: she scrambled some eggs, and warmed up some potatoes. Then suddenly she pulled out a bottle of pure alcoholic spirits from under the table. We had been friends for almost ten years and I could never have imagined that she would so much as take a drop of wine. And here she was with pure spirit!

"Well?" She noticed my embarrassment. "I guess I didn't want to embarrass you before. I was afraid that you might be scandalized. But now you're all grown up and a priest yourself. I know you won't judge me. We old folks need to drink to keep our blood going."

She poured herself a shot of about thirty grams full—a little tumbler of pure spirit—and downed it in one gulp with great pleasure. This was extremely surprising for me but revealed yet another side to the life of this great nun, a life not to be comprehended solely by simple "arithmetical" laws.

St. Seraphim's relics today.

The Candle

*I*N A BELOVED treasure chest, among the relics of St. Seraphim, the nuns used to lovingly keep a little candle. Whenever Mother Frosya would display the saint's relics to pilgrims, this little candle was kept off to the side and nobody noticed it. So once I asked her what was so special about this little candle. And she told me this story:

The nuns had been keeping this candle since the days of St. Seraphim himself. He gave them this candle before his death and told them, "With this candle one of you will greet my body, for it will be carried out and buried in Diveyevo. For my relics will not be resting in Sarov, but will come to you in Diveyevo."

After his death in 1833, St. Seraphim was buried in Sarov Monastery. It was there that people began to revere his memory, and thousands of pilgrims streamed to Sarov from all over Russia. In 1903 St. Seraphim was canonized, and his remains were placed in the Holy Trinity Cathedral in Sarov in a magnificent shrine. Now, of course, Orthodox believers had been told the prophecies of St. Seraphim about the transfer of his remains, but it all seemed rather murky, especially after the Revolution, when it was believed that his remains had been destroyed. It was therefore more conveniently believed that the prophecies had no more than a symbolic meaning.

But Mother Frosya related that in 1927, just before the closure of the Diveyevo Monastery, blessed Maria Ivanovna had gathered together all of the sisterhood of Diveyevo and in the presence of all of them had taken in her hands the sacred candle that had been left her by St. Seraphim. Then she prophesied that the last of the sisters gathered here—the very last of those nuns left alive, out of all those murdered and tortured sisters who yet remained true to their Lord God—would yet greet the relics of St. Seraphim in this place, Diveyevo, with this very candle.

When Mother Frosya told me the story there were only about ten of the original nuns of Diveyevo still living. Each year their numbers grew fewer. But the survivors all ardently believed that the prophecy would

Diveyevo today.

come true. Finally, out of all the nearly 1,000 nuns who had lived in the monastery before the Revolution, only one sister was still alive—Mother Frosya.

In the 1990s the Diveyevo Monastery was restored, and she moved from her home on Lesnaya Street to a cell in the monastery. Also, in 1990, the remains of St. Seraphim of Sarov, which had been thought to have been lost forever, were suddenly found. With magnificent triumph in a Procession of the Cross that went through all of Russia, the holy relics were brought to Diveyevo.

When an assembly of bishops headed by Patriarch Alexiy and accompanied by thousands and thousands of people and the singing of choirs brought the relics of St. Seraphim into the Diveyevo Monastery Cathedral, Mother Frosya was standing, waiting for them by the door with the candle, which she had lit.

Mother Frosya died on February 9, 1997, on the day our Church commemorates the new martyrs and confessors of Russia. She was just such a martyr and confessor, just like Father John (Krestiankin), who died on that same feast day, five years later.

The monastery on the Solovki Islands.

On the Feast of the Baptism of the Lord, All the Water in the World Becomes Holy

A story that may end up in a future *Prologue*

WELL-KNOWN FATHER confessor in Russia was asked how he had performed the Divine Liturgy during his long years of imprisonment. The elder answered:

"Many priests knew the text of the Liturgy by heart. We could find bread even if it wasn't wheat bread, usually without difficulty. We had no choice but to replace the wine with cranberry juice. Instead of the altar with the relics of the martyr on which Church rules require us to serve the Liturgy, we would get the fellow convict-priest among us who had the broadest shoulders to help us. He would strip to his waist, lie down, and then we would say the Divine Liturgy upon his chest. Everyone in the concentration camps of the Gulag was a martyr liable at any moment to die for Christ."

"Tell us, Father, how did you make the water holy during the Feast of the Baptism of the Lord?* After all, the prayers during this service for the sanctification of the water are read only once a year, and they are very long indeed."

"But we had no need to remember all those prayers by heart. For if in just one place in the Universe, the rite of the sanctification of the waters is performed in an Orthodox Church, then through the aid of the Holy Church 'the nature of all the waters'—all the water in the world is thereby made baptismal and holy. In that day we would take water from any source, and it was incorruptible, blessed, Theophany water. And like all Theophany water, it would keep and not go bad for many years.

---

* This Church feast is also called the Theophany, or in the Western Church, Epiphany. —TRANS.

The Great Sanctification
of Water in an icy lake.

"Specialists in anti-religious propaganda recently asserted that the reason why Theophany holy water does not go bad is that the priests secretly place bits of silver, either in strips or coins, or crosses. Ecclesiastical wits have responded to this by a riddle:

"'How many ions of silver are there in one liter of Theophany water if its sanctification took place in a hole dug through the ice in the middle of the Volga River at a place where the width of the river is one kilometer, its depth is seven meters, and its flow rate is five kilometers per hour, and if the cross dipped by the village priest into the water, due to the penury of the church in which he serves, is made of wood?'"

Любитъ Гдь врата Сіонѧ паче всѣхъ селеній Іаковлихъ

By the gates of the Pskov Caves
Monastery. View from inside.

Father Avvakum and the Religious Affairs Commissioner from Pskov

O NE SUMMER EVENING the watchman of the Holy Gates of Pechory Monastery, old Father Avvakum, announced to us all in the refectory after evening prayers that he would no longer let nonbelievers into the monastery. Enough is enough! He was sick of the simpering, shamelessly dressed young tourist hussies walking hand-in-hand with their godless boyfriends who stink for a mile from cigarette smoke. One day it's Communists with holy rollers, the next it's those newfangled "ecumenists," and the next day it's Zionists locked in embrace with the Mujahideen! Time to put an end to it!

No one paid the least mind to the old man's grumbling, but somebody asked him: "And how would you be able to know whether or not the person before you is a true Orthodox believer?"

Avvakum thought about it carefully for a moment. But only for a moment. "Anyone who can read the symbols of the faith I will allow in. If not—wander around the walls, but you've got no business in our monastery."

Everyone laughed at the old man's words and soon forgot about them. But next morning, when after services the monks went about their tasks, they were surprised to notice that it was unusually empty in the monastery. Pious pilgrims were wandering around the churches crossing themselves, and familiar grannies had come to be blessed, and wanderers with their wanderers' bundles on their staffs were resting after the Liturgy, and the holy fools were running around near the well. But the normally pestiferous crowds of tourists had disappeared somewhere. It was like a scene from ancient Holy Russia! It seemed that Father Avvakum had worked a miracle and had truly kept his word.

And so it was. Since the crack of dawn when he had assumed his post as the watchman of the Holy Gates, Father Avvakum had demanded that anyone who tried to come in to read aloud the ancient Nicene Creed, articulated by the fathers of the first Ecumenical Councils that took place in Constantinople during the fourth century. His calculation was remarkably simple: any true Orthodox believer would definitely know this text by heart.

From 5:30 until 10 in the morning, not one of the visitors to the monastery had any trouble reciting the Creed. But after 10 o'clock, the first two buses had arrived from Pskov. Naturally, not one of the Soviet tourists had been able to pass Father Avvakum's simple test. All of them complained and threatened him as they stood frustrated before the locked gates of the monastery. But for an old soldier like Father Avvakum, who had finished the war at the siege of Budapest, these threats were nothing if not ridiculous.

Yet another tour bus rolled up. Out came a group of foreign tourists. By noon there was a large and absolutely enraged crowd milling about the locked gates of the monastery. That crowd was of course noticed by the chief overseer for religious affairs of the Pskov Provincial Communist Party Committee, Nikolai Alexandrovich Yudin, who was driving up in an official black Volga sedan on his way to have lunch with the monastery's abbot.

Everyone in the monastery pronounced the name of this officer in an exaggerated way: "Yudin"—as in "Judas." It was not that this overseer for religious affairs was worse than any of the others, but simply that any overseer over Church life by definition was a symbol of the enslavement of the Church. Actually, to be fair, it must be said that Nikolai Alexandrovich was a rather kind fellow. Although he had worked for many years in the organs of "state security," he had not been made cruel from an excess of power. That said, he was nonetheless the complete master of the fates of all the clergy who were under his department's supervision. On his own whim he could remove any priest simply by taking away his so-called "registration"—which would mean that that priest no longer had any right to work in the Church. And that was the least that he could do. The enmity of the overseer could absolutely result in an extremely unpleasant range of choices for the priest, given the power that any worker in the KGB had to do almost anything he wanted to someone whom he considered dangerous to the Soviet state. Therefore all abbots of the monastery, not to mention simple priests, would rush to the office of the overseer as soon as they were summoned.

All, that is, except for our abbot, Archimandrite Gabriel. He was the only one to whom Yudin would come himself if any question needed to be solved. Why was this the case? I think it was because our abbot knew how to comport himself with a certain indisputable air of authority. Also, Father Gabriel was incredibly strong and independent. And strict. Whatever he decided—happened. He always got his way.

Of course, there were certain poisonous tongues who alleged that overseer Yudin was actually going to the monastery "to be called out on the carpet" because our abbot's rank in the Secret Service was actually higher than his . . . Actually, while that is nonsense, it is understandable that monastery abbots in those days could not avoid having ties or at least relationships with representatives of the power of the state.

When he saw the outrageous mess in his "bailiwick," Nikolai Alexandrovich Yudin immediately got out of his car. He quickly found out what the trouble was and loudly pounded his fist on the ancient iron-gilded oak planks of the doors. "Who's on duty there? Open up at once!"

"Recite the Symbol of the Faith!" the old monk growled from behind the gates.

"What?" The overseer could not believe his ears. "What Symbol? What Faith? Open up at once, I'm telling you!"

"Recite the Symbol of the Faith," said the grizzled monk implacably.

Nikolai Alexandrovich was already gasping for breath. "Who do you think you are? What insolence! I am Yudin! Open right now, or you'll regret it!"

"Read the Symbol of the Faith!"

This inspired dialogue continued in just this fashion for another ten minutes.

Finally, looking at his watch, the overseer began to yield. "I beg you to let me in. I'm already a whole fifteen minutes late to see the abbot. Can you imagine how displeased he'll be?"

There was a brief pause from behind the gates. Clearly, old Father Avvakum could imagine the unhappy fate of someone who had kept Archimandrite Gabriel waiting. "Indeed." He sighed with sympathy. "I don't envy you." But then he once more implacably said: "Recite the Symbol of our Faith."

"But I don't know your symbol of faith!" said the overseer. "What on earth is it?"

Father Avvakum once more thought deeply to himself, and then made a decision. "All right. Let it be so. Now repeat after me." From behind the gates emerged the words to the ancient symbol of our Orthodox faith, the words of the Constantinople Nicene Creed.

"I believe . . ." Father Avvakum intoned.

"I believe . . ." The overseer nearly choked on his words as he stared at the tourists in humiliation.

"In one God, the Father," said Father Avvakum triumphantly.

"In one God, the Father," said the overseer resignedly.

"The Almighty!"

"The Almighty!"

"Maker of Heaven and Earth!"

"Maker . . . of . . . Heaven and Earth!"*

The overseer of the Communist Party Regional Soviet's People's Commission for Oversight of Religious Affairs for Pskov Province publicly declared the final dogma, expressed in the prayer: "I look for the resurrection of the dead, and the life of the age to come. Amen." Then the gates slightly opened up a crack, and the bureaucrat was let into the courtyard of the monastery.

Raging at his inquisitor through his teeth and burning him up with his eyes, the overseer raced ahead to the abbot's office, where the abbot was waiting for him in an extremely irritated mood. "What is your excuse, Nikolai Alexandrovich, for keeping me waiting half an hour?" our abbot reproached his guest.

"It wasn't me!" The overseer was in a rage by now. "It's because of the mess you have going on here. You put some madman at your gates. He won't let anyone in unless they read some sort of symbol of the faith! There

---

* The entire Creed is: I believe in one God, the Father Almighty, Maker of heaven and earth, and of all things visible and invisible: And in one Lord Jesus Christ, the Son of God, the Only-begotten, Begotten of the Father before all ages, Light of Light, True God of True God, Begotten, not made; of one essence with the Father, by whom all things were made: Who for us men and for our salvation came down from the heavens, and was incarnate of the Holy Spirit and the Virgin Mary, and became man; And was crucified for us under Pontius Pilate, and suffered and was buried; And rose again on the third day, according to the Scriptures; And ascended into the heavens, and sitteth at the right hand of the Father; And shall come again, with glory, to judge both the living and the dead, Whose kingdom shall have no end. And in the Holy Spirit, the Lord, the Giver of Life, Who proceedeth from the Father, Who with the Father and the Son together is worshiped and glorified, Who spake by the Prophets; In One Holy Catholic and Apostolic Church. I Confess one Baptism for the remission of sins. I look for the Resurrection of the dead, And the life of the age to come, Amen.

were buses full of tourists waiting outside! Angry foreigners are there, fussing and fuming! Can you imagine the scandal that's brewing?"

At this the abbot got nervous. He immediately summoned the Father Manager to find out what was going on and settle things down. He asked that Avvakum be summoned at once to the abbot's office for punishment.

When Avvakum walked into the dining room, the overseer had been calmed down with a some honeyed words from the abbot, plus a heaping table and a good dose of French cognac the abbot kept handy just in case.

When he saw Father Avvakum, the abbot broke into a rage as he rose from his chair. "What have you done? Without my permission, willfully making up your own rules in the monastery?"

Now, making up one's own rules instead of just obeying is truly a dire sin for a monk. The abbot was absolutely correct here. And Father Avvakum immediately realized his sin. He rushed to the table and threw himself at the feet of Father Gabriel.

"I've been wrong! Forgive me, Father Abbot!"

"Get out of here! Making up your own rules!" The abbot was so enraged as he thundered over the prostrate monk that the walls shook. He even kicked Avvakum with his boot.

The overseer was beside himself with vengeful delight. But once the overseer had left, the abbot once again asked Father Avvakum to come and see him. No sooner had the latter entered the room then he again prostrated himself at his abbot's feet.

"Very well! Excellent! Good for you!" Father Gabriel generously offered Father Avvakum a bottle of Napoleon brandy. "Here, have some!"

That evening Avvakum and a few other elderly monks who were also former soldiers had the chance to experience the abbot's legendary cognac.

The Black Poodle

ΥOU WOULD HARDLY think there is anything interesting or important about the sanctification of an apartment or a house. But during this modest ceremony, even if only for a short time, people are nonetheless in the presence of the Lord God. That may be enough for someone who before that time had been far away from the Church to suddenly discover striking and hitherto unknown horizons.

In the life of every person, sometimes once, and maybe even several times, sooner or later certain events will occur that, no matter how you try, cannot be interpreted rationally. Actually, if you truly wish to deceive yourself, you can decide to consider these incidents just random if unbelievable coincidences or even just a feverish imagination. However, if these unimaginable stories take place when there were other witnesses around, that task becomes a lot more difficult. Of course, even here there is always a chance to write off all that has taken place as, say, a collective hallucination, a chimera.

But no matter how we try to explain, forget, or better yet to simply laugh off our mysterious spiritual experiences, we will never be able to fully free our memory of the powerful onrush into our everyday consciousness of a different reality.

What happens next, whether we meditate on what has happened or prefer to pretend that nothing has happened at all, will depend upon us. But the human soul after death, once it is separated from its body and presented to a new world, will no longer be able to blame someone else for not having been forewarned. It will not be possible to shout like a schoolchild: "We were never taught this! We were never assigned this!"

We were taught, and we were assigned this. And everything we needed to know was explained to us. Although it must be said that sometimes, for all their significance, events like these may be quite ironic and even amusing.

In the beginning of the 1990s just about everybody laughed at our irreligious public standing through long services in Orthodox churches and keeping a serious demeanor. They tried as hard as they could, but

263

crossed themselves very clumsily, did not know how to bow in prayer, and quite obviously did not understand much of what was going on. It was also very popular to make fun of anyone who invited priests to sanctify their homes and apartments. "How stylish!"—people would quip sarcastically.

But I must admit it always gave me joy to see these "candleholders," as the sarcastic wits used to call them. I felt joy for them, because however clumsily, still in fact they were appearing before the Lord God with dedication and humility. Such goodness does not pass unnoticed. Even those least skilled in prayer will absolutely receive from God particular spiritual bounty, and will make discoveries of wonders that have been personally destined for them—wonders that the sarcastic know-it-alls cannot even begin to dream of.

I used to have a good friend named Oleg Alexandrovich Nikitin, who was a decorated scientist in the field of energy during the time of the Soviet Union. In the 1990s he was the director of an institute for the management and repair of a major electrical grid that stretched across eleven time zones, from the Far East to Kaliningrad. Oleg Alexandrovich and his colleagues were extremely interesting people, but had little to do with ecclesiastical life, to put it mildly. They were typical Soviet scientists, and old-fashioned enterprise managers. Nonetheless, they started to come to church from time to time.

When they came to services, these comrades would stand there like columns. Or like candleholders. They would huff and puff and break out in sweats, but they would stick to it and get through it—even though it was quite a feat for them to stand straight through a church service lasting an entire hour and a half.

One day Oleg Alexandrovich invited all his friends and colleagues to a housewarming party for a new small dacha, or country house, in Kaluga Province. He had been building it for several years, and it was finally ready to receive guests. He asked me to sanctify the new dwelling place. After the sanctification ritual there was supposed to be a friendly banquet. As a gift I brought the Nikitin family an old-fashioned samovar and some country jam to be served with the tea.

I should say that at that time most people in our country were quite confused about religious matters. Great masses of people ranged in their delusions from dyed-in-the-wool atheism to belief in newspaper horoscopes and belief in flying saucers and aliens. Oleg's daughter Elena, who was a very pretty and very well educated girl, even believed in something she called "applied magic." There was nothing particularly surprising about this after decades of state-sponsored atheism. (Although similar things, I must admit, were abundant in Russia even before the Revolution.)

When I got to the dacha, I was met at first by a black toy poodle. I really love dogs, but this creature seemed to be incredibly hostile to me. Barking at me furiously, the poodle lunged at me and tried to bite my leg and roughed up the edge of my cassock, leaving me no choice but to give it a good kick with my shoes. Its owners were extremely surprised by how their little dog was behaving, and Oleg's daughter raced to pick it up and console it in her arms.

I cautiously tried to stay out of reach of this creature, for it was still struggling to get out of Elena's arms, and still snapping its canine teeth at me. I immediately warned them when we were going to sanctify their house that the dog could not be inside the building. And it was not only because this tiny little Cerberus had immediately won my displeasure. The fact is, there is a rule of the Church, and I informed its owners of this rule.

"It's a very strange rule!" Elena was bitterly offended. The hysterical poodle was her darling.

"A dog is considered to be an unclean animal." I explained this gloomily.

Elena was even more offended. "What about cats? Are they also unclean animals?

"No. Just dogs. Dogs and pigs."

The last bit was my spite talking. Pigs had been considered unclean animals long ago, even during the time of the Old Testament, even though now Orthodox believers eat pigs with great pleasure. But I had been really irritated by this spoiled poodle.

At this Elena became outraged. "Pigs! How can you even possibly compare them to dogs?"

Oleg's wife rushed to defend her daughter. "What? Now after our house blessing we're not to be allowed to keep our dog in our house?"

"Of course you will, but there are reasons why the Church considers the dog an unclean animal. We weren't the ones that created this rule, and we aren't the ones to change it. Now this doesn't mean that you have to drive your poodle out of your house. But in any case we're not supposed to do the blessing ceremony with the dog in the house. So while we do the ceremony you're going to have to lock it up somewhere—firmly."

Elena was not satisfied. "Can't you at least explain why the Church considers the dog an unclean beast? Why such discrimination? In other esoteric teachings there is nothing of the kind. This is completely random and made-up nonsense!"

"Nothing is random," I answered. "And as for other esoteric teachings, do you really think that it's a coincidence that you happen to be so interested in mysticism while you happen to keep a black poodle in your house?"

"And what's so strange about that?"

"Let's start with the fact that Mephistopheles appeared to Faust in the form of a black poodle."

"Excuse me? Who? Mephistopheles?"

"Exactly. The demon from Goethe's *Faust,* which is Goethe's rendering of an ancient Western legend. When Faust decided to sell his soul to the Devil, Mephistopheles appeared to him in the shape of none other than a black poodle."

"And you are seriously talking about Mephistopheles? In our time?"

"For anyone who has carelessly decided to play with evil mysticism, the story of Mephistopheles is relevant in our time and in any other time as well. The truth is that your amusements are actually extremely dangerous. Mephistopheles quite cruelly sinks his hooks into those who lightheartedly entrust themselves to him. So it's no accident that a black poodle has settled himself in your home."

"He never settled himself. I was the one who bought him! And in an elite Moscow club!"

"Very well. But you didn't buy a lapdog, or a toy terrier, or even a white poodle, no. You bought a black poodle!"

The guests by now were getting extremely curious and could not conceal their interest in our argument. Elena burst out laughing.

"Father, you must be joking! What does Mephistopheles have to do with anything here? It's just that you are an Orthodox priest, and you don't like it when people explore the spiritual world by paths that happen to be different from yours, although you don't know anything about them! And now you're picking on my dog! Maybe you just got so scared when she nearly bit you that now you're ready to tell us about devils in hell and frying pans and you're trying to scare us with Mephistopheles!"

It was not easy to argue with this girl. But Oleg Alexandrovich helped me. He grabbed up the shrieking poodle in his arms and dragged it out to the woodshed. Meanwhile I, not without interior doubts, began to prepare for the sanctification ceremony. Thank God, there were no esoteric images, pictures, or symbols in the house. Otherwise I would have had to face the long ordeal (which I have faced before) of convincing them to take them down from the walls.

The guests and the hosts stood together during the sanctification. When the rite was over, we all could unmistakably feel that something ineffable had really changed. It is always this way after a house blessing. Elena and I somehow had softened as we looked at each other. At the end everybody sang as best he could the traditional Russian song wishing their host "Many years!"

One of the energy science professionals who lived next door asked me to sanctify his home as well. Of course I could not refuse, but Oleg Alexandrovich warned me to hurry up because it was time to sit down for the celebratory banquet.

I stepped out into the garden and ran into a guest of the house-warming party who had come late. With difficulty, his driver was carrying some enormous gift wrapped in a white sheet.

The other house blessing took about forty minutes, after which I rushed back to the home of Oleg Alexandrovich eagerly anticipating a delightful meal. But hardly had I walked into the living room when I came upon the most disconcerting scene: all the guests were pale and terrified, standing stunned in silence. As for the Nikitin family—Oleg, Galina, and Elena—they were pale as sheets.

The first thought that came into my head was that maybe there had been a little fire caused by the candles burned during the sanctification rite. I looked around worried for traces of fire. And suddenly in the corner I saw . . . Mephistopheles! Yes indeed! It was Mephistopheles himself! For real, a very skilled sculpture out of black brass and about half the height of a man. Mephistopheles had been sculpted like a Spanish nobleman, with a sword and cape and a subtle yet powerfully contemptuous sneer on his lips. The black poodle sat right next to the sculpture. He was passionately rubbing himself against the cold brass. I felt goose pimples on my skin.

"What is that?" I whispered horrified, remembering our recent conversation. Judging by the expression on their faces, none of the others had forgotten what we had been talking about either.

The late guest whom I had run into was Leonid Vladimirovich Makarevich, the director of the enormous Moscow Eletrozavod Factory. He

A Photo of Oleg Aleksandrovich and Galina Dmitrievna Nikitin.

had brought as his housewarming gift this extremely expensive sculpture, which his driver had carried into the house, wrapped up in a sheet, as I had been leaving.

Later, when Leonid Vladimirovich had triumphantly removed the sheet, the guests had all been petrified. Their astonishment and horror were only intensified when the black poodle, who had already been freed from his confinement, had suddenly run up to the sculpture, sniffed it, and sat down beside, affectionately rubbing himself against the brass, as if he were a cat. It was this very scene that I had entered upon when I walked into the living room. Meanwhile, for the umpteenth time, Makarevich was asking in complete amazement and indignation: "Listen! Can somebody please finally tell me what's going on here?"

All at once and all together, interrupting each other excitedly, we explained to the bewildered Leonid Vladimirovich the whole strange tale. At first he suspected that we were just playing a trick upon him, but in the end he had to believe us. The sincerity of our nervousness was all too palpable . . . And the behavior of the poodle seemed absolutely weird.

Oleg Alexandrovich and his entire family made their excuses to Leonid

Vladimirovich and then turned to me and begged me to please take the sculpture away—anywhere—and get rid of it.

Makarevich tried to protest weakly. "Oh, come on, guys! It's just a coincidence!"

"Indeed, it certainly is a coincidence!" Oleg Alexandrovich heatedly concurred. But then he turned to me and repeated: "Father Tikhon, I beg of you to please take that thing out of here at once." Makarevich at this could only wring his hands.

We put the sculpture in the trunk of my car. Immediately, everyone's mood improved and we sat down to dinner.

When I got home I completely forgot about the sculpture. Indeed, I was driving it all around Moscow for another couple of days. Finally I remembered just what an object I happened to have with me in the trunk of my automobile. So I and my friend Father Anastasius one late evening brought this bronze Mephistopheles to the banks of the Yauza River and drowned him in the water.

Of course, it is a silly story. And it's certainly just a strange coincidence. However, after this coincidence, Elena ceased to dabble in esoterica. And Oleg Alexandrovich Nikitin decided to come to church. He did so, however, according to his own particular calendar, and would stubbornly appear in church exclusively on the commemoration days of the icon of the Mother of God of Kazan. But that is another story—yet to come.

Sergei Fyodorovich Bondarchuk.

A Christian Death

$\mathcal{W}$ORKING AS A priest sometimes offers a perspective available to no one else. I'm not even speaking here about the privilege of serving the Divine Liturgy, of standing before the throne of God in the moments of the celebration of the Eucharist. This is a joy beyond all description. But, even beyond performing the Liturgy, the priesthood has certain exclusive opportunities for discovering humanity and the world that those outside the priesthood cannot even begin to contemplate.

Often during the last minutes of the life on earth of a Christian, his or her priest is with the doctor. But the priest is the only witness of the last confession. I am not speaking about what the dying person specifically repents of: people's sins are usually fairly similar. But the priest gets to be a witness, and even sometimes a participant, in the remarkable event of the revelation of God's will to a person.

* * *

Ancient tradition has preserved these word of Christ: "In whatsoever things I apprehend you, in those I will judge you." The clergy has long believed that if before a person's death he is able to take Holy Communion, that person's soul immediately goes up to God, without undergoing any ordeals after death.

I have often been struck by how various persons (of whom there are quite a few examples) could go to church all their life and even be monks, or priests, or even bishops, and yet somehow circumstances before their death were such that they died before receiving Communion. Others never went to church at all, and lived as unbelievers, and yet in their final days they not only revealed true deep faith and repentance, but, even beyond all expectations, the Lord vouchsafed them Communion of His Body and Blood.

I once asked Father Raphael (Ogorodnikov) about this. He sighed and said: "Ahh! To take Communion before death! One can only dream about such things. Personally I believe that if a person lived his entire life

271

outside of the church, but in the very last moment repented and took Communion, that the Lord has undoubtedly given him this gift for some secret virtue. For compassion, for example."

Reflecting a bit more, Father Raphael then corrected himself: "Although . . . What am I talking about? What mortal can claim to know the mind of the Lord? Let us remember that verse from Isaiah the prophet: 'For my thoughts are not your thoughts, neither are your ways my ways, saith the Lord.' Sometimes we are too cruel in our judgments of non-churchgoers. The fact is that we simply do not know anything."

In the fall of 1994 my classmate from film school, Dmitri Talankin, visited me in the Sretensky Monastery. We hadn't seen each other for many years, but he brought sad news. Our former professor, the great actor and film director Sergei Fyodorovich Bondarchuk (winner of the 1968 Best Foreign Film Oscar for his monumental epic *War and Peace*), was dying and near death already.

Bondarchuk was a friend of Dmitri's family, and so Dmitri sought me out to hear his confession and give him Communion before his death.

I hadn't seen Sergei Fyodorovich since my student days, but I knew that his recent years had been darkened by harassment and persecution by colleagues in the movie industry. He had endured it all stoically. Bondarchuk was not only extremely versatile in his talents, but also a very strong and courageous man. However, his health had become irreparably frail.

As for the spiritual life of Sergei Fyodorovich, he had been baptized in childhood, but then he had been educated and had lived in an atheist environment. Only in his final years had he come to some understanding of God. But his religious teachings had been gained not from the Church, but from the religious writings of Leo Tolstoy, whose genius he revered. As is well known, Tolstoy at the end of the nineteenth century offered the world a religion that he had basically created for himself. Several generations of Russian intellectuals went through the temptations of Tolstoyan mysticism. Many of them transformed their relationship to their idol into something akin to real religious reverence.

Dmitri told me that in the past few weeks Sergei Fyodorovich's physical sufferings had been aggravated further by strange spiritual torments. He was receiving "visitations" from long-dead people whom he had known well, famous actors and colleagues in the movie industry, appearing before him as if real. But now they were appearing before him in the most monstrous and horrific forms possible, tormenting the patient, and giving him no rest either by day or night. His physicians tried to help him, but without success. Tormented by nightmares, Sergei Fyodorovich tried to find refuge in the religion of Tolstoy. But the strange visitations tormenting his consciousness only became worse and tortured him even further.

I was met in the Bondarchuk apartment by Sergei Fyodorovich's wife, Irina Konstantinovna Skobtseva, and their children, Alyona and Fedya. A melancholy gloom had settled over their home. Everyone seemed to be weighed down by suffering, and not just the dying man, but all his family as well.

Sergei Fyodorovich was lying in a spacious bedroom whose curtains had been tightly drawn. His illness had changed him visibly. Across from the bed, looking right at the patient, there hung a large and beautifully executed portrait of Tolstoy.

After greeting Sergei Fyodorovich, I sat by his bedside and could not at first even begin to find the words to express our gratitude as graduates of the National State Cinematic Institute for our beautiful memories of his lectures. Happy to hear of my gratitude, Sergei Fyodorovich gratefully clasped my hand. This cheered me up, and I was encouraged to proceed to the main goal of my visit.

I said that I had come in order to remind him of the precious teaching that is kept and passed on by the Church from generation to generation. The Christian Church does not only believe, but absolutely knows that physical death is not by any means the end of our existence, but is instead the beginning of a new life for which the person is predestined.

This new life is endless and is open to those who have filled themselves with God our Lord, Jesus Christ. I told Bondarchuk about the beautiful and remarkable world after death that is endlessly good and full of light to which our Savior will lead anyone who trusts himself unto Him with all his heart. And I told him that one needs to prepare for this great event of dying and transition into a new life.

As for the horrible visions that had so cruelly been torturing the patient, I tried here to set forth the basic teachings and experience of the Church about the reality of the influence upon us of the evil spirits. Modern man has difficulty accepting this theme. However, Sergei Fyodorovich had clearly felt the reality of the presence in our world of these pitiless spiritual entities for himself, and so he listened to me with great attention. At the threshold of death, once someone approaches the boundaries between this world and the next world, the previously impermeable barrier between the two worlds can dissolve. Unexpectedly one can begin to see a new reality. One of the greatest shocks is often the fact that this revealed new reality can be aggressive and truly awful.

People who are separated from the Church do not understand that because of their sins and passions for which they have not yet repented, they can be prey for these evil spiritual entities, which the Orthodox Church calls demons. These demons were in fact torturing the dying man, partly by taking on the visages of persons whom he had once known. The goal of these demons is to frighten us, to make us feel terror, powerlessness, and utter despair. Their goal is to make sure that the soul passes into the other world in an agonized state of hopelessness, despair, and the absence of belief in God or any hope of salvation.

Sergei Fyodorovich listened to all of this with noticeable emotion. It was plain that he had already understood and thought about much of what I said. When I finished, Sergei Fyodorovich said that he wished to confess his sins with a full heart and to receive the Holy Mysteries of Christ.

Before I could remain alone with him there were two important things I needed to do. The first was fairly easy: Alyona and I opened the heavy curtains and let the sunshine stream into the room through the windows. Then I stepped out with Sergei Fyodorovich's family into another room and closed the door. I explained to them as best I could that the ceaseless grieving and despair of his loved ones only worsens the spiritual pain of a dying man. When someone we love goes into another life, of course, this is a sad event, but it is not by any means a cause for despair. Death is not only an occasion for grief about the person who is leaving us behind, but also a sacred moment for us Christians, because it is the transition to a new life. Our role was to help him get ready for that most important of transitions with all of our energies. And therefore we absolutely should not present ourselves to him in mourning and despair. I asked Irina Konstantinova and Alyona to prepare a celebratory meal, and bade Fedya to deck the table with the best drinks available in the house.

I went back to Sergei Fyodorovich and told him that now we would get ready for the confession and Communion. "But I have no idea how that's done," Bondarchuk admitted to me confidentially.

"I'll help you. But just one thing: do you believe in the Lord God and in our Savior Jesus Christ?"

"Yes! Yes! I do believe in Him!" Sergei Fyodorovich pronounced these

Irina Konstantinovna, Sergei Fyodorovich, Alyona, and Fyodor.

words with all his heart. Then, as if remembering something, he murmured to me: "But I . . . I've . . . always been asking Tolstoy for help."

"Sergei Fyodorovich!" I broke in heatedly. "Tolstoy was a wonderful and great writer! But he will never be able to defend you from these horrible visions! Only the Lord can do that!" Bondarchuk nodded.

It was time to prepare for the sacraments of confession and Communion. However, as before, the portrait of his beloved genius was on the wall opposite him like an icon. There was no way that I could place the gifts of the Eucharist for Communion on the commode beneath the portrait of that writer. It was unthinkable! In life, Tolstoy had not only refused to believe in the sacraments of the Church, but he had openly and cruelly mocked them. Indeed, he had with particular refinements satirized even the very sacrament of Communion. Bondarchuk knew and understood all this no less than I did. With his permission I carried the portrait into the living room. And this was the second important thing that needed to be done.

The Bondarchuk family had an ancient icon of the Savior in a tarnished silver frame. Fedya and I placed it in front of Sergei Fyodorovich's eyes, and he finally, leaving behind all that was temporal and temporary, fulfilled the sacrament to which the Lord by His Providence had been leading him for years and decades. Bondarchuk confessed before God all the sins of his life profoundly, courageously, and sincerely. After this the whole family walked into the room, and Sergei Fyodorovich, for the first time since distant childhood, partook of the Holy Mysteries of Christ.

Everyone was amazed with what feeling he did this. Even the expression of pain and suffering that had never gone from his face had suddenly vanished.

Having completed our main task, we set a beautiful table for a feast right by the bedside of the patient. Fedya poured everyone a little bit of red wine as well as some of his father's oldest and best cognac. We had a real peaceful and joyful feast, as we congratulated Sergei Fyodorovich with his first Communion since so long ago, and the upcoming mysterious journey or "the way of all flesh" on which he was soon destined to embark.

Before I left I had another moment alone with Sergei Fyodorovich. I wrote a simple Jesus Prayer on a little piece of paper and left it in front of him: "Lord Jesus Christ, Son of God, have mercy on me, a sinner." Sergei Fyodorovich did not know any prayers. And of course in his condition he could not learn anything more complicated. But nothing more complicated was needed.

Then I removed my monastic prayer rope* from my own arm and taught Sergei Fyodorovich how to use it. And we said goodbye.

Several days passed. Alyona Bondarchuk called me and told me that her father's condition had changed markedly. He was no longer being tormented by dreadful visions. He had calmed down and was somehow visibly resigned from suffering in this world. Alyona told me that she often saw how her father would be lying there staring for hours at the icon of the Savior, or, having closed his eyes, whispering a prayer at each knot of his prayer rope. Sometimes he would press the little cross at the end of the prayer rope to his lips. This meant that his physical pain was becoming unbearable.

Another week went by. I was invited by the chief of the department of neurosurgery of the Moscow Province Hospital to bless the operating room and intensive care unit. When I got there in the morning, Dmitri Talankin and Fedya Bondarchuk were waiting for me. Sergei Fyodorovich had been brought to the Central Clinical Hospital, where the doctors had declared that he might die any day now. I had the Holy Gifts of the Eucharist with

---

*   The prayer rope is the Orthodox form of a rosary, made with yarn or cord. —TRANS.

me, ready to give Holy Communion to the sick, and we immediately went to the Central Clinical Hospital.

Sergei Fyodorovich was suffering unbearably. When I came up to him he opened his eyes slightly to let me know that he recognized me. He had the prayer rope in his hand. I asked him if he wished to receive Communion. Sergei Fyodorovich nodded, almost imperceptibly. He was already unable to speak. I read the prayer of absolution of sins over him and gave him Communion. Then his whole family and I kneeled by his bedside as we read the Canon for the Departure of the Soul.

The Church has one particular prayer and rite that is known as "when a person suffers very long in sickness." This prayer is read if the soul of the dying person is taking a long and torturous time to leave the body. It is used when a person wants to but cannot die.

When I saw the state the patient was in, I read this prayer right by his pillow. In this prayer the Church commends its son into the hands of God, asking that he be freed of suffering and worldly cares in this temporal life. Making the sign of the cross over Sergei Fyodorovich for the last time, I bade him farewell. Dmitri Talankin and I departed the hospital room, leaving the dying man in the company of his family.

No matter how sad the sight of the sufferings of someone about to die, life has its own demands. Dmitri and I had not had a single bite to eat all day. Therefore we decided to go to Dmitri's family's home on Mosfilm Street.

We were met at the doorstep by Dmitri's parents Igor Vasilyevich and Liliya Mikhailovna, who were in tears. Alyona had just telephoned them to say that Sergei Fyodorovich was no more. Right there and then in the apartment we served the Orthodox requiem.

Perhaps we could end the story of the Christian death of the remarkable man and great artist Sergei Fyodorovich Bondarchuk on this note—were it not for one highly unusual occurrence that was conveyed to us by Dmitri's parents. To be honest, I thought for a long time about whether it is even worth telling you this detail. I do not know how even churchgoers will be willing to accept the story Dmitri's parents told us. Will they not just dismiss it as a fantasy—or perhaps just coincidence? But in the end, this story was and shall remain a sacred family story known to the Talankin family, and they authorized me to relate it.

There are certain strange but absolutely real events in our lives that to outside observers will seem like nothing more than mere chance or

The grave of
Sergei Fyodorovich
Bondarchuk.

absurd invention. But for those who undergo these events, they will always be a genuine revelation, completely changing their entire lives and outlooks on the world.

I will therefore not edit out the detail from my chronicling of that day. And I will convey all that was related to me by two absolutely healthy and normal people—the People's Artist of the Soviet Union, celebrated director Igor Vasilyevich Talankin, and his wife, professor Liliya Mikhailovna Talankina—exactly as Dmitri and I heard it.

No sooner had we completed the first requiem for Sergei Fyodorovich when Dmitri's parents told us in an unsettled matter that something extremely strange and incomprehensible had happened just a few minutes before Alyona Bondarchuk had called them. They had been sitting in their room and still did not know about the death of their friend. Suddenly, they could hear a growing cawing and cawing of ravens. The sound got louder and louder and became almost deafening. It seemed that an innumerable flock of ravens was flying over their home.

Surprised by this, the husband and wife walked out onto their balcony and beheld a scene the likes of which they had never laid eyes on before. The sky was choked by a black cloud of birds. Their sharp cries had become unbearable. The balcony looked out on a wooded park and onto the hospital where, as the Talankin family knew, their friend lay dying. The numberless horde of birds was streaming out precisely from that place. The sight of the horde suggested a thought to Igor Vasilyevich, which he suddenly stated with absolute conviction to his wife: "Sergei has just died. Those are demons which have just fled away from his soul."

He said it and was himself surprised by what he had said. The flock of birds flew up over them, and disappeared among the clouds hanging over Moscow. Several minutes later Alyona called.

Everything that happened on that day—both the death of Sergei Fyodorovich, and the strange sight that happened at the moment of his death—Igor and Liliya Talankin conceived of as a message to them from their dying friend. No one was able to convince them otherwise— not friends, not Dmitri and I, nor even their own intellectual skepticism. Although, as far as I can remember, the Talankin family never again told any kind of stories of any events that might have anything to do with mysticism. I had the fortune to baptize them, and gradually they became Christians of deep and devout faith.

Marshal Georgiy Konstantinovich Zhukov with his daughter, Maria.

Marshal Zhukov's Mother-in-Law

*T*HE DAUGHTER OF the celebrated Marshal Georgiy Konstantinovich Zhukov was a parishioner of our monastery. Once she told me with sadness that her grandmother on her mother's side, Klavdia Yevgenievna, who was eighty-nine years old, had not received Communion since she was a little child. To make matters worse, Klavdia Yevgenievna had already for several years been suffering from Alzheimer's disease. Things had gotten so bad that she could not recognize her own beloved granddaughter. She would look at Maria Georgievna and ask her: "Who are you? Where's my granddaughter? Where's Masha?"

Maria Georgievna wept in floods of tears, but the doctors told her nothing could be done.

Therefore it was not so easy to understand whether or not Klavdia Yevgenievna wished to confess and take Communion. It was impossible to tell whether she wished to have a priest in her room. Maria Georgievna appealed to the priests she knew, but they merely wrung their hands.

To give Communion to an old lady without even knowing whether she believed in God was not something that anyone was willing to do (since Klavdia Yevgenievna had been a member of the Communist Party and an atheist all her adult life). Maria Georgievna and I thought about this unusual situation for a long time but could not come to any solution. In the end I couldn't find anything better to say than this:

"You know what, Masha? It's one thing to discuss our meager human reasoning. It's another if we approach your grandmother with Holy Communion. Maybe the Lord will resolve the situation Himself. Otherwise we are out of options." Maria Georgievna agreed.

But actually, it was one thing to make the suggestion, and quite another, to be honest, to really believe there was any hope. Therefore, I must admit, to my shame, that I postponed visiting the sick old lady for quite a long time. I didn't feel right about appearing with the Holy Eucharist before somebody who more likely than not had absolutely no comprehension of why I was even in her house. What's more, there was always something urgent coming up—one thing after another.

Maria Georgievna then demonstrated some of the celebrated military decisiveness that she had inherited from her father, Marshal Zhukov. There was just no refusing her. In fact, I was beginning to be ashamed of my faintheartedness. We then decided that we would do two things at once: bless the apartment of Marshal Zhukov, and try to administer confession and Communion to Grandma—if, of course, she herself wanted this and correctly understood the point of my visit. This last was an important point. Masha warned me that her grandmother might just get angry. What's more, it turned out that she absolutely could not abide people who were dressed in black! As if things weren't hard enough already! I had to have a white cassock sewn for myself quickly.

Finally, we set off to sanctify the apartment of Marshal Zhukov and to give Communion to his mother-in-law. I would like to point out that this was no ordinary mother-in-law. She might have been the only mother-in-law in the entire history of humanity to whom her son-in-law (and we all know just how demanding Marshal Zhukov was of everyone around him) publicly expressed his gratitude in the dedication of his book of memoirs.

Carrying the Holy Gifts in a receptacle for their safekeeping, I walked into her room with what I must admit was a good deal of trepidation. A wizened little old lady of neat and pleasant appearance was lying in bed. I looked at Masha with shyness, approached the bed, and said: "Uh . . . hello, Klavdia Yevgenievna."

Grandma stared up at the ceiling with an empty and scattered look. Then she slowly turned her attention to me. And the expression in her eyes became completely different.

"Father!" She exclaimed with joy. "At last you've come! I've been waiting for you for a long time!"

I was not expecting this. I had been told that the old lady was by now far gone, and had long since lost her mind (let's call a spade a spade) . . . And now—suddenly—this! Utterly confused, I turned to Maria Georgievna.

Well, if I was confused, Masha and her friend whom she had asked along for the blessing of the apartment were utterly dumbfounded! Masha cried and ran out of the room, while her friend told me that nothing even slightly like this example of ordinary reasoned speech had been heard coming from Klavdia Yevgenievna's lips for three full years.

Marshal Zhukov at the victory parade May 9, 1945.

Meanwhile the old lady was insistent. "Father! What took you so long to come here?"

"Forgive me, please, Klavdia Yevgenievna!" I spoke with all my heart. "I am very sorry. But now I am here."

"Yes, yes. Now you and I must do something very important!" Marshal Zhukov's mother-in-law said. But then she added with anxiety: "Except I don't remember. What should we do?"

"You must say your confession and take Communion."

"Absolutely right. Only please help me."

We were left alone. I sat down on the little chair by her bed, and with some prompting from me, of course, Klavdia Yevgenievna over the course of the next half-hour sincerely and fearlessly confessed all her sins, starting from the time when she had been a ten-year-old schoolgirl—which was the last time she had ever been to confession. What's more, it appeared that she had such a prodigious memory that I could only be astonished.

When Klavdia Yevgenievna was done with her confession, I invited

Claudia Yevgenyevna with her granddaughter Maria. Photo dates from 1977.

Masha and her friend into the room, and I recited the concluding prayer for the old lady. She was sitting up in bed and absolutely beaming with delight.

Finally we gave her Communion of the Holy Mysteries of Christ. It was astonishing, but when I began to read the prayer commonly administered before Communion: "I believe, O Lord, and I confess . . . ," then Klavdia Yevgenievna herself placed her arms crosswise over her breast, just as custom has it. It appeared the memory from her last Communion in childhood had come back to her.

We gave Grandma a piece of blessed Communion bread dipped in holy water, and Klavdia Yevgenievna lay back in bed, calm and at peace, munching toothlessly on it with great pleasure.

Then we began the blessing of the apartment. When I went back into Klavdia Yevgenievna's room carrying a cup of holy water, she took the rather hardened piece of blessed bread out of her mouth and nodded her head at me in recognition.

After the apartment blessing, Masha, her son Egor, her friend, and I sat down to have a bite to eat. Our conversation went on perhaps for an hour and a half.

As I was leaving to go home, I walked in to say goodbye to Klavdia Yevgenievna. The old lady was still lying in bed, but I immediately noticed that something was not right with her face. The left side of her face had gone dead and seemed frozen somehow. I yelled for Maria Georgievna. She raced to her grandmother's side, and started asking her what was wrong, but Klavdia Yevgenievna did not answer. We thought that she must have suffered a stroke.

That in fact is what had happened. Her words of repentance during confession had been the very last words that Klavdia Yevgenievna had uttered in this life. She died soon afterwards. With the permission of His Holiness the Patriarch, we served her funeral rites in our Sretensky Monastery. The Ministry of Defense issued a special military command for the burial with full honors for the mother-in-law of Marshal Zhukov.

Archimandrite Claudian.

Archimandrite Claudian

IN THE TOWN of Staraya Russa there served an old priest named Archimandrite Claudian (Modenov). He was well past eighty years old, but he had an absolutely phenomenal memory. He not only personally knew almost all the bishops of the Russian Orthodox Church, but also most of the ordinary priests, especially those of the older generation. What's more, he could also say with exactitude when each and every one of them had been ordained, what their wives' maiden names were, how many years this or that monk had been imprisoned in the Gulags, and under what criminal code article, and in which camps. In short, Father Claudian was a walking ecclesiastical encyclopedia.

We happened to be together by the altar during a service in the Holy Trinity Monastery. Two well-known Metropolitans were unhurriedly walking before us. "Look at how imposingly those boys are walking!" Father Claudian remarked.

"What boys?" I asked in surprise.

"Right there—in front of us."

"Those are Metropolitans!"

"They're just little kids to me," Father Claudian remarked jokingly. "I led both of them around the Holy Table in the altar during their ordinations." (When a priest is being ordained, he is led around the Holy Table three times.) In other words, Father Claudian had been a senior priest during the service of the Liturgy when those young deacons, now archbishops, had first been ordained.

We novices were extremely skeptical and critical of the so-called "ecumenical" activities of certain clerical authorities. Once, Father Claudian became an involuntary witness to such a conversation. When he heard our condemnations and insolent words, he stamped his foot passionately and stated in a commanding voice: "Silence! You don't know what you're talking about! How dare you judge a bishop?"

Father Claudian died on the Feast of the Nativity of the Mother of God. On that day he served Divine Liturgy and communed of the Holy Mysteries of Christ. Then he took people's confessions and served a funeral.

287

When he got home he was tired and went to bed, and, taking out his prayer rope, remembered all of the people whom he had known during his long life. Usually just from memory he could name about 2,000 people for the repose of whose souls he would pray daily, and that included only the departed. Once he had done this, he asked that his apprentice, Deacon Vasily Sereda, come to say goodbye to him. But he didn't wait for him, and died with his prayer rope in his hands.

He was buried in the caves of the Pskov Caves Monastery. He had often traveled there to pray and to have a chat with Father John.

A schema-monk in the Pskov Caves Monastery.

Death of a "Stool Pigeon"

To be on death's doorstep is a strange and mysterious time in the life of a human being. Some of us, like Sergei Fyodorovich Bondarchuk, experience that the boundaries between our world and other worlds begin to dissolve. And people who have lived ascetical lives sometimes receive visions from the Lord that had previously been denied to them.

In the Pskov Caves Monastery there lived an extremely elderly schema-monk named Father Cyprian. There seemed nothing particularly special about him. He had left the world for the monastery at an already advanced age, and it seemed his monastic existence had been hardly noticeable. There was, however, one rather unpleasant circumstance: he was suspected of informing on the brothers to the abbot. Whether or not this was really true I do not know. Maybe somebody had reasons for thinking this. Or maybe the rumors had spread because Cyprian was always wandering around the monastery, hunched over and shuffling his feet, and he had a knack for appearing everywhere, suddenly, out of nowhere. In any case, various people called him a stool pigeon outright. Father Cyprian himself took this all in good stride. But not long before his death we began to notice surprising things about him.

One morning the abbot left the monastery on some business. I had been assigned to keep the watch on Dormition Square. One of my tasks was to immediately open and close the gates for cars that would enter and leave. But there was really only one car according to the rules that was allowed in through this narrow gate onto Dormition Square, and that car belonged to the abbot. If the watchman was late in opening the gates, and the abbot was forced to wait for even a second, punishment could be swift.

But now, however, since I knew that the abbot had left for Pskov, I decided to go down to the cowshed where my friend Sergei Gorokhov was doing his work. We were warming ourselves in the sun and had gotten into an animated discussion, when all of a sudden Father Cyprian hobbled up, leaning on his staff, suddenly stopped, and then turned to me and yelled: "Hey! Georgiy! You better hurry up and open the gates. The abbot's coming back and you'll be in trouble!"

291

In the Pskov Caves Monastery.

Sergei and I looked at each other skeptically. What was Father Cyprian talking about? The abbot had just left, and there was no way he could have made it to Pskov already, not to mention come back. There were no signs whatsoever of any approaching car.

"Go! Run, run! Or else you'll be punished!" Again Father Cyprian yelled at me and even rattled his staff.

I didn't believe him, but I thought I'd humor the old man, so I said goodbye to my friend and casually meandered back to my post on Dormition Square. Imagine my surprise when suddenly behind me I heard the familiar honking of a horn. There could be no doubt about it: the abbot's car had gone through the lower gates of the monastery and in less than a minute would be on Dormition Square. For some reason the abbot had returned home in a hurry.

I ran as fast as I could back to my post and barely managed to get there in time to let the car pass through the gates as I was supposed to.

That evening in our novices' cell, we discussed how it was possible that Father Cyprian had known the abbot's car was going to be returning to the monastery. At the moment he had warned me, the abbot's car had still been over two kilometers away from the monastery, out of sight or hearing. My friends began to recall that they had noticed Father Cyprian making similar surprising observations.

When the ascetic schema-monk grew sick, we began visiting him in the St. Lazarus Hospital wing. To be honest, we were all hoping that now that he could foresee the future he would tell us something particularly wise and important. But Father Cyprian would look at us with his kind eyes, and with his life force fading he merely smiled at us and repeated: "God bless you, my children!"

The recently restored Church of the Kazan Icon of the Mother of God in Ryazan Province.

Stories Like This Happen in Moscow Today

O LEG ALEXANDROVICH NIKITIN was not a particularly churchgoing fellow. You have already read the story about the blessing of his house and about the black poodle and the sculpture of Mephistopheles that had been given to him as a gift for the occasion. Yet, for many years, Oleg Alexandrovich lobbied with dedication for the restoration of a destroyed church—the Church of the Icon of the Mother of God of Kazan in Ryazan Province. What it was about this church in particular that attracted him I cannot say. But twice a year on the summer and winter festivals of the Kazan Mother of God, he would always attend the service in the ruined church where our monks from the Sretensky Monastery would come to serve the Liturgy. Several times Oleg Alexandrovich confessed and took Communion there. This continued for many years, but there was no further movement whatsoever on his part towards the direction of the Church.

It so happened that exactly on this day, the summer feast day of the Icon of the Kazan Mother of God, the Lord took Oleg Alexandrovich out of this world. On that day, July 21, 2003, Nikitin for some reason did not come to services in the church—and it turned out that there was an emergency. That evening we learned that Oleg Alexandrovich was no more; he'd been in an auto accident in Moscow Province because his chauffeur could not handle the steering.

But I want to tell the story about how Oleg Alexandrovich managed to surprise us, his friends, even after his death.

Several months after he died, he appeared in a dream to his daughter Elena. There was nothing particularly strange about that, but this dream was so specific that Elena remembered it in detail. In the dream Oleg Alexandrovich appeared to his daughter with the following request: "Please give Demirtchan my congratulations today, because today is his birthday." I ought to mention that Oleg Alexandrovich had always been very attentive to his friends, and would never forget their birthdays.

The Church of the Kazan Icon of the Mother of God, before its restoration.

But both in the dream and after waking up, Elena had no idea what her father was talking about. "Who is Demirtchan?" she wondered.

However strange this request might seem, she and her mother Galina Dmitrievna Nikitina decided to call Oleg Alexandrovich's close friend and colleague, the former Deputy Minister of Energy, Viktor Vasilyevich Kudryaviy. He immediately and without any difficulty answered the women's questions, because at that very minute he was setting off for a party celebrating the eightieth birthday of a colleague of his and of Oleg Alexandrovich's: Kamo Serobovicha Demirtchan.

Oleg Alexandrovich's request was, naturally enough, complied with. Viktor Vasilyevich Kudryaviy announced to the guests at the party that he had a particularly important assignment that had been given to him from beyond the grave, and to everyone's general astonishment, he congratulated the dumbfounded Demirtchan on his birthday on behalf of Oleg Alexandrovich Nikitin. Stories like this happen in Moscow today.

The Holy Hieromartyr Hilarion.

Lyubov Timofeyevna Cheredova

*W*HEN WE BEGAN to restore the Sretensky Monastery, a rather serious problem developed for us: among the parishioners there were almost no old women. All our parishioners were either young or middle-aged. When the first grandmothers began to appear, we were so happy that we were willing to wait on them hand and foot. What joy! The coming of the grandmothers meant that old Muscovites were beginning to accept our monastery.

Among these grandmothers was Lyubov Timofeyevna Cheredova. In 1996 with great ceremony we celebrated her birthday—she had turned 100! But this was not the main thing. Lyubov Timofeyevna turned out to be the last living spiritual daughter of the previous Abbot of the Sretensky Monastery, the martyred Archbishop Hilarion. In the 1920s, displaying incredible courage she had tried to follow Archbishop Hilarion into exile. But she couldn't follow him all the way to the Solovki Islands concentration camp in the White Sea, where the archbishop spent the greater part of his imprisonment. Lyubov Timofeyevna was part of a group that bravely buried that courageous and unbroken spiritual leader. All her life she was profoundly devoted to Archbishop Hilarion and maintained a remarkable spiritual unity with him until her final days.

Lyubov Timofeyevna never married. I never found out whether or not she was a secret nun, but she certainly lived a true life of sacrifice and asceticism. It is quite possible that Archbishop Hilarion secretly administered monastic vows to her during those dark days of the Church, but that with the conditions common for the time she never reveal her secret to anyone.

Lyubov Timofeyevna never doubted the holiness of her great spiritual father, and she fervently prayed to the Lord that she might live to see the day when he would be canonized.

While Lyubov Timofeyevna had sufficient strength she used to visit the monastery. We would send a car for her, and then in the church we would give her a chair to sit down in, so that she could pray throughout the entire service. She had a perfect memory of the services that Archbishop Hilarion had once given in the cathedral, and so we considered her presence in the resurrected monastery to be a particular blessing from the monastery's great former abbot whom she so revered.

For several years we prepared materials for the canonization of the holy martyr Hilarion, but it must be said that we were afraid that Lyubov Timofeyevna might not live to see that much awaited hour. The time had come when she already could not visit the monastery. We began to visit her home to give her Communion. On each visit she would ask us, full of hope, how the canonization procedure of her spiritual father was proceeding. By now she was already 102 years old.

At that time we were restoring a small side altar of our monastery church, and we had set up an iconostasis there. One of the icons that we ordered for it was an image of the Holy Hieromartyr Hilarion.* Of course, we were somewhat ahead of ourselves, because the canonization had not yet taken place, although ecclesiastical law states that an icon is considered sanctified only when it is inscribed with the name of the saint whose image it bears. Our icon had not yet been inscribed and was awaiting the moment when the Church authorities would approve the canonization of this holy martyr, our former abbot and heavenly patron. In any case, our iconostasis was established, and our church became the only one in Russia bearing an iconic image of this man, who, even if he was not yet canonized, was extremely revered as a new martyr by the people of the church.

Finally, just before a plenary session of the Commission for the Canonization of Saints, Metropolitan Juvenal, its chairman, told me that the case for the canonization of Archbishop Hilarion had been practically decided. The next day I went to see Lyubov Timofeyevna and I told her the joyful news.

"I knew that I wouldn't die until I heard these tidings!" She was barely able to speak.

It was like the story in the Gospel of Luke about St. Simeon, of whom it had been foretold that he should not see death before he had seen the Lord's Christ. And when Jesus was brought into the Temple, "then he took him up in his arms, and blessed God, and said: 'Lord, now lettest Thou Thy servant depart in peace, according to Thy word, for mine eyes have seen Thy salvation.'"

Several days later Lyubov Timofeyevna left us to be with the Lord.

---

* In Orthodox tradition, a martyred clergyman is called a hieromartyr. —TRANS.

Lyubov Timofeyevna.

Her body was brought into the Sretensky Monastery for the funeral service, which was held right in that little side altar where we had just installed the iconostasis with the image of Archbishop Hilarion. Our oldest parishioner was lying in state right opposite the image of her spiritual father. And if in 1929 she had been present at the archbishop's funeral, now it was his icon standing by his spiritual daughter and accompanying her upon "the way of all flesh."

On February 11, 1998, at about 11 o'clock in the morning, precisely during the funeral of Lyubov Timofeyevna, the Commission for the Canonization of Saints in Novodevichiy Monastery formally decided to forward materials and documents for the canonization of Holy Hieromartyr Hilarion to the highest council of the Russian Orthodox Church. When this joyful news was communicated to the Sretensky Monastery by telephone, the coffin with the body of Lyubov Timofeyevna was carried around our cathedral to the accompaniment of ringing bells and singing of the hymn "Holy God, Holy Mighty, Holy Immortal, have mercy on us."

Donskoy Monastery. The cemetery.

The Metropolitan's Daughter

*T*HERE ARE CERTAIN sins that can be healed by repentance. But then there are particular sins against the Church that will so alienate a person from God that there is not even any repentance possible for them.

Once when I was serving in the Donskoy Monastery, a tall middle-aged woman stopped me outside the church. "Father, may I pray for my dead father?" she asked.

"Of course you may!" I answered hurriedly, as I was running off somewhere. But then I nonetheless stopped and checked with her. "Please forgive me, but who was your father?"

"My father was a Metropolitan," the woman replied.

Amazing! "A Metropolitan?" I was so astonished that I repeated her words. "What was his name?" "Metropolitan Alexander Vvedensky," the woman replied.

This was even more amazing. The Russian Church has an excellent recollection of the name of this priest, Alexander Vvedensky. He was one of the leaders of the so-called "renovationist" movements in the Russian Church in the 1920s and 1930s. Vvedensky and his followers were willing to revolutionize the fundamental rules and canons of the Russian Orthodox Church at the behest of their Communist overseers. Many denunciations to the secret police, and much collaboration in the murder and repression of Orthodox believers, martyrs, and bishops, lay on their conscience. These "renovationists" had created a schism in the Russian Church, and the sin of those causing schism, according to St. John Chrysostom, can never be purged, not even by the blood of martyrdom.

The woman who had approached me was named Tamara Alexandrovna. Vvedensky had married for a second time after he became a renovationist Metropolitan—something strictly forbidden by Church canons—and out of his marriage a son and a daughter had been born.

"How can I possibly advise you?" I finally said to the woman. "You are your father's daughter, and so of course . . . you cannot *not* pray for him. Indeed, it is your duty. But as for us, we cannot pray for your father during the Liturgy. He deliberately broke with our Church. And as far as we know, he never repented or tried to reunite with the Church in any way whatsoever. However, you absolutely can and should pray for him at home in private prayer."

That was our decision. The woman came back to the monastery a few times. It turned out that she was an extremely kind and heartfelt Christian who sacrificed and gave of herself profoundly to help the sick, the homeless, and the elderly. I believe that this was actually her active form of prayer for her father.

Once she came to me and begged me to give Communion to her elderly mother, who was the second wife of Alexander Vvedensky. We agreed that next morning I would come to church an hour before services to be able to give her extra time for confession. Tamara told me that her mother had never confessed or taken Communion in any Orthodox Church, and had only ever been to services during those years when her husband had been in charge of the so-called "renovationist" movement. Of course, it was not possible to call such services sacraments.

But that morning I waited for them in vain. Tamara called me, very much upset, and told me that when she and her brother had come for their mother, she had pulled a blanket over her head and had categorically refused to go anywhere, even though the night before she had been ready to confess and take Communion. But I knew that old folks often can be capricious in this way, and so I said that I would take the Holy Gifts with me and give her Communion at home.

Regretfully, Tamara refused. "That's impossible, Father," she said to me. "You cannot come into her apartment."

"What do you mean I can't come into her apartment?"

"You simply cannot come in."

"But why not?"

Tamara explained that in her mother's apartment there were lots of cats. So many cats indeed that no one even knew how many: they kept giving birth and even dying in her apartment. For many years the old woman had not allowed anyone to even clean in her apartment. The only people brave enough to cross her threshold were her own son and daughter.

I shuddered to myself as I imagined the scene. On top of everything else I had a particular reason for really not wanting to go to this house: since childhood I have always had a terrible allergy to cat fur.

But Tamara found a solution. She said that tomorrow she would bring her mother to her brother's apartment, where we would be able to give her Communion peacefully. And so it was decided. However, late that evening, Tamara called to tell me that a few hours earlier her mother had just died.

Bulat Okudzhava, the famous bard.

How Bulat Became Ivan

O LGA, THE WIFE of the great bard Bulat Okudzhava, came to visit Father John (Krestiankin) in the Pskov Caves Monastery. While she was there she complained to Father John that her famous husband had never been baptized and had no desire to be—he was utterly indifferent to religion.

Father John told her, "Don't be sad, he will be baptized. You yourself will baptize him."

Olga was very surprised about this and she asked, "But how can I baptize him?"

"Just like that. You will baptize him!"

"But what shall I call him? After all, Bulat is not an Orthodox name."

"You will name him after me, Ivan," said Father John, and sped off about his own business.

Many years later, Bulat Okudzhava was dying in Paris. Just a few minutes before his death, he told his wife that he wished to be baptized. It was already too late to summon a priest. However, in such circumstances, anyone, even a member of the laity, may baptize a dying man.

She simply asked her husband: "What shall your name be?" He thought about it for a moment and said, "Ivan." So Olga herself baptized him with the name of Ivan (or John).

But it was only when she was standing over his dead body that she remembered that some fifteen years earlier in the Pskov Caves Monastery, Archimandrite John had foretold all this to her.

Father Nicholas.

Father Nicholas's Prediction about My Monasticism

*I*N THE FIRST YEAR after my baptism, I often visited the parishes of my new friends, Father Raphael and Father Nikita. Although I was quite often in the monastery by that time, I had no thoughts of becoming a monk myself.

On the contrary, I was seriously planning to get married. My fiancée was probably the prettiest girl in all of Moscow. In any case, lots of people thought so, and that was very flattering to me. The wedding was already being planned. And so I was not only enjoying all my new impressions from the revelations of the spiritual life, but I was also dreaming of future happiness.

I used to go fishing, and I smoked fish I had caught in the smokehouse. I would lie in the sunshine, looking forward to my upcoming family happiness. What's more, I was thinking how nice it would be in the fall to sit somewhere on the south bank of the Moscow River enjoying some beers with my friends, as we ate this fish that I had just caught and dried with my own hands.

A whole warm summer passed by in such daydreams.

Then somehow Father Nikita and Father Raphael were going to visit the elder Father Nicholas, who lived on the island of Zalit in Lake Pskov. The elder was over eighty years old, and he had spent the better part of his life as the presiding priest on this remote island of fishermen in Lake Pskov. I decided to go with my new friends, although not without some inner dread: after all, this was a clairvoyant elder—what if he knew all about me?

But in my first minutes of acquaintance with Father Nicholas, all these fears vanished. The priest was remarkably kind and hospitable, and took great care of us as he housed us in his humble little cottage, not far from the church. He gave us tea and fed us generously. My friends the priests secluded themselves with him for conversation and advice. Meanwhile I had nothing in particular to ask him.

309

As we were saying goodbye we all walked up to the elder for his blessing, which he gave to all of us with his love. When it was my turn to be blessed, Father Nicholas suddenly grabbed me by my forelock and either jokingly or seriously began to drag me with some force by it, saying all the while: "Don't drink! Don't drink! You absolutely mustn't drink!"

Now in those years I must admit that I certainly was partial to a drop or two—especially in the company of my friends. This was not something that was obvious just by looking at me. I looked much younger than I was back then. But the elder did not let up. Then he lifted up my head by my hair and stared into my eyes.

"Are you a monk? Not yet? You need to go to the monastery!"

The monastery? I laughed right in his face. What was this mad old fellow talking about? I was getting married soon. I tried to tell him about this, but Father Nicholas shut my mouth with his hand as if he already knew what I was going to say.

"Be quiet! Be quiet! You need to go to the monastery!"

Again I laughed. "No way!"

But the elder again did not let me get a word in edgewise. "Listen to me, little Georgiy, when you will be living in the monastery you will be visited by temptation. But don't let it get you down!"

He began to tell me in detail about some sort of weird ordeal the abbot of the monastery would be inflicting as a test upon some monk . . . Only ten years later would I understand that he was actually talking about me, but back then I listened to Father Nicholas's strange speeches with condescension, and took them as nothing more than the ravings of an old man.

Finally, Father Nicholas blessed me and bade us go in peace. He accompanied us to the dock. As our boat was sailing away, the elder yelled after me, "Georgiy, be loving to everyone!"

This strange missive sank into my memory for a long time, as did the face of that elder on the banks of his island with his long gray hair waving in the wind as he bade us farewell with the sign of the cross.

Father Raphael advised me to take Father Nicholas's advice seriously, but I merely scoffed in reply. Then I forgot all about what had happened, as it hadn't made any sense.

However, when I got back to Moscow, my relationship with my fiancée somehow broke up of its own accord. Our feelings cooled, and then eventually disappeared. Both of us were actually glad about this. Meanwhile, more and more I began to feel the need and the longing to go to the monastery, to be there, to pray there, and yes, to live there. After several months I already knew for sure: nothing except the monastery and service to God interested me anymore in this life. And then with surprise I remembered the words of Father Nicholas, to whom the Lord later brought me back again many times.

An Old Believer.

A Chapter That May Be Skipped by Readers Who Don't Know Church History

*W*HAT ELDERS THERE used to be in Soviet times! A friend of mine who was an Old Believer* recalls how once he was sent to some provincial capital (Kuibyshev or Sverdlovsk, it doesn't matter which now) by the central directorate of the Ancient Orthodox Church on some Old Believer business. At first, as was required in those days, my friend went to the Provincial Executive Committee of the Communist Party to visit the overseer for religious affairs.

That overseer was named Ivan Spriridonovich Tolstopyatov. He sat down his guest from Moscow in his office, and interrogated him in detail about the reasons for his visit, and about conditions among the Old Believer communities. He asked for quite exact details even about the South American Old Believer communities. It was only after he'd found out everything he wanted to know that he explained how to get to Clara Tsetkin Street, where the Old Believer Church was.

Having said goodbye to Ivan Spriridonovich Tolstopyatov, my friend went out into the city and soon found the little street and the wooden house he was looking for, which had been turned into a church with an onion dome and a cross. Nearby on a bench, an old grandfather about ninety years old with a neatly trimmed long beard was sitting in the usual half caftan. Grandpa was warming himself in the sunshine and praying with his leather Old Believer prayer rope, or "little ladder," as they call it because of its step-like form. He looked at the newcomer with the benevolent indifference of someone who had seen it all before.

"Greetings, Father!"

---

* Church reforms were introduced by Patriarch Nikon into Russian practice between 1652 and 1666. Many Russian Orthodox did not agree with the reforms, and a schism occurred, which became known as the "Old Believers" or "Old Ritualist" schism. The Old Believers call themselves simply "Orthodox," and the members of the Patriarchal Church "Nikonites," after the reformer. —TRANS.

Painting by Isaac Levitan.
Over Eternal Peace (fragment).

"Hello to you too, if you're not joking."

"Are you in charge here?"

"Sort of." Grandpa didn't bother to object.

"So how do you save your souls here? Does everyone go to church?"

"The old folks do."

"How about the youngsters?"

"The youngsters prefer to go dancing and to the movies."

"M-hm. And besides you and the Patriarchal Church, what else do we have in the city?"

"Two and two of all flesh, like the animals in Noah's ark," said the old man stoically. "There's us, and the Patriarchal Orthodox Church of the Nikonites, and the Catholics and the Baptists and the Jews and the Muslims. And all of us are governed by one indivisible authority—Ivan Spriridonovich Tolstopyatov!"

Father Adrian.

Exorcism

ONLY ONCE IN my life did I attend an exorcism—but that was more than enough. It was performed by Father Adrian: literally devilish and inhuman cries and shouts eerily resounding in a church packed full of people. The people were growling, bleating, squealing, and crowing. Some were cursing so vilely that I wanted to cover my ears. Others were spinning on the ground like tops and slamming themselves with force onto the floor—and in all these cases it was obvious that these people absolutely had no desire to do what they were doing. One well-educated and obviously intellectual man with a face that seemed scared to death was running around the church oinking and snorting like a pig or a wild boar, and finally collapsed with exhaustion only after he was forcibly grabbed and dragged to the priest, who sprinkled holy water on him.

The Russian word for exorcism is *otchitka,* meaning a "reading-out" —a prayer rite for the driving out of demons. It is frightful to describe this procedure, and even more frightful to be present during such things. How Father Adrian was able to stand it, I have no idea.

Father Adrian began his monastic path in the Holy Trinity Monastery. There he was also involved in exorcisms, but secretly, so that no one would notice. They took place in a little church far off the beaten paths of the tourists. It is said that one day high-ranking Soviet authorities arrived at the monastery and, unfortunately for themselves, wished to inspect all of the sites of the monastery without any exceptions. This included the out-of-the-way church from which strange yells were emerging.

There was no refusing such high-ranking officials, so the monks brought them into the church, where a sluggishly speaking and extremely disheveled Father Adrian happened to be saying the exorcism prayers. The visitors were petrified when they saw people rolling around on the floor and screaming with savage voices. But imagine the shock of these high-ranking Soviet guests when one of the ladies who had come along with their group, who happened to be herself a very high-ranking official, suddenly began to hiss and meow like a cat in heat, screaming and rolling around the floor of the entire church—on top of which she began using such language that even experienced men of the world have never heard anything more revolting.

Later this lady came back to visit the monastery. This time she was all alone. She sought out that same thick-tongued Father Adrian and asked him just one question: what had been wrong with her?

Father Adrian, being a simple man, answered her very simply: "You have a demon inside you. That's what's causing your troubles."

"But why is this demon inside of me in particular?" The lady was quite indignant.

"Well, don't ask me, ask him," Father Adrian replied, pointing with his finger at an icon of the Last Judgment—especially at a frightful image of a horned and repulsive creature. However, when he saw how his visitor turned pale, he hastened to calm her down. "No need to kill yourself about this. Maybe the Lord let this happen so that he might lead you through sickness back to faith."

Father Adrian had grasped the truth. The lady began to visit the monastery frequently, confessed all the sins of her life, and took Communion. The demonic attacks ceased and were never repeated. Soon Father Adrian said that she no longer needed to attend any exorcisms: her belief in Christ, her new life according to God's commandments, and her participation in the sacraments of the Church all were sufficient to drive out any spiritual filth from the human soul.

However, Father Adrian himself began to have problems soon after this, because this lady took no measures to conceal her new attitude towards religion. The big scandal was only resolved when under very serious pressure from the authorities the abbot of the monastery sent Father Adrian far away to the provincial Pskov Caves Monastery, so that high-ranking and responsible Soviet comrades could now make their tourist excursions to the Holy Trinity Monastery in peace, drinking libations with the steward, and reasoning with profound condescension that "maybe there is something in this Church stuff."

* * *

A brief digression. Once there was a still-young bishop who was remembering past years. He remarked that the Church administrators of his generation had defended the interests of the Church at the cost of their livers. He said this and wept—whether it was because he felt so sorry for

The Holy Trinity-St. Sergius Lavra.

himself, or because he really had begun to have liver problems.

But I will never cast a stone of aspersion on such bishops and priests. First of all, of course, that is because I myself am not without sin. But second of all, all these bishops and priests simply had no choice but to entertain these important government bureaucrats and overseers for religious affairs at their ecclesiastical refectories. And these priests, who had no choice but to abuse their livers with Party visitors for the good of the Church, were the ones who were not only taking care of the economic and political and administrative support system of the Church, but they were in fact the ones giving Fathers John, Cyril, Naum, and Adrian the opportunity to serve, and to spread their blessings to the millions of parishioners and pilgrims who were coming to their churches and monasteries. So let us not criticize them, please, for they did their job as best they could.

In the Holy Trinity Monastery there was a famous cellarer named Father N. The brotherhood there still remembers him kindly to this day. They remember both his kindness and goodness as well as the fact that he always took upon himself the labor of dealing with the outside world, keeping the other monks of the monastery free from such burdens. In cases when the monastery was again visited by yet another "inspection" or high-ranking and precious guests, who needed to be taken care of and pampered, everyone knew that "Father N. will handle it."

* * *

But let's get back to our exorcism. Many years later I was told by psychiatrists how in pre-Revolutionary Russia they distinguished psychologically ill patients from those who were suffering from demonic possession. The doctors would use a simple method: they placed in front of the patient several cups of ordinary water and one cup of holy water. If the patient calmly drank water out of all of the cups, he was sent to the hospital. But if he refused to drink from the cup with holy water, and then began to scream and yell and go into trances, then he was sent to be cured by the exorcist.

Exorcism, or the driving out of demons from a person, is not only a nerve-racking but also an extremely dangerous procedure. Witnessing just a single such rite is enough to convince oneself of this fact. However, all of these remarks relate to real exorcisms. For it must be said that without doubt there are cases of fake possession, or cases where the patients are really only just psychologically ill people. There are also particularly revolting cases, where people are playing games of "exorcism" and claiming to be "healers."

Thank God, however, this happens quite rarely. The Holy Hierarch Ignatius Branchaninov wrote scathingly about cases of "soul-destroying simulation and pathetic comedy where old men take it upon themselves to act the role of the ancient holy elders, without having any of their spiritual gifts."

Demons are like parasites in the human body. You may not know about them, and may not even believe in their existence, but they truly do act as parasites on our souls and, imperceptibly to their hosts, control their thoughts and deeds. In turn these people may not understand why such strange, horrible, and senseless things are happening to them, and why all their life has been transformed into a miserable process of extricating oneself from one mistake into another. The Church has all the methods for healing and curing these broken fates. But the key thing is that a person can only be cured by changing himself. The prayer of a priest may have some effect, but it is only an aid.

Naturally, not all priests are capable of carrying out the rite of exorcism of demons. Father Adrian was practically the only one who did such work during the 1980s. Supposedly there was also a Father Vasily in Vask-Narva, Estonia, who could also do it.

Archimandrite John (Krestiankin) was quite skeptical about this practice. And not because he thought it was incorrect, but because he believed that negative influences from the spiritual world on a person could only be healed by personal repentance, confession, and the taking of Holy Communion. That said, he did not contradict the usefulness of the actual prayer rite used to drive out demons, but he was concerned that those who came to be exorcised were only really there to be healed by others, but without doing anything on their own for healing. And in spiritual life it just doesn't work that way.

* * *

An exorcism is not only a very difficult but also a very dangerous matter, as I have said. As a novice I once had some occasion to be in Father Raphael's parish at the patronal feast of his village church, dedicated to St. Mitrophan of Voronezh. Several priests from neighboring parishes arrived for the Evening Vespers. One of them was a priest who really surprised me.

First of all, his entire mouth was filled with gold teeth (that is how those with money used to replace teeth in Soviet times). Second of all, when we all lay down to sleep in the only room available to us—some on beds, and some simply on the floor—he took off his cassock and put on a special white cassock just for sleeping. When I asked him why, the priest answered me seriously that I was just a boy and so I could sleep in my underwear and in a T-shirt, whereas he as a priest was obliged to go to sleep in a cassock. What if that very night should occur the Second Coming of Jesus Christ? What was he supposed to do, as a servant of the Lord—greet his Lord in his underwear? At the time I was very pleased by his faith.

Even more interesting was how he got his gold teeth. Generally this is a great rarity for priests. Well, one or two teeth is fine, but for the entire mouth to be full of gold . . . this is unusual. I could not hold back my curiosity and asked him where he got such beauty from. And the priest, settling his legs by the bed in his white priestly nightgown, told us the story by the light of the night light by his little nightstand.

In his worldly life he had been the manager of a network of provincial cinemas. In the course of such highly placed and lucrative activity, he had been able to fill up his mouth with gold to his heart's content. He liked having his mouth full of gold. And yet, notwithstanding his job, he was a pious man. He lived together with his aged mother, and they had a father confessor—an elder in some distant parish in Belgorod Province. Time passed, and this elder gave him permission and blessing to get ready to enter the priesthood. Within a year he was ordained, and appointed as priest and rector of a country church not far from a local regional center.

He served there for ten years. He buried his mother. From time to time he would visit his father confessor and also the elders of the Pechory Monastery near Pskov. Then one day a young girl from the local regional center was brought to him, suffering from a terrible case of demonic possession. At first the priest absolutely refused to carry out the rite of exorcism, protesting that he was not ready to undertake such a great task. But in the end the girl's mother and all the rest of her family managed to convince him. Understanding that it would be a very serious thing, the priest spent an entire week in fasting and prayer, and only then for the first time in his life carried out the appointed rite. The girl was cured.

The priest was very happy both for the girl and for himself. He was happy for the girl because the child had truly ceased to be tortured and suffer for the sins of her parents. And he was happy for himself because he realized that he wasn't such a simpleton after all.

Two weeks passed. And one evening after dinner the priest was relaxing in his armchair by the window when he opened the local provincial newspaper to check out the news. He read an amusing article, then put down the newspaper and . . . was petrified with horror. Standing right in front of him was—*him*. The very same demon whom he had driven out of the young girl. He was merely standing there and staring right into the priest's eyes.

Just one look at this creature was enough to make the priest leap out the window and run as fast as his legs could carry him—anywhere. The priest was a portly man, and out of shape, but he only relaxed after his legs had carried him a couple of kilometers away. Without bothering to go home, he went straight to Pskov, borrowed money, and went to visit his old father confessor, Archimandrite Seraphim Tyapochkin.

At first the elder scolded his spiritual child for taking matters into his own hands. It is forbidden to perform an exorcism without the particular blessing and prayers of one's father confessor. Our priest had arrogantly and casually neglected this rule. Furthermore, after temporary victories achieved not through our grace but through the grace of God and the prayers of the Church, there can be no relaxing, reading of newspapers, and vainly feeling good about oneself for one's spiritual triumphs. The elder reminded him of the words of St. Seraphim of Sarov that, if God would allow it, the Devil would destroy the world out of hatred in an instant. At the end of their talk, the elder warned his spiritual child to be ready for new ordeals. Just one mere glance at the Enemy of Mankind would probably not exhaust his torments. The Devil would without doubt find a time to take cruel revenge on the arrogant and spiritually weak priest who had dared unprepared to do battle "with the forces of evil." The elder promised to pray for him and sent him back.

Six weeks passed. The priest was beginning to forget about what had happened when one night he heard a knock on the door. The priest lived alone. When he asked who had come so late, and what was it that these visitors needed, the answer came from the other side of the door that someone was dying in a neighboring village and urgently needed to take Communion. The priest opened the door, and immediately several people began to attack him. They beat him savagely and then tortured him, demanding him to tell them where he kept his money. The priest showed them everything he had except for the place where he kept the keys to the church. The villains took all that they could and then finally pried the gold out of his teeth with tongs.

Parishioners later found their priest. He was barely alive, and was in so much pain that he could not even scream, but could only moan. The priest spent several months in the hospital. And when the bandits were found and the priest was asked to identify them, as soon as he saw them, he could not control himself but burst into tears like a baby.

But they rightly say that time heals all wounds. The priest got better and once again began to serve in his church. The parishioners were grateful to the priest for not having betrayed where he kept his keys, and therefore having heroically kept their church free and unharmed from attack by these bandits. They therefore took up a collection of money to get new gold teeth for the priest. I don't know whether it was the taste of the gold that he liked, or whether the priest just couldn't imagine himself anymore without gold teeth.

* * *

Valery Postoyev, the boy around whom everything caught fire.

I myself was only once involved in a similar kind of matter. But, of course, it was not an exorcism, just the continuation of the baptism of a young boy that had not been finished by the unknown priest who had started the procedure.

At that time I was serving in the Donskoy Monastery. I was approached by a man of about forty, a lieutenant colonel of the police named Valery Ivanovich Postoyev. He was a nonbeliever, and had not even been baptized, but he had nowhere to go except the Church. He had an only son also named Valery to whom unthinkable things were happening. In the presence of this boy all kinds of objects started to light on fire—all by themselves. Whenever Valery would appear, everything would start to burn: refrigerators, pillows, tables, beds, chests of drawers . . . The Postoyev family ceased to pay visits to others, because within twenty minutes of their visiting, fires broke out. For the same reason they could not let their boy go to school.

Valery was looked at by everyone: doctors and psychics and officers of the FSB* and various other secret organizations of state security—all in vain. Various newspapers ran sensational stories with photographs of

---

* The FSB was the reorganized, post-perestroika KGB.—Trans.

the boy and the fires he had caused. But the parents had no desire for such glory. "Just in case," they even had had their son baptized. Desperate, the policeman wandered into the Donskoy Monastery. Someone had suggested that he pray at the recently discovered relics of the revered Patriarch Tikhon. That is where I met him.

I couldn't understand why it was that the fires hadn't stopped occurring after the baptism. At least, not until I asked the question: how long did the boy's baptism take? The lieutenant colonel answered that it all had taken less than half an hour.

Normally the baptism of one person takes a lot longer. And so I understood everything: the priest who had performed the sacrament had omitted certain ancient prayers, which in the Church are known as exorcism prayers. There are only four of them, and several of them are quite long. Unfortunately, it does happen that certain priests, especially those who as they would say today are of a "modernistic" bent, omit these prayers, believing them to be unnecessary. Yet it is precisely through these prayers that the Church, by the power given to it by God, asks for the deliverance of the human soul from the ancient evil lurking and nestling within. But our modernists believe all of this to be strange and archaic. They are afraid to seem anachronistic and ridiculous in the eyes of their parishioners—although I have never once noticed that these prayers during baptism raised a hint of a smile even among people who were little connected to the Church.

I wrote to Father John about Valery Postoyev, and he answered me that I needed to finish reading the exorcism prayers from the baptismal rite that had been left out by the previous priest. And that is precisely what we did in the Church of the Donskoy Monastery. From that very day the fires ceased. Lieutenant Colonel Valery Ivanovich Postoyev was baptized himself, and all of his family then became our parishioners. The young boy is long since grown up and is now also a police major—in fact, he works as a teacher in the Moscow Police Academy—but keeps the memory of what happened to him in the past through photographs of fires in his family's apartment.

Service for the taking of monastic vows in Sretensky Monastery.

A Sermon Given during a Service for the Taking of Monastic Vows in Sretensky Monastery

OUR LORD EXPECTS faith from us. Faith, and nothing more. Faith in the spirit of God. Faith in our faith. Faith in Christ.

Today in our monastery we have a special occasion—a new monk has appeared in this world. In detail we heard from the Scriptures today; the Lord has placed a child before him and has said: "Verily I say unto you, except ye be converted and become as little children, ye shall not enter the Kingdom of Heaven."

Everyone after taking his vows appears before the Lord like a child, innocent—with a new life opening before him. And now it all depends on the monk himself: will he remain as pure of heart as a child standing before his Savior? From our teachings we know that the innocent boy set before the Lord was the future St. Ignatius, who suffered martyrdom for Christ, and yet remained true to Him in spite of everything. Or will he choose a different path, and be true only to his own desires that he will hold up as a law for himself and the entire world? Will he try to deceive everyone, and in the end deceive only himself?

Our Lord expects faithfulness from us. And from you, our new brother monk! Faithfulness above all. To your monastic vows. To obedience. Faithfulness in humility. Faithfulness to your commitment to love above all else in this world our Savior and Lord Jesus Christ, and to prefer nothing and no one else in this world to Him.

If you can remain true to this, your new covenant with God, which you have made today upon taking your vows, then many people will come through you to salvation and eternal life. Yet if, God forbid, the human heart and the heart of the monk are focused on himself and not upon the Almighty, if we do not keep faith with God, then the very worst possible thing that could happen to us will occur—the senseless life of a monk. And there is absolutely nothing worse than that! But you have been given all the weapons you need to help you to victory.

The Lord has encouraged you with the remarkable words that you have heard upon taking your vows. We have all prayed for you. A remarkable and beautiful path is opening before you. It is full of struggle and of temptation, but it is also full of incomparable meaning, joy, and happiness that the rest of the world simply cannot comprehend.

May God help all of us brothers and sisters to be faithful to our calling. After all, the vow of faithfulness is not just for us monks alone. As St. Ephraim the Syrian wrote, the Lord does not seek the monk or the layperson, the scholar or the simpleton, the rich man or the pauper, but only the heart that thirsts for God, full of a sincere desire to be true to Him and His commandments! May God give us understanding of this faith, for it gives our lives meaning. In exchange for our faith in Him, Christ gives His disciples and students everlasting joy and strength and courage to surmount all temptations we will face as we go through life. Amen.

* * *

Postscript: The monk for whom the sermon was given left the monastery within five years. There are no mechanisms within our Church to compel anyone to remain in the monastery. Here in the Sretensky Monastery over the past roughly twenty years we have had three such cases. When we are told that this is not very much in comparison with the other monasteries, we do not believe it. Even one such occurrence is truly a tragedy for the monastery, first of all for the monk himself who has betrayed his own vows.

One can't help feeling terribly sorry for these people. Church canons prohibit them from being buried in a Christian cemetery, and they are treated the same as those who commit suicide. Their marriages are not recognized by the Church. I have had occasion to read theological rules and canons such as these, and often it seemed that they were just too cruel.

But once I heard not a theological commentary, and not a paragraph from the ancient canons, but just one small quatrain, from which I understood that the laws of the Church merely confirmed the sorry state into which a monk who has recanted from his chosen path plunges himself. Of course, the Lord is merciful, and repentance is available to all.

And yet listen to how Arseny Chanyshev, a professor in the philosophy department of Moscow State University and the author of several books of commentary about classical philosophy, summed up his life. He was not a monk. He had no cause to repent for having violated vows that he had given to God. But he was the son of a monk who had abandoned his faith. And here is his quatrain.

> I'm a monk's son, a child of sin.
> I am the breaking of a vow
> And cursed by God for this somehow:
> My life is naught but dust and din.

The Tale of the Prodigal Bishop

From *The Prologue*

*I*N A TOWN in Byzantium there was once a bishop who was very much beloved by the townsfolk. But then something terrible happened: whether through his own weakness or lightheartedness, or through the conniving of the Devil, this bishop fell into the sin of fornication.

On a Sunday when the entire town had gathered for the Divine Liturgy, the bishop addressed the people, and removed his bishop's stole, the symbol of his episcopal rank, and said: "I can no longer be your bishop, for I have fallen into the sin of fornication."

At first silence reigned in the crowd. Then sighing was heard all over the church. People stood and cried. The bishop was also crying as he hung his head and looked at his parishioners.

Finally the people calmed down a bit and asked: "What will we do now? We still love you. Therefore put your vestments back on and serve the Liturgy, for you will always be our bishop and our pastor."

To this the bishop replied: "Thank you for your generous words, but I truly can no longer serve as your bishop. By the laws established by our Holy Fathers, a bishop who has sinned as I have is no longer worthy to serve the Divine Liturgy."

The people answered him: "We know nothing about your laws. No doubt they are very important and all correct. But we have come to love you for all those years during which you have served us in our town. All kinds of things happen in life. So put on your vestments and serve. We forgive you."

The bishop laughed bitterly: "Yes, you have forgiven me. But I will never forgive myself, nor will the Church ever forgive me. I can never be forgiven before God. Therefore make way for me. I will walk into the desert to weep and to repent of my sins."

But the crowd only grew tighter and did not even let their bishop leave the podium. "No!" The crowd was insistent. "You are our bishop! Put your vestments back on and serve!"

The interior Basilica of St. Apollinarius the New, Ravenna, Italy.

The standoff continued till late in the evening. The people would not back down, and the unhappy bishop had no idea what he should do. When he finally comprehended that the people would not let him go, he said: "All right! Have it your way! But I will stay only on one condition. You must all now leave the cathedral, and I will lie down upon the threshold of the door. And as you come back into the church, you must all walk over me so that you will all know what a sinner I am, and how worthless I am."

On this point the bishop was no longer willing to compromise, and it was the people who had to back down. Everyone left the church, and the bishop lay down on the threshold of the door. Each and every one of his parishioners, from the oldest to the youngest, with horror (and many with tears in their eyes), walked back into the church, wiping their feet on the bishop.

And finally, when the very last parishioner was inside the church, everyone heard a voice thundering from heaven: "For such great humility, his great sin is forgiven!"

The subdeacons clad their bishop again in his holy vestments, and he served the Divine Liturgy.

*Patriarch Tikhon
in his patriarchal vestments.*

The Relics of Patriarch Tikhon

O NE OF THE many mysteries of ecclesiastical life in Soviet times was what had happened to the remains of the Holy Patriarch Tikhon, who had been buried in 1925 in the Small Cathedral of Moscow's Donskoy Monastery. In 1946 during his funeral, Metropolitan Nicholas (Yarushevich) of Krutitsa and Kolomna sadly pronounced: "We have just prayed over the grave of His Holiness. But his body is not here."

There was every reason to be certain of this. It would not have been surprising to anyone if the remains of Patriarch Tikhon had been destroyed. For if Orthodox believers revered the deceased head of the Russian Orthodox Church as a saint, the hatred felt for him by the Bolsheviks was exceptional, even against the background of hysterical anti-religious Soviet persecution. In a "list of enemies of Soviet authority" published back then by the newspaper *Izvestiya*, Patriarch Tikhon was listed as number one.

The rumor was that in 1927, after the Donskoy Monastery had been closed, Soviet authorities, fearing that his remains might become an object of reverence, removed his coffin from his grave and burned it in a crematorium. There were other reports that the remains of His Holiness had been secretly spirited out and reburied in the German cemetery in Lefortovo. A third version was that the monks, fearing that the authorities would desecrate the remains of the Patriarch, secretly reburied him in a hidden necropolis somewhere in the Donskoy Monastery.

All these theories grew into a real conviction that was solidified when in 1932 the leader of the Soviet-supported group of ecclesiastical renovationists, the self-styled Metropolitan Alexander Vvedensky, appeared before his supporters in the vestments of the Patriarch himself. Muscovites immediately recognized these garments as having been sewed specifically for Patriarch Tikhon in the famous factory of the Olovyanishnikov merchant brothers. And Patriarch Tikhon had been buried in these vestments.

Yet hope lingered that the remains of this Patriarch beloved by the entire Church would one day be found.

* * *

335

When monastic life was revived in the Donskoy Monastery, one of the first requests of the then still small brotherhood of that monastery to their leader Patriarch Alexiy II (since Donskoy Monastery is Patriarchal) was a petition to undertake a search for the remains of the Patriarch Tikhon. His Holiness joyfully blessed them to undertake these labors. If only we had known then what events would arise from this, and how beautifully everything would end!

Δ. Voedensky in the "patriarchal" garb.

Soon afterwards a convenient occasion for the task arose. Restoration work had begun on the small Cathedral of Donskoy Monastery. The church was closed for several months, and so it would have been a good time to start looking . . . But it didn't happen, as for various reasons the search was always put off, and now the repairs were already complete. Services began in the church once again, and it seemed that we had missed our opportunity. To be honest, at that time we did not take sufficiently seriously the directives of the Patriarch.

Thus we had quite foolishly neglected his blessings because of various "other causes and circumstances." We would soon have to pay for that, and very dearly. But as always, the Lord directed our mistakes to our general enlightenment—and to the triumph of His true holy servant, the new martyr, Patriarch Tikhon.

It was November 1992. The repairs were complete, and the abbot of the monastery, Archimandrite Agathadorus, set off on an official trip somewhere and left me in charge of the monastery as the presiding monk. There might not have been too many worries upon me, though, if it hadn't been for a very unfortunate conflict with certain strange people who had seemingly come out of nowhere and begun to pester us. They represented themselves as priests and laypersons from the Russian Orthodox Church Abroad, although, as it turned out later, they had absolutely no relationship to it whatsoever. They were constantly trying through arguments and disorder to get their way no matter what—and wanted to have their own church services in the monastery, come what may, without the blessing of the Patriarch! We tried to convince them and dissuade them as best we could that this was not allowed, and finally when we understood that there was no reasoning with them whatsoever and it simply could not be helped, we decidedly removed these uninvited guests, and set them out on the other side of our gates. Naturally they were very bitter at us for this.

November 18 was the day on which in 1918 the Holy Hierarch Tikhon had been elected the Patriarch of Moscow and all of Russia (of the three possible candidates, the lot was cast to him). I was sick on the anniversary of that day, but nonetheless I served the Liturgy and also a commemorative funeral service, because it was also the anniversary of the death of my friend Father Raphael. November 18, it must be said, is generally an extraordinary day for me: on that day Father Raphael was killed in 1988; and on that day in 1993, Valentina Pavlovna Konovalova, the Moscow merchant woman and spiritual daughter of Father John, died. And this particular story that I am in the middle of telling also took place on November 18.

On the occasion of these services, it happened to be the first time in my priestly career that I had personally prepared the reserved Holy Gifts for Communion of those who were ill. According to the Church canons, this is supposed to be done on Holy Thursday.

However, on the night before, my friend the sculptor Vyacheslav Mikhailovich Klykov came to me, urgently requesting that I give Communion and Divine Unction to an acquaintance of his who was ailing. But it had turned out that there were no reserve Holy Gifts in our church. It seems that we had never prepared them in our church at all.

Thank God, everything worked out with Klykov's friend. In the night I gave him Extreme Unction, and in the morning a cleric from a different church gave him Communion. In order that nothing of the kind ever happen again, under the direction of our oldest hieromonk Father Daniel, I prepared spare Holy Gifts and placed them in a special receptacle upon our altar.

After the evening service my friend Zurab Chavchavadze came to visit me and brought me a gift, a jar of raspberry jam, our Russian cold medicine. We were drinking tea when the night watchman reported to me with alarm that there were several firemen by our gates whose commander was asserting that they needed to urgently enter our monastery to dowse some fire.

"Is something burning in our monastery?" I asked with surprise

"Certainly not!" the watchman assured me. "If anything is burning I believe it is inside the firemen's commander's head."

I grasped the situation at once. Not far from us there was a fire brigade whose leadership was friends with Father Agathadorus. One of its officers was very fond of sitting up nights with Father Agathadorus and philosophizing about life. Already once before, during his bout of alcoholic philosophizing he had tried to break into the monastery in the middle of the night. It seemed that this story was repeating itself.

I hung up and a minute later there was yet another call. The watchman alerted me that the firemen were insistent. This was too much. Zurab and I had to put on our coats and in my feeble condition, and even after the raspberry jam, I had to bundle up warmly and go find out what was wrong.

"What happened?" I yelled loudly so they could hear beyond the gates.

"Fire! Fire! You have a fire!" they called from over there.

"Maybe you'll think of a funnier reason for visiting?'

"We received an emergency call!"

"It must be some mistake. Come see for yourself," said I, opening the gates.

Two fire trucks with full crews were standing on the other side of the monastery walls. Several firemen in bright fire helmets walked into the monastery. They themselves were quite upset.

"Some woman called. We thought she was calling from you. She said there was a fire in the Donskoy Monastery."

To prove to them that it absolutely had been a misunderstanding, I asked them to walk with me around the monastery. We went to the central square. It was late twilight, but one could still see quite well. All seemed quiet and peaceful, with no reason to be alarmed. "You see?" I smiled as I turned to the firemen.

And then just at that moment in the windows of the Small Donskoy Cathedral bright flames blazed, and we could hear the sound of smashing glass as orange flames and clouds of black smoke came billowing through the window frames.

The firemen rushed to their fire trucks. Zurab and I were stunned, with our mouths hanging open, and then we began to shout like madmen: "Fire! Fire!" And we ran to the church.

The fire trucks raced past us, but the church was already all ablaze. The

The Small Cathedral of the Donskoy Monastery after the fire.

fire kept growing through the windows, as the gloomy column of smoke climbed into the evening sky of Moscow.

I will not describe that terrible night at length. The firemen only let us into the church after two o'clock in the morning. The sight that met our eyes in there was truly frightful. The walls and ceilings were charred, as were the icons, the cases, everything . . . Everything was covered in water, and one could scarcely breathe—there was a terrible stink of carbon monoxide everywhere.

One of the firemen drew me aside and led me into the heart of the church. As he did so he offered his first conclusions about the reason for the blaze. He asserted that the fire had broken out right at the grave of the Patriarch Tikhon. And because the walls of the church had been painted with flammable oil paint, the fire had spread in minutes.

"But this is really strange!" The firemen pointed to the iconostasis. Although the wooden frames and icons had been somewhat blackened with soot, they hadn't even been slightly charred. The iconostasis had been completely preserved. In the altar area as well there was absolutely no damage, other than a bit of soot.

When I returned from looking around and spoke to the officer, he explained to me that he was utterly bewildered by this fact. "Everything around the iconostasis is completely burned, and yet it is not damaged in the least. Is it made of wood, or is it metal?"

"It's made of very ancient wood."

"Then why didn't it burn? This is very strange!"

Then I suddenly remembered and said: "Oh! Just this morning we put the Holy Gifts on the altar table!"

"You put what?"

I tried to explain. The officer listened politely and then with a gentle cough asked: "And you seriously believe that this has some kind of effect on the preservation of wood from fire?"

"I don't know. I'm just telling you that this morning we put the Holy Gifts there on the altar table!"

"A-ha. Sure!" the officer drawled skeptically. "Actually, sometimes these things happen. Everything around may burn up, and then for some reason some objects are spared. You never know what's going to happen."

The investigation began that very day. It turned out that the fire had indeed originated by the grave of Patriarch Tikhon. The window is always kept slightly opened. Investigators believed that someone who wished us ill had thrown something like a Molotov cocktail through the window. The walls, being covered with oil paint, had immediately burst into flame, and the fire had begun to spread through the church. During the subsequent commotion, the arsonist had had sufficient opportunity to exit the monastery along with its last visitors and remain unnoticed.

We also found out how the fire had so quickly been discovered. One of our parishioners who lived right across the street from the monastery used to like to read her evening prayers right on her balcony. It was she who had fortunately noticed the flames in the window of the little church and had immediately called the fire brigade.

A day later in the burned out church we held the Vigil Service in honor of the Archangel Michael. The choir sang the hymn "Praise the Name of the Lord" as I censed the church and as the worshipers, standing together amidst the charred remains of the church and soot-covered walls, could not hold back their tears. But it was out of the question that we would hold the services in any other church of the monastery. We couldn't let people think that this difficult trial was going to defeat us, or that the Lord would fail to transform our sorrow and grief into joy, and into a triumph of faith and hope in His Providence, unfathomable though it might be to us. That was precisely what I said in my sermon to the parishioners that evening.

So again we had to repair the church. It had been less than a week since the restorations, but now this time we had a second chance to search for the relics of Patriarch Tikhon.

Once again we asked His Holiness the Patriarch for permission to excavate the church, and he gave his blessing, on condition that we act with due care and prudence. We understood his concern. Various people had tried to convince him not to allow the search to take place at all, especially given how unlikely it was that we would ever find any remains of the Holy Patriarch. Worse, if the rumor were to spread that there had been a search for the relics of Patriarch Tikhon and nothing had been found, we were advised that there would be all kinds of problems. Schismatics and enemies of the Church would immediately spread rumors that the holy prelate Tikhon himself had not wanted his remains to be buried in the Patriarchal Church. But thanks be to God, Patriarch Alexiy firmly stated that if we were to find the remains, it would be a great celebration, but if we didn't, we would not attempt to conceal this fact.

The arsonists were never found. Various members of our brotherhood and certain parishioners tried to imagine who it might have been, and even then they somehow pitied them and commended them and their souls to the merciful judgment of God. What's more, looking back now with the benefit of time, we can see how this evil act of arson somehow coincided with the Lord's plan. For it was during the second and much lengthier restoration of the Small Donskoy Cathedral that the relics of the Patriarch Tikhon were found.

It was the evening of the feast of the Meeting of the Lord. We started by saying prayers by the grave of the Patriarch Tikhon, and then began our excavation. Very few people even knew about this: His Holiness Patriarch Alexiy II, several monks, Archimandrite Cyril from the Holy Trinity Monastery, Archimandrite John from the Pskov Caves Monastery, and those whose help we had asked for: Vyacheslav Mikhailovich Klykov and several of his stonemasons and assistants, and also the artist Alexey Valeryevich Artemyev. Our group leader was the learned archaeologist Sergei Alexeyevich Belyayev. He had been responsible for the location of the remains of St. Ambrose of Optina, and had also carried out excavations in the Monastery of Diveyevo and in the Chersonese peninsula, where there used to be Scythians, as well as ancient Greek colonies.

We began by removing the gravestone. After the fire its marble had become practically brown. As we got about thirty centimeters deeper we found a massive marble slab inscribed: "His Holiness Tikhon, Patriarch of Moscow and all Russia." That was precisely the title of the Russian Orthodox Patriarchs at the beginning of the twentieth century. This find inspired us, as we began to dig deeper, and as we reached one meter more in depth we saw what we had been looking for: the stone vault of a hidden crypt. But as we reached again to remove several stones from the vault of the crypt, I cautiously inserted a burning candle into the cavity that had been formed and glanced inside. The crypt was empty. All the candlelight was able to reveal were the dusty remains of an old spider web.

When I told my friends this, everyone was let down with exhaustion, and for a while we just sat there silently. Then one after another they raced to check whether what I had told them was really true. Had I perhaps made a mistake? Perhaps in the quite roomy crypt there were a few relics or remains of the former remains that had survived the violation of the grave of the Patriarch? But there was absolutely nothing there at all. Our worst fears had been confirmed.

As we calmed down, we decided to document the size and condition of the crypt. But as we were measuring its length, the measuring rod, which was two meters long, unexpectedly quivered to the right and the left. The same thing happened with a rod that was eight meters long. We hurried to investigate this underground structure and soon understood that we had found not a crypt, but a portion of the heating system of the church, containing stone pipes placed under the floor through which the hot air from the stove was conducted. The heater was significantly wider in the area by the Patriarch's grave, so that it truly did resemble a crypt. Or perhaps the grave was even deeper? Perhaps what we had found was actually a false crypt, specially built this way to deceive the Bolsheviks into believing that the coffin with the body of the Patriarch had already been stolen and buried somewhere else?

Then suddenly Father Daniel brought us a very old man, who asserted that he supposedly knew for sure that the holy prelate Tikhon had been buried exactly five meters to the east of what had been marked as his grave. Our opinions were split after this, and so the next morning we went to visit His Holiness, to ask for his blessing and advice on what to do next. Having listened to all we had to say, the Patriarch blessed our continuing efforts in searches in the same place.

At last by nightfall we finally found the real burial vault of the Patriarch. There could be no doubt about it. It was a very powerful structure covered by an enormous slab, which to our great fortune had not remained whole but was made up of several massive stone sections. We were able to lift up one of them. I lay on my stomach and inserted a candle inside. I remember how I was suddenly struck by a smell of spring freshness emerging from this underground crypt. Everyone gathered round. In front of me was a thin oak coffin of extremely refined carving, whose description I already knew very well. On it there was a marble inscription. By the flickering light of the candle I read: "The Patriarch of Moscow and of all Russia, Tikhon."

We could not believe how lucky we were. Father Agathadorus immediately left to call Patriarch Alexiy. It was already quite late, near midnight, but the sessions of the Holy Synod had only just finished. Twenty minutes later His Holiness came to Donskoy Monastery. By the time he arrived we had lifted up the other slabs above the vault, and greeted the Patriarch with the sound of bells ringing in celebration. It was midnight, and sounded almost like Easter.

It is difficult to convey our feelings that night as we stood by the open rediscovered grave of the Patriarch Tikhon. We could not believe that it was all over and that his relics were really there in front of us. I am sure that Patriarch Alexiy felt the same way. But then he said to me: "Nonetheless we had better look—are those truly his relics?"

I donned my priestly stole, because one can only touch remains when one is clad in priestly attire, and lowered myself back down to the crypt. Removing the nails lifting up the carved lid of the coffin, I felt my heart pounding as I put my arm inside. My fingers gingerly touched first fabric, and then a shoulder. "He's here!" I cried out as loud as I could

"Enough! Come back! Come back! And close the lid quickly!" I heard from above the voice of the Patriarch quivering with emotion.

This took place on February 19. Three days later His Holiness the Patriarch, the members of the Holy Synod, and the father confessors of the Holy Trinity Monastery, Father Cyril and Father Naum, came to our monastery. When the weathered lid of the coffin whose carving was collapsing was lifted up, we saw with our own eyes the preserved remains of the Holy Patriarch Tikhon covered by his velvet Patriarchal mantle.

Several days later we washed the holy relics according to an ancient rite, garbed them in new Patriarchal vestments, and placed the relics in a specially prepared shrine. The Patriarch was wearing the very same famous

The relics of Patriarch Tikhon under his patriarchal mantle.

vestments that had been made in the factory of the Olovyanishnikov merchant brothers. After this for a long time we could not understand how it was possible that these same vestments had also been on the false Metropolitan Vvedensky.

In spite of the fact that it had been very humid in the crypt, the body of Patriarch Tikhon, which had been lying in the earth for sixty-seven years, had somehow been almost perfectly preserved. It was remarkable that by contrast one of his *panagias,* or pectoral icons, resting on the breast of Patriarch Tikhon, though it had been made from the ivory of a mammoth tusk, had been completely dissolved into dust over the years. Only the silver frame of the *panagia* had survived.

We could not help remembering the verse from the Psalm: "Many are the afflictions of the righteous: but the Lord delivereth him out of them all. He keepeth all his bones: not one of them shall be broken." And yet not just the bones of the Holy Patriarch but most of his body had been preserved as well. Likewise preserved were the great Patriarchal *paraman,*[*]

---

[*]A *paraman* is a piece of cloth worn on the monk's back; it bears a depiction of the cross, and states: "I wear on my body the wounds of Jesus Christ my Lord."

At the acquiring of the relics.

his prayer beads, and his monastic *paraman,* his baptismal cross, and a gold *panagia* that had been presented to the Patriarch once by the Bishop of Yaroslavl and the parishioners of that diocese. We even found a piece of a palm frond (for the holy prelate Tikhon had been buried on Palm Sunday)—and found as well a little bottle of aromatic rose oil with which the body of the Patriarch had been anointed before his burial.

Sometime later our archeologist Sergei Alexeyevich Belyayev was able to get to the bottom of the mystery of why the "false Metropolitan" Alexander Vvedensky had been seen wearing the Patriarchal vestments. It turned out that in the Olovyanishnikov Factory two sets of vestments had been made. Now the one that truly belonged to the Holy Patriarch Tikhon is on display in the museum of the Donskoy Monastery in Moscow.

Zurab Chavchavadze and Father Euphemius in the destroyed church of Grozny.

How Prince Zurab Chavchavadze and I Broke the Lenten Fast

I N 1998, Alexander Ilyich Muzykantsky, the Prefect of Moscow's Central District, where the Sretensky Monastery is located, told me about his trip to Grozny in Chechnya, and about the frightful conditions being endured over there by what was then already a very sparse Russian Orthodox minority. I and the rest of our brotherhood asked the Patriarch, His Holiness Alexiy II, for his blessing to take up a collection for the support of our beleaguered brothers, and after just three days we had filled an enormous truck full of food, clothing, and medicines. Our parishioners also collected a fair amount of money, which we supplemented from our own funds in the monastery, and so we had amassed what was a good sum in those days. It was very touching to see how people sometimes gave away their most precious possessions, considering it to be their chiefest joy to sacrifice for their fellow believers.

Alexander Ilyich Muzykantsky, on behalf of the Moscow government, was able to agree with the government of Aslan Maskhadov, the warlord of Chechnya at that time, that we could travel there and distribute aid for Easter to our fellow Christians in Grozny. The director of the Patriarchal workshops in Sofrino also passed along everything that the bombed-out and looted Church of Grozny would need in order to be able to hold Divine Service again.

We were supposed to set out on our trip on Holy Monday, at the beginning of Orthodox Holy Week. The day before we planned to leave, I called my friend Zurab Chavchavadze and asked him to look after my mother in case anything should happen to me on my trip. But Zurab said he would definitely come with me. He said that his great-grandmother Princess Nino Chavchavadze had been kidnapped by the Cherkessians, the people of modern-day Chechnya, at the end of the nineteenth century, but had later been set free. He thought that was a good omen for a successful voyage to those parts. In the end I had to agree, and my dear friend and I departed for Grozny, having asked for the prayers of His Holiness the

347

Patriarch Alexiy, of Father John, and of other elders of the Pskov Caves Monastery.

The scene when we got there was horrific. Grozny had been bombed to bits and lay in ruins. We could not find a single multistory house that had been spared. We had the greatest of difficulties in bringing a few bottles of sacramental wine through Chechen customs, because in Chechnya the absolute Islamic ban on alcohol had been imposed. Thank God we were able to smuggle the money through because I put a money belt around my body, which was not searched. This money was needed to give to ethnic Russian residents of Grozny. For several years they had not received salaries, subsidies, or pensions. Some of the money was meant for the priest, and another portion was for mothers who were searching all over Chechnya for their sons who had been kidnapped.

We stayed in the headquarters of the official delegation of the representative of the President of Russia in Chechnya. It was located in a small area beyond the northern airport, and consisted of just two old wooden barracks. The official representatives of the Russian government were in the first set of barracks. Several generals and officers were living there, and Zurab and I were lodged there. Sixty Special Forces soldiers were housed in the second barracks. Their job, as I was later informed, was to hold out in case of attack for at least fifteen minutes, while the officers were destroying code machines and documents.

We were received very warmly. One of the officers was assigned the task of accompanying us. However, we were honestly warned that if any difficulties arose, this officer would not be able to help us very much, although he might die heroically for our sake. Maskhadov, the Chechen leader, had also assigned us a protection unit of four heavily armed Chechen guards. In response to our question about their loyalties and whether they could be trusted, we were told that everything would be all right, provided they did not sell us for bounty somewhere along the road. Zurab and I decided, so as not to let this worry us, to consider this just a joke.

All day until late at night we delivered food and clothes and money. We gave part of the food and medicines to a children's home. In the utterly ravaged Church of the Archangel Michael we met its priest, Father Euphemius, and agreed that we would serve the Liturgy together two days later on Holy Thursday. Several hundred of the surviving Christians of Grozny were expected to gather for the services. The government had utterly abandoned them. The sufferings that they had endured over the

The Church of the Archangel Michael, Grozny.

past years cannot be even remotely described. We were happy to be able to help at least in some way.

The degree of hatred after the war was so bitter that Russians were forbidden even to keep the tiniest garden so that they could at least feed themselves. As we were walking around the city, people literally spat on my priestly robes, but Zurab and I tried not to notice this, so as not to provoke even worse reactions.

For the convenience of the rest of our charity operations, Zurab and I were offered a chance to shelter not in the Russian government's official representative office, but in a location in the city and without an accompanying officer. Naturally, the officer was categorically against this idea, but Zurab and I decided to entrust ourselves to the will of God and to the honor of the representative of the Chechen government. The officer guarding us warned us that he could not be responsible, and that he had no choice but to leave us. Then we were driven to a place on the outskirts of Grozny. It was a private house.

Naturally, it was nerve-racking. But everything worked out all right. We were greeted with warmth and hospitality by a large Chechen family whose head was an influential man in these parts, an engineer who had grown up in Russia. During the long evening talk we learned about another side of the tragedy of war, which had affected a multitude of simple Chechen families. Meanwhile, we were able to finish almost everything we needed to do. Well after midnight, after I had cleaned my frequently spit-upon priestly garb, and having prayed as powerfully as we could, Zurab and I fell asleep.

In the morning it was Holy Wednesday, and we set off with our same group of Chechen guards on our way back through the destroyed city. Today it seemed that our guards were more warmly disposed to us. Perhaps it had made a favorable impression on them that we had not been afraid to risk death by sleeping in a stranger's house for the sake of our humanitarian mission. We got back to the Northern Airport, where the Russian base was, only late that night, exhausted by many adventures (one of which, unfortunately, was an hour-long chase after our car by a group of armed fighters that even our Chechen guards had no knowledge of).

As we were walking back to the barracks, Zurab and I couldn't wait to sip hot tea with bread and read the service for Holy Thursday that we had brought from Moscow, as well as its rules for Communion, before collapsing to sleep till the morning. If only we had known what was waiting for us in the barracks!

At the door the officers greeted us impatiently. They embraced us in a bear hug and announced that the soldiers, after having lost any further hope of seeing us alive, had prepared a major ceremonial feast to celebrate the fact that we were unharmed and well.

As soon as we walked into the barracks, we were petrified: an enormous table had been set along the entire length of the barracks. That table was absolutely groaning with food: steaming lamb chops, roast suckling pig, mountain trout, fish from the Caspian and Black Seas . . . Next to this banquet on a bookcase stood a paper icon in a frame before which was lit a paraffin candle. Our hosts had done absolutely everything they could do for us. We looked with horror on this gastronomic abundance, and at the joyful faces of the officers who practically fell on themselves in their eagerness to push us forward to the table.

"I can't, I can't . . . I have never in my life broken the Lenten Fast!" Zurab murmured.

What could we do? Try to explain the strictness of Holy Week? Lecture these people who would have done everything they could to guard our lives with all their hearts about the fact that not only meat but even oil was forbidden at this time according to Church rules? I must admit, neither Zurab nor I even in our worst nightmares could imagine being so inhospitable. Somehow we both felt that all our absolutely correct explanations in this context and time would be incomparably more sinful before God than taking the unknown risk of breaking the fast.

That long and beautiful banquet, so full of genuine Christian love, will be remembered by both Zurab and me for the rest of our lives.

In the years that followed, our monastery and its brotherhood had several occasions to be in Chechnya and in other military garrisons. If our voyages coincided with the Lenten Fast or any other fast, we took special care in advance to warn our hosts about our gastronomical limitations.

Gustave Doré's Illustrations of the Bible.

You Cannot Serve God and Mammon Both

O NCE KOLYA BLOKHIN and I decided to earn some money. Kolya is now a well-known Orthodox writer, and then was a dissident who had just gotten out of a labor camp after five years as a political prisoner. (Kolya was imprisoned for five years under article 139 of the criminal code for illegal distribution of Orthodox literature.)

It was 1988. Kolya suggested that we make reprints (illegally, naturally) of the Bible with illustrations by Gustave Doré. This book had not been republished in Russia for many decades and was of course sorely needed. In this sense, what we were doing was absolutely correct.

On the other hand, for an edition of one thousand Bibles we could at that time earn a quite tidy sum of money for those days, which certainly would be nice for both Kolya and me. We both understood this perfectly. And in this sense what we were doing had nothing to do with piety, and it was simply business.

There wasn't a single library in the country where the Bible with illustrations by Gustave Doré was available. I told Metropolitan Pitirim about our idea, and he got very excited about it as a publisher—even though it was quite a dangerous undertaking at that time. He gave me that fabulous book from his home library, and warned me that it was very precious to him because it had belonged to his deceased father, who was a priest. I solemnly swore that I would keep the book safe and gave it to Kolya for a week to make copies.

A week later I called him and asked how things were going. He replied that he needed another three days. Three days later he told me with distress that there were problems and he would need another week. A week later, it was the same thing: Kolya was not returning the book. Meanwhile, Metropolitan Pitirim wanted to know when he could get his Bible back and when the edition would be ready.

I yelled at Kolya over the phone for about ten minutes, but for somebody who had undergone torture and interrogation in prison, a mere scolding was nothing. He explained to me as if I were a little kid that he totally understood everything, but that, come what may, he needed yet another week, at which point the book would be returned to the Metropolitan safe and sound. But yet another week passed, and he did not return the book.

I was in despair and did not even know how to look the Metropolitan in the eye. To try to understand what was going on I went to see a common friend of Kolya's and mine—Victor Burdyuk, who had been sentenced to the same jail term with Kolya on the same case.

"Oh! He's sold it!" Once Victor had heard my story, he was certain of this.

"He couldn't have sold it! That's impossible!"

"It most certainly is possible. He sold it, and he's drinking the proceeds right now. Come to think of it, he's been on a binge lately. He's always drinking cognac, cognac . . . All the time!" I should say we were aware that our friend had this flaw. If he touched the bottle, nothing could stop him—especially after five years in the camps.

Victor sympathized with my terrible predicament, and together we rushed off to see Kolya. Being a truthful man, Kolya immediately owned up to everything and repented. He had sold the senior cleric's Bible on the very day that he had received it from me. Forty minutes later, to be exact. That was the amount of time needed to go to Kuznetsky Most and sell the book for 500 rubles in the famous Moscow black market by the Bouquinist Antique Bookstore. When I asked him in despair why he had done this, Kolya replied drunkenly that the Devil had made him do it. Victor Burdyuk didn't ask him about anything; he knew his friend a lot better than I did.

The situation was getting really catastrophic. It was practically impossible to buy such a book. And where would we get the money? Even if we were amazingly lucky enough to find another copy, we were reliably informed that it would cost us no less than 1,500 rubles. At the time that sum of money for me was simply astronomical—not to mention the fact that Metropolitan Pitirim would immediately understand that it was not his father's book. Nonetheless I scoured the pawnbrokers and loan sharks of Moscow . . . but in vain, as I had absolutely nothing to pawn as collateral.

Next Monday, in three days, I was supposed to appear before the Metropolitan. There could be no further putting off the meeting. And so I

Nikolai Blokhin.

bought a train ticket and went to Pechory to see Father John. Fortunately it was the weekend.

However, in Pechory I was shocked by the news that Father John had locked himself away in retreat and was not seeing anyone and had not seen anyone for days. The news that he was not receiving anyone crushed me. In such a terrible moment, would he really not give me a single word of advice?

In despair I went to Father Raphael's parish and told him of my bad luck. And here I got lucky. Father Raphael was a man who never became depressed under any circumstances. He thought depression to be the most foolish of the seven deadly sins. He began by laughing at my lack of faith, and reminded me that I had forgotten the simplest and best-known means for solving my problems: to read the Prayer Rule for Lost Things.

His words truly shocked me. How could I have forgotten? Everyone knows perfectly well that there is a time-tested way of finding something that has been lost: recite the fiftieth (fifty-first, in the King James Version) Psalm of King David and then the Nicene Creed, or the Symbol of the Faith, and what you seek shall be found.

Metropolitan Pitirim.

By the way, not so long ago this rule really came in handy for me. Irina Vladimirovna Krutova, wife of Alexander Krutov, editor-in-chief of the magazine *Russian Home,* bought a new car. I read the rite of the blessing of a vehicle over it, and then the next day the car was stolen. The police told her that this was one of the most commonly stolen models of cars, and more likely than not it had already been stripped for spare parts. But unlike me, Irina immediately remembered the special prayer. She merely laughed at the policeman's words and began to recite the prayer. The next day they found her car—only the ignition lock had been ripped out.

And I had forgotten about this prayer! Moreover, Father Raphael had been absolutely right. In my despair I had completely forgotten that I needed to turn not to Victor Burdyuk, nor to secondhand booksellers, nor to Moscow pawnbrokers, but to the Lord God Himself and no one else! But Father Raphael reminded me about all of this in the nick of time.

That evening at the Vigil, the next morning at the Liturgy, and on the train ride back to Moscow I never stopped reciting the Psalm, "Have mercy upon me oh God, according to great mercy," and the Creed, "I believe in one God, the Father, the Almighty, Maker of Heaven and Earth . . ." I kept praying until the morning, when I fell asleep in my train wagon to the rolling sound of the train wheels. The Lord even provided for me to be alone in the train car so that I might pray undisturbed.

Next morning, when I came straight from the train station to the Patriarchal publishing department, Victor Burdyuk himself was waiting for me . . . with the book! Wrapped in a satin cloth and completely unharmed! It was the very same book that belonged to the Metropolitan, given to him by his father the priest. Victor didn't tell me how he had managed to find it. One look at his exhausted face was enough to dissuade me from asking. I gathered from several hints that Victor had asked for the help of various unsavory acquaintances from his previous life behind bars.

I returned the book to Metropolitan Pitirim. Thank God, he didn't even scold me. His was true nobility, sympathy, and Christian love.

With joy I immediately called Father Raphael. "You see, Georgiy Alexandrovich, how close the Lord is to us in our travails!" Father Raphael exclaimed with emotion!

How could I not see?

Kolya Blokhin went on to drink those 500 rubles. Yet eventually our relationship was restored. But, of course, I didn't print anymore books with him—except for his own stories that he wrote in jail, which I would later publish in our monastery's own publishing house.

Since that time I have thoroughly learned the teaching: you cannot serve two masters, God and Mammon. What's true is true. If you do not try to mix the unmixable, then the Lord God will send you all that you need at just the right time. And this is not just my experience. A friend of mine once got into a similar situation, only the stakes in his case were much higher. From time to time I even call him and I ask him: "Would you like to save your soul and earn a million?" And then he answers: "Absolutely!" And we both understand that it's just a joke.

A painting of an angel over the Dormition Church, Pskov Caves Monastery.

Yet Another Breaking of the Rules

(Or how Father Raphael proved to be an angel)

The rules of the Holy Apostles set forth that a priest who has struck someone must undergo canonical punishment and is forbidden to serve as a priest.

THIS STORY TOOK place in 1977. Father Raphael was still a young monk who had only just taken his vows in the Pskov Caves Monastery. One sunny summer morning in a beautiful mood he'd walked into its Dormition Cathedral to serve the Liturgy. However, the first people whom he saw there were three drunken hooligans. One of them, as his mates roared with encouragement, actually lit his cigarette from the lantern of the Icon of the Holy Virgin Mary.

Father Raphael remembers what happened next only dimly. As the parishioners who witnessed the event recalled, the young monk grabbed the laughing smoker in a headlock (and Father Raphael was physically an extremely strong man), dragged this fellow outside into the courtyard of the cathedral, and then struck him such a blow that the witnesses still talk about it to this day. Only then did Father Raphael come to his senses.

As if in a slow motion film, he saw the unfortunate hooligan knocked off the ground and flying over the cobblestones, and then crashing onto the ground, lying still. His terrified mates rushed to his help, and then, with one look at Father Raphael, they dragged their comrade away as fast as they could from the cathedral out towards the monastery's gates. But Father Raphael, realizing that he had done something irreparable and now could not properly serve the Liturgy, bowed his head and dashed to the cell of Father John, his father confessor.

Father John at that moment happened to be finishing a series of monastic prayers. But Father Raphael tore into his cell without knocking and threw himself at the feet of his elder. In despair, he confessed his crime and begged for forgiveness for this sin, asking for advice as to what he should do now.

359

Father John.

Father John listened attentively and then scolded his pupil severely: "Why are you trying to crawl beneath my vestments for absolution? It wasn't you who struck him! It was an angel!" Nonetheless he read the prescribed prayer of forgiveness, blessed Father Raphael, and sent him off to serve the Liturgy.

Confession.

The Story of the Egyptian Cat

N O DOUBT ABOUT IT, people love to make fun of and criticize priests. Therefore it was very unexpected for me when once, during the time when I was still serving in the Donskoy Monastery, a parishioner named Nikolai walked up to me and said, "Now I have understood that the very best, very greatest, most patient, and most beautiful people in the world are the priests!"

I was surprised at this. I asked him what had suddenly led him to these thoughts. Nikolai replied:

"I have a cat. A very good, intelligent, and beautiful cat. But he has one peculiarity: whenever my wife and I go to work he gets in our bed and, excuse me, craps in it. We've tried everything we could to train him out of this habit. We've begged and we have punished him—but it's all to no avail. We even erected a whole barricade to guard our bed from him. But when I got home, I saw that the barricade had been scattered, that the cat once again clambered onto the bed and had once again done its dirty little deed. I was so furious that I grabbed that critter and just smacked him! At this, the cat was so upset at me that he climbed under the chair, and just sat there, sat there and cried. Yes, he really cried, crying, for real . . . It was the first time I've ever seen such a thing. He really had tears coming out of his eyes. Just at that moment my wife comes home and she says to me: 'You ought to be ashamed of yourself! And you call yourself a Christian? I'm not even going to speak to you until you go to the priest and repent for your frightful, horrible, utterly un-Christian act.' And so I had no choice, and besides my conscience was tormenting me anyway. The next morning, I went to the monastery to say my confession. I was confessed by Father Gleb. I waited my turn and told him everything."

Father Gleb was a very kind middle-aged priest from the Holy Trinity Monastery, who was then serving temporarily in the Donskoy Monastery. Usually during confessions he would stand behind the lectern, take his beard into his fist, and listen to the sins of his parishioners. Nikolai related his melancholy tale with a full heart, spilling out everything. He tried not

363

The Small Cathedral of the Donskoy Monastery.

to conceal anything and therefore he spoke for quite a while. The Russian word for cat is *kot*.

When Nicholas was finished, Father Gleb was silent for a bit, sighed, and then said: "Hmm! Yes! It certainly is a bit awkward. But I'm not quite understanding. Does this Copt* study in the university? Don't they have dorms there?

"What Copt?"

"You know. The one that lives with you. The one you're having problems with."

"And then it struck me," Nikolai continued, "that Father Gleb, who was slightly deaf, had humbly been listening for ten minutes to some ridiculous story about a Copt who for some reason lived in our apartment, yet craps in our bed, and whom I had savagely beaten, and who had then been so upset that he crawled under a chair and sat there and wept. And when I realized he was still listening, that's when I understood that the most beautiful and incomprehensibly patient, generous, and great people in this world are our priests!"

---

* A Copt is a member of the ancient Coptic Church, established in the first century in Egypt.—Trans.

Archimandrite Abel.

Andrei Bitov

O NCE WHEN I was on my way to see the Patriarch, I dropped by the office of my friend Archpriest Vladimir Vigilyansky, His Holiness's press secretary.

We had only just started to drink tea when we were joined by Paul, the Archbishop of Ryazan, who needed to kill some time before his meeting with the Patriarch. Soon Father Vladimir's cell phone rang, and he stepped out into the corridor so as not to disturb us with his conversation. When he got back he looked quite surprised, and he told us that his caller had been his friend Andrei Bitov, the famour writer. Before his ordination, Father Vladimir had been a well-known journalist and a member of the Writers Union.

Andrei Georgievich Bitov had been baptized in Georgia by a priest who was called Mamao Tornike in Georgian, and to whom certain Moscow intellectuals often paid visits. But after his baptism Bitov did not often go to church. However, his late mother had become a deeply religious woman. She had died about a year ago. And now Bitov was calling Father Vladimir about his mother. She had appeared to him in a dream the previous night.

All day Bitov had been under the deep impression caused by that dream. And finally he decided to ask advice of his friend the priest.

In the dream his mother had been very strict. She had said to her son, "Andrei, you must do what I tell you. You must confess your sins and take Communion."

"It is difficult for me to confess to our priests. It's always a problem for me." Her son answered just as they all do. "The Russian intelligentsia does not change even when it's dreaming!" I managed to think, not without a certain degree of wry affection. But Father Vladimir continued his story.

Bitov's mother who had appeared in the dream was unrelenting. "You must go to Ryazan Province. There is an old monk there, an Archimandrite," she said firmly. Then she named a rare and extremely ancient name, which Bitov immediately in this dream forgot. "You must go to this monk and confess and take Communion!"

That was the end of the dream. In the morning Bitov woke up, but

Daur Zantariya and Andrew Bitov.

everything that he had seen in the dream was firmly fixed in his memory—except for the terribly rare and ancient biblical name of the monk—a monk whom he now for some reason had to go see. Bitov thought about it for a long time. It all seemed strange and ridiculous. But his mother had insisted. In the end he decided to call Father Vladimir Vigilyansky, his old friend.

When Father Vladimir heard what Andrei Georgievich had to tell him, he remarked: "Try to remember the name of that Archimandrite."

"It's impossible. I can't. All I remember is that he lives somewhere in Ryazan Province. And his name is something out of the Old Testament."

"Naum?" Father Vladimir asked, having in mind a rather famous father confessor from the Holy Trinity Monastery.

"N-no, not Naum."

"Then it must be Abel!" Father Vladimir was certain. "We don't have any other elders with Old Testament names."

"Yes! It is Abel! Exactly!" Bitov was overjoyed. "But how did you know?"

"Lots of people know Father Abel."

"And where does he serve?"

"In the Monastery of St. John the Baptist near Ryazan."

"Exactly! Mama told me that I needed to go see the monk Abel in Ryazan Province!"

"And it just so happens that in my office right now there are two people sitting with me." Father Vladimir continued. "One is Archbishop Paul, who heads the diocese of Ryazan. And the other is Archimandrite Tikhon, whose monastery's agricultural community is near Ryazan. And he was just telling me how he had recently visited Father Abel. So you see, Andrei, God himself has commanded you to go see Father Abel as soon as possible, and finally make your confession and take Communion. If your poor mother had no choice but to come to you in a dream, believe me that's no joke at all!"

"Yes, I know, I know," Bitov replied. "But it's all so strange."

Father Vladimir continued: "I will ask Archbishop Paul to put you up in the monastery and take you to see Father Abel. It's about a three-hour drive from Moscow. Is it agreed?"

"Of course!"

But in fact he tarried and he dallied and delayed for several months, and did not go as agreed. And soon six months had passed. And by then Father Abel had passed and gone on to be with his Lord.

Bishop Basil Rodzyanko.

His Eminence the Novice

$\mathcal{T}$HE RUSSIAN BISHOP Basil (Rodzyanko) died on September 17, 1999, in Washington, D.C. In reality, Bishop Basil had simply been waiting for this moment to begin a journey for which he had been preparing his whole life. Indeed, Basil often spoke about it, but no one seemed to understand. His interlocutors preferred to ignore it or to express their sympathy by saying: "Why, Vladyka"—this is what Russians call their bishops, an affectionate word meaning "Sovereign," "Master," or "Your Grace"—"you have a life ahead of you! God is merciful!" But the bishop himself looked forward to his journey onward with impatience and with lively interest.

The thing is that even during his life he had always been an inveterate traveler. Moreover, I would say that traveling was his true mission and true way of life.

The beginning of his journey, without a doubt, was his birth in the aristocratic estate of Otrada, which was his family patrimony. The boy who was to become the bishop Basil was called Vladimir (Volodya) by his parents. The newborn boy's paternal grandfather was Mikhail Vladimirovich Rodzyanko, the chairman of the State Duma of the Russian Empire. And his mother came from two ancient princely lineages of the highest rank: the Golitsyn and the Sumarokov families. Indeed, many noble Russian families were in close or remote kinship with this particular servant of God.

In 1920 the bishop undertook his next real journey. At the time he was only five years old. The road was long—by land and by sea, through Turkey and Greece and on into Serbia. The family was forced to leave because the new leaders of Russia were not willing to let the former chairman of the Imperial State Duma and his family live in peace. The Rodzyankos settled in Belgrade, and this is where the future bishop was raised.

He was fortunate to have wonderful teachers. The cream of the Russian émigré community had congregated in Yugoslavia. Among them were his immediate mentors, the Holy Hierarch John (Maximovich), who thirty years later was to become the distinguished Archbishop of San

371

Francisco, and sixty years later would be known as a saint to the Russian Orthodox Church Abroad, as well as the great Primate of the Russian Orthodox Church Abroad, Metropolitan Anthony (Khrapovitsky). These were both spiritual giants, and they had a powerful and positive influence on their young pupil.

Yet there was another teacher who was no less important in the life of the future bishop—one whom Volodya could never forget. This was his tutor, a former officer of the White Army. No one but little Volodya knew that his tutor was constantly beating him and torturing him, and torturing the poor boy very skillfully too, hitting him without leaving any traces. This miserable officer nursed intense hatred for Mikhail Vasilyevich Rodzyanko, his little student's grandfather, believing him to be at fault for the destruction of Russia. He had no way of venting his anger at the grandfather, and so, alas, he made the poor little grandson pay for all of it.

Years later, the bishop recalled: "My mother not long before her death said: 'Please forgive me for unwittingly letting that man torture you when you were a child.' 'Mother, this was God's will,' said I. 'And if it had not happened to me when I was a child, I would have never become who I am today . . .'"

When the bishop was already in his declining years, God gave him the chance to return to the Imperial village of Tsarskoye Selo. There Bishop Basil had received permission from the Church authorities to serve the Liturgy in the Church of the Feodorov Icon of the Mother of God, a church especially beloved by the Tsar's family. When the service was over, the bishop came out to the people and confessed the guilt he had felt since his childhood solely because he had been the grandson to his beloved grandfather. The bishop said: "My grandfather only wanted the best for Russia, but as a feeble man, he often made mistakes. He was at fault when he sent his parliamentarians to his Imperial Majesty asking for his abdication. He didn't think that the Tsar would abdicate both for himself and for his son, and so when he learned that this is what had happened, he cried bitterly and said, 'Nothing can be done now. Russia is lost.' And so he unwillingly became responsible for the tragedy of the massacre of the Imperial Family in Yekaterinburg. This was an involuntary sin, but a sin nonetheless. And so now, in this holy place I am asking for Russia, for her people, and for the murdered Tsar's family to forgive my grandfather and to forgive me. And as a bishop, with the authority given to me by God, I forgive him, and release his soul from this involuntary sin.

* * *

The Rodzyankos settled in Yugoslavia. Vladimir grew into a kind, tall, and very handsome young man. He received a brilliant education, and fell in love with a wonderful girl who became his wife. And at the age of twenty-five he was appointed to serve as a priest in a Serbian Orthodox Church. When the Second World War began, Father Vladimir Rodzyanko fearlessly participated in the fighting against the Nazis. And when the Communists came to power, he remained unhesitatingly in Yugoslavia while most of the other White Russian émigrés fled the country. Father Vladimir served as a priest in his Serbian parish and he believed it was wrong to leave his congregation, even if he were under the threat of prison or death.

He was not killed, but he was sentenced to spend eight years in a camp. Tito's camps were no less terrible than those in the USSR. Fortunately, Tito soon got into an argument with Stalin, and to irritate his former patron, he let all the White Russian émigrés he had imprisoned out of the camps. As a result the bishop was let out of the labor camps after just two hard years and was allowed to leave the country. And so he immediately began his further travels.

At first he came to Paris to his spiritual father, Archbishop John (Maximovich). Then he was sent off to London to serve at a Serbian Orthodox Church. While in London he began to host religious programs on the BBC Russian language radio service. And through this program many, many generations of citizens of the USSR learned something about God, about their holy Orthodox faith, and also about the history of their Church and their country.

Time passed and Father Vladimir became a widower. The Church blessed him to take his monastic vows and he received a new name, Basil, and became a bishop. Soon afterwards, Bishop Basil undertook a new journey to the United States, where he converted thousands of Protestants, Catholics, and atheists to the Russian Orthodox faith.

But as it happens, he ended up like a fish out of water, not so much for his energetic missionary activity as for his conflict with a very powerful lobby—a group who advocated certain practices that have no place in the Orthodox Church. As a result, Bishop Basil had to retire on a very modest pension. But even this uninspiring event led to the continuation of his heartfelt dreams of wandering and became a reason for renewed activities. During those years, new opportunities for travel to Russia had opened up, and the bishop rushed back to his native land, which was so scary yet so important to him. I happened to witness a part of the events that took place during his return.

* * *

Bishop Basil appeared in my life and in the life of my friend, the sculptor Vyacheslav Mikhailovich Klykov, because of an astonishing and unexpected encounter. It happened in 1987 just before July 17, the anniversary of the Tsar's family's death. Vyacheslav Mikhailovich and I had wanted to serve a requiem for the repose of His Imperial Majesty before, but during prior years it had been impossible, and the idea represented an unsolvable problem. Going to a church in Moscow and just asking a priest to serve a requiem for Tsar Nicholas II was clearly unthinkable. Everyone knew that word would get out, and the very least punishment that such a brave priest could expect for such a deed would be dismissal from the Church. Having services in a private home was impractical, as many friends would have wanted to attend.

It so happened that during those days Vyacheslav Mikhailovich Klykov had just completed the monumental gravestone for Alexander

Bishop Basil on the road.

Peresvet and Andrei Oslyabya—two famous warriors, schema-monks who had been sent to fight for the victorious army of Dmitri Donskoy at the Battle of Kulikovo Field in 1380, in which Russia freed itself from the yoke of the Tatars. After a long confrontation with the local Soviet authority, a memorial gravestone for them was finally placed on the grave of these heroic monks in the former Simonov Monastery, the site of the famous Dynamo Factory during Soviet times.

And suddenly I had a thought—since there already had been an issuance of official approval for sanctifying the gravestone for Peresvet and Oslyabya, we could insert a requiem for the Tsar's family during the service. They would definitely send someone from the KGB to spy on us, but the spies would be unlikely to understand the subtleties of the memorial service in Church Slavonic anyway—for them it would all simply be one long church service.

Vyacheslav Mikhailovich liked this idea. Now there was only one small problem: trying to find a priest brave enough to be willing to carry out the memorial service. Because there were, after all, quite serious risks. Perhaps not the greatest of risks, but risks all the same. And if any of the snoops and stool pigeons caught on to what it was that we were planning on doing . . . we preferred to not even think about this. On the other hand, we didn't want to get any of the priests we knew into any trouble.

And then one of my acquaintances mentioned to me that Bishop Basil Rodzyanko had recently arrived in Moscow from America. Many of us had heard about this bishop, and some of us even knew about his radio broadcasts by the "voices of the enemy." As we thought about this, we came to the conclusion that we would never be able to find a better candidate for serving the requiem for the Imperial Family.

First of all, he was a White Russian émigré. Second of all, since he was a foreign citizen, the risk he would bear would be far less than the risk that our local priests would be facing. The KGB wouldn't really be able to do anything particular against him—probably. At a minimum, we thought it would be easier for him to get out of any pickles he might get himself into—after all, he was an American. That's what we told ourselves. Lastly, as it used to be said in a slightly cynical but popular line from a poem of those days: "Grandpa is old and he doesn't care." In fact, when push came to shove, we just didn't have any other candidates.

Anyway, that evening, Vyacheslav Mikhailovich and I went to the Hotel Cosmos, where Bishop Basil was staying with a group of Orthodox American pilgrims. The bishop came out to meet us in the lobby of the hotel . . . We were amazed! Before us stood a remarkably handsome, tall, elegant old man with a surprisingly kind face. To be more exact, he was the very model of a nobleman and an elder, without any irony or sentimentality, a perfect example of the best people of the times of old. We had never seen such grand prelates. There was something noble about him that we could sense—it was the old unspoiled Russia and her culture so long lost. This was a completely different bishop from all the other bishops with whom we had ever had dealings before. It's not that those other bishops we knew were worse. No! But this one truly was a completely different bishop, from a completely different Russia.

Vyacheslav Mikhailovich and I suddenly were ashamed of ourselves for trying to put such a grand, kind, defenseless, and trusting dear old man into danger. After we first met him and said a few general words, we excused ourselves, stepped to the side, and before having broached the main subject of our conversation, agreed between ourselves that we would insist that the bishop think very carefully before agreeing to our suggestion.

In order to have our conversation the three of us went out for a walk on the street, to be further away from the KGB microphones in the hotel.

But as soon as the bishop heard why we had come to see him, he joyously stopped right on the sidewalk, and, grasping my arm as if he were afraid that I was going to run away, he not only gave his full agreement, but passionately assured us that we had been sent to him by the Lord God Himself. While I was rubbing my elbow, trying to figure out whether or not I would have a big bruise beneath my sleeve, everything was explained. It turned out that on this date every year for the past fifty years, since the time he had first become a priest, our bishop always said a commemorative memorial service for the Imperial Family. And now here he was in Moscow, and for several days he had been trying to figure out where and how he would be able to say this memorial service for the Tsar and his family even here in the Soviet Union. And suddenly we had turned up out of the blue suggesting our pious adventure! The bishop saw us as neither more nor less than angels, sent to him by Heaven. As for all our warnings about the dangers, he merely swept his hands indignantly.

There were only a few other questions, which Bishop Basil resolved instantly. According to ancient Church canons, a bishop who arrives in another bishopric could not celebrate Divine Service without the blessing of the local presiding bishop—and in Moscow, that meant the Patriarch himself. But the bishop told us that on the evening before, His Holiness Patriarch Pimen had already allowed Bishop Basil to have private supplicatory services and requiems. This was exactly what we needed. Furthermore, we needed a choir for the service. But it turned out that almost all the pilgrims who had arrived with the bishop sang in their local church choirs.

In the early morning on the anniversary of the murder of the Imperial Family, we all met by the entrance of the Dynamo Factory. Klykov and I had brought about fifty friends, and there were also about two dozen American pilgrims. For the most part these were Orthodox Anglo-Saxons who had converted to Orthodoxy but who spoke only English and Old Church Slavonic. We had to figure out something urgently, because if our "minders" became aware that foreigners had entered the territory of the factory, this could also cause us major headaches. Therefore, in order to make sure we would be okay, we were forced to scare our American Orthodox brethren half to death by warning them that they might end up in the basements of the Lubyanka Prison if they so much as said one word other than singing during the services. By the way, once the bishop began the services, they actually were quite an excellent choir, and they sang the entire service entirely by heart, almost without any accent.

The representatives of the administration of the factory and some gloomy minders conveyed us along through very long corridors and passageways until we reached the place where the monks Peresvet and Oslyabya were buried. My heart trembled when I saw with what suspicion those plainclothes minders were staring at this elegant bishop, and at his terrified, silent, but otherwise extremely not-Soviet-looking flock. But somehow, everything went okay.

Klykov's memorial sculpture for the warrior monks Peresvyet and Oslyabya was remarkably beautiful: acetic, restrained, and yet majestic. We began with the consecration, and then, in a way that the official minders watching us could not understand, subtly switched into the funeral service. The bishop then gave the service with such passion, and his parishioners sang with such generosity of spirit, that it seemed the whole service was over in a minute. The bishop was careful not to say the words Tsar, Tsarina, or Crown Prince, but instead said the service for the fallen Andrei Oslyabya and Alexander Peresvet, praying also for the murdered Nicholas, the murdered Alexandra, the murdered boy Alexey, and the murdered young girls Olga, Tatyana, Maria, and Anastasia, as well as those who were murdered just for being close to them.

It's hard to say whether those folks and plainclothes understood or not. I cannot quite rule it out. But none of them gave any sign of having understood. And they even thanked us when we took our leave—sincerely, as it seemed to me and Vyacheslav Mikhailovich.

When we left the territory of the factory and once more emerged into the city, Bishop Basil suddenly came up to me and hugged me, with a great affectionate bear hug. Then he said some words that will remain in my memory forever. He said that he would be grateful for what I had done today for the rest of his life. And although I myself didn't really understand what it was that I had done that was so extraordinary, it was extremely pleasant to hear these words from the bishop.

And it was true: the bishop for the rest of his life treated me with the most affectionate consideration and reverence, which became for me one of the most valuable and undeserved gifts ever given to me by God.

* * *

In those days the truth about the martyrdom of the Tsar and his family was only just coming out. Yes, there had been some books published overseas, and a few of the older generation of Russian Orthodox Christians had related what had happened—and these accounts, sparse as they were, were the source of what learning we could glean about the new martyrs of Russia.

At that time, quite furious arguments were raging about the fate of Nicholas II and his family. Various people whom I very much respected were rather skeptical about the idea of elevating the Imperial Family to the status of saints. One of these skeptics was the wonderful Metropolitan Nicholas of Nizhny Novgorod, who was as well as a professor at the Moscow Theological Academy, Alexey Ilyich Osipov. I had nothing to answer against the objections of these highly worthy individuals. Except for one thing: I just knew that Tsar Nicholas and his family had in the end been saints.

This happened about two years after my acquaintance with the bishop, during one of the most difficult moments in my life. I was still just a novice, and I was in an unenviable state of mind when I wandered into the Donskoy Monastery to visit the grave of Patriarch Tikhon. I did this on the anniversary of the murder of the Imperial Family. In that year memorial services were said for him, but for the first time not in secret. And from

The entrance to the Pskov Caves Monastery.

the bottom of my heart I began to pray to these Imperial martyrs, asking them, if indeed they had attained holiness before God, to help me.

The memorial service ended. I left the church still in a despairing and quite heavy state of depression. By the doors of the church I met a priest whom I had not seen in several years. Without any small talk or questions from my side he immediately started talking about the subject and immediately resolved all my doubts. He calmly and clearly told me exactly what I needed to do. This without exaggeration in many ways influenced my further fate. And the question about how or whether the Imperial Family should be revered never arose further in my heart—no matter what I was told afterwards about the undeniable flaws, mistakes, foibles, and sins of the last Russian Emperor.

Of course, our own religious experience means relatively little if it has not been confirmed by the Church. But fortunately for me, the fact of the canonization by the Russian Orthodox Church of the martyred Tsar Nicholas II and his family gives me the right to recognize my own small personal experience to have been truthful.

Among my acquaintances no one has ever doubted that for Russia the monarchy is the most organic and natural form of government. This is true even though we were more than skeptical about various active and scattered monarchist movements of the time.

Once when I was working for Metropolitan Pitirim, serious people dressed up in pre-Revolutionary officers' uniforms walked into the publishing department where I worked. On their uniforms Imperial medals and orders were gleaming, including crosses of St. George—the very highest of Tsarist honors.

I was very surprised and asked: "What made you decide to put on such medals? After all, they were only ever given out for extreme personal bravery in the battlefield."

My guests assured me that they had indeed won these medals honestly on the battlefield. They said that they wanted to speak to the Metropolitan immediately. The Metropolitan, to my surprise, received them, and attentively heard what they had to say with great curiosity for a whole hour and a half. The theme of their visit was hardly without controversy: these guests were demanding that the Metropolitan give them all kinds of assistance in the matter of the immediate restoration of the monarchy. But when Metropolitan Pitirim had shown them out, he remarked: "Give you a new Tsar now, and you'll shoot him again within a week . . ."

* * *

After this, every time Bishop Basil came to Russia, he always called me ahead of time. I was always glad to accompany him on one of his amazing new adventures and pilgrimages. Indeed, the bishop always had innumerable occasions for these. Although, strange as it may sound, the bishop never once undertook a single one of these journeys of his own free will.

He told me one particular story about this. In 1978 his wife Maria Vasilyevna died. The death of his wife was a terrible blow for Father Vladimir. He had absolutely loved and doted on her. The loss caused something that not infrequently happens to real, open-hearted Russian people: Father Vladimir began to drink. The bishop told me about this sad period of his life with a clear heart, explaining it as his most difficult ordeal, the worst he had ever been forced to undergo.

He became a real alcoholic. Fortunately, because of his incredibly strong constitution, large size, and great strength, for a while his drinking did not affect his ability to carry out his priestly duties or his radio broadcasts. Father Vladimir used to drink a powerful Balkan vodka popular in Serbia known as *raki*. It's not clear how this all would have turned out, because neither his father confessor, nor his family, nor his friends could do anything about Father Vladimir's drinking.

Things might have been absolutely terrible, had not the departed spirit of his wife Maria Vasilyevna, who in life, as they say, had been a woman of great spiritual strength and prayer, appeared from the other world in a dream to make her husband shape up. Father Vladimir was so shocked by her appearance, and particularly by the severity of what his wife had to say to him when she appeared, that he immediately pulled himself together after her supernatural scolding. His particularly Russian disease was cured instantly.

Well, he did stop drinking. But he also had to somehow live on. His children by that time had already grown up. And naturally, there could be no question of a second marriage. By the canons of the Orthodox Church, second marriages are forbidden to the clergy. In the event that a priest who is a widower remarries, he is forever stripped of any right to serve in the priesthood. But, even beside these rules, Father Vladimir had been so attached to his former wife and had loved her so deeply that the portion of his own heart that had known earthly love remained entirely devoted to Maria Vasilyevna until the end of time. Father Vladimir began to pray devotedly. And the Lord answered his prayers.

After the death of Father Vladimir's father confessor (Archbishop John Maximovich), his new spiritual father became the Metropolitan of London, Anthony (Bloom) of Surozh, an old friend of the Rodzyanko family. It was he who informed Father Vladimir that the hierarchs of the Orthodox Church of America were delicately yet insistently petitioning him to try to talk the widowed priest Father Vladimir Rodzyanko into taking monastic vows, after which he should be sent to the United States to serve as a bishop in the capital city of Washington, D.C.

Father Vladimir knew all too well that true service as a Church hierarch has nothing to do with honors and rank, but instead with a multitude of ceaseless daily cares, and with the complete impossibility of ever having a moment to yourself, as well as with constantly bearing an enormous load of responsibility almost incomprehensible to laypeople. Furthermore, poverty is also the inescapable lot of a Russian bishop in the diaspora, even dire poverty. By this time he had nearly reached the age of sixty-six, forty years of which he had spent in the priesthood.

But Father Vladimir accepted the suggestion of becoming a monk and then a bishop as the will of God, and as the answer to his own prayers. He agreed. The hierarchs of the American and British Orthodox churches shook hands, and the fate of Father Vladimir was decided.

However, right before taking the monastic vows, the future monk asked his spiritual father, Metropolitan Anthony of Surouzh, an unexpected yet heartfelt question. "Well, Your Grace, I will now receive the monastic vows from you. I will undertake for the Lord God and His Holy Church the great monastic vows gladly. As for the vow of chastity, I totally understand what it means. I fully accept the vow of poverty as well. All the vows related to prayer are also perfectly clear and acceptable to me. But as for the vow of obedience—here I can't understand anything!"

"What are you talking about?" Metropolitan Anthony was very surprised.

"Well, I mean," Father Vladimir reasoned, "instead of starting me out as a simple monk, you're immediately making me a bishop. In other words, instead of being a novice and obeying the commands of others, my job will mean that I'm the one who will have to command and make decisions. How then do I fulfill the vow of obedience? To whom will I be a novice? Whom will I obey?"

Metropolitan Anthony grew thoughtful for a moment, and then said: "You will be in obedience to everyone and anyone whom you meet on your journey through life. As long as that person's request will be within your power to grant it, and not in contradiction with the Scriptures."

Father Vladimir was very pleased by this commandment. But later it turned out that people who made the acquaintance of the bishop did not have an easy time of it all in dealing with his constant willingness to carry out his decisive and unequivocal fulfillment of this monastic vow. Partly I'm referring to myself. Sometimes, the bishop's understanding of his holy vow of obedience would prove to be quite a trial for me.

For example, we might be walking together through the streets of Moscow—on a miserable day, through the pouring rain. And we are in a hurry to get somewhere. And suddenly an old babushka with an old string shopping bag called an *avoska* ("perhaps bag") stops us.

"Father!" She quavers in the voice of an old woman, not realizing of course that she's speaking not just to a simple priest, but to a bishop, no less—and what's more, a bishop from America! "Father! Please can't you help me? Please, bless my room! This is the third year that I've been asking our Father Ivan, and he still hasn't come. Maybe you'll take pity on me? Will you come?"

I hadn't even managed to open my mouth, and the bishop was already expressing his most passionate willingness to carry out her request, as if his whole life long he had only been waiting for the chance to bless Grandmother's little room somewhere.

"But Your Grace," I say desperately. "You don't even have the slightest idea where this room of hers might be. Grandma, where are we going?"

"Oh, not far at all. Just the other side of town—in Orekhovo-Borisovo. It's only forty minutes by bus from the last stop on the Metro. Really—it's not that far," she warbles joyfully.

And the bishop, canceling all our important plans (since it was impossible to contradict him in such situations), would first traipse headlong all the way to the other end of Moscow, the largest city in Europe, to a church where a friend of his gave him the necessary vestments and utensils needed for a house blessing. (Of course, I tagged along with him.) All the while Grandma, beside herself with joy (Lord only knows where she got her strength) and unable to contain her happiness, ceaselessly told the bishop all about her children and grandchildren who never visit her anymore . . . Then, after the expedition to the church, off we went in the other direction, jam-packed like sardines in the crowded Moscow Metro at rush hour, standing all the way and with several long walks to change train lines through the jam-packed corridors, and then standing that way as we rode all the way to the end of the line, on the very outskirts of Moscow.

From there, just as Grandma had promised, it was a forty-minute bone-rattling ride in a dusty old bus, also crammed full to overflowing. But finally the bishop blessed and consecrated Grandma's little room, all eight meters square, on the ninth floor walk-up of some hideous Communist project housing. And he did it with sincerest prayer, majestically, and triumphantly, just the way he always performs any divine services. Then he sat down with the ecstatic Grandma (actually, both of them were ecstatic about each other) and praised to the skies her humble offerings— little Russian pretzels called *sushki,* and tea over-sugared with sickly-sweet cherry jam, full of pits . . .

Then, with immense gratitude, he accepted as an honor and did not refuse the crumpled one ruble note that she stealthily handed to her

Bishop Basil blessing the faithful in Russia.

"Father" as she said goodbye. "May the Lord save you!" she called out to the bishop! "Now it will be sweet for me to die in this little room!"

* * *

Time after time I was able to observe how Bishop Basil gave entirely of himself in carrying out his "task of obedience as a novice" to absolutely anyone who would ask for his help. What's more, it was plain to see that beyond his sincere desire to serve people there was an inner and still more secret desire, known but to him alone.

As I meditate upon this I recall that the Russian word for a novice's monastic obedience, *poslushanie,* derives from the verb *slushat* (to listen, to obey). Gradually I began to grasp that it was through this humble vow of service and obedience, remaining a novice even upon attaining the rank of a very senior cleric, that our sovereign Bishop Basil taught himself how to sensitively hear and to obey the will of God. Because of this his entire life was nothing more nor less than one constant search for the knowledge of the will of God, one mysterious yet absolutely real conversation with our Savior, in which He would speak to mankind not with words, but with the circumstances of this life, while granting unto His listeners the very greatest reward there is—a chance to be His instrument in this world.

*　*　*

Sometime in the summer of 1990, during one of the bishop's visits to Moscow, a young priest who looked like an old-fashioned grenadier came to meet the bishop, and immediately asked him to come serve in his parish. As usual the bishop did not need to be asked twice; meanwhile, I realized we were in for a few problems.

"And just where is your parish?" I asked the young priest gloomily. From my tone of voice the young grenadier understood that I was hardly his ally. "Oh, not far . . ." came his unfriendly reply to me. This was the usual answer always given to us whenever we were being asked to sweep at once across the vast expanses of our endless Motherland!

"You see, Georgiy? He says it's not far," said the bishop, trying in vain to calm me down. "Well, not too far," clarified the young grenadier.

"Where exactly?" I demanded to know. The young priest began to stammer a little. "It's quite a lovely little church, built in the eighteenth century. There are hardly any in Russia like it! It's in the village of Gorelets . . . Not far from Kostroma . . ." My forebodings, as it turned out, were entirely justified.

"I see," said I. "And how far is it from Kostroma to your Gorelets?"

"It's maybe about 150 kilometers. Or probably more like 200 . . ." admitted this young priest. "It's between Chukhloma and Kologriva, to be exact . . ."

I shuddered. Then I began to think out loud. "Let's see . . . four hundred kilometers from here to Kostroma . . . then 200 more . . . by the way, Bishop, do you have even the foggiest idea what kind of roads there are over there between this fellow's Chukhloma and Kologriva?"

I tried to grasp the last straw of hope. "Listen, young priest! Have you received the blessing of the Bishop of Kostroma for this bishop to come visit you? Because by our Church law, without your bishop's blessing, our bishop is forbidden to give any service in another bishop's parish!"

"Without our bishop's express permission I would never have come," the young grenadier pitilessly assured me. "All the required blessings have already been received well in advance from our bishop."

And so this is how Bishop Basil ended up on a rut-filled, bumpy, winding "road" in the middle of nowhere en route to a lost village deep in the forests of Kostroma Province. Father Andrei Voronin, as our young grenadier was called, actually turned out to be a remarkable, devoted servant of the Church, as so many of those who came calling to us in those years proved to be. He had graduated from Moscow State University, the top university in the country, but had put aside career prospects in order to restore a ruined church, and create a parish, school, and a beautiful summer camp for children. The trip to his village, however, truly was long and arduous, and we, his travel companions, were soon thoroughly worn out.

But then our car suddenly came to halt. Literally a few minutes ago there had been an accident on the road: a truck had run head-on into a motorcycle. There was a dead man lying right in the dust of the road. Standing over him, numbed with grief, stood a young man. Nearby, the truck driver listlessly stood smoking a cigarette.

The bishop and his companions hurriedly got out of the car. There was already nothing that could be done to help. This cruel senselessness of how sometimes things are in the life of this world, this awful picture of irreparable human grief depressed all of us who happened to be there at that minute on the road.

The young motorcyclist, clutching his helmet in his hands, was weeping. The dead man had been his father. The bishop embraced the young man and said: "I am a priest. If your father was a believer, I can say the necessary prayers for him."

"Yes, yes!" The young man began to cover from shock. "Please do whatever is needed! My father was an Orthodox believer. Although . . . he never used to go to church. They got rid of all the churches around here. But he used to say that he did have a spiritual father. So please, do whatever is required!"

They were already taking the necessary ecclesiastical vestments out of the car. The bishop could not restrain himself and gently asked the young man, "How did it happen that your father never went to church, and yet had a spiritual father?"

"It just happened that way . . . For many years my father used to listen to religious broadcasts from London. They were made by some priest named Rodzyanko. And my father considered this priest his spiritual father, even though he never saw him once in his life."

The bishop sobbed and wept and got down on his knees before his spiritual son who had just died.

* * *

Wanderings . . . Near and far, truly they are blessed, as are all of those who are followers of our Christ, for indeed our Lord God Himself was once a wanderer among men. His very life was but one long wandering . . . From the world above the clouds down to our sinful earth. And then amidst the fields and valleys of Galilee, and through the blazing deserts and the crowded towns, and then on to His dealing with the descendents of human souls, throughout all of the world that He has created, and with all of its people, who have forgotten that they are His children and heirs.

* * *

It may be that the bishop also loved to travel because, in all his wanderings, surprises, and sometimes even dangers, he always felt a particular closeness to God. It is no accident that in every service the Russian Orthodox Church contains a prayer for "those who are voyaging and traveling" or "for those in peril on the sea." This particular closeness to God that comes during travel may be one reason why even in this modest volume there are quite a few stories that have to do with travel. How many amazing, unexpected, and unforgettable events have taken place during all our voyages?

We have honestly always had the complete and utter "service and faithful obedience" in keeping with the monastic vows of this unforgettable bishop. In 1992, I was with Vyacheslav Mikhailovich Klykov and our wonderful old friend, the scholar Nikita Ilyich Tolstoy, chairman of the International Foundation for Slavic Literature, as we prepared the pilgrimage of a large Russian delegation to visit the Holy Land, in order to bring back to Russia for the first time Holy Fire from the Church of the Holy Sepulcher in Jerusalem.*

After the Easter service in Jerusalem our pilgrims were supposed to come back by bus to Russia bringing the Holy Fire from the Church of the Holy Sepulcher through various Orthodox countries en route: Cyprus, Greece, Yugoslavia, Rumania, Bulgaria, the Ukraine, Belarus, and finally home to Moscow.

---

* The miracle of the Holy Fire is an annual event in which the Patriarch of the Orthodox Church in Jerusalem enters the Holy Sepulcher with thirty-three unlit candles he has bound together and emerges with them lit. Both the Sepulcher and the Patriarch are thoroughly searched by civil authorities before the event to exclude the possibility of any technical igniting. The first written record of this event, which occurs on Saturday of Passion Week according to the Orthodox Christian calendar, dates back to 870 A.D.

Bishop Basil carrying the Holy Fire.

Nowadays, the Holy Fire is specially brought for the Easter Service by airplane to many cities in our country. But back then, since it was the very first time, the trip with the Holy Fire involved all kinds of worries and complications. It was supposed to take an entire month. His Holiness Patriarch Alexiy II sent two Archimandrites—Pancratius, who is now a bishop and the Abbot of the Monastery of Valaam, and Sergius, who was later appointed Bishop of the Diocese of Novosibrsk.

One of the participants in our pilgrimage was supposed to have been Maria Georgievna Zhukova, daughter of the commander of Soviet forces in World War II, Marshal Zhukov. But suddenly on the evening before we were supposed to leave she fell ill. We had to urgently find someone who could travel in her place. Complicating matters even further was the problem that it would be impossible in such a short time to arrange for visas for such a large number of countries. And then once again we remembered Bishop Basil, who happened to have just arrived in Moscow on that very day.

To our great shame we didn't think about the fact that the bishop had already turned seventy and it might be not so easy for him to live for a whole month on a bus—not to mention the fact that he had all kinds of things to do in Moscow. The main thing for us was that the bishop, as always, would agree. The second thing was that the question of visas would be resolved by itself: the bishop was a citizen of Great Britain, and with his passport, he did not need a visa for any of the countries we would be visiting.

Best of all, with the participation of Bishop Basil, our pilgrimage had acquired a spiritual director—the kind about whom we could only dream. We even regretted that we hadn't thought about him earlier. In addition to all of the other good things about him, the bishop, unlike many other participants of our pilgrimage, was fluent in English, German, and French, Serbian, Greek, Bulgarian, and a fair bit of Romanian.

And so His Holiness Patriarch Alexiy II blessed him to be the leader of our pilgrimage group, which filled the heart of our bishop with joy in the feeling of extraordinary responsibility. Furthermore, thank God, the bishop's health remained favorable throughout the trip. One of our participants, Alexander Nikolayevich Krutov, would bind up the bishop's aching legs every day, and make sure he didn't forget to take his medicines. In short, as Bishop Basil himself said, Alexander took care of him like a devoted mother.

I remember how then before our trip we all helped him pack and prepare, and with what relief we set out on our long journey. All our problems had been solved!

The problems began again as soon as our pilgrims needed to cross through any country's border control. Our delegation was supposed to cross through the border control exactly in accordance with the list that had been given to these authorities in a group visa. On that list was Maria Georgievna Zhukova. But there was now Bishop Basil (Rodzyanko) to take her place.

The first problems began when we got to Israel, a land famous for its scrupulous rigor in all issues of security, border control, and customs matters. Israeli security services in the airport immediately asked this unusual group of Russians to step aside and began to call us out each by name. There was no problem with the first names in the group visa, such as Archimandrite Pancratius and Archimandrite Sergius, Alexander Nikolayevich Krutov. But then when they called out the name Maria Georgievna Zhukova, suddenly instead of her they saw Bishop Basil, who politely smiled at the Israeli border agent and bowed to him.

"Wait a minute!" The agent was confused. "I called out Maria Georgievna Zhukova."

"Maria Georgievna Zhukova is me," said Bishop Basil naively.

"What do you mean that she is you?" The agent got annoyed. "Who are you?"

"I? I am the Russian Bishop Basil."

"Maria Georgievna Zhukova is a Russian bishop? Listen, this is not a place for joking! What's your real name?"

"You mean on my passport? Or—?"

"Of course your name on your passport!" the agent snorted.

"My name on my passport is Vladimir Rodzyanko."

"Maria Zhukova, Bishop Basil, and now Vladimir Rodzyanko! Where are you from anyway?"

"Actually, I live in America," the bishop began. "We can explain everything to you!"

Other members of the delegation tried to assist. But the Israeli border agent rebuffed them. "All others are requested to keep quiet!" Then he turned once more to the bishop. "Let's see if I get this straight. You say you are a Russian bishop, but for some reason you live in America? Interesting. Let's see your passport."

"I have a British passport," said the bishop cautiously, as he handed it over.

"What?" Indignantly the border guard shook the list of the group visa and waved it in the face of Bishop Basil. "Where are you listed in this group document?"

"How should I explain?" The bishop tried his best, himself somewhat surprised and smiling. "The thing is, in this document I am listed as Maria Georgievna Zhukova."

"Enough nonsense!" said the Israeli border guard. "Just tell me who you are! And right now!"

The bishop was genuinely upset to have been the cause of so much trouble for this young officer. Of course, notwithstanding his natural modesty, he also did not like being yelled at. "I am a Russian Orthodox cleric, Bishop Basil," he answered with a dignified air.

"So you are Bishop Basil? Who then is Vladimir Rodzyanko?"

"That's also me."

"Well then, and who is Maria Georgievna Zhukova?"

"And Maria Georgievna Zhukova is also me." The bishop waved his hands vaguely.

"Hmm! And you live—where?"

"In America."

"And your passport is?"

"My passport is British."

"And on this list you are . . . ?

"And on this list I am Maria Georgievna Zhukova."

This delightful little scene was repeated every single time we crossed a national border. However, notwithstanding all these difficulties, Bishop Basil was utterly happy. It had been his dream to pray at Easter time in the Church of the Holy Sepulcher. And he was overjoyed that after so many years of separation he could be—even if only for a brief visit—back in his beloved Yugoslavia. What's more, he faithfully executed the important task that he had been given, as head of our mission of pilgrimage to the Holy Land, and, on his return to Moscow, on the day of Saints Cyril and Methodius, was able to participate in the Procession of the Cross, right next to Patriarch Alexiy, around the Dormition Cathedral in the Kremlin on Slavyansky Square, solemnly carrying the receptacle of the Holy Fire as he did so.

* * *

Although the bishop never said as much out loud, it had always been his fondest dream to serve Russia and the Russian Orthodox Church. He had been brought up this way. Once we were able to make arrangements with Channel 1, the Central Television Station, to record a series of broadcasts—discussions about God and the Church, about the revered saints of old, and about the new martyrs of Russia, about the Russian Diaspora, and about the fate of Russia itself.

Bishop Basil was not feeling well, but he raced to Moscow and worked day and night with all of his fading strength on these broadcasts. These turned out to be the first discussions on these themes that had ever been shown on what was then still Soviet television. These programs provoked immense interest among their viewers and were repeated many times. Wherever the bishop appeared later, people would come up to him expressing their gratitude for having acquired faith thanks to his programs. For the bishop these words were his very highest reward.

Much of the ecclesiastical history of the twentieth century was revealed to us in a completely new way by Bishop Basil. Somehow at one point an argument began about what was then a popular theme—the ecclesiastical authorities under the Soviet regime. Some of the speakers were quite bitter in their condemnation of their collaborationist mentality, expressing thereby feelings not just aggrieved, but poisonously inimical towards them. The bishop listened to the arguments silently. When these fearless judges of the Russian bishops of the past appealed to him to support their position, which they considered self-evident, the bishop merely told them one story:

In the beginning of the 1960s when he was still just a priest named Father Vladimir, he was visited in his apartment in London by Metropolitan Nicodemus, chairman of the foreign relations department of the Russian Orthodox Church. In order for them to speak, they actually needed to lie down on the floor, so that the Secret Service agents tailing Metropolitan Nicodemus, and never once leaving him alone, would not be able to record their conversation through the windows.

Lying on the floor, and whispering softly as he could, Nicodemus told Father Vladimir that the Soviet authorities were planning any day now to close the ancient Pochaev Monastery (the foremost Orthodox monastery in the Western Ukraine). The Church hierarchy back in the Motherland had already exhausted all its possibilities to stop this from happening. Nicodemus therefore begged Father Vladimir to organize special broadcasts on BBC Radio and on the Voice of America to put pressure on the Soviet government not to eliminate the Pochaev Monastery. Both Metropolitan Nicodemus and Father Vladimir perfectly understood what a risk the Metropolitan was undergoing in appealing to Father Vladimir with such a request.

But by the very next day, the theme of the threat to the Pochaev Monastery was the lead topic in the religious broadcasts of the BBC and the Voice of America. Thousands of letters of protest from all over the world flew in, addressed to the Soviet government. All of this was perhaps decisive in influencing the authorities to change their minds and once again allow the Pochaev Monastery to continue with its activities.

In 1990 Bishop Basil and I had the good fortune of finally visiting Pochaev Monastery. It was his first time there. He served Divine Liturgy and was able to meet with all the people who together with him had been participants in the dramatic events that had taken place thirty years previously.

* * *

What else can I remember about the bishop? Somehow every one of his visits always coincided with some extraordinary event: the thousand-year anniversary of Russia's conversion to Christianity, the bringing of the Holy Fire to Russia for the first time, the first Memorial Service for the martyred Imperial Family, the first religious programs on the Central Television Station. But as the bishop himself liked to say: "Whenever I stop praying, the amazing coincidences stop happening."

The visit of the bishop to Moscow in the summer of 1991 was no exception. He had come as part of a large delegation from the United States attending the first global summit of Russian-speaking communities. Representatives of the Russian émigré community from many countries and of all different political persuasions were officially invited to Moscow for the first time. The government planned this meeting to mark a new stage in the development of post-Communist Russia.

A large number of people arrived. They included various émigrés who had forever decided to have nothing at all to do with the Soviet Union. There were so-called "White Guards" who would never believe that anything good whatsoever could come out of the land of the Soviets, and there were even certain representatives of Vlasov's Russian Liberation Army, famous for siding with Hitler against the Soviet Union during the Second World War, and mercilessly punished for this after the war. How anyone had convinced these people to attend remains a mystery to me! Maybe in spite of everything they truly missed their Motherland . . .

The Intourist Hotel was booked full to overflowing. Various émigrés and their families wandered around Moscow, looking at the city and the faces of the people. They were all amazed to see how interested everyone was in meeting them. What amazed them even more were the high hopes, in some cases rising to the level of unbounded fantasies, with which they were received. At the time there was no shortage of well-meaning souls who truly believed in the myth that "we will be helped from overseas." As to this, I wish to say that if anyone on behalf of the Russian émigré community truly contributed to Russia's spiritual renaissance not just in words but in deeds, it was the ever modest retired Bishop Basil, along with several tireless laborers from the émigré community—bishops, priests, and laypeople.

The main event of the first global summit of Russian-speaking communities was Divine Liturgy in the Dormition Cathedral in the Moscow Kremlin. After long decades in which service of Divine Liturgy in the cathedrals of the Kremlin had been forbidden, a service was held and presided over by His Holiness Patriarch Alexiy II. Bishop Basil also assisted the Patriarch at these services. Unfortunately, a week before flying to

Moscow, he had broken his leg at his home in Washington. But he could not miss such an event—and so, with his leg in a cast, and hopping about oddly on crutches, he stood through the whole service, as well as all the events, barely able to catch up with the crowd of Russian émigrés moving around from place to place.

Then on the early morning of August 19, 1991, on the day of the Transfiguration of Our Lord, several dozen buses crowded with Russian émigrés from every continent set out from the Intourist Hotel. These buses brought the tourists to the Kutafyev Tower of the Kremlin. With tears in their eyes, hardly believing what was happening, they proceeded through the Kremlin Gates to the Dormition Cathedral, where His Holiness Patriarch Alexiy II with all his bishops (including Bishop Basil, hobbling on crutches) began the Divine Liturgy.

However, as is well known, this was precisely the day, August 19, 1991, of the attempted coup against Gorbachev and his government. Indeed, this coup was taking place exactly at the time that His Holiness the Patriarch was praying in the Dormition Cathedral. And so when these émigrés, touched to the depths of their hearts and full of joy after the conclusion of the Liturgy, left the Kremlin, they were astonished to see not tour buses waiting for them, but a thick line of armored personnel carriers and tanks and soldiers with machine guns.

At first nobody knew what was going on, but then someone cried out: "I knew it! Those Bolsheviks have deceived this again! It was all a trap!"

The confused soldiers in their ranks surrounding the Kremlin looked around at this quite confusedly. Another of the émigrés cried out: "I warned you! I knew we shouldn't have come! They tricked us! It was a trap, a trap! All of this was arranged on purpose!"

Just at this moment an officer approached these panicked émigrés. He had been given orders to protect these members of the foreign delegations. His orders were to accompany the delegates to Lubyanka Square, where there were buses waiting for them on the instruction of the troops who would surround the Kremlin. These buses were supposed to take these foreigners as quickly as possible to the Intourist Hotel.

"Comrades, do not panic!" The officer's voice rang out with authority and command. "You are all instructed in an organized manner to proceed to the Lubyanka! These soldiers will accompany you now!" As he spoke, the officer pointed to a squadron of troops armed with machine guns.

"No, no, no! We don't want to go to the Lubyanka!" The émigrés' panic was only increasing at the mention of that dreaded place.

"But they're waiting for you there," said the officer with good-natured surprise. This only increased the terror further.

"No! Anywhere but the Lubyanka! Absolutely not!" Everyone was yelling.

Several times the officer tried to reason with the crowd, but it was all in vain. So finally he gave the order to his troops, and they, energetically pushing these émigrés, sometimes with the barrel of their machine guns, and sometimes with their burly arms, forcibly drove them on towards Lubyanka Square.

Everyone was so utterly shocked that they forgot all about Bishop Basil. He was left alone by himself on his crutches by the Kutafyev Tower, surrounded by soldiers and armored personnel carriers. Up to this point, no one had even heard about the coup. People who were accidentally in the vicinity of the Kremlin might be guessing as to what was going on, but at this point certainly no one knew for sure. But many people began to recognize Bishop Basil and asked what they should do . . . So there was an entire crowd gathered around the somewhat confused bishop, who was a head taller than everyone else.

Meanwhile the émigrés who had been driven forcibly on to Lubyanka Square finally understood that they had been brought to their tour buses, which would be taking them to their hotel, and not to the prison and the dreaded basements of the KGB. Then suddenly they remembered about the bishop! The bishop's secretary Marilyn Swezey ran out of the tour bus and courageously ran back towards the Kremlin, fearlessly approaching the tanks of the armored personnel carriers in that foreign land, trying to rescue her dear Bishop Basil.

She recognized him immediately. He looked like a gray-haired prophet towering above the crowd in the center of the ever growing protest meeting. Marilyn stretched out her arm to him and briefly but convincingly talked him into taking the only route towards certain safety . . . to go with her towards the Lubyanka . . .

But the bishop on his crutches was physically unable to walk that far. He told Marilyn that he would go but somehow transport would need to be arranged for him. Marilyn dashed out of the crowd of protesters and looked around. There was no transport available except the armored personnel carriers of the soldiers with their engines humming. Marilyn walked up to a young officer and in her broken Russian with bits of

English mixed in explained that there was an old priest from America who was unable to walk and urgently needed to be transported to the Lubyanka Square.

But the officer shrugged his shoulders and waved his hands: "What transport can I offer you? Only a tank. Or maybe an APC . . ."

But suddenly Marilyn noticed that not far away from the tanks there appeared to be a car that might be sufficient for transporting the bishop. "How about that Jeep over there?"

"The police van, you mean?" The officer was happy to help. "All right, we can give him a lift in the police van! Let me work it out with the cops!"

For some reason this officer felt true compassion for the fate of this foreign bishop. And so the van, which had been brought up with the intention to arrest the crowd of protesters against the coup, instead drove through the crowd, in the center of which the bishop was standing towering above everyone else. Marilyn followed the officer and two policemen as they approached. Yelling above the crowd and the racing engines of the tanks, Marilyn told the bishop that they were being taken to the Lubyanka.

Everyone together—the policeman, the officer, and Marilyn—grabbed the bishop and dragged him through the crowd. When they saw this, the crowd became extremely nervous. "What's going on? Are they arresting the priest?" The crowd grew utterly indignant.

When they saw policeman taking an old priest on crutches and with a cast on his leg and putting him in a black van, the crowd became so furious that the people immediately began to cry out in defense of the bishop. "It's starting all over again! They're already arresting priests! No! We won't let them arrest that good father! We will die for him!"

"No, no!" The bishop tried to calm the crowd and get away from his own rescuers. "Let me go, let me go . . . It's all right. I want to go to the Lubyanka!"

Those soldiers barely managed to put the bishop with his crutches and his leg in a cast into the police van and to drive off with him through the now utterly furious crowd of protesters. As the bishop looked out the window of the police van, tears of gratitude started rolling down his cheeks. "What a wonderful people! What a great country!"

Soon the bishop was met on the Lubyanka Square by his faithful parishioners.

* * *

Even in the last years of his life, when he was ailing, he always yearned for Russia and visited as often as he could, ever hoping to serve his native land.

The bishop was already quite ill when he visited Moscow for the last time. He spent several weeks in bed. Natalya Vasilyevna Nesterova, in whose home he was staying, took tender care of him. But I understood that the bishop possibly would never come back to Russia again, and therefore asked the brothers and nurses to sit by his bed in vigil, and ordered that he be attended to around the clock by monks and novices of our Sretensky Monastery. That way the young monks could converse with the bishop, ask his advice, and pose questions to him, questions that only an extremely spiritual, wise, experienced priest could answer.

More likely than not my monks were not the best nurses. Probably they asked the poor ailing bishop too many questions and wanted too much advice and too much of his failing energies. And yet just as for these young novices it was extremely useful to spend these days and nights with this elderly bishop, so it was extremely important and pleasant for the bishop to spend time with those who one day would be taking his place in the Church. He was actually happy that even at the cost of wearing himself out he was able to answer their questions, teach them, give them the benefit of his experience and knowledge, and yet again provide service, that service for which he had always lived and without which he would not have been who he was.

* * *

On his final voyage, away from the country in which he was living and on to the long-awaited Kingdom of Heaven, Bishop Basil embarked all alone. He was found one morning on the floor of his room in Washington, no longer breathing. The bishop had lived in this little room for many years. It was a tiny studio, and yet in addition to housing the bishop, it had somehow also contained a house church, a radio station, a library of decades of sermons and writings and radio and television broadcasts, a hospitable refectory for parishioners who frequently came to visit, and a study. Somehow there was even space for visitors. Guests from Russia would often show up at the bishop's home to spend a night or two—or sometimes even a week . . .

Even after his death, the bishop did not deny himself the pleasure of traveling a little bit.

His family could not at first figure out where it was that he should be buried. Some said he should be buried in Russia—his Motherland, after all. Others wanted to bury him in England, next to his wife, whom he had so dearly loved. Others suggested Serbia, a land that had always been close to his heart. I can only imagine what joy filled the soul of the bishop as it was hovering above this scene in the heavens: he would truly have enjoyed any one of these journeys! But in the end his body was brought from Washington only as far as New York: one of his relatives insisted that he be buried in the Orthodox convent of New Diveyevo, which is located not far from the city. However, for some reason the burial did not take place there and the bishop was brought back again to Washington. Here his worldly wanderings finally came to an end. The bishop was laid to rest in the Orthodox Christian section of Rock Creek Cemetery.

Sometimes during his life the bishop used to call himself "the reposed bishop." That is because under his status he was merely a retired bishop, who had been fired (or sent "into retirement," a phrase that in Russian sounds like being "laid to rest") from the American Autocephalous Church. A bishop who has been "retired" in fact is no longer really a bishop, and no longer makes any official decisions about formal ecclesiastical matters. That is why the bishop from time to time used to joke about himself that he was "the reposed Bishop Basil."

But he was indeed a real bishop! He truly governed without borders the human souls who crossed his earthly path. He did so with the indefatigable force of that remarkable power which to this day continues to bless those who had the joy of knowing Bishop Basil and experiencing his unforgettable and irreplaceable goodness, faith, and love.

The Foolish Townsfolk

*I*N A LAZY, sleepy Byzantine town that had seen better days, the townsfolk had become so shameless in their self-indulgent brazenness that they did whatever they wanted, breaking all moral laws and canons, without the least thought for the reproaches of their good old bishop, no matter how he begged them to reform their ways. The townsfolk merely laughed at the elder and waved him off as they would a pesky fly.

Finally the old bishop died. A young new bishop was appointed, who began to live with such sybaritic excess that even the townsfolk who thought they had already seen everything shuddered to observe him. Suddenly they missed their good old meek, elderly bishop.

Unable to stand any longer the constant extortion, corruption, humiliation, beatings, and most incredible and riotous disorder of the new bishop, the citizens of the town cried out as if in unison: "Why, oh Lord, have You sent us such a monster?"

They had no idea how to pray properly, but after a long period of prolonged and piteous yelping, the Lord appeared to one of the town fathers and replied: "I tried to find someone worse for you, but couldn't."

The St. John the Baptist side-church in Sretensky Monastery.

Liturgy Is Served No More Than Once Each Day on Any One Altar Table

*H*ow the Lord preserves us priests from our own mistakes, how He spares us from our carelessness and absentmindedness and sometimes our foolishness!

There is a strict rule in the Church: in each church only one Eucharist may be celebrated at one altar table during the course of one day. The monks at our Sretensky Monastery love to have services in the middle of the night. They love being able to pray in monastic seclusion without any distractions. Lay parishioners do not attend these nighttime services, except for those whom we ourselves invite.

Once during the Lenten Fast I set aside some time to serve the Liturgy of the Presanctified Gifts at night. And although in order to prepare for such services one must strictly fast all day, and neither eat nor drink for almost a full twenty-four hours, several of our oldest and most loyal parishioners asked to come and take Communion during that evening service.

I spent all day working in our agricultural community in Ryazan Province. When I got back to the monastery late at night, I went at once to our church. Since as a general rule the Liturgy was served at the main altar table in the morning, I was supposed to serve in the side-church of St. John the Baptist, where services are held rather rarely.

Everything had been made ready for the services. Four of our first-year students sang from the choir. Six of my friends who had prepared to take Communion that night were praying in the little chapel.

However, from the first minutes of the service I felt something unusual. I was seized by an insurmountable sense of alarm. I couldn't pull myself together: I confused routine priestly refrains, had difficulty reading from the prayer book, mixed up prayers that I had long since known by heart, and somehow was quite unable to take in their meaning. The same strange

403

thing was happening to the choir. Superb though they are, at times they were singing outright badly, now and then missing notes, mispronouncing words, starting over, coming in at incorrect measures, or simply guessing. . . . It was unheard of. Finally, when it was time to draw back the altar curtain and open the Holy Gates, I had no more than touched it when the curtain with its rods collapsed with outrageous noise onto the floor along with a heavy bracket.

Never in my life had anything like this happened before! I had no choice but to stop the service. Completely at a loss, I stepped out of the altar. Everyone who was there was just as upset as I was. Completely unable to guess what I should do, I asked the first-year choirboys—just in case—whether by any chance there had already been a service here in the Chapel of St. John the Baptist today.

The first-year choirboys answered: "But of course! We already sang here for the Liturgy that was held here at four o'clock in the afternoon. It was served by our Father Treasurer."

I hung my head in shame. Had it gone on just a bit further, I would have served a second Liturgy in one day on one altar table! "Why didn't you tell me about this earlier?" I yelled at my students.

"But we didn't know that it's forbidden to celebrate the Liturgy twice at one altar table!" The first-year students looked at each other defensively and with embarrassment. "We haven't covered that yet."

As if it weren't bad enough that I had messed up, I had yelled at the youngsters! Some superior I was! After all, it had been my responsibility to warn our dean in charge of scheduling services that I was going to serve a Liturgy that night. I shouldn't have so casually assumed that here in the Chapel of St. John the Baptist no one would have already served the Liturgy of the Presanctified Gifts. Fortunately, the most important sacramental portions of the Liturgy had not yet been performed. I set up the portable altar table in a neighboring altar and finished the service there.

When we gathered for the evening meal, over and over again we pondered what had happened and were struck by how the Lord had preserved His church from our mistakes and possibly even our involuntary but serious sin. How is it possible after that not to thank God for His patience and care for us?

After this incident we firmly decided that henceforth all services in our monastery would be strictly controlled by the dean in charge of scheduling. We could not count on further curtains and brackets falling every time.

Or worse, what if they were to fall on someone's head? It is not even to be thought of!

But what should we say? One must never blame anyone else for our own failures to comply with our obligations and individual responsibilities in life to the Lord. In the words of the Russian proverb, "Put your trust in God, but don't stop working." Although, to be honest, we always secretly count on Him. He will not abandon us. He will protect us. He will preserve us.

Cutting the hay the traditional way, with a scythe.

How We Bought Our Combines

*I*N THE SUMMER of 2001 a young man named Yaroslav N. applied to join our Sretensky Monastery. He was descended from a family of Russified Germans. He had been born and bred in the Altai Mountains, and had immigrated with his parents to Germany. There he had received German citizenship. Thus, to our surprise, he had two passports: a Russian one and a German one. There was more than a month left before the entrance exams, and the young man asked whether during that time he could live in the monastery. I asked him what he knew how to do. It turned out that he had studied accounting in Germany.

"So you know how to deal with accounting programs?" I was very happy to hear this.

"Of course, Father! Computer programs are my specialty!"

That was exactly what we needed at the time. We gave Yaroslav a workplace in the accounting department, and he began to work for us so well that we could not have been more contented.

I should mention that that year we had decided to allocate all the money earned by the monastery from the books it publishes to buying agricultural equipment. We have a skete in Ryazan Province where we go for monastic retreat. All the farms or collective farms in the surrounding area had gone to rack and ruin over the past decade or were in such a state of decay that it was truly painful to look at the dying villages around us.

One winter evening, farmers from the neighboring village had come to our skete. These people had been driven to the furthest depths of despair. They told us that they hadn't been paid one kopeck of their already miserable salary for the past three years. There was no equipment left on the farm except for a ramshackle and half-broken tractor and an old Soviet-era Jeep-like car belonging to the chairman. The collective farms' cattle had not been fed and for lack of fodder would have to be sold to a slaughterhouse within a week for almost nothing at all. In certain families the children were being fed nothing more than steamed animal fodder. We shuddered to hear all of this, and we couldn't refuse our neighbors when they asked us to take over their completely collapsed farms and help them.

To our complete horror, they begged us, "Please take us on—even as serfs!" It was quite obvious that they were utterly desperate and had absolutely no one else to whom they could turn.

Well, we took them on, but it was easier said than done. As we acquainted ourselves with the problems of these farms, we understood that we would have to rebuild everything from zero, starting entirely from scratch. Even after we paid them their salary and purchased fodder for the cattle, it was not enough: in any case huge sums of money would be required to buy the minimal agricultural equipment needed to get the farms running again—$200,000. We decided to save up this money ourselves, by putting off repairs to the monastery and also by postponing various of our publishing projects.

We did not deposit our savings in the bank. We had all too vivid a memory of the financial crisis and default of 1998. Our parishioners, some of whom were quite savvy in matters of finance, suggested that we save our money for the purchase of agricultural machinery not in rubles, but in dollars. And they suggested that we keep them not in a bank account but in a safe hiding place.

The Father Treasurer and I found such a place. We drilled a niche in one of the rooms of our bookkeeping department, installed an excellent safe in the niche, and then hid the key to the safe in the bottom drawer of the desk under a pile of old copies of the *Journal of the Moscow Patriarchate.* Then we hid the key to that drawer under the floorboard! We were utterly delighted with ourselves and were certain that now the money we had saved would be safer than if it had been deposited in Sberbank (the Russian state savings bank).

By fall we had saved up $180,000. We needed just a little more and soon we would be able to order grain harvesting combines and tractors and sowing machines. We were already leafing through catalogs of agricultural machinery, and discussing which brands would be more effective for future harvests. But then on September 14, 2001, as I was setting out for our farm in our car, I received a telephone call from the Treasurer of the Monastery. His voice was trembling from anxiety and he was barely able to speak:

"Father . . . only please don't get alarmed. There's no money in the safe. And Yaroslav has also disappeared. Please come back as soon as possible!"

When I came back to the monastery, things were exactly as he had said: there was no money in the safe, and Yaroslav was gone. However, both keys were neatly back in the places where they were before, in the bottom drawer of the desk and under the floorboards.

However devastating this blow was, we still had to do something. I telephoned our parishioner Vladimir Vasilyevich Ustinov, who at the time was the Chief Prosecutor of the Russian Federation. Vladimir Vasilyevich came to the monastery and brought several detectives with him. The detectives did their thing—interrogations, dusting for fingerprints, inspection of the scene of the crime—and meanwhile the Father Treasurer and I wandered dispiritedly about the monastery waiting for their results.

Finally Vladimir Vasilyevich asked me to step into our Father Treasurer's office. As soon as I walked in I could see by the expression on everyone's face that there was no good news. Gesturing me to have a seat, Vladimir Vasilyevich said:

"It was a good thing that you sat down just now, Father. Try not to be nervous, and prepare yourself for what we are about to tell you. This so-called 'student' Yaroslav N. has already left Russia. There is no doubt that he took the money. And if that is the case, then unfortunately there is nothing that we can do to return it."

"Why is that?" I whispered.

"Because the thief is a citizen of Germany," Ustinov patiently explained, "and Germany will never hand over one of its citizens to us, just as we have never handed over any of our citizens to them."

"But he's a criminal!" I said, amazed at this.

"Indeed he is," Ustinov sighed, "but there are certain rules that are not made up by us, and we can't change them. Never in the entire history of Russian or Soviet jurisprudence has there been one single case when the government of Germany has handed over one of its citizens to us for a criminal trial."

"And where is this Yaroslav?"

"Probably at home in Germany. After all, he has a German passport. Therefore he calmly sailed through the green corridor in customs (for "nothing to declare") with all your money. Nobody's going to thoroughly inspect a citizen of Germany. You understand this; you've flown overseas. Now of course we will start a criminal case, and we will file a report with Interpol. But the best thing you can do, Father, is not to waste time and nerves. Forget about this money altogether and start saving up once again for your agricultural amusements," the Chief Prosecutor concluded.

From these words I nearly lost the gift of speech. "How are we supposed to just forget? That was $180,000! Those were all our combines! No, Vladimir Vasilyevich, we can't just forget about it!"

"Believe me, there is nothing we can do."

"Well, if there's nothing you can do, then we . . . we will pray. If neither the government nor the police can help us, the Mother of God will protect us."

Those were my words, but I was shaking inside. The fact is that there was no source of hope but prayer. I told our brotherhood everything that had happened, and together we began to pray. First and foremost we prayed to the icon in whose honor our monastery has been founded, the icon of the Holy Mother of God of Vladimir.

Two weeks passed. Front-page headlines were already screaming with scandalous stories of how a million dollars had been stolen from the Abbot of the Sretensky Monastery. Then suddenly one truly bright day Vladimir Ustinov drove back to our monastery. He looked not only surprised but actually shocked.

"Can you believe it, Father? That thief of all your combines has actually been found!"

"Really? They found him?" It was so surprising that at first I didn't even believe it.

"Yes, can you imagine? This morning we received a report from Interpol; strange as it may sound, that scoundrel has been detained at the border crossing in Frankfurt on the Oder."

Ustinov told me that Yaroslav had driven from Russia through the Ukraine and Poland and was finally passing into Germany. He had passed through German customs at the border town of Frankfurt on the Oder numerous times, and because of his German passport had never had any problems. Indeed, he would never have had any problems this time, had his crossing not been on September 14, 2001—in short, on the third day after the infamous terrorist attacks in New York and Washington. Seeking terrorists, the alarmed German border guards began inspecting everyone from head to toe, their own citizens as well as foreigners. And so it happened that they found on Yaroslav's person $180,000 that had not been declared and whose honest origin he of course could not explain. These funds had been confiscated from him, had been duly registered, and had been sent for safekeeping to the prosecutor of Frankfurt on the Oder.

Scarcely had Vladimir Vasilyevich finished telling me the news when I cried for joy. "When will the funds be returned to us? We're going to Frankfurt immediately!"

"I don't want to upset you, Father, but the thing is . . . they won't return the money to you," Ustinov sighed.

"Why not?"

"I was trying to explain: first of all, we can't prove that this is the same money he stole."

"Why can't we? One hundred and eighty thousand dollars was stolen from our monastery, and they found $180,000 on him there. Yaroslav N. disappeared from us here when these funds were stolen here, and he is there when the funds are found on him! It all fits! And I'll bet the fingerprints—"

"All of this may fit here," said the prosecutor with sympathy, "but only a court will consider these facts. And the court will never convene."

"What do you mean it will never convene?"

"I mean that the Germans will postpone it and postpone it forever. And that Yaroslav will figure out some explanation for the funds one way or another. Besides, the court case has to be held in the presence of the accused, and of course there's no way that he'll ever show up for his own trial."

"I thought they'd arrested him at the border."

"Not at all. They merely confiscated the funds, but they let Mr. N go. Father, do not have any illusions. Be glad at least that that scoundrel was not able to use your money."

"Glad? What consolation is that? He may not be able to use those funds, but neither can we! And we need to buy combines!"

"Well, that, Father Tikhon, is beyond my control."

"All right then," I sighed once more. "We'll keep praying!"

"Pray as long as you like!" Ustinov got angry. "But you should know that in their entire history neither the Germans, nor the French, nor the British, nor the Americans have ever extradited any of their criminals to us, nor have they ever sued them for crimes committed on our territories. Nor will we ever give them any of our criminals! Never!"

"Well, then, we will pray!" I repeated.

Nearly a year elapsed. This happened to be a period when we were restoring our complex but extremely important relationship with the Russian Orthodox Church Abroad. And it happened that Archbishop

Mark of Berlin and Great Britain invited me to Munich to prepare a summit meeting between Patriarch Alexiy and Metropolitan Laurus, the Chief Hierarch of the Russian Orthodox Church Abroad.

His Holiness the Patriarch blessed my voyage and I flew off to Bavaria. I was met by Archbishop Mark's closest helper, Father Nikolai Artemov, who came to greet me at the airport and drove me back to the residence of the archbishop, the tiny Monastery of St. Job of Pochaev on the outskirts of Munich.

It turns out there are over eighty million inhabitants of Germany. But the very first person I saw when I got out of the car in that little monastery was—Yaroslav N.! I lunged for him and grabbed him.

I must admit that my memory of what happened next is a bit foggy. Yaroslav was so surprised to see me that he didn't even resist. Before the very eyes of Father Nikolai, the bewildered monks, and Archbishop Mark himself, I dragged Yaroslav into the monastery, shoved him into some room, and locked the door behind me.

"What are you doing, Father Tikhon?" Archbishop Mark reproached me, beside himself with astonishment.

"This man stole an enormous sum of money from us!"

"It must be some mistake. He's going to be working in our monastery as an accountant."

A crowd of monks gathered around us. Finally it occurred to me to put myself in the place of the astonished Archbishop Mark. Some priest he had never met before arrives from Russia, the former Soviet Union, and suddenly grabs a citizen of Germany and locks him up in someone else's monastery!

So I told the archbishop and his monks the story of what happened with Yaroslav. But I could see that they couldn't believe me. Then I asked for permission to make an overseas telephone call and dialed the Chief Prosecutor in Moscow.

"Vladimir Vasilyevich! I've caught him!" I yelled through the telephone.

"Caught whom?" Ustinov's voice sounded discouraged.

"What do you mean—whom? The thief, of course, the same one who stole our money!"

"Wait a second . . . what do you mean you caught him? Where?"

"In Munich!"

"In Germany? Are you joking? How could you possibly have found out where he was?"

Archbishop Mark.

"Well . . . I got out of the car, and I looked and there he was. I grabbed him, dragged him into the monastery, and locked him in a cell."

There was an unpleasant pause. For a moment I was afraid that Ustinov thought I was pulling his leg. But a minute later I realized that this was not the case, because from the other end of the line there came a real yell. "You let him go at once!"

I was petrified. "What do you mean let him go?"

"Release him immediately!" It seemed that Ustinov was yelling loud enough for all of Moscow to hear. "Have you any idea what you've just done?"

"Vladimir Vasilyevich! How could they possibly just let him—"

The prosecutor didn't listen to me at all. "You have deprived a citizen of Germany of his freedom. And on German soil. You will be sentenced to two years for that. And we'll be going crazy trying to spring you from jail! Let him go at once! This minute! And let him run wherever his feet will carry him!"

I thought for a moment and said, "No, I won't! The Lord sent him to me. How could I possibly release him now? Do what you want with me,

Vladimir Vasilyevich! But I'm holding him here until the police arrive."

And I insisted on my position no matter how loudly Ustinov yelled. And there was nothing he could do to change my mind from where he was sitting in his Chief Prosecutor's office in Moscow. Finally, he relented: "Very well, right now I will call German Interpol. But if you get arrested, don't say I didn't warn you!"

Soon enough the Bavarian representative of Interpol drove up to the monastery. However, instead of arresting Yaroslav, he began to interrogate me. Our conversation went as follows.

"Have you been carrying out illegal investigations on German soil?"

"What investigations?"

"How did you find this man?

"I got out of the car and I saw that it was Yaroslav! So I grabbed him!"

"So you've been tracking him? Following him? Trying to determine the subject's whereabouts?"

"Of course not. It's just that the Lord delivered him to me."

"Excuse me, who?"

"The Lord!"

"Excuse me once more. Who?"

"The Lord God. He has delivered him into my hands!"

"Yeah, right!" The Bavarian looked at me as if I were crazy.

He then asked in great detail about the entire case. Then he repeated all his questions. Gradually the disbelief on his face began to be replaced by enormous astonishment. Finally he said, "You know, if it really happened just the way you're telling me, I'm willing to offer you the position of director of Bavarian Interpol."

To this I replied: "Thank you, but I already have another civilian job. I'm the chairman of a collective farm and therefore I cannot accept your kind offer."

* * *

The effect of these events that had been so utterly unpredictable, happening one after another, also could not help but form a stunning impression on Yaroslav.

First, the money he stole had suddenly been confiscated—and not just anywhere, but in Germany, when it had seemed to him that all dangers were in the past, and he had already been celebrating in his mind his spending of this money, feeling his complete triumph. Second, this had happened at the customs point at Frankfurt on the Oder, a place that Yaroslav had selected on purpose because he had crossed the border there many times before without incident. And he had been caught by me in the monastery in Munich, where he had already almost managed to get himself a job . . . as a bookkeeper! And finally, his confinement was not just anywhere, but once more in a monastic cell—very much like the cell in Moscow from which he had so improperly fled a year ago.

What's more, I believe that all these coincidences began to weigh on the conscience of the young man for his sad and ill-considered deed in our monastery. After all, he knew all too well what the purpose of this money was and just how difficult the saving of it had been, and I have no doubt that in fact deep down he felt pain and shame no matter how he tried to justify himself in his crime.

But most important of all, he felt the action in the world not just of the Church, but of the mysterious and benevolent Providence of the Lord. And this truly amazed Yaroslav. And he began to think deeply. In the end he confessed to everything and took responsibility.

He was held in pretrial confinement, and then after a while there was a trial. Yaroslav was sentenced to four years in jail for his theft, and he served the full term of his sentence in Bavaria. The monks and the novices of the Monastery of St. Job of Pochaev in Munich visited him all the time and helped him as best they could.

Meanwhile the Chief Prosecutor's office and the Ministry of Justice of Russia, in accordance with protocol, worked out an arrangement with the German Justice Ministry. And finally, by a decision of the German court, the $180,000 that the German prosecutor of Frankfurt on the Oder had been keeping safe was transferred to representatives of our Justice Ministry, which traveled to Frankfurt especially for the occasion.

Early in the morning of July 6, 2003, these representatives brought a box with this money to our Sretensky Monastery and gave it to our Father Treasurer, who signed a receipt for it. It was a day of our patronal feast, the celebration of the Icon of the Vladimir Mother of God—that same icon before which we had prayed to the Virgin Mary for a favorable ending to the misfortunes that had befallen us.

I did not need to think about the theme of the sermon for our celebratory Liturgy. I just told our parishioners the story and jubilantly showed the entire church the box that had just been brought to us that morning. And soon we bought the agricultural machinery we needed.

Mount Tabor in Israel.

Vasily and Vasily Vasilyevich

I N T H E B E G I N N I N G of the 1990s from time to time there used to appear a parishioner of ours in the Donskoy Monastery. We will call him Vasily. He was a stout and solid man, a successful businessman and without doubt a religious believer. Yet he had a certain peculiarity. He had stubbornly made it his motto to do only that in life which had been particularly advised for him by priests and elders agreeable to his own intentions—no matter what. He had read about this practice in some books somewhere.

And what was wrong with that, you might ask? Well, the thing is that if a priest would advise Vasily to do something that he didn't feel like doing, he would immediately set off in search of different spiritual advisors, until at length they would give him the "blessings" he sought for whatever it is that he wanted to do. Then Vasily would calm down and immediately recognize that particular agreeable priest as his only true spiritual advisor.

We tried as we might to shame him out of doing this. But Vasily was very headstrong and merely smiled cunningly at all our fatherly reproaches. Although we do have to admit that he certainly did have a fervent belief in these "blessings" (even if they had been, sad though it is to confess it, occasionally purchased by his generous donations).

Vasily was already raising three little daughters, but he had long been dreaming passionately of a male heir. He had even thought of a name for him: Vasily. In honor of St. Vasily (Basil) the Great, of course. Not in his own honor, as some sinners, always eager to condemn others, might think!

Now and then Vasily would sneak up to all the priests in our monastery and beg them to give him some kind of particular blessing so that his wife would finally bear him a son. We reasonably answered him that there can be no such blessings, and Vasily should pray devoutly so that the Lord as He saw fit might grant Vasily's wish. But Vasily was absolutely not satisfied by such answers. No indeed, he wanted guarantees! He would take our priests off to the side and cajole them, trying to convince them to give "the right blessing." He would even whisper of his willingness to pay them any money as long as a boy would be born to the family. When he didn't get anything of what he wanted from us, he set off for Pechory, but there the result was the same.

Everybody decided that he would finally calm down. But we didn't know him well. Instead, Vasily went off in search of "real" priests, "real" spiritual fathers and elders. And naturally, especially as he was willing to pay, he found them rather quickly.

As a wise man keenly observed, "It is very easy to become an elder; it is enough to wish you were." Meaning, it's enough to knit your brows, put on majestic airs, earn somewhat of a reputation for uncompromising spiritual rebukes, begin to prophesy little by little, and give people blessings right, left, and center. And for such a "miracle worker" people will go a long way. Of course, it goes without saying that such a person is not by any means an elder, but merely a flatterer.

In short, Vasily returned to Moscow and tried again, with a horde of blessings and prophecies for the birth of a son, to make them come true. And soon enough his wife truly did get pregnant.

Not long before she was supposed to give birth, Vasily decided to make a pious pilgrimage to the Holy Land. And, naturally enough, all three of them would go: he himself, his wife, and his long-awaited heir, Vasily Vasilyevich, who was still in his mother's womb.

It was the peak of summer. Even a healthy person at such a time finds it difficult to be in the Holy Land because of the blazing heat. Now imagine the state there of a woman in the last month of pregnancy! But pious Vasily was uncompromising. He had decided that he and his true heir must absolutely traipse over all the holy places.

And so they visited the Holy Sepulcher. With his son and wife in tow, he climbed up to Golgotha. Vasily was happily talking to his heir, slapping his wife with his palm on her belly, and finally he said: "Vasily Vasilyevich! Can you feel it? We are on Golgotha!"

Then they went off into the Judean desert. They wandered and wandered about the sacred paths utterly blazing with heat. They climbed up to the Mount of Temptations. Here too Vasily addressed his little son, saying: "Vasily Vasilyevich! We are on the Mount of Temptations!"

Just before leaving the country they even climbed up Mount Tabor. Like a real pilgrim Vasily naturally refused the Arab taxis beckoning to the tourists and climbed up to the summit of Mount Tabor through the blazing heat on foot. From there, looking out over the gorgeous view from the height where the Transfiguration of Christ had once taken place, he cried out: "Vasily Vasilyevich! We are on Mount Tabor!"

In Ben-Gurion Airport it became clear that Vasily's wife was about to go into labor. But they decided that of course she should give birth only in Moscow. Things were even more complicated by the fact that Israeli customs would not let Vasily onto the plane. In the Holy Land, he'd made a habit of taking little holy relics along with him as souvenirs. What sort of relics are holy to an Orthodox pilgrim? A rock from the Mount of Temptations, some water from the Sea of Galilee, some water from the Jordan River, some sand from the Judean desert, a rock from Nazareth, a piece of soil from Bethlehem, and so on and so on. Other pilgrims were more modest in whatever souvenirs they took—for example, a tiny twig from a tree in Galilee or a pebble from Jerusalem—but Vasily had amassed at least thirty kilograms' worth of holy stones, earth, and water.

But if for him these were holy relics, for the surprised Israeli border police these were attempts to remove soil and water samples from the entire territory of Israel without permission to do so. This was the first time they'd ever seen such a thing. And they categorically refused to let Vasily leave for Russia with such a load. However, Vasily categorically refused to return home to his Third Rome without his holy relics from ancient Jerusalem.

Finally the customs police understood that they were dealing with, to put it mildly, quite an eccentric. And they thought about it and realized that there would be no irreparable harm to the security of the state of Israel if they let him go with a bit of dirt and rocks and leaves . . .

Finally he got on the plane, and in Moscow straight from the airport they brought his unhappy wife in an ambulance to the hospital. And there she gave birth at once—to a girl.

There was no describing the shock felt by our hero.

"They switched him!" he screamed. "Those dirty doctor-saboteurs! Where is my Vasily Vasilyevich? I got a blessing! The elders promised me we would have a son! Give me back my Vasily Vasilyevich!"

And so our story ended. Vasily soon disappeared from my field of vision. I don't know how he is now. I hope he pulled himself together. Perhaps, finally, he prayed himself a male heir. Otherwise, I hope that he is happy that the Lord has blessed him and his family through the birth of so many wonderful representatives of the fairer sex.

Hieromonk Raphael.

The Life, Amazing Adventures, and Death of Father Raphael, the Shouting Stone

O UR HERO WAS born in the little town of Chistopol on the river Kama in 1951. His father was the director of some sort of Soviet enterprise, his mother was a housewife, and his older brother was a leader of the Communist Youth League and a romantic believer in the just and beautiful future of Communism.

Nothing out of the ordinary seemed to be foretold in the ordinary Soviet life of Boris Ogorodnikov. He was the best sportsman in his high school, and hanging around with him was always cool and fun, and all the girls in his class were in love with him. When Boris graduated from school, he went straight into the Army and heroically served for three years on Damansk Island in the Amur River, during the height of the bloody undeclared war between the USSR and China. He returned home to Chistopol safe and sound, with medals for bravery and with the stripes of a sergeant. Next up for him were supposed to be undergraduate studies in an institute. Boris decided to enroll in the Automotive Construction Institute in order to learn how to build beautiful new cars and then to drive off in them all over, forgetting everything else in the world.

But then it so happened that this demobilized border guard somehow got into his hands the Book of Books, even though there was no way it was ever supposed to have been accessible to him or those of his generation. A severe and well-planned state machinery ceaselessly did what it could to prevent such mishaps from occurring. But it seems that somebody made a mistake somewhere. And so our hero secluded himself by the riverbank with curiosity, and with some distrust began to look at this Book. He opened it. He began to read its first words:

"In the beginning God created Heaven and Earth . . ."

How quickly worlds collapse! Just a moment ago he had been a model Soviet youth with an impeccable past and a no less impeccable shining

Communist future. But now suddenly he had neither past nor future left. The present had begun.

"Behold, I will make all things new." This is not only a promise but also the serious warning of which the Bible foretells, that Book of Books which, verse by verse, chapter by chapter, Boris Ogorodnikov, the future Father Raphael, read by the river Kama.

But he didn't know what was happening to him at the time. Boris suddenly had many questions, and he tried to ask them of the local priests. But they were afraid of the young man and so they shunned him. It was a difficult time, when priests had a right to talk freely only with old grandmothers who would soon be dying anyway.

Boris set off for Moscow to enter the Automotive Construction Institute, which no longer interested him. In the capital he began to go to churches where he would pose the questions that were so unexpectedly arising in his mind, questions whose answers he had waited for from the priests of Chistopol in vain.

But everywhere he met with the same caution and distrust, until he came upon a secluded little church on the south bank of the Moscow River. Here, to his astonishment, the priest spoke to him for a whole two hours. Boris stayed in the church, earning his living by working as a night watchman and guarding the territory entrusted to him as if it were the most important border in life.

As for the Bible, that Book which had so powerfully transformed his life, Boris, to the great surprise of the parish priests, managed to read it twice in a short period from cover to cover. The head priest in the church even cited the young man as an example to his other colleagues.

"We who were called upon to study and communicate the word of God are lazy and faintheartedly silent," the rector rebuked his other priests. "But this lad, who never even received any Christian upbringing and wasn't even supposed to know anything about God until the day he died, displays true zeal and faith. Such youngsters shame us priests of God in our timidity, laziness, and silence about Christ. Fathers, what will our answer be? What will happen to our Church with such pastors? But the Lord is alive. And the prophecy of our Savior is coming true: 'if these become silent, then the stones will cry out.' This simple lad happens to be that very same shouting stone. And we are looking for miracles somewhere!"

Boris said nothing to his parents, but instead of preparing for the Automotive Construction Institute he started to prepare for the seminary.

He passed his entrance exams in the Moscow Theological Seminary with flying colors. But naturally he could not enroll. With his heroic Army background, and as a member of the Communist Youth League, with his bright, shining Soviet future before him, any enrollment in the seminary in those years was simply out of the question.

The responsible "comrades" who controlled access to seminary education in those days immediately met with Boris. They felt guilty for having neglected him, for having allowed a model Soviet youth to even take the entrance exams for the seminary. These comrades severely demanded that the young man cast off this religious mania and return to normal life.

They pushed the young man with the sweetest of temptations, and threatened him with the direst of punishments. In reply Boris would only look somewhere off into the distance towards some place known only to him, and finally, after two days of nonstop pressure, he handed over a sealed envelope to the men who were desperately trying to talk him out of what was in his heart. They opened it eagerly, only to find a declaration from Boris Ogorodnikov withdrawing from the Communist Youth League for "religious reasons."

At this, the comrades got so angry that they promised Boris all conceivable problems and unpleasantness in the future: at work, at school, whether free or no longer free . . . They promised jail sentences or lifelong confinement in the psychiatric asylum. Basically, they promised him that he would endure absolutely the worst that this life had to offer, both now and in the future. Rejected for religious reasons, these comrades began to use apocalyptic language themselves—even about the future life. Yes, having been mobilized to the religious front, these persuaders had involuntarily absorbed the spirit of mysticism.

But for Boris the only conclusion to be drawn from these promised terrors was just one thing—he would not be allowed to enroll in the seminary. Thus, on the advice of the head priest of the church that had sheltered him, he set off for the Pechory Monastery near Pskov, having no idea what might be awaiting him there.

But He who had so powerfully taken into His hands the life and fate of young Boris Ogorodnikov knew everything: every footstep, and every footstep of the men He had arranged would greet him.

Boris was immediately distinguished from the throng of pilgrims by the Great Abbot Alipius. The responsible comrades whose job it was to oversee the Pskov Caves Monastery warned Father Alipius under no circumstances to disobey their command to keep hands off this heroic border patrol soldier. Archimandrite Alipius was given their dire warnings even as he was himself terminally ill. He listened attentively. The very next day he issued a decree accepting the novice Boris Ogorodnikov into the monastery. This decree may have been the very last order ever signed by Archimandrite Alipius. Soon afterwards, he died, and the novice Boris was made a monk by the new abbot, Archimandrite Gabriel.

The "responsible comrades" lost no time in warning and threatening Father Gabriel that it was his obligation to do everything to ensure that Boris Ogorodnikov leave Pechory in short order. The abbot replied soothingly that he certainly did understand the complications inherent in the situation that had developed, and he promised that he would do everything he could for the young lad. And in fact he was true to his word, because several days later he himself administered monastic vows, and a new person came into this world—the young monk Raphael.

In response to the thunder and lightning of the outraged and indignant comrades, the abbot replied with a very reasonable argument. In his desire to maintain the stability of the state and not

Archimandrite Alipius.

disturb the general peace, he had made the youth a monk, since that was the best decision for everyone. How was that? Very simple. The older brother of this new young monk Raphael had recently become a well-known dissident. Foreign radio stations reported his opinions through the length and breadth of the Soviet Union. So if you wanted his younger brother to be expelled from the monastery he would almost certainly join Alexander in his battle against Soviet authority, and that would be almost certainly be worse for everyone.

And indeed Alexander Ogorodnikov did (just like his younger brother) strive with audacity and courage for freedom and spiritual meaning in this life, fearlessly embarking upon the most dangerous journey—the search for a higher purpose. True, he had taken a different path, and yet he was headed for the same place. What the abbot had said about Alexander being a dissident was absolutely true, and the comrades knew it all too well.

The soul of young Alexander Ogorodnikov, in its thirst for justice, had come through passionate spiritual searching to the point where he (also a former leader of the Communist Youth League) joined another community of passionate believers in a shining future. This time he was on the other side of the barricades, for now he tried to organize dissident Christian seminars in Moscow.

The "responsible comrades" had reacted predictably to the creation of spiritual barricades against the Soviet state. Alexander was arrested. While he was under arrest incredible pressure was put on him, but though they tried with every means available to force him to change his mind, they failed. Finding that they were unable to break him, they sent the young man away for nine years to continue his searches and meditations for higher truth in a prison camp for political prisoners called "Perm 6," which had the reputation of being one of the most severe camps of all in its treatment of its prisoners of conscience.

In the end, the reasonable arguments of the abbot made an impression on the responsible comrades. And so the young monk Raphael was left in the monastery, and he was soon made deacon, and then a hieromonk. And Father Raphael became the happiest man in the world.

Boris Ogorodnikov was the first man to whom Archimandrite Gabriel, upon becoming the Abbot of the Pechory Monastery, administered monastic vows. He gave him the name Raphael in honor of the Archangel. The abbot's own heavenly patron was also an Archangel—Gabriel. Such things do not simply just happen in monastic life: it was evident that the abbot was particularly counting on this young and fervent and devoutly faithful monk. In any case, throughout the thirteen years that Father Gabriel served as abbot of the monastery, he never named anyone else in honor of an Archangel.

Upon taking vows, each new monk is given over to serve under the guidance of an experienced spiritual father. The first spiritual father of Father Raphael was Archimandrite Athenogenes, a monk who was already very advanced in years, and who had gone through persecution, wars, imprisonment, and exiles. Yet Father Athenogenes was feeling his ninety-eight years but lightly, with all the force and majesty of a new man transformed by faith and internally united with his Christ, his God and Savior. Father Raphael's time with his first spiritual father was quite short: Archimandrite Athenogenes soon left us to meet his Lord. Father

Father Athenogenes.

Raphael related two particularly memorable stories about him.

When all the brotherhood of the monastery gathered in the large refectory to celebrate Father Athenogenes's name day, or the commemoration of his patron saint, he listened to their words of respect and reverence and stood for a long time silent, a tiny figure hunched over with age; everyone waited for his response with bated breath. The elder looked at all the monks standing in front of him and spoke: "What can I possibly say to you, my brothers? I just love you all."

And then all the monks who were gathered in the refectory—even the sternest monks—simply stood there and wept.

The second story begins with the fact that Archimandrite Athenogenes, right up until his death, used to perform rituals of exorcism, or as they would say among the people, he would "read out" or drive out the demons who were tormenting terribly sick and suffering people. Sometimes it was sufficient to bring the agonized victim, overcoming his despairing resistance, kicking and screaming into the cell of Father Athenogenes for the demons to leave, unwilling even to cross the threshold of his door. And the sufferer would awaken and pull himself together, not even able to believe that he had finally been freed of many years of suffering.

However, far more often, the cure required long pastoral labors and particular Church prayers from Father Athenogenes. This extremely difficult, and indeed for many reasons extremely dangerous, service would exhaust the elder to the very utmost.

Once during the bath day, Father Raphael was helping his spiritual father to wash himself in the monastery bathhouse. It was always the task of the young novices to help out the elderly monks with such care. Father Raphael for a minute had turned away in order to put soap on the brushes and sponges, and when he turned around again he was terrified to see his elder hanging in the air, hovering above the bench of the bathhouse. But then, before his very eyes, he saw Father Athenogenes slowly and surely come back down to the stone bench, at which point he asked his novice with some irritation: "What? You saw? Quiet, you fool. Don't tell anyone. It was the demons. It's just that they wanted to dash me against the stones. But the Holy Mother of God would not allow this. Keep quiet, and do not tell anyone else about this until I am dead."

"Behold, I will make all things new." These words came true time and time again in the life of Father Raphael. Like most of the new monks he gradually began to discover for himself the limitlessly mysterious but utterly incomparable new world of which he had had his first glimpse when he sat by the banks of the river Kama, when he had begun to read the Book of Books, of which he had previously had no knowledge.

This new world Father Raphael had joined was full of joy and light, and governed by its own particular laws. In this world the help of the Lord would always come when it was truly needed. In this world wealth was ridiculous, and glamour and ostentatiousness absurd, while modesty and humility were beautiful and becoming. Here great and just souls truly judged themselves to be lesser and worse than any other man. Here the most respected were those who had fled from all worldly glory. And here the most powerful were those who with all their hearts had recognized the powerlessness of their own unaided humanity. Here the true power was hidden with frail elders, and it was understood that sometimes it was better to be old and ill than to be young and healthy. Here the youthful would leave behind the usual pleasures of their friends and mates in the normal world, and do so with no regrets, as long as they would not have to leave this special world without which they could no longer live. Here the death of each became a lesson to all, and the end of earthly life was just the beginning.

* * *

Once Father Raphael so decidedly and powerfully was taken from his former life, he then joyfully gave unto God everything: his ordinary human happiness, his ordinary human pleasures, his career, and even his own passionate freedom. But there was one thing that he proved simply unable to give up . . . Oh yes—this is something about which we cannot be silent, no matter how much we might like to. It might sound ridiculous, but there was one passion that Father Raphael simply could not give up— his passion for speed! Yes, yes! Just that!

But first I will have to tell you that after he lived in the monastery for six years, Father Raphael was exiled to an obscure country parish. The reason for his exile was again his elder brother.

By this time Alexander had become world-renowned as a dissident. He had already spent several years in confinement, the majority of that time in severe solitary confinement. The reasons for such severe punishments were nothing more than the outrageous and simply unthinkable demands (for that time) that Alexander had made to the prison camp officials. Alexander insisted that he be allowed to keep the Bible in his prison cell, and that he be allowed to meet with a priest for confession and taking of Communion. Needless to say, of course, the prison camp bosses refused his requests, upon which Alexander also refused to live according to their rules. When they ordered him to stand, he would sit. When they demanded him to answer, he would be stubbornly silent. You may surely understand that for such unheard-of defiance, truly enviable courage was required. Throughout his nine years of imprisonment, he lived two years on hunger strikes, and more than a third in solitary confinement. (It should also be noted that in the end Alexander was victorious in his battle, and he became the first Soviet prisoner ever allowed to keep the Bible in his jail cell, and to receive visitation from a priest.)

Father Nikita.

Father Raphael.

When Alexander was being prosecuted in court, Father Gabriel allowed Father Raphael to witness the trial and even secretly gave money to support his family. But after the trial, Soviet authorities began making merciless demands that the brother of so famous a dissident be removed at once from the monastery.

In the end, either the abbot decided not to exacerbate the conflict with the authorities, or the relationship between Father Gabriel himself and this young firebrand monk had somewhat worsened (very likely both), but finally Father Raphael was exiled to a sleepy country parish. It was not even reachable by bus. It was several kilometers' walk from the nearest neighboring village. Later he was transferred from there to a place just as remote, though slightly more populous: the Church of St. Mitrophan in the little village of Lositsy, where no more than ten people would come to church every Sunday.

Father Raphael's only possession besides an icon, a pair of books, and his monk's robes was a tape recorder. But what a tape recorder! It was a large foreign-made transistor tape recorder. In the Moscow commission stores of that time it cost a whole fortune—1,000 rubles. This valuable thing had been given to him as a gift right on the eve of his exile. From his jail cell Alexander had asked his friends to give his younger brother his tape recorder in order to be of some material support to him.

Father Raphael and his "Zaporozhets."

And this is how Father Raphael's dream of a car was realized. He sold the tape recorder at once, and used the money to buy a ramshackle old Zaporozhets car at the automotive market in Pskov. The car was an absolutely revolting dirty orange color.

Father Raphael began to repair this half-destroyed piece of junk. He dove deeply into the loins of this Zaporozhets and emerged from its belly into the light of day only after a month. That old car, after his loving work, became something quite incredible. I have no idea how he did it, but he managed to make it capable of going 150 kilometers per hour. There was only one thing left to do: to change that horrible color. Father Raphael left for Pskov in a horrible orange-looking little monster and returned to the village practically in a limousine, painted in the black colors of the government, with white curtains on its back windows.

When he was asked why he had chosen to paint the car black, Father Raphael explained that in the mechanic's shop there had been only two colors: black and red. Naturally, he had chosen black, the monastic color, especially since it was unthinkable that he would be driving around in a car the color of the Communist flag.

I believe that this was the only Zaporozhets in the entire USSR that was painted the black color of a government vehicle. No one else in his right mind would have thought about painting such a jalopy black, adding white curtains to the back windows (which at that time was truly a characteristic of government bureaucrats' automobiles). It is a little sad to admit this, but this act of Father Raphael was more than a prank, but was a deliberate act of youthful defiance—hooliganism.

Father Raphael was particularly fond of making fun of high-ranking provincial Party officials. He would get on the tail of one of their black Volga sedans, and then when they tried to lose him, would step on the gas of his jet-propelled Zaporozhets jalopy and stream ahead like a bolt of lightning. And if that Volga happened to belong to Comrade Yudin, the Pskov Provincial Overseer for Religious Affairs, the day had not passed in vain.

Deacon Victor.   *Hieromonk Nikita.*

The Parish House in Lositsy
and Its Inhabitants

*T*HE PARISH HOUSE of Father Raphael in the village of Lositsy was a simple one-room wooden cottage. But everything else about the place was extraordinary.

On the stove there lived an incorrigible old geezer—crazy, possessed Ilya Danilovich, a powerful old fellow who nonetheless almost never clambered down from the comfort of the stove. I never met anyone like Ilya Danilovich either before or since. Whenever he would begin to tell a story (and it didn't matter whether it was about something that happened long ago or something that had just happened yesterday), his listeners would hear him out with rapture, understanding that they were in contact with something totally unique: Ilya Danilovich was gifted with a truly epic state of mind. In all the history of the world, perhaps only a few men were ever so naturally endowed at epic storytelling: Homer, Tolstoy, and crazy Ilya Danilovich.

He had a phenomenal memory. If he chanced to be relating something from his own military past, he would list the names of all the officers and all the soldiers, all their ranks, their dates of birth and dates of death, the names of their wives and fiancées, and the names of their home towns and villages. He could remember what weapons they fought with, whether it was a .375 caliber rifle or a howitzer. Ilya Danilovich described everything with no less fascination and loving detail than that with which the Shield of Achilles was described in *The Iliad*.

Ilya Danilovich had come to religion in a very peculiar way, and it was precisely due to his having been possessed. Because, as Father Raphael explained, without his possession Ilya Danilovich would have stayed a handsome young cavalier who feared nothing in this world and lived entirely according to the laws of the flesh, and would never have come to God of his own free will. And the desires of his flesh, according to Ilya Danilovich, were so powerful that even leaving aside his amorous exploits (which were considerable), he was so moved by his senses that once in 1941 when he was

433

Ilya Danilovich on a boat near Lositsy. He is carrying a Psalter.

standing sentry by the front line, he felt such hunger that he followed the smell of beef stew all the way to the enemy's trenches. The Germans at first were stunned, but they didn't shoot. They decided to wait until this crazy Russian fell into their trench. And when they realized why the crazy lad had come, they gave him beef stew and oatmeal. And so not only did Ilya eat his fill, but even stuffed his helmet and pockets with oatmeal for his hungry comrades. (Such incidents happened in the war, though they were rare.)

When he got back from the war, the brave soldier did not put off until tomorrow what he could do today, but immediately chose for himself the most beautiful woman to be his bride. But quite soon it emerged that his choice was flawed: his young wife's character, and particularly the character of his mother-in-law, were remarkably nasty. Ilya Danilovich was sad, but divorce in those days, and especially in workers' villages, was just not done. He quickly, however, found other ways to console himself. Ilya worked as a driver on long-distance journeys, and as he told me his story, he related with repentance that not only on his long-distance routes but even in his own village he soon had mistresses. His wife quickly found out about it. However, neither scandals, nor pleading, nor scoldings from provincial Communist Party committees, nor the judgments of his comrades had any effect on Ilya in the least. At this point his bitterly offended wife decided to take the most extreme measure.

She went to a sorceress, and that witch, as they say among the people, "sentenced" or "did" Ilya to death. I remember myself how skeptically I listened to this portion of Ilya Danilovich's tale, but he didn't even bat an eyelid, and kept on telling us what happened next.

One evening as he was returning home late from another one of his long-distance journeys, he approached the gate of his cottage and saw an unknown woman in his yard. What was most surprising about this woman was the fact that she was no less than five meters high. Her head could reach the roof! She was older than middle-aged, and straight-haired with a very long braid, and dressed up in an old-fashioned *sarafan* (peasant dress). This female giant paid no attention to Ilya but paced around the house muttering something under her breath, and then effortlessly stepped over the picket fence and disappeared completely into the darkness.

Ilya, like any normal Soviet person, had absolutely no belief whatsoever in mysticism. What's more, he was absolutely sober. Therefore, when his initial shock passed, he assumed that he had just been seeing things, being tired out from a long and arduous drive.

As he walked into his house, he saw his wife and mother-in-law carefully fussing over a generously decorated dinner table. This struck him as a very strange, since Ilya could never once remember having been the subject of such attention and devotion from these perpetually complaining and cantankerous women before. But they courteously sat him down, and his mother-in-law poured him some vodka, and an unprecedented feast began.

Ilya remembered the unusual vision he had just seen in his yard and he asked the women if anything out of the ordinary had happened before he had arrived. The women amiably scoffed, waved their arms, and assured him that nothing out of the ordinary had or possibly could have happened. The vodka flowed in even more abundance than before, and Ilya soon forgot about everything.

He awoke early next morning in his bed. His wife was not next to him. Ilya decided that it was time to get up. But to his amazement, he was unable to do so. His hands and feet would not obey him. Terrified, he began to scream, but instead of a real scream all he could manage was a weak groan. Within an hour (which seemed to Ilya a terrifying eternity) his wife and mother-in-law returned with yet another woman who seemed remarkably like the woman whom he had seen yesterday in his garden. Only now she was normal in height. They paid no attention whatsoever to Ilya's groans, but instead unabashedly looking at him wandered around him muttering whispered incantations to each other. Then they left, and Ilya was once more all alone and helpless.

Only later that evening did his wife return once more, only this time in the company of the local doctor. Ilya listened to her weeping in floods of crocodile tears, describing how her husband had returned home from his trip, had drunk way too much, had fallen asleep, and was now completely unable to get up. The next day they took away the patient to the regional hospital. He spent more than a month there, but the doctors could not figure out the cause of his strange ailment, and so they released Ilya, wizened and emaciated and dried out like a woodchip, to die at home.

At home a real nightmare was waiting for him. His wife and mother-in-law did not even begin to conceal their victories, and joyfully awaited the death of the wayward husband who had wronged them. One time when Ilya was really feeling terrible, his wife even invited the coffin maker to their home, and helped him to measure her husband who, though unable to speak, was still breathing.

Though not understanding what was happening to him, Ilya was reconciled to the thought of his impending death, and awaited his inevitable end almost meekly. But then Ilya's old friend who had served with him in the war found a moment when the women weren't home and brought along a priest dressed in civilian clothes. He suggested that Ilya be baptized even on his death bed, and that he turn to God for help. Ilya was so sick that he barely understood what all of this meant, but with the only movement still left to him—a slight nod of the head—he expressed his agreement.

After his baptism no miracles occurred, except for the fact that despite all odds, and to the utter astonishment of the doctors, Ilya did not die. His wife and mother-in-law were beside themselves with rage. Nearly a month passed, after which Ilya with extreme difficulty was able to somewhat lift himself up from bed and barely speak a few words. Otherwise his condition remained horrible. But then his friend who had served with him on the front came and collected Ilya, packed him up into a train, and brought him on slow trains through the entire country, changing trains in city after city, to the Pskov Caves Monastery, to the elder Archimandrite Athenogenes.

Ilya had come to a strange and unfamiliar world unlike anything he had ever known. But after speaking to Father Athenogenes, after which he followed up by his first confession and taking of Communion, he was, so to speak, resurrected. Within one week Ilya was completely well, walking on his own two feet, and each day getting better and better. He had very much in common with the elder. Both of them were simple people, of peasant origins. Therefore, when Father Athenogenes told Ilya that his wife had had a spell cast on him, and that he, having no spiritual defense, should have actually died, Ilya believed him at once. Why shouldn't he have believed him, when the only one in this world who had been able to save him was this ancient monk?

Ilya Danilovich never came home again. He became a holy pilgrim. From time to time he lived and worked in the monastery, and other times he wandered on foot through all of Russia from church to church. It'd been a long time since he had had an internal passport. Gradually he began to get older, yet he remained physically strong and healthy. He was in this state when I met him living in Father Raphael's parish house.

* * *

Yet another inhabitant of the parish house in the village of Lositsy was the monk Alexander. He had begun as a student of the Bryansk Pedagogical Institute but, having discovered faith several years before, had also dropped everything and become a pilgrim wandering from church to church all over Russia. Although, thank the Lord, nothing remotely like the story of Ilya Danilovich had ever happened to him.

Alexander had ended up in the Pskov Caves Monastery but within two years became part of the group of monks who had rebelled against Father Gabriel, and so he left to go on pilgrimage again. Eventually he found refuge at the parish house of Father Raphael.

At the time Alexander was twenty-eight years old. But all over his hands and arms were weals and calluses caused by his many years of studying karate. We used to wander the fields and forests together. For walks we would make light staffs or walking sticks of walnut wood. Or so I thought. All of them were slightly curved, like the twigs of the trees they came from, and only Alexander's staff was ideally straight, and painted an elegant black. Once when we were resting I decided to take a closer look at this beautiful thing, and then I discovered to my great surprise that I could scarcely even lift it. The staff turned out to be an enormously heavy steel rod. When I

Father Alexander, now Father Roman.

asked Alexander what he needed such a powerful weapon for, the monk replied that this staff gave him the chance to at least somewhat stay in physical shape.

Father Alexander was taciturn. Throughout all his spare time he used to read the writings of the ancient fathers of the Church. He would sleep in a little closet-partition, walled off by a slab. Alexander would lock up his partition with a key, which was a little strange, considering that Father Raphael closed the entire house with only a latchkey. But one time I was alone in the house washing the floors and Alexander went out somewhere and forgot to lock up his closet. Unable to curb my curiosity, I had a peek inside. It contained a coffin, made of crude wooden planks. From sheer shock I was so surprised that I ran out of his little shelter as fast as I could.

When I pulled myself together, I asked Ilya Danilovich what it meant. From the top of his stove, Ilya answered that Alexander slept in a coffin because he believed that a monk should always remember death. Apparently many holy men did the same thing.

In spite of his severe ascetic ways, Alexander composed many excellent poems and music to accompany them. Some of his songs are now well known, are reproduced on CDs and cassettes, and are published in many songbooks of the most famous songwriters. The monk Alexander has long since finally taken his full monastic vows and has been given a new name, Father Roman—in honor of the ancient Byzantine holy poet Roman the Melodist.

Back then in Lositsy he used to create and sing his songs in the evenings, accompanying himself on his own guitar—when Father Raphael permitted. (Although he considered this activity not at all monastic, he nonetheless sometimes loved to listen to Alexander.)

Here is one of Father Alexander's songs:

Oh, my friends, it is already evening.
And the moon up above us does gleam
Let us cease for a moment our speeches,
Let us cease for a moment our feast.

There's no rain, no skies black as a pall.
No winds blow, there's no rustling, no fuss.
It's as if nature, heeding our soul's call
Has flung open fall's beauty for us.

And perhaps, though I will not foretell it,
On a hard road a pilgrim somewhere
Under night's sweet confession is seeking
New hope that his end is soon there.

All the forest now quivers with blessing
And the pond quivers incense of mist
Peace be on you, oh wanderer questing,
And on those who grant shelter and rest.

Who are you, unknown wanderer thoughtful,
How much longer the road which you trace?
Why I am so entranced by your mournful
And blissful and luminous face?
All the spiritless gloom of life random
Holy prayers dispel from your heart.

Maybe soon I will also abandon
All things, take my rod up, and start

On your road, of directions quite heedless
With a staff and with crosses endowed.
And I'll welcome the wilderness nearest.
And I'll give a wide berth to all towns.

We recorded his songs on a tape player, and I later brought them to Moscow. Once many years later I was sent on an errand to Patriarch Pimen, to his residence on Chisty (Pristine) Lane. While I was waiting there in the foyer, I was surprised to hear this song by Father Roman emerging from the Patriarch's own rooms. Patriarch Pimen was himself an excellent singer and was therefore a keen judge of true religious creativity.

* * *

There were two other frequent guests in the parish house of Lositsy: the monk Nikita, Father Raphael's closest friend; and the Deacon Viktor.

Father Nikita had also taken his monastic vows in the Pskov Caves Monastery. He had run away from a home where no one loved him in Leningrad at the age of thirteen, when he had still been a young Pioneer. Father Nikita used to say, "Even back then I understood that in this world a person is needed by no one else except himself and the Lord God." It remains a mystery how a young Pioneer thought of this on his own, but somehow or other the young lad soon found himself taking refuge in the parish house of the remarkable ascetic monk Father Dositheus in the village of Borovik, sixty kilometers from Pskov. There he grew up under the guidance of that elder, raised on the Psalms, on the ancient patericons, learning his vocabulary from the lives of the saints and from ascetic books written in the fifth century: the Ladder of Divine Ascent, and Abba Dorotheus. He had virtually no knowledge of worldly life.

The boy no longer went to school, but grew up extremely intelligent, very kind, very well educated in his own way. What's more, he was tall, strapping, remarkably handsome. Before he was drafted into the Army, Father Dositheus sent him for a year to the Pskov Caves Monastery, so that he could be brought up to speed a little bit with the twentieth century. It was there that he became friends with Father Raphael. And when he got back from the Army, he immediately petitioned to become a monk. In the same year that Father Raphael was exiled from the monastery, Father Nikita's elder, Father Dositheus, asked Metropolitan John of Pskov to allow the boy to remove himself to a hermitage, which was a little home two kilometers from the village of Borovik, near the woods and swamps of Pskov. The Metropolitan, well aware of the elder's pious and ascetic life, gave his blessing to this seclusion, and so he appointed Father Nikita, who knew the Church of Borovik and the people who attended it, to a priestly position that had opened up there.

Thus, the two young monks were placed in parish houses some 200 kilometers apart from each other. When either of them got the chance, they would visit the other, each in the other's church. They would pray together and serve the Liturgy together and help each other with whatever domestic tasks were needed.

Finally, one other frequent resident of the village of Lositsy was the recently ordained Deacon Viktor, who had been sent to the parish to Father Nikita in order to receive his practice as a deacon. Father Viktor had only recently gotten out of jail. He had been in the camps as a political prisoner for seven years. The deacon had very much wanted to become a monk, but Metropolitan John, a very wise and kind elder, was only able to obtain the permission of the Provincial Overseer for Religious Affairs for this former political prisoner to become a deacon—and even then only in the most remote and desolate parish, nowhere near a populous monastery. It must be said that in those days the appointment of a former political prisoner even to the position of deacon was a quite extraordinary event.

Father Viktor emerged from the prison camps with an unshakable faith in God, and full of contempt for the ordinary difficulties of ordinary life, and with such a cheerful spirit that from his never-ending store of jokes and humorous stories we literally used to fall to the floor from laughter. Of course, this last factor did not seem quite monastic, and we tried to struggle against it with all our might. But all our might could only hold out until the next story from Father Viktor. He also brought to our pious life some of the lexicon of prison, from which, in spite of all our reproaches, he was never quite able to free himself.

More than anyone it was goodhearted Father Nikita who suffered from the paucity of Deacon Viktor's catastrophic vocabulary. Deacon Viktor had made an enormous impact in this quiet little nook with his laughter and incurable optimism—and even his unbearable jailhouse slang, some

Father Nikita.

of which, to our horror, Father Nikita soon also picked up.

Father Viktor for some reason immediately acquired the nickname "the Little Elder." This was quite surprising in and of itself, since we never gave nicknames to anyone. But somehow for this veteran of the Soviet penal system, the nickname arose spontaneously and seemed to just fit him.

I remember one autumn I came to the village of Borovik to visit Father Nikita. The food and money that I had brought from Moscow was quickly exhausted, since I was not the only guest here. Other youngsters visiting there and utterly famished after the Dormition Fast—a strict two-week fast before the Feast of the Dormition of the Holy Mother of God—included Father Raphael, the monk Alexander, Deacon Viktor, and the possessed wanderer Ilya Danilovich. The last was actually thirty years older than we were, but he had a fierce youngster's appetite all the same.

Having soon completely devoured everything that had come from Moscow, and having eaten our fill of the new harvest of apples (to the point of allergy), we were all beginning to feel a little glum. And we decided as a last resort to travel to Pskov to ask Metropolitan John to give us some money for food.

This bishop at that time was probably the oldest hierarch in the

Russian Orthodox Church. One can only imagine what tribulations he had experienced in his life! But this tall, powerful, completely gray-haired man was remarkably kind—especially to monks. So we were certain that he might grumble and complain but he would never say no to us. For forty years the Metropolitan had remained in his bishopric involved exclusively in ecclesiastical affairs. He was the only bishop in the entire Russian Church who had the privilege of not being obliged to travel to Moscow, even for the local ecclesiastical assemblies, which everyone had to attend. It seems that they had long ago forgotten about him. The Metropolitan knew Father Nikita very well, and was very fond of him, since he had taken part in his upbringing from the time he had run away from home to the parish house of the elder Dositheus.

There is no doubt that the Metropolitan had a very good idea of the penury in which his monks in the remote parishes were living. He knew it well, but nonetheless sent them to serve there. For it was only because Divine Services were still served in these churches that the authorities did not dare to close or destroy them. Therefore he had monks or unmarried priests serving in practically all of the remote parishes of the diocese of Pskov. Married priests, especially those with children, would not have been able to survive there. Father Nikita told us that he with great difficulty made only twenty-five rubles a month. Nor were his parishioners any less poor, so they were unable to supplement his meager salary with donations. On the contrary, the priests used to help out these generally retired old peasant women whose children and grandchildren had all too often moved to the towns and completely forgotten about them. Sometimes they would chop wood for them, other times they would fix their roofs, and sometimes, with their own last pennies, they would buy these abandoned grandmothers food and medicine.

For priests, a little bit of money might be earned when the country folk, who were almost all not religious, would come to church to have a child christened or to have a funeral and burial. But monks did not think about money. Or rather, to be completely honest, they thought about money only after everything else.

Having borrowed a ruble for the bus trip, for greater piteous effect we traveled in one group to see the Metropolitan, leaving only Ilya Danilovich to look after the church, because throughout Pskov Province it seemed there were brigands who used to specialize in robbing churches. There were not many people on the bus, and the four of us—Father Raphael,

Father Nikita, Father Viktor, and myself—spread out and made ourselves comfortable. The other passengers looked at us with interest and with sympathy. In those years it was quite a rare thing to see young monks so casually traveling in the Soviet Union in monastic garb and with staffs.

We finally made it to the bishopric. However, we had so immersed ourselves in conversation that we nearly missed our stop in Pskov. At the last second, Father Viktor noticed where we were and roared (so loudly the whole bus could hear): "Fathers! Quick! Make tracks and whet your horns!"

Even as we leaped out of the bus, we did manage to notice the shocked faces of the other passengers. But we couldn't think about them. The object of our pilgrimage lay before us, and even though the street was named for the Bolshevik Jan Fabricius, it was the site of the Metropolitan's diocesan residence. (The Soviet government was particularly fond of locating the spaces it allocated for religious leaders either in some "Second Communist Dead-End" or else in a "Karl Liebknecht Street."*)

The Metropolitan received us in his office, deeply ensconced in his armchair. Each of us walked in and received his blessing, and then mournfully bewailed his plight. The Metropolitan listened to us, but did not stir. This made us nervous immediately. Perhaps he wanted to hear the circumstances of our penury in more detail, or perhaps he didn't have very much money himself. Whatever the reasons, we became very nervous indeed. Father Raphael even pushed me—the smallest and thinnest of our number—ahead of the rest of us, but this had no effect. Then suddenly Father Nikita began to speak to the Metropolitan.

Father Nikita was no orator; what's more, he had a terrible stammer. But now, perhaps from true hunger, he found inspiration: "Your Grace!" he began despairingly. "Whassup, for real, eh? We're down to our last whatsits, man. Our arms will drop off. We've got no cash, we've got no grub—teeth on the table—don't need 'em! We'd sell 'em for food if we could. And we've not even got any c-corpses!"

The Metropolitan froze in his chair. But we had been pleased by this speech, and we nodded our heads fervently.

Of course, Father Nikita in his nervousness had somewhat thoughtlessly used some of the vocabulary he had acquired from Father Viktor. And in his reference to the dead he was of course not referring to cannibalism but to the fact that the only funds that he ever came by in the church were for

---

* Karl Liebknecht (1871–1919) founded the Communist Party of Germany. —TRANS.

The Church in the Village of Borovik, where Father Nikita Served.

saying funerals of parishioners. Of course, the way it came out was a bit too striking and colorful of an appeal for such an elderly prelate.

"Father, my dear . . . Where on earth did you learn such words?" The utterly stunned Metropolitan turned to Father Nikita.

The Metropolitan had not heard such expressions for sixty years, certainly at least not since his own imprisonment in the 1920s. At this point our "Little Elder" Viktor stepped forward to take the full blame on himself.

"Your Grace, it's me, an old jailbird, always yapping my prison slang in front of him, and I can't seem to kick the habit. It's all my fault," he said with profound self-reproach, even beating himself against his own breast.

But it seems the speech of Father Nikita had produced a profound impression on our Metropolitan. He ponderously lifted himself up from his chair, walked to the table, grunted a little, and removed 100 rubles from a drawer. We couldn't even have begun to dream about so much money!

The Metropolitan of Pskov played with the bank notes as he held them

Deacon Victor.

in his hand, perhaps wondering whether this sum was not too much, but he did not stoop to trifling and handed the money over to Father Raphael, as he was the oldest. As he blessed us for our return journey, he nonetheless said, "As for you, my dear Nikita, I suggest you do more reading in Old Church Slavonic!"

Father Nikita fervently promised to reform himself, and we left the Metropolitan's house delighted. Life could go on! It happened to be Wednesday—a fast day, so we couldn't splurge on ice cream, but we were willing to wait until tomorrow. We bought food for ourselves and the country grandmothers in our care, and then we went home.

But the next morning we received a telegram from the directorate of the bishopric, stating that by a decree of Metropolitan John, Deacon Viktor was hereby transferred from the Church of the Protection in Borovik to the Church of the Archangel Michael in the village of Tolbitsy. The priest who served in that church was the well-respected old priest Father Andrei. And it seemed the Metropolitan's reasoning was simple. The jail slang of Deacon Viktor would certainly have no influence on Father Andrei, for that intellectual and highly educated priest had been imprisoned for his faith in the labor camps, it seems, for no less than twenty years. In spite of this, no one had ever heard him utter any of the words and phrases that so often colored the ears of the listeners of our Little Elder, Deacon Viktor.

*A village church,
Pskov Province.*

An Incident on the Road

LATE ONE EVENING we were sitting in the little wooden parish house all covered in snow in the village of Borovik, sipping tea with Father Nikita. Outside, a bitter frost of thirty degrees below zero Celsius was drawing cracks in all our windows. It was past eleven o'clock at night, but nobody wanted to go to sleep. "Why don't we go visit our Little Elder Viktor in Tolbitsy?" Father Raphael suggested.

Naturally I was overjoyed to agree to his suggestion that we visit our Little Elder Viktor, the most cheerful fellow in the world! Father Nikita refused to drive with us, as he wanted to stay home and record all the songs of Father Alexander onto the cassette tape recorder that I was planning to take with me to Moscow. Alexander was helping him and therefore also didn't want to go with us. Ilya Danilovich, the possessed, was reading the Psalter and had no reaction whatsoever to our idea.

Father Raphael went outside to warm up the motor of his doughty Zaporozhets, and to turn on the heater (which in a Zaporozhets works separately from the main motor). When we were ready to go, the temperature in the car was such a sauna that Father Raphael and I set off only in our cassocks and raced off in his black Zaporozhets to see the Little Elder Viktor. We had a drive ahead of us of about sixty kilometers.

It was a very frosty, starry night. We raced along, lighting up the snow with our headlights, now and then skidding around the turns. The summer tires of the Zaporozhets had been worn out even in the summer, and there was no replacing them. In spite of the lateness of the hour, our Little Elder received us with his usual good cheer. We sat down to his feast of white bread with jam and chatted merrily till about two in the morning. None of us had to serve the Liturgy that morning, and so we were not afraid that we might sleep late for once.

Finally we set off to go home. When I stepped outside in nothing but my cassock, I nearly froze to death. The bitter cold had become even more bitter. We decided not to even wait until the inside of the car had warmed up, and flew homeward towards Borovik.

But for some reason the heater wouldn't turn on at all. The frost seemed to bite quite through us. Several times Father Raphael stopped us and tried to do something with that cursed heater, but in vain. If he had driven like a madman before, now from the cold he was racing as fast as he possibly could. And so we drove on down the desolate road in an icy black freezer, shivering and champing our teeth from the cold.

Suddenly our Zaporozhets wildly swung off to the side of the road. Father Raphael, now rigid from the cold, could do nothing to stop the skidding of the car along the ice into a rutted snowdrift, and so we flew into a ditch, raising a cloud of snow.

The car did not turn over but had sunk deeply on all sides into the snow. It was only with great difficulty that we could open the doors and crawl outside. The Zaporozhets was two meters off the road, and covered in snow up to its windows. We could immediately see that there was no way we would be able to drag the car back out by ourselves.

Our situation was becoming more desperate by the minute. We were standing at three o'clock in the morning on an absolutely desolate and deserted country road wearing nothing but our cassocks in a frost of thirty-five degrees below zero Celsius. There was no place to walk to. The nearest village was fifteen kilometers away. If we were lucky, the first cars were likely to pass no sooner than six o'clock in the morning.

As I realized all this I became truly scared. "Father!" I exclaimed, shivering throughout from fear as well as from the bitter cold. "How could it be? We will die like this! Maybe we ought to pray somehow? But what should we ask for? Lord, help us drag our car from the snow? Somehow it doesn't sound right!"

Father Raphael suddenly looked at me so severely that for a second I forgot about the cold. "Shame on you, Georgiy Alexandrovich!" he said indignantly (Father Raphael always called me by my secular first name and patronymic, my name before tonsure). "How can you possibly doubt that the Lord will not aid us in such a moment? Pray for help at once!"

All this was said with such infuriated and demanding passion that he even stamped his foot, and I obediently crossed myself and began to murmur awkwardly: "Lord, help us! Do something, or we will freeze to death and perish here!" Father Raphael also crossed himself and then immersed himself in prayer.

And suddenly . . . At first from a distance, and then, ever and ever more clearly, we heard the divine singing of some kind of motor. From utter surprise and astonishment I was quite petrified. I would like to repeat and emphasize that neither on the way to Father Viktor's nor on our return home had we seen so much as even one automobile. Father Raphael and I exchanged glances, and I realized that he was no less astonished than I was.

The sound of the motor grew and grew, and finally from around the corner a Moskvich sedan came puttering up. We waved our arms like madmen and the car stopped.

In hearing our prayer, the Lord had sent four Angels to save us in the incarnation of four drunken officers returning home from some party. With great effort the six of us together managed to drag out our Zaporozhets from the snow and back onto the road. Father Raphael poured out some gasoline for the officers from his jerrycan. It turned out that they had been almost completely out of gas. With all our hearts we thanked these soldiers, and they thanked us, and then we drove as carefully as we could back home to Borovik.

We were so struck by what had happened that we were silent for most of the way home. Finally, Father Raphael said: "Now you can see, Georgiy Alexandrovich, how quickly the Lord hears the prayers of simple laypeople!"

By this he meant that the Lord had saved us because of my prayers. As always, Father Raphael was modest and never lost an opportunity to be humble. Or maybe by now he felt all too profoundly the truth that humility is the only reliable fulcrum of real spiritual life.

After this little trip I caught a really nasty cold and spent three days lying on top of Father Nikita's big Russian-style brick stove. But Father Raphael didn't even sneeze—not even once!

The hieromonk and hermit, Father Dositheus.

On Humility

$\mathcal{F}$ATHER RAPHAEL NEVER missed an opportunity to humble himself before anyone—even the first passerby whom he came across. But this always happened completely naturally, as if a matter of course, and it certainly never looked forced. On the contrary, one might say that he eagerly looked for chances to be humble. One might say this is because with his sensitive soul Father Raphael discovered an amazing secret: from humility even the simplest of sinners comes closer to God. And closer immediately, at once. And so, even in trifles, he always tried to find opportunities to humble himself.

For instance, when we sat down to eat, Father Raphael would immediately first take the worst and most rotten apple for himself, and distribute the best apples to us. Or else, whenever I would come to visit him in his parish house, he would immediately give up his own bed to me and he himself (ignoring my protests) would sleep on the floor. And he didn't do this because I was some visitor from the capital. The very same reception in his parish house could be expected by any old wandering holy fool or sexton from the neighboring parish.

Once Father Raphael and I came by train to Pskov. A frozen rain was drizzling down the northern sky. But as soon as we got down onto the platform, some gypsy beggar came up to pester us: "Priest! Priest! Help me out! Give me three rubles at least!"

It was falsely believed (thanks to anti-religious propaganda) that priests always have money, although in fact we usually never had a penny on us at all. I explained this to the gypsy, but he wouldn't go away. "What do you mean you have no money? You must have something! Priest! Priest! Give me something at least."

Father Raphael stopped and looked attentively at the beggar. The beggar was wearing tattered and torn shoes. Father Raphael sighed and without saying another word began to remove his own excellent box calf boots, which a fellow soldier had given to him one month ago. "Father, what's wrong? Are you ill?" The gypsy grew frightened.

But Father Raphael had already removed these light, high-quality boots and given them to the shocked gypsy. He also neatly put down his excellent foot bindings for these boots and proceeded to practically skip on barefoot through the puddles.

"Man! Man! What a man!" The gypsy called out his astonished approval through the entire station.

Father Raphael's humility extended, by the way, only to certain defined boundaries. The boundary was actually quite clear. He would endure any humiliation with respect to his own self, but he would not or could not abide any insults against the Lord God and His Church.

Once Father Raphael, Deacon Viktor, the monk Alexander, yet another friend of ours, the slightly blind Father Seraphim, and I were walking one late evening through Pskov. Our monastic attire drew the attention of a drunken company. At first we attracted nothing but mockeries, but these soon grew to insults and actual threats. Father Raphael was physically incredibly strong—something like a clumsy young bear. Father Viktor was also no weakling, and after his time in jail was well acquainted with how to behave in situations like these. Father Seraphim was simply a giant, in spite of his semi-blindness. Finally there was the monk Alexander, who was the most outstanding fighter among our group, as he had several black belts in karate. My meager school days' third prize in boxing counted for nothing in a company like this.

But not replying to this onslaught from the hooligans, we continued to calmly make our way through the town. Even when clumps of earth and even sticks began to fly our way, we tried not to pay any attention to this. The barrage continued: each time their aim was successful it provoked not only laughter but the most vulgar cursing. The monk Alexander was already shaking with indignation. Finally he could bear it no more and with a quivering voice meekly asked Father Raphael for permission to hang back and have a little talk with these deluded young men. But Father Raphael simply kept walking casually as if nothing were wrong.

Finally the hooligans became completely emboldened when they saw that neither insults nor clumps of mud would provoke any reaction. At this they began to blaspheme against God and the Virgin Mary. Father Raphael stopped.

"I may not answer," he sighed, "because I am a priest. Father Viktor is a deacon, and is also forbidden to answer. Father Seraphim and Georgiy Alexandrovich will stay in reserve. Ah well, what can we do if you're the only one left, Father Alexander?"

There was no need to prompt the monk Alexander twice. He ripped off his monastic belt, tore off his robes, and in his long baggy pants, loose long shirt, and boots, he turned on the hooligans with fury. There were several of them, and they stopped with surprise. In the next moment the monk Alexander uttered a savage, barbarian war cry and whipped through the air in a whirlwind of kicks. That drunken company received a savage beating. The luckless hooligans scattered every which way, wiping the blood from their noses and holding onto their teeth that had been kicked out of their mouths. We tried to draw Alexander back from them, and for our pains received some pain in return until his frenzy died down. Finally we calmed down our hero with difficulty, though it was like trying to get a bull terrier to release his grip. Once we were certain that it would not be necessary to call an ambulance for the wounded hoodlums, we dressed up the monk Alexander in his robes again and proceeded on our way.

Of course the story is hardly the best example of humility. But in the monastic life of Father Raphael there was a multitude of live examples of true humility: for instance Archimandrite John (Krestiankin), who became Father Raphael's spiritual father after the death of Father Athenogenes. There were others to whom he also humbled himself—for example, Hiero-monk Dositheus (Pashkov), who had brought up Father Nikita.

Father Dositheus had also been a graduate of the Pskov Caves Monastery. Like many of the other monks of the monastery, Father Dositheus had gone through the entire war as a soldier. Having liberated their own country and half of Europe from the Nazis, these young warriors had paid their debt to society in full, and had decided now to serve the Almighty God. They clearly knew and understood why they had come to the monastery, and were ready now to engage in mortal spiritual combat for themselves and for their living and dead companions—those who had not been called to fight this unseen yet crucial spiritual war between good and evil.

Father Dositheus was truly a great monk, though he was hardly noticed in the monastery. This is usually a reliable sign of an elevated spiritual warrior. He ended up in his parish as part of his obedience to his bishop, who had once sent him off to serve in the Church of the Protection in the village of Borovik. He was sent back there again and again, and eventually he was made the parish priest in this village that was nestled among the woods and swamps.

When Father Dositheus went into reclusion in an abandoned little house about two kilometers down the river, on an island in the swamps, he would paddle back to the church on Saturdays and Sundays in a dugout canoe-like boat that he had carved out of a pine log. (Nobody else but the elder Dositheus was able to navigate in that craft for more than ten meters without turning over.) On all other days Father Dositheus would remain in complete seclusion.

Into that utterly secluded little retreat Father Dositheus dragged the trunk of an oak tree with a hollow that he had carved out of its inside. The elder would clamber into that hollow for hours and hours, repeating the Jesus Prayer to himself, retreating even from his own retreat, as it were, in his thorough renunciation of all things worldly. But the mysterious recluse had entered into his retreat from the world not from any loathing for the world, but precisely because with all the power of his intensely loving soul he cared for this world, and wanted to protect it with his passionate prayer and with his nameless labors for others, which were only discovered later, long after his death.

When we were going through Father Dositheus's belongings after he was gone, we found that he had left us a typewriter as well as four manuscripts that he had personally typed of the New Testament, as well as the ancient spiritual texts, the Ladder of Divine Ascent, and the works of St. Isaac the Syrian. At this time, all such spiritual literature had been nearly destroyed, and his legacy was truly a treasure.

In his clairvoyance, Father Dositheus was able to predict, long before it happened, the departure of the ten unhappy monks from the Pskov Caves Monastery, and indeed frequently dropped hints about this event. He did not approve of their rebellion, and indeed, condemned it, but he felt pity for them, foreseeing how they would later be in need, and even began to prepare food for them: grains, cans, and other stores. Father Dositheus's pension as a war veteran was ridiculously tiny, yet he did not stint in helping others, and when these ten monks left the monastery and were shunned by others, these foodstuffs he gave them helped them to survive.

The local country drunkards spread it all over the neighborhood that the priest was getting a big pension. And one day three big strapping hoodlums, known brawlers and thieves from the nearest town, paddled up in a boat in order to rob him. They burst into the elder's cell, threatening his life, and demanded his money and everything he had.

Father Dositheus replied: "Take whatever you want, but first I will

The oak trunk with its hollow in Father Dositheus' house.

bless you." He then made the sign of the cross over them, blessing them in the priestly manner. In that second the ruffians were seized with such a terror that they raced out the door and scattered in panic.

The elder was tall, skinny, and gaunt, and yet until very late in life was endowed with uncanny strength. For a very long time, he was completely able to manage in his hermitage all by himself. Only in his final years was he helped by Father Nikita and Father Raphael.

One time the three of them prepared firewood for the winter. The two young monks dragged the logs, while Father Dositheus cut them with an ancient hand saw. Only when the two youngsters were thoroughly worn out did the elder agree to also take some rest. Father Raphael decided to weigh in his hands the antediluvian hand saw that Father Dositheus had been using, and he was amazed by how heavy it was, which made the casual lightness of his movements with it over the past hours all the more amazing, since Father Dositheus had been working without stopping at all.

That very day, as Father Raphael told me, they went together with the elder to the barn to get some tools, when suddenly the young monk saw a swamp adder right next to his bare foot. He was terrified, and then he heard the calm voice of the elder: "Don't worry, she won't hurt you. Grab the chisels and let's go."

Once I asked Father Nikita whether this ascetic elder of his had been a very severe person. Nikita answered by telling me about one incident. At the time he had been a sixteen-year-old boy, and had suddenly for some reason become relentlessly angry and had even yelled at Father Dositheus. The elder threw himself at Nikita's feet and in tears began to beg his forgiveness for having allowed his ward to have gotten into such an unholy state of rage.

Father Dositheus left us for our Lord on Holy Thursday. That morning he paddled up in his boat through the bitterly cold waters and the spring winds straight to the church, where he confessed, took Communion during the service, and once more paddled back to his hermitage. The next day his body was found in the river. Next to it they found the overturned logboat. When the autopsy was performed in the morgue, the pathologists were surprised not to find any traces of food in his intestines. Father Nikita explained that the elder had not taken anything except water and Holy Communion for the entire forty days of the Lenten Fast. In the police report of his death, they wrote it up as "drowned in the river as a result of complete physical exhaustion."

Father Dositheus was buried during Holy Week in the caves of Pskov Caves Monastery. When Father John approached his coffin, he took one look at his dead friend and, waving his arms wide, exclaimed: "They killed you, my dear Dositheus!"

And indeed, it soon became known around the neighborhood that drunken hunters from the local town were even boasting about the fact that as they were speeding down the river in their motorboat, they had knocked the frail old priest into the frozen water, just for a lark . . .

All his life Father Dositheus had aimed for a goal that is awarded only to the most select few even among God's elect on earth—namely, to find his own Golgotha. We ordinary people cannot comprehend such reasoning, but later, we found among the papers of the elder the following little poem that he wrote for himself:

Keep your Golgotha in mind.
Always remember the time
When for the sake of your kind,
Christ gave redemption divine.

Much about the way he lived was beyond our ken. But there was one thing about which we could have no doubt. In the final moment of his life, God let him pronounce the prayer from Golgotha of His Son, Jesus Christ, about those who crucified and tortured Him, and about all of humanity: "Father, forgive them, for they know not what they do."

Father John (Krestiankin) has called Father Dositheus the last of the great Russian hermits.

Father Raphael, at tea.

How Father Raphael Drank Tea

$\mathcal{P}$EOPLE HAD DIFFERENT attitudes towards Father Raphael. There were some who simply couldn't stand him. There were others—many more, actually—who said that Father Raphael had miraculously transformed their entire lives. For example, one of the three young monks who were murdered in Optina Monastery on Easter Day in 1993, the Hieromonk Vasily (Roslyakov), said of him: "It is to Father Raphael that I owe my monasticism, my priesthood, and my all."

What was the secret of the uncanny influence that Father Raphael held over the souls of others? What else did he do besides his ordinary work as a country priest, singing, saying services on feast days and on Sundays? It is not hard to answer this question. Those who knew him well will answer that most of his time in this life Father Raphael spent just drinking tea. With everyone, absolutely everyone who visited him. That's it. He drank tea. Although . . . no, sometimes he would also repair his black Zaporozhets car, so that he would be able to go visit somebody—and while visiting, drink some tea! Now that is truly all! That was his life.

From the point of view of the outside world Father Raphael was truly a complete idler. Some people even called him that. But it seems that Father Raphael had his own particular agreement with the Lord God. Therefore, everyone with whom he drank tea sooner or later became an Orthodox Christian, all without exception! From the most passionate atheist and the intellectual most disillusioned with ecclesiastical corruption to the most desperado criminals devoid of all morals . . . I don't know of a single person who after meeting Father Raphael did not afterwards decisively change and turn back to the spiritual life.

This is even though, to be honest, Father Raphael could not even manage to utter the simplest of sermons. At his best he would say: "Mmmm, hmmm, Brothers, Sisters, the thing is . . . Greetings with the Feast, dear Orthodox Christians!"

Once we in fact shamed him and convinced him to say a proper sermon for his church's patronal feast. He became very enthusiastic about this, but the results were such a mess that we all nearly died of shame,

461

although Father Raphael himself was quite pleased with his own efforts.

But if you chanced to drink tea with him on his little table in his country parish house, he became completely transformed, especially when people exhausted with suffering and heartache from their lost lives in this world came and sought him out. To be able to deal with such an endless flow of visitors, often capricious, often offended at everything and everyone, often rude and insistent, invariably with heaps of insoluble problems and ceaseless questions, would have been impossible for a normal person. But Father Raphael endured everything and everyone. Actually, he didn't even endure them—that's not really the right word, because he never even felt slightly burdened by it. In fact, he enjoyed this time that he spent drinking tea with absolutely anyone, always telling stories, always remembering something interesting from his life in the Pskov Caves Monastery, or talking about his old spiritual mentors, the elders of Pechory. Anyone sitting down to drink tea with Father Raphael found that once he had gotten going, it was impossible to tear oneself away.

Although, let us be honest, merely conversing with people who have gotten themselves hopelessly lost in this cold world, and what's worse, in their own selves, is not enough to transform them. For transformation, you need to show them hope, show them the opening to a new life, a new world, in which meaninglessness, suffering, and cruel injustice do not triumph, but where, reigning omnipotent over everything, are faith, hope, and love. And then you need to not only show them this new world from afar, pointing towards it, but you need to bring them to this world by yourself. You need to take them by the hand and place them before the Lord God Himself. Only then will they recognize Him, the One Whom they have long truly loved deep inside in their hearts, their one and only Creator, Savior, and Father. Only then will life truly be transformed.

But the whole question is how to get into this remarkable world. It cannot be done by any ordinary human methods, nor by any human earthly power, nor by any "connections." You can't buy your way into it for any sum of money. You can't get a scouting report on what it's like there—not even with the help of all the Secret Services and intelligence agencies there are. What's more, it turns out that you can't even get into this world by your credentials, not even if you're a graduate of the seminary, not even if you have obtained the rank of priest or even bishop.

But you could easily get into this world by taking a spin with Father Raphael in his black Zaporozhets. Or else this world would suddenly open itself to anyone who was sitting next to him, just drinking tea in his modest little parish house in the remote little village of Lositsy.

Why was this the case? Simply because Father Raphael was a genius at guiding people to this uncanny world. God for him was real, the One for Whom he lived, the One with Whom he lived, and the One to Whom he dedicated every moment of his entire life. And to Whom he therefore brought all those whom the Lord had sent to visit and drink tea with him in his ramshackle little cottage.

That was what ceaselessly brought people to Father Raphael. And particularly in his later years there was quite a throng gathered around him. Both Father John and several spiritual fathers in Moscow used to send young people to learn from him. Father Raphael was pleased to receive them all, and there was no one in his home who left feeling unneeded or unwelcome.

He was able to simply turn most people's ordinary way of looking at things inside out. Somehow in his own unique lighthearted manner (jocular, so that people would not take Father Raphael too seriously, nor would he take his own self too seriously), he knew how to give such exact yet unexpected answers to the questions posed him by his visitors that he would sometimes leave them catching their breath at how suddenly he had perceived and understood the truth in their lives. This ability of his could reveal itself in the slightest of trifles.

Once we picked up, in his Zaporozhets, a hitchhiker on the way to Pskov. But instead of being grateful to Father Raphael, this angry eccentric began to rail for all the world against all priests: "You priests are all crooks! How do you make your living? By swindling grandmothers!"

As usual, Father Raphael listened to this abuse good-naturedly, but then replied quite earnestly: "You know what? You try and swindle a grandmother. She is old and experienced. And usually she has lived quite a life . . . Do you really think it's so easy deceiving her? You must've heard this phrase at your Communist Party meetings, and now you can't help repeating it like a broken record. But seriously, go and try and deceive her."

Our passenger was stunned by this thought. "Hmm! I never thought about that. Just you try and fool my grandma, or, say, my mother-in-law!"

After this, for the rest of the whole journey, he bombarded Father Raphael with questions about everything under the sun, but mostly about ecclesiastical quandaries, about the Church feast days that he didn't understand, and customs that his grandparents used to keep. In parting, Father

Raphael invited him to come by the parish house to drink tea . . .

Another time Father Raphael was walking by the cemetery and he happened to hear on the other side of the fence a woman screaming, howling, wailing with pain over a grave. Father Raphael's companions felt very uncomfortable at hearing her horror and despair. "How frightfully that servant of God is weeping," somebody said.

But Father Raphael replied: "No, that is no servant of God. That person weeping there is not an Orthodox Christian. An Orthodox Christian would not be grieving over a grave with such terrible despair."

He might, quite without intending to offend, still unerringly tell a sanctimonious priest: "What a snout your face looks like today! Were you watching television all day yesterday?"

Or he would answer a young girl who asked him which priest she should turn to for her confession: "Pick the very fattest one there is. He will be able to realize his unworthiness, and will calmly listen to your confession without getting distracted."

Once on the eve of Pentecost, Father Raphael and I and Ilya Danilovich went into a grove together to gather young birch twigs, so as to decorate the church as is the custom for this feast day. But as we were beginning to chop the little trees, I suddenly felt pity for them. Here in this grove, the tree had grown and grown, and now we were chopping it down, ending its entire life so that it could decorate our church for some two days. My sadness angered Father Raphael. "You don't understand anything, Georgiy Alexandrovich! The little birch will be simply overjoyed to be decorating the Temple of God."

But Father Raphael could easily speak this way not only on behalf of a few trees, but of the entire universe. I remember how one spring night together with Father Nikita we were walking along a beautiful forest path not far from Borovik. The stars in the heavens at that late hour were so magnificent that we could not help but marvel at them. I thought to myself: "Is it really possible that this beautiful, endlessly uncanny Universe with its endless number of worlds and galaxies is made by God only for us people living on this tiny little planet, so ridiculously insignificant in comparison with the infinity of the Universe?"

I shared my lyric musings with my companions, and Father Raphael decisively and unhesitatingly resolved all my doubts. "There is no intelligent life anywhere except on Earth," said he. Then he explained. "Because if there were intelligent life somewhere else, God would have definitely revealed this to Moses, when he wrote the book of Genesis. And Moses would have at the very least hinted about this to us. Therefore, have no doubts whatsoever, Georgiy Alexandrovich, the universe was created by God only for mankind!"

"Why then all these infinite myriad stars and galaxies above us?"

"So that we, in looking at them, could grasp the omnipotence of God."

This, however, was not all! Sometimes Father Raphael would answer not only for the universe, but for God Himself! Once a conversation started about whether there were any people in this world whom the Lord does not love. Everyone amiably hastened to give the correct and expected answer that of course "the Lord loves everyone." But Father Raphael suddenly said: "No, that isn't quite true. The Lord does not love cowards!"

Father Raphael's relationships with people were as simple as could be. Once a neighbor brought Father Raphael a jar of pickles. "Please accept them, Father! They've gone bad anyway."

"All right, give them to me," he agreed. "If you feel bad about throwing them away, I'm happy to do it for you."

One woman from Moscow came to visit Father Raphael, but she always refused to put on a head scarf as required before entering a church or the parish house. Father Raphael growled at her strictly: "Again entering without a head scarf? What do I have to do—nail the doormat to your head?" That young woman got so scared that she never took off her head scarf again. They say she even used to sleep in it!

We were always struck by how Father Raphael put up with those who insulted or hated him—and in his life there were quite a few such people, including some of his brother priests. But Father Raphael never allowed himself to say one negative word about them, indeed, would not even allow anyone to use a negative tone of voice in referring to them. In fact, he never condemned anyone. Well, now and then he would grumble against the Soviet regime. He had had his own special relationship with it.

In those years Soviet authorities and government officials in general were always hovering around us and pestering us and sometimes seriously made it hard for us to live. On the other hand, in some way the government really didn't exist for us. We simply lived our own lives, not paying any attention at all to it. Therefore, we didn't quite understand, for instance, those religious dissidents whose main purpose in life was the struggle with

Soviet authority. For us it was somehow completely obvious that Soviet authority would someday live itself out and collapse with a magnificent crash. That is not to say, of course, that it could not seriously ruin our lives, putting some of us in jail, for example, or into insane asylums, or subjecting us to all kinds of persecution, or even getting us killed. But we believed that unless it was the will of God, nothing of the sort could possibly happen anyway. In the words of the ancient ascetic Abba Forstus: "If God wishes me to live, He knows how to make this happen. But if God does not wish me to live, then why should I live?"

From time to time Father Raphael took pleasure in teasing the provincial and local authorities of Pskov. Especially when he was supposed to be the head priest and at the same time the only priest in some isolated village church. As part of his instructions, he was supposed to write reports about the number of baptisms and marriages that he performed each year. In these reports Father Raphael listed such enormous four-figure statistics of married couples and baptized children that, in reading about these thousands, the local Soviet for Religious Affairs group utterly panicked. Finally they realized that he was just pulling their leg, and the Pskov Regional Soviet decided to get its revenge with full hatred and cruel persecution, to really pay back Father Raphael for his mathematics, as well as for his speedy black Zaporozhets with its white curtained windows, and also for the hundreds and hundreds of people who used to come to his parish house for tea. But Father Raphael never got depressed even during the several times per year when, on the orders of the bureaucrats in the Soviet for Religious Affairs, he was arbitrarily transferred from one remote place to another to another to another. And he even liked to tease his tormentors.

In those years we often used to complain about how little religious literature there was in Russia. It was not only forbidden but actually a criminal act to publish religious literature other than the miserly small editions allowed for all of Russia of a few of the holy books. We even once fantasized about how we would set up a clandestine printing press in the little island hermitage of Father Dositheus where we would secretly print religious literature. We got so carried away by these dreams of ours that we even began to discuss this future publishing house with many of our acquaintances.

Then on the eve of November 7 (the anniversary of the Bolshevik Revolution) Father Raphael traveled to Moscow for some spare parts for his car and stayed at my house overnight. We decided that we would travel together back to his parish house, because thanks to the holiday and weekend I would have almost a week off.

That evening Father Raphael was sitting in my room, whiling away the hours till our train and chattering with his friends on the telephone. But there was always a rattling and crackling on the line. Having decided that the reason for this was wiretapping by the KGB, Father Raphael began to really plaster the Soviet government with criticism. "Why, those idiots can't even figure out how to put normal listening devices on the telephone line!"

I became alarmed at this, and hinted to him that it was all too possible that our telephone was being wiretapped. This irritated Father Raphael even further, and he yelled into the telephone receiver: "And now they've gone and scared Georgiy Alexandrovich to death! Never mind, you godless Commies, you Bolsheviks! Soon enough the Soviet system will collapse! Meanwhile we will get ready, we will publish books, we will set up a clandestine printing press in a hidden hermitage! We will end up baptizing and marrying you all in church, you Bolsheviks, you Commies!"

And so on, and so on . . . By now I had gotten so unbelievably nervous that I was past even caring, and ceased to even listen to him.

As always, we dashed off to the train station at the last minute. For Father Raphael it was simply the height of style to be able to leap with one leg on the stepladder of the last car of the train as it was already leaving the station. Otherwise it was no fun. Until then he would simply drive all of us crazy. We would warn him: "Father, it's time to go. Our train leaves the station in an hour."

"What? A whole hour? Fill up the chifir-tank!"

By this he meant the teapot. "Chifir-tank" was a prison camp expression that had been brought to us by Father Viktor. (Chifir is prison camp slang for an extremely potent brew of highly caffeinated and deeply steeped tea drunk by the camp inmates.)

So we put on the kettle and we sat down to drink tea, accompanied by the nervous sighs of all the companions who had the occasion of traveling with Father Raphael on the same train. "But Father! There's just half an hour left until the train leaves the station, and it'll take us at least twenty-five minutes to get there," his companions would complain in despair. "All right then. Just a few cups more," he would reply indefatigably.

If someone didn't break out into complete hysteria, everything usually went just fine somehow. I know of only one case when Father Raphael asked with surprise: "Why are we still sitting around? We might be late!"

Even though there were several occasions when we actually did have to watch the train leaving the station, accompanying it with our eyes instead of being on board, nonetheless this amusement of his would repeat itself every time.

That evening, after his telephone monologue about clandestine printing presses on the island hermitage, we made it to the train just on time. We got to Pskov and immediately from there set out to go see Father Nikita. We had brought him books and food, and setting out together for his village parish house, we began to read aloud a brand-new book that we had only just acquired in Moscow, entitled *The Elder Silhouan.*

It was a clear November day, with a light frost on which the sun was sparkling. That morning the first thing we did upon arriving at his house was to pray. Then we sat down once again to listen to the book. However, our peaceful reading was suddenly interrupted: we heard the sharp screeching of wheels as several cars at once raced up to our house. This wheel screeching was quite surprising for a sleepy corner as remote as the village of Borovik. We looked out the window and realized that "they" had come for us. Policemen and plainclothes officers in their typical long coats and black fedora hats were pouring out of two Volga sedans and one police van. They were going to arrest us.

To be honest, I was utterly frightened. So was Father Nikita. On the other hand, Father Raphael, Ilya Danilovich, and Father Viktor were calm as could be. Only the Little Elder had a somewhat sarcastic expression on his face because he knew beyond a doubt just who our "visitors" were.

"Everyone freeze! Stay right where you are! Show us your documents!"

With this bellow, our local cop, a potbellied fellow whom we all actually knew quite well, blundered and bored his way into the house. All our other guests, of whom there were no less than six, stared at us menacingly. They fingered but did not draw their pistols.

"Document check! Everyone present your documents at once!" Our normally good-natured local cop bellowed so loudly that one of his comrades in plainclothes had to calm him down—it was too much even for them!

The only one whose documents actually got checked was me. Several of those plainclothes agents started to ask me questions. Who was I? At what address was I officially registered? Where did I work? Why was I located here so far from home without having registered my arrival with the local authorities first as required? This was the first time I had ever been mixed

Father Nikita by his own church.

up in such circumstances, and I had no idea how to answer. But as scared as I was, I was even more scared that my friends might notice my cowardice.

I was unexpectedly rescued by this same local cop. Once more he yelled. And this time he asked something far more incriminating.

"Where is the clandestine printing press? Confess your guilt! Answer at once! We know all about it! It's pointless to conceal anything!" He was yelling like a fire alarm, and his face was getting redder and redder before our very eyes.

At first we just looked at him with surprise and had no idea what he was talking about. What printing press? What were we hiding? Nothing! But then it occurred to me and to Father Raphael that the reason for all of this was all the joking babbling Father Raphael had been doing among our friends and perhaps on the telephone about that same infamous printing press.

The outraged policeman continued to rant and rave. "We know everything. You have a printing press. In an underground hermitage. No one move! All right, step outside! Outside, I said! Everyone step outside, and take your belongings! Now show us the way! You're in charge here!" He yelled, pointing his finger right into the breast of Father Nikita! "Let's go! Now! Show us where it is!"

"He's not going anywhere," Father Raphael replied calmly. "And none of us is going anywhere."

"What-at?" The guardian of law and order was so shocked that he stammered. "Nor are we going to show you our printing press." Father Raphael added. He spoke calmly about the printing press as if it already existed in reality. I immediately understood that he had a reason for this.

For twenty minutes more our uninvited guests demanded, threatened, and convinced us to admit everything, to bring them to the hermitage and show them the forbidden printing press. But, following Father Raphael's lead, we remained stubbornly silent.

Finally the entire uninvited company gathered in the yard to take counsel among themselves. When they came back, they declared that they would find this printing press without our help. However, they demanded that we explain to them how to find the hermitage.

Unexpectedly Father Raphael began to explain to them how to get there. However, he pitilessly explained to the detectives how to get there by the very longest and most difficult path—a fifteen-kilometer trek through the bogs, woods, brush, briars, and swamp.

It was the beginning of November. The swamp in these parts was sometimes quite deep and thick with mud, and sometimes also concealed by a thin layer of ice. Our excited guests sped off on their unfortunate path and disappeared. I even felt sorry for them and asked Father Raphael: "What if they drown in the swamps on the way?"

"Oh, they won't drown," he replied, "but they will save each other heroically."

It was eight o'clock in the morning. We drank cup after cup of tea, chopped wood for a little old lady who was a parishioner of Father Nikita, and cleaned up the church . . . A nasty frozen rain was falling, but we even managed to get in a nice little stroll, then we enjoyed lunch listening to the rain, and wondering to ourselves how our local Sherlock Holmes types were getting along in "detecting" our nonexistent printing press.

It was only after seven o'clock, well after the gloomiest of Russian twilights had set in, as we were cheerfully sitting around the samovar, that our morning "visitors" burst into our house again. But how awful they looked now! They were soaked from head to toe, frozen, exhausted, muddied, infuriated, and they looked so pitiful that we almost offered them some piping hot tea.

"Where's the printing press?" This time it was a plainclothes officer who asked, but not with the demanding tone of this morning, but more like a pitiful and hopeless whimper.

"What printing press?" Father Raphael asked them, very confused.

"The underground one," said the plainclothes officer, beginning to understand that he'd been played for a fool.

"Oh, an underground one! Do you mean to tell me that you searched the hermitage and didn't find anything?"

"I get it," said the plainclothes officer. "Give us a nice hot cup of tea."

"They'll give it to you in the village Soviet," Father Raphael answered amiably.

"I get it!" The plainclothes officer repeated darkly. But then as he was saying goodbye he warned Father Raphael: "Just you wait! You'll be sorry for this."

The plainclothes officer carried out his threat. A week later Father Raphael was transferred to a new parish. Two months later, he was transferred to a new one again. But Father Raphael was not sorry. Although he could never really get used to this.

* * *

We never had a car in our family, and therefore as we were racing across the broad distances and plains of Pskov Province with Father Raphael in his black Zaporozhets, I used to think that his style of driving was absolutely normal. It was only much later that I began to guess that this was far from the truth. Actually, though, the truth was that Father Raphael was an excellent driver, and back in his youth in Chistopol, he had won not only bike races, but provincial auto rallies as well.

Father Raphael braked only to stop the car. Otherwise he raced straight ahead. He tried not to use the brakes too often in order not to—in his own words—wear out their brake shoes. He was capable of fixing the steering wheel, at times suddenly, even while the car was still going—actually removing the steering wheel itself and fiddling with the steering mechanism and driving all while his car was still speeding ahead. Then, and only at the last minute, he would replace the steering wheel and make a turn. I had gotten used to this eccentric style of driving, but his other passengers would sometimes be scared speechless, to the point of feeling ill.

Once Father Raphael and I set out for Pskov. About seventy kilometers from the town we picked up a priest who was hitchhiking by the side of the road. We knew him quite well—it was Father Georgiy, an artist from Petersburg who had become a priest and had left the big city for a parish in the diocese of Pskov. I got into the back seat, while Father Georgiy sat down next to Father Raphael. And we zoomed off.

Father Georgiy immediately began to clutch with all his might at the elbow rests, staring uneasily straight ahead. We understood that our new companion simply wasn't in a talkative mood, and so we continued to chat about our own problems. After a while Father Raphael commented that the car was leaning strangely to one side, and again there must be some trouble with the ridiculous steering wheel.

In the middle of the road, on a straight patch, he, without slowing down, as usual, calmly removed the steering wheel and stuck his head into the steering mechanism of the car. While doing this, he as usual thundered in condemnation against the Soviet authorities for not being able to produce a normal car.

We were getting close to a turn in the road, and I warned Father Raphael about this. He glanced up the road, made a slight correction in the steering mechanism, and began at last to put the wheel back on. But for some reason the wheel didn't go back in its place smoothly. "Father, we're nearing the turn," I remarked, meaning that without a steering wheel we would be unable to make the turn.

Father Raphael hurried up but did not decrease his speed. At the last moment he managed to put the steering wheel back on, turned sharply, and we neatly but safely avoided a dangerous section of the road. Having once more complained about the calamitous state of the Soviet auto industry, he switched to another no less fascinating topic. We had already forgotten about everything that just happened, and were dashing off further down the road, when suddenly we heard an absolutely inhuman shriek of despair emerging from the throat of Father Georgiy:

"Stop! Sto-oooooop!"

Father Raphael was so shocked by this horrible shriek that for once in his life he sacrificed his principles and stepped on the brakes. "What's wrong, Father?" Father Raphael and I asked very alarmedly, and in unison.

Instead of answering, Father Georgiy jumped out of the car. Once he was back on the road, he stuck his head through the door and screamed. "Never! You hear me? Never, never, never again, will I ever sit down in your car!"

At this we begin to understand that from the very moment he had got in the car and especially as the repair of the steering wheel had taken place en route, Father Georgiy had been in a nearly catatonic state of fear. We asked for his forgiveness, and promised to drive slower and more carefully, but Father Georgiy adamantly refused to step back into the black Zaporozhets. Instead he moved away with eyes blazing at us, and started trying to flag down other drivers.

*   *   *

In spite of what one must admit was a certain puckish quality of pranksterism about Father Raphael, we all noticed not only the incredible effectiveness of his prayers, but the power of his priestly blessings. Once I got into an argument with him. At this point I can't even remember what it was about, but I was really sore. We happened to be present in the Pskov Caves Monastery for the feast day of the Dormition of the Holy Mother of God, but I was so angry at him that I decided to go back to Moscow at once, not even waiting for the service commemorating the Burial of the Holy Shroud of the Virgin, which is performed in the monastery on the third day after the Dormition. Before leaving for Moscow, I tried to express nothing but indifference and independence as I nonetheless went to Father Raphael to get his blessing for my journey home.

"How dare you, Georgiy Alexandrovich, walk out on the burial service of the Mother of God?" he asked me in astonishment. "There's no way that I will give my blessing to that. Pray with us this evening service for the Virgin Mary's burial service, and then you can leave with my blessing."

"Oh, yeah?" I was still furious. "Have it your way. But just so you know, the main holy day, the Dormition, is over. Well, I'll just get the blessing of some other priest in this monastery."

I said this, turned around, and walked away. But it was my bad luck to find nobody. Not one single priest, not one, anywhere in the monastery. They were all preparing somewhere for the long evening services, or out doing their tasks. And there was very little time left before the train. Thus, forgetting about blessings, I ran for the bus. But at the bus station, yet another travail was waiting for me: there were no tickets left for Pskov. But even this wouldn't stop me. I asked the ticket lady to do something for me, and finally she found me a ticket on the most inconvenient trip possible. Technically, according to the schedule, the bus might just make my train, but instead of going to Pskov directly, it would make a wide arc around all the neighboring villages. I got into the first row by the window, and soon was staring out moodily at the rainswept wooden houses and melancholy northern pastures.

I was in a foul mood. Worse could not be imagined. First of all, I was torturing myself for having quarreled with Father Raphael, whom of course I loved deeply. Furthermore, my conscience was torturing me for having indeed had the unheard of gall to have walked out on the burial service of the Holy Mother of God. And without having even received any blessing for my journey? . . . "Is this what I have come to?" I heard the voice of conscience reproach me in my head, even as we were shaking and rattling in that antediluvian puttering old bus.

The bus had completed its tour of the neighboring villages, had already turned onto the road for Pskov and was gathering some speed. On the highway right by my window, a red Zhiguli car started to pass us. I watched without paying much attention and noticed how after passing us he suddenly turned back to the right and was too close to the wheels of our Icarus bus. There was a horrible screech of metal and squeaking brakes, as the passengers were hurled forward. Everyone screamed. And I screamed loudest of all, as the horrible truth struck me: "It's all because of me!"

It may sound foolish or ridiculous, but when I remember that story from long ago, I remain convinced that everything that happened then was because of my sins, my stubborn pride, my lack of humility and obedience. For the time being, though, no one paid the least attention to my shout.

The momentum of our bus dragged that car ahead on the asphalt for several meters more. Then we stopped. Our driver opened the doors and ran to the aid of the car, which was now totaled. The bus was literally hanging over the breast of the crushed Zhiguli. All the passengers ran out after the driver. Everyone was horrified at the sight of the Zhiguli. Suddenly its door squeaked open slightly and an enormous black Newfoundland dog crawled out. The hound whimpered pitifully, and then took to his heels down the highway. I have never seen a dog, even when totally frightened, ever quite tuck in its tail as this dog did—in this case, curled all around its throat.

A girl of about twelve clambered out of the car after her Newfoundland

... Thank goodness! She was safe and sound. "Prince! Prince! Come back to me!" she yelled, and ran after the dog.

Our driver had to help the driver of that wrecked car to get out. There was nobody else in the car. It appeared that the man somehow had also amazingly managed to avoid any serious harm. He had only been slightly concussed after the accident, and there were scarlet bruises on his face. The poor fellow's Zhiguli, however, was totally ruined.

All the passengers got out of the bus, relieved that in the end we were all alive and well. But I became only more and more bitter and headstrong about my own fate. Together with about another dozen of my traveling companions I tried to hitch a ride on other cars or buses, hoping to be able to make it to Pskov anyway. I was utterly downright cursed in my stubbornness. I was determined. I would have my way after all. I was going to go to Moscow now, no matter what!

So I raised my hand and jumped up and down on the highway at the passing cars for about fifteen minutes, but nobody stopped, probably realizing that there were just too many people trying to get to Pskov. In the end I looked at my watch and realized that in fact there was no way that I was going to be able to make my train under any circumstances.

A few minutes later, right by the scene of the accident, a regularly scheduled bus stopped on its route away from Pskov and asked if anybody wanted to go to Pechory. There were no other alternatives, and so in the end I was delivered back to the place from which I had so shamefully run.

The service for the Burial Shroud of the Virgin Mary was already under way. By tradition, the service took place under the open skies on Dormition Square outside St. Michael's Cathedral. I sought out Father Raphael. He did not seem the least bit surprised to see me again. "Ah, Georgiy Alexandrovich, there you are!"

"Forgive me, Father," I said.

"How about after the service we go visit our Little Elder?" I nodded, stood next to him, and we were not distracted from our prayers any further.

* * *

Once (when I was already serving as a novice in the publishing department of the Patriarchate) Metropolitan Pitirim asked me to bring his relatives to Pechory Monastery: his sister, her daughter, and his two grandnieces. The Metropolitan's sister Olga Vladimirovna was a very talented architect, and her daughter was also studying architecture, while the little girls were just finishing school. All of them of course were very religious people, but they had only had contact with Moscow priests and bishops. They had never seen anything at all like Pechory in their lives.

They set off for Moscow after seeing the monastery and meeting Father John, chock-full of impressions. I had told them so much in the train about my wonderful friends Father Raphael and Father Nikita that when we got close to the village of Porkhova, where Father Raphael happened to be serving at the time, all the women said that they would be so pleased if they could somehow see such amazing priests. I answered that just about anything could be expected from Father Raphael and Father Nikita. So it was absolutely possible that we might just run into them at this very moment. The ladies looked at me somewhat skeptically, but just in case, I stepped into the corridor to have a look—what if my unpredictable friends

The feast of the Dormition in Pskov Caves Monastery.

truly did happen to be there by the train station?

And naturally, "what if" came true! The stop at the village of Porkhova was two minutes long. Just as the train had already begun to slightly lumber forward, in his inevitable style, Father Raphael with Father Nikita in tow raced up to the platform, and as I yelled at them, waving my arms, they leapt with their usual aplomb onto the stepladder of our moving train wagon.

It turned out that they were also going to Moscow, to pick up new spare parts for the car, and they only had one third-class ticket for the two of them. But I happened to have a spare ticket, since I had purchased tickets for an entire train compartment.

When I triumphantly demonstrated my two dear friends to these ladies, they at first could not believe that this was the very same Father Raphael and Father Nikita about whom they had just been hearing so much. The ladies invited the priests to sit down with them at the table, took out all their food for a little feast, and ordered tea.

Tea! As he reached for his tea-glass holder, Father Rafael felt himself entirely at home. The ladies besieged him with questions, often asking in detail about the difficulties of living in remote parishes in the desolate woods of Pskov Province. "In Father Nikita's village, sometimes the bears walk right up to the front porch of the church!" Father Raphael beamed as he gulped down his beloved tea.

"Do the bears really walk right up to the front porch of the church?" the ladies asked Father Nikita, who felt very shy to be asked this question. Stammering somewhat, he replied honestly: "About five years ago there was a rabbit who hopped up the steps of the porch of my church. In the retelling of the story by Father Raphael, that rabbit has gradually been transformed first into a fox, then into a wolf, and now today he has been promoted to bear."

"The truth is, the most dangerous animals are the bear and the wild boar," Father Raphael continued. "It only seems that a wild boar is really just a pig who noses around in the earth and grunts and oinks, or that a bear is just a cute little teddy-bear with real fur. But the truth is far more dangerous. The bear is a frightful, cunning, and pitiless beast. It pounces on the human being so powerfully that with one swipe of his claws, it can break everything, indeed, even tear one's scalp off one's head, right off, just like that, with one swipe!"

Such a picturesque vision was certainly rather disconcerting. But it seemed that Father Raphael noticed its effect on his listeners, and so he decided to cheer them up. "Ah, but there is one way to protect yourself from a bear."

"What way is that?" It was Olga Vladimirovna, sister of the Metropolitan, who asked, and with such hope in her voice that it seemed as if she were destined tomorrow to set out on a trek through dark woods that were teeming with hungry bears.

Father Raphael did not need to be asked twice, and told her, as if in great confidence: "The instant you see a bear, you must stop right there in your tracks and just wait. If the bear isn't hungry, he will growl a little bit, and then he'll go away."

"But what if the bear is hungry?"

"Well, in that case . . . that's a bit worse. Then you'll have to run as fast as you can."

"Run? But where?"

"As far as the eyes can see! But of course you'll need to understand that the bear will run after you, and much faster."

"So what should we do?" In their despair the ladies cried out.

"There's only one thing you can do. Quickly climb a tree, higher, higher, don't even think about it, and don't look down, but just keep climbing higher and higher and higher!"

The ladies just stared at Father Raphael, listening to him with bated breath. It was obvious how clearly they could imagine themselves scampering for dear life up a tree trunk, saving themselves from the clutches of a hungry beast. But Father Raphael was not finished. "However, the bear will immediately climb up after you," he warned them.

"So then what should we do?"

"You will have only one way left to save yourselves. After you have climbed up as high as you possibly can, tear off your jacket and hurl it right in the bear's face. The bear won't understand that it's just a jacket, no, he'll think that this is you. And as he tears into it with all four limbs and claws, he'll lose his grip on the tree trunk. And then he'll fall smack down on the ground! Crashing with all his weight on the ground, he'll break his neck! And then without hurrying, you can calmly climb back down to earth, and step with your boot triumphantly on his big fat belly!"

Everyone was smiling, imagining this happy ending. But Father Raphael would not let his listeners relax. "It's actually far more dangerous if you run into a wild boar in the woods," he continued, wiping the smile off the faces of his listeners. "A wild boar is a terrible mechanism of muscles like steel and tusks sharper than razor blades. If he throws himself against some luckless human being, then he will definitely devour that person entirely, down to the very last fragments of clothing. Why, he'll even eat up the dirt on which little bits of human fat have dripped out. The person will vanish entirely from the universe, gone in a flash, just like that! Although . . . there is a way to save oneself from a wild boar."

"And what way is that?" The nice ladies from Moscow asked, quivering.

Father Raphael.

Father Raphael looked protectively at all of us, like a schoolteacher with a bunch of kids, and asked us a question. "What do you do if you meet a wild boar in the woods?"

"Run as fast as you can," the ladies replied amiably. Then they whispered in terror: "But won't the wild boar probably run after us?"

"Correct!" Father Raphael praised his students. "So what do you do next?"

"Find the closest tree and climb up as high as we can?"

"Exactly!"

"And will the wild boar climb up after us?"

"No," Father Raphael assured his listeners. "Wild boars do not climb trees."

"That's good news!" The ladies were very pleased to hear it. But they had been premature in their relief.

"Wild boars do not climb trees," Father Raphael continued authoritatively. "But they also never abandon their prey. The boars will get you in another way. They'll begin to dig, and dig, and dig deep into the roots of the tree in which you've taken refuge. That boar will dig and dig, not eating, drinking, or sleeping, digging and rooting until the tree you're in crashes down."

"Oh! What shall we do?" the women cried out in utter despair. But Father Raphael consoled them. "There is a solution. And it's the only one. You need to find the very thickest branch on your tree and crawl out along it, crawling as far as you possibly can from the tree trunk. Keep going. Because the wild boar is an incredibly strong animal, but he is also incredibly stupid. He'll keep digging and digging right under his prey, right under you, that is, day and night digging, digging, digging . . . Two days, three days, maybe even four days straight. You just need to hang onto your branch without letting go. Finally the wild boar will dig himself into such a deep hole that he'll collapse from exhaustion and die in it. Then you just need to cautiously crawl back to the tree trunk and climb back down onto the ground."

Many years later, I met these ladies again, and we remembered that train trip, and those hours we had spent together with Father Raphael, as remarkably light, joyous moments. Of course, these intelligent women had understood perfectly that the country priest had just been teasing, simply pulling the legs of these fine Moscow ladies, but it was quite all right, because he was so cheerful, so funny, so gently and amiably joking . . .

Later I met Father Raphael briefly in Moscow. He was unusually remote and lost in his own thoughts. And then he was no more.

Everyday Saints

"O UR PRIEST CRASHED in a Mercedes! Our priest crashed in a Mercedes!" The little boys were yelling outside the windows of Father Raphael's house.

We sat in his room and somehow knew it was true. The mystery of death teaches us a lot. Much can also be learned from the circumstances in which this mystery unfolds. And so Father Raphael's death also taught us a lot. In the end, he died as he lived, teaching us even as he always had taught us, by the way, without superfluous preaching or commands.

I think he must have felt his death coming on soon, because about a year before it happened, Father Rafael bought a burial shroud from the church store and hung it above his bed. From that time on he became more serious and taciturn. We all noticed this. This was even though the stream of people visiting his little house in the little town of Porkhova where he had served for the past three years never ceased, and indeed, only grew noticeably bigger. In fact, it got so big that a priest whom he knew growled at him, "What on earth have you got going on in your place? Cats? Girls?"

Indeed, the parish house of Father Raphael was crammed full of both. It was always jammed with young people, with their spiritual and ordinary everyday problems in life. Quarreling couples whose arguments had brought them to the edge of divorce would travel to see him all the way from Moscow. Just about anyone and everything might be found in his house. We were already used to the fact that Father Raphael was able to speak to everyone naturally and with ease. And yet, everyone jealously believed that he and he alone had his own special relationship with good Father Raphael.

Indeed, the relationship of our pious parishioners to their beloved priests might sometimes be characterized by just one word: "merciless." Father Raphael felt the full force of this, but he took such things for granted. In his own time he too had pestered his elders, especially Father John, and so he felt that being pestered now was only fair and proper payment in return for the salvation of his soul. "What else are elders and priests placed on this earth for if not for this?" he used to say.

Only in the wee hours of the night would Father Raphael lock himself away in the tiny little chimney-corner of his little cottage (which was the only part of the parish house that was off-limits) and collapse in exhaustion onto his bed. He would lie there for a while, and then pray until dawn.

As for the "cats and girls" that the priest referred to, there certainly were quite a few cats in his house, although he didn't spoil them particularly. Sitting on a wobbly stool, he would stroke his favorite one with his foot. She had shown up in his home after her "March strolls," and he would say to it gently: "You sinful little girl, you've been out on the town!"

And then he would answer himself, on her behalf, as it were. "No, Father. You're the one who's a monk, who has taken vows. But I'm just a beast, and I am free of sin."

Now as for the girls, I must admit honestly that even in his monastic period lots of girls had fallen seriously in love with Father Raphael. That's not even beginning to speak about the time when he lived in Chistopol, before he lived in the monastery. Back then there was just no getting rid of the girls—they were all over him. Oh yes, the world did not easily release its grip on young Boris Ogorodnikov!

When he was still young, Father Raphael used to love to race on a motorcycle. One time—and this was already after he had found God—there was one girl who so totally overpowered him with strong feelings that he even took her with him on his beloved motorcycle, daredevil racing on it as fast as he could. And then, when it was flying ahead fast, he turned around to face her suddenly and said: "Kiss me now!"

"Idiot!" she screamed out in terror, and fell out of love with him at once.

But Father Raphael himself was full of faith in God, and so overflowing from all his heart in sheer love for Him and Him alone that there really was no room left in it for anyone else. Father Raphael was a true monk—even if he was a bit of a hooligan. In fact, he worried more about the girls who had fallen in love with him than they ever did for themselves.

No, that was not the human frailty that was Father Raphael's chief temptation. The temptation instead was something you might consider nothing more than a trifle, a completely unserious whim. But there is this law in spiritual life: a monk must have no powerful desire for anything except God. There are no exceptions. It doesn't matter what that desire might be, whether for higher rank, or more knowledge, or better health, or for some material thing, or even to become an elder, or to obtain spiritual

Father Raphael.

gifts. Everything will come of itself, if such be God's will. Now of course Father Raphael knew this law perfectly well. Yet he had a very passionate dream.

His modesty and humility touched everything about his life except, strange though it might be to say this, his automobile. Here he could not control himself. He raced along the roads of Pskov Province in his black Zaporozhets with such elation that he must have felt some kind of incredible sense of freedom. Father John repeatedly warned him about this during their meetings: "Now be careful! Don't get too carried away with your car!"

Father Raphael would only grunt and giggle in embarrassment at this. But everything stayed the same. Finally, he truly got carried away with one dream—to buy himself a foreign car no matter what . . . and noticing this passion, and the overweening desire it provoked in his spiritual son, Father John became very worried indeed.

He categorically ordered his charge to give up this passion, and pleaded and argued with Father Raphael to drop this whim. Father John advised him that if he wanted to buy a new car instead of his old jalopy, he should be content with the simplest and cheapest possible car befitting his monastic modesty.

But here Father Raphael managed to interpret the words of his father confessor to match his own desire. Passionately he rationalized both to us and himself that by buying a fancy foreign car he was obediently and absolutely literally carrying out a blessing that he had been given: buying himself a car. Just a car. Just any old car. But no reasonable person could call any Soviet means of transportation a "car." The best such a Soviet claptrap could be called was a mechanized cart, a crudely modified Bolshevik means of barely getting from place to place—but not a car!

If a person truly and utterly wants something, even against his own best interests, the Lord will patiently and at length through various people and new circumstances plant obstacles and try to dissuade the person from the needless and fatal goal. But when we are stubbornly implacable in our desires, then God steps aside and lets our blind and powerless freedom take its course. And this spiritual law began to act even in the life of Father Raphael.

It so happened that he greatly helped out a man who had very serious family problems. Indeed, he helped this man so much that he saved the man's marriage and family. Out of sheer gratitude this person either gave him or sold him for a purely symbolic price (I can't remember exactly) his old Mercedes.

The car was colored bright red. Nonetheless, Father Raphael was beside himself with joy over this present. We did not miss the opportunity to remind the happy owner of the fancy foreign car of times in the past when he had assured us that nothing on earth could ever persuade him to drive a car in the color of the Communist flag. In response to this Father Raphael answered somewhat arrogantly that we didn't understand anything: his car was really colored in the ideal color of Orthodox Easter . . .*

For a whole year the Lord postponed misfortune. Father Raphael had always been generous and was never mean. At the very first request he

---

* The color red is associated with Orthodox Easter, and Easter eggs are colored red. According to tradition, St. Mary Magdalene handed a red egg to the Roman Emperor Tiberius as a symbol of Christ's resurrection from the dead.—TRANS.

lent his Mercedes for a week to our common friend Nikolai Filatov. In a matter of days, his friend managed to ruin the car in an accident, somehow even totaling the motor. A very lengthy and extremely expensive repair was needed. But even this did not stop Father Raphael.

Almost a year went by, as some cooperative mechanic workshop in Moscow fussed and fixed up that ill-fated Mercedes, while Father Raphael worked overtime on house blessings, baptisms, and so on to earn money, ran around here, there, and everywhere, borrowing every penny he could to pay for the repairs. It pained us to see all of this, but there was nothing we could do. We all thought, let it be, this too shall pass, he'll get his car and play with it for a little bit, and then he'll come back to us as the same old Father Raphael we all know and love.

Finally his dream had come true. The Moscow workshop had created exactly the car of his dreams. They had replaced the motor and engine completely. They had put in new tires. They had even repainted the body of the car in black monastic colors. Finally Father Raphael took out his "beloved" Mercedes windshield wipers, and . . .

On the morning of November 18, 1988, he got into the car of his dreams and raced off home to his parish house. He crashed at very high speed on the 415th kilometer of the Moscow-Leningrad Highway near Novgorod.

Father Raphael was buried in accordance with the Church canons three days later. It was his name day. It was the feast day of the Archangel Michael and of all Angels and Archangels. Many times Father Raphael had said, "Let me die as long as I die in the bosom of the Church! It is the greatest possible happiness for any Orthodox Christian to die in the bosom of the Church. Liturgies will be served for him. The Church has an awesome power to lift up sinners even from the very depths of hell."

A multitude of people, shocked and feeling lost with unexpected grief, came from all over to be at his funeral. Father John, to whom the spiritual children of Father Raphael turned with indignant grief, asking dumbfounded why all this had to happen, answered them all in a letter: "The earthly wanderings of Father Raphael have ended. But for the Lord there are no dead; for the Lord all are alive. He alone knows whom and when to summon from this life."

Not long before that frightful day, Father Raphael had come to visit Father John. The little house in which he was living in Porkhova had been dilapidated for ages, and so Father Raphael had asked his spiritual father for blessing and advice: should he try to replace the house, or should he buy a new house?

Father John had answered him with weariness: "It doesn't matter whether you repair it or buy a new one. Just make sure to choose a home right opposite the altar."

Father Raphael of course felt his conscience gnawing at him for having ignored the advice of his father confessor about his automobile. So he obediently went around all the houses that surrounded the village church of Porkhova. Nobody wanted to sell.

When Father Raphael was killed in a car crash and it was being decided where he would be buried, everyone was certain that he would be buried in the caves of Pskov Caves Monastery, since he was a monk of that monastery and had taken his vows there. But instead Archbishop Vladimir, who by now had replaced Metropolitan John in the diocese of Pskov, gave his blessing for Father Raphael to be buried at the place where he had last served, by the Church of Porkhova. And it was there that he was laid to rest—right opposite the altar.

* * *

Ten years after the death of Father Raphael, Father Nikita died. He had suffered more than anyone else from the loss of his best friend. Possessed Ilya Danilovich took his monastic vows in our Sretensky Monastery and became Father Isaiah. He left us for our Lord four years ago. That cheerful jailbird, our Little Elder Deacon Viktor, finally had his most devout wish granted—he took his monastic vows, also in our Sretensky Monastery. Now he is a monk named Father Nilus, and serves as a priest in a remote parish of Pskov Province in a village named Khokhlovy Gorki. Father Roman, once the monk Alexander, has been living for many years in Father Dositheus's old hermitage on an island in the swamps in a remote part of Pskov Province. Not long ago we published a little book of his beautiful poems.

* * *

I named this last chapter of my book "Everyday Saints." Yet my friends were all ordinary people. There are many like them in our Church. And of course they are very far indeed from canonization. It's quite out of the question. Yet, at the end of the Divine Liturgy, when the great mystery of the Eucharist is finished and the Holy Gifts are placed upon the altar table, the priest proclaims: "Holy things are for the holy!" What this means is that the Body and the Blood of Christ are now being taken in by holy people. But who are these people? They are the people who are now in our Church, priests and laypersons alike, coming here to us with faith and waiting for Communion. They do this because they are faithful Christians who are yearning to draw closer to God. It turns out that in spite of our frailties and sins, we, the people who compose the Church on earth are, to God, also saints.

In our small company, Father Raphael was without doubt our elder brother. This is not even because he had already been an ordained priest for seven years when we first met him, and that seemed then to be an incredible span of time. The main thing about him then and always was that we could see in him an absolutely remarkable example of living faith. One cannot confuse such spiritual strength with anything else, no matter what other eccentricities or frailties a person may otherwise be weighed down with.

Why did we all love Father Raphael so much? He was an awful prankster, he couldn't say a sermon to save his life, and very often it seemed

he busied himself a lot more about his car than he did about us. And yet now that he is no more, how my soul still pines for him! More than twenty years have passed now since his death.

* * *

In those occasional hours when gloom and despondency steal upon me and seek dominion over my soul, or when the same thing is happening to people who are very close to me, I remember that everything that happens is in some way connected to the unfathomable Providence and will of the Lord.

One ascetic monk once told me that every Orthodox Christian could relate his own Gospels, his own Glad Tidings about coming to know God. Of course, no one would compare such testimony to the books of the Apostles, who saw the Son of God alive on Earth with their own eyes. Yet still, though we are frail and feeble sinners, we remain His disciples, and there is truly nothing more beautiful in this world than the contemplation of the remarkable unfolding of the Providence of our Savior in His divine will for the salvation of this world.

I have related these stories to the brotherhood of the Sretensky Monastery, and then later to my students, many of them during sermons. I am grateful to all my listeners. They were the ones who urged me to sit down and write this book.

I would particularly like to ask forgiveness from my readers for having had to speak about myself in this book. But otherwise it is impossible to bear witness to stories I have experienced in the first person. As Archimandrite John (Krestiankin) once wrote:

"My scattered and episodic recollections are not really stories about myself, but are really more just like illustrations of various situations in life. Now that the patchwork quilt of events has been set down, and I have rewritten and reread it, returning in my mind into the past, I have found myself time and again beholding with loving amazement the splendor of God's compassion."